Oracle Press™

Oracle Essbase & Oracle OLAP: The Guide to Oracle's Multidimensional Solution

About the Authors

Michael Schrader, Director, Business Intelligence and Performance Management Architecture at Oracle Corporation, is an internationally recognized expert in the fields of data warehousing; extract, transform, and load (ETL); business intelligence (BI); online analytical processing (OLAP); enterprise performance management (EPM); and database administration. He has more than 30 years of IT experience, specializing in Oracle since 1987. Michael graduated with an MBA from Ohio University and a Master's degree in Data Processing from the University of Denver. He is a certified Oracle Professional DBA (OCP) (Oracle 7, 8, 8*i*, 9*i*, 10*g*, and 11*g*).

Michael is a frequent speaker at major Oracle and BI conferences, such as Oracle OpenWorld, Independent Oracle Users Group (IOUG) Collaborate, Oracle Development Tools User Group (ODTUG), and the BI & PM Conference; as well as regional conferences, such as the Rocky Mountain Oracle Users Group (RMOUG). He has written articles for the *Journal of Management Excellence*, produced the white paper *Understanding an OLAP Solution from Oracle* for Oracle Corporation, and coauthored *Oracle Data Warehousing Unleashed* (Sams, 1997).

Dan Vlamis has been developing OLAP applications since 1986, when he graduated from Brown University with a Bachelor's degree in Computer Science. He worked with Express at Information Resources, Inc. (IRI), where he led the back-end team that wrote Oracle Sales Analyzer in Express. In 1992, he left IRI and moved to the Kansas City area, where he founded Vlamis Software Solutions, Inc., which has led more than 200 OLAP implementations. Dan has been a frequent speaker at major Oracle conferences such as Oracle OpenWorld, IOUG Collaborate, and ODTUG for over a decade. As an Oracle Business Intelligence, Warehousing, and Analytics (BIWA) board member, he chaired BIWA Summit 2008. Dan was a contributing author to *Oracle8i Data Warehousing* (Oracle Press, 2001). Recognized by Oracle as an Oracle ACE, he is often featured in *Oracle Magazine*. Dan is a customer advisory board member for Oracle BI and OLAP-related products, and he consults with Oracle Product Management regularly. Dan enjoys covering BI and OLAP through his blog at www.vlamis.com/blog and can be reached at dvlamis@vlamis.com.

Mike Nader has been working in the BI and EPM space for more than a decade, starting in logistics and distribution in the client sector, and moving to Hyperion (in Connecticut) in 2000. He has worked with Essbase for the past nine years in a variety of roles, which span both Hyperion Solutions and Oracle. These include curriculum development, technical instruction, product management (as part of Hyperion's engineering organization), and technical field strategy. Mike has also worked on a number of field services engagements with Essbase and surrounding technologies. He has been certified in Essbase since version 6 and has been on the committees to write the certification exams since version 7.*x*. Mike is also a recognized expert on Oracle's Smart View Office integration. Currently, Mike is the Global Domain Expert for Essbase and Analytics with Oracle's Enterprise Performance Management and Business Intelligence team.

Chris Claterbos has been an Oracle DBA since 1984. Over the past 24 years, he has also been a data architect, developer, and project manager for numerous companies. He has managed numerous data warehouse and BI implementations. His most recent work includes several Oracle Express and Oracle OLAP-based analysis systems. Chris speaks and teaches at several national conferences every year, including IOUG Collaborate and Oracle OpenWorld. He has participated in several software beta programs, including the betas for Oracle Database 10*g* and Oracle Database 11*g*, and also serves on advisor boards, such as the IOUG Conference Committee. He was a contributing author to *Oracle8i Data Warehousing* (Oracle Press, 2001). Chris is currently Consulting Manager for Vlamis Software Solutions, Inc., specializing in data warehousing and BI implementations, using Oracle Business Intelligence editions, Oracle OLAP, Java JDeveloper BI Beans and ADF, Oracle Warehouse Builder, and related products. Chris regularly contributes to the Vlamis Software blog at www.vlamis.com/blog and can be reached at claterbos@vlamis.com.

Dave Collins began his career some 25 years ago at Arthur Andersen & Company, as a Program Manager for the company's worldwide budgeting application. The application was hosted via Comshare, a time-sharing and software provider. Dave joined Comshare, working as a consultant, instructor, and sales engineer. The move to Comshare also provided an introduction to Essbase. Dave also worked at several partners specializing in Essbase implementations and education, and then joined Hyperion. Today, as a Director, Analytics at Oracle, Dave is responsible for assisting in strategic opportunities and sales readiness globally.

Floyd Conrad has been working in the finance and accounting field for more than 20 years, and with Oracle's Hyperion Enterprise Performance Management System as a customer, consultant, and sales consultant for more than 15 years. He is a certified Oracle Hyperion Planning Professional. In his current role as Senior Director of Performance Management, Floyd is responsible for leading the team of Integrated Business Planning Experts, and assisting in strategic opportunities and global product sales support. Additionally, Floyd acts as a conduit between the global field sales organization and Development and Marketing.

Mitch Campbell is a Global Domain Expert for Business Intelligence at Oracle. He has more than ten years of experience with decision support systems, Essbase, and many BI reporting tools. As part of the Technical Strategy team for the Oracle Global Business Unit for Enterprise Performance Management, Mitch works with strategic accounts and global pre-sales product readiness, and acts as a liaison with the Product Management and Engineering organizations at Oracle.

About the Contributors

John Baker is Director of Analytics for Oracle's Enterprise Performance Management and BI Global Business Unit, specializing in Essbase. With a background in both IT and accounting, John worked with Essbase for more than ten years in various roles in the UK, before joining the global team. He has helped numerous prospects realize the value of Essbase and supported some of the largest Essbase implementations for several high-profile clients.

Andy Lathrop is a Solution Specialist for Oracle's Crystal Ball Global Sales Unit. Andy enjoys using, communicating, and teaching Crystal Ball's unique decision-support capabilities, which are useful across many industries and applications. Andy also has experience in discrete event simulation and marketing return on investment analysis, as well as mathematics and computer science, teaching at the college level. Prior to joining Oracle, Andy worked in the Army Corps of Engineers, Accenture, and the nonprofit sector. He holds Bachelor's and Master's degrees in Operations Research from the U.S. Military Academy and the Colorado School of Mines, respectively.

Tim Tow, Applied OLAP, Inc. Founder and President, is highly respected in the Oracle Essbase community for his prolific contributions to public forums as well as his Essbase blog. He was designated as an Oracle ACE Director based on his contributions to the community and his extensive knowledge of the Oracle Essbase APIs. Tim also serves as the Treasurer of the Oracle Development Tools User Group and a member of its Board of Directors.

About the Technical Editors

Denis Desroches, Consulting Solution Specialist, is a Principal, Enterprise Planning, with Oracle Corporation. Since 1993, Denis has supported organizations with the selection, implementation, and knowledge acquisition of scorecard, performance management, and activity-based management solutions. He has spoken about these topics throughout the world on numerous occasions, and is a coauthor of *Scorecard Best Practices: Design, Implementation, and Evaluation* (Wiley, 2007). Previously, Denis was a Professor of Mathematics and Business Systems at Seneca College of Applied Arts and Technology in Toronto, Ontario. He has a Bachelor's degree in Mathematics from the University of Waterloo and a Bachelor's degree in Education from the University of Western Ontario.

John Paredes is the president of OLAP World, Inc, incorporated in 1998, and dedicated to helping companies benefit from BI systems. He has more than 15 years of experience developing analytical systems based on Express/Oracle OLAP. John is the author of *The Multidimensional Data Modeling Toolkit: Making Your Business*

Intelligence Applications Smart with Oracle OLAP (OLAP World Press, 2009). He holds a Bachelor's degree in Electrical Engineering from Rice University and a Master's degree in Statistics from Yale University.

Fred Richards is a Senior Director for Oracle BI. Fred has 15 years experience working with advanced analytic technologies, including EPM, analytics, OLAP, and BI. He has built analytical applications to help run multibillion dollar operations, and has marketed and managed BI software at Oracle, Hyperion Solutions, Jinfonet Software, and MicroStrategy. Prior to his career in software, Fred worked at ORBCOMM, the U.S. Department of Energy, Thermo Electron Corporation, and Westinghouse Electric Corporation. Fred holds a Bachelor's degree in Mechanical Engineering from Vanderbilt University, and a Master's degree in Engineering and Policy and a J.D. from Washington University in St. Louis. He is also a coinventor on nine patents related to the integration of OLAP and telephone networks.

Michael Valianti, Principal Applied Engineer, OLAP Server, Oracle Corporation, has served as an Applied Research and Performance Engineer for more than 12 years in Oracle OLAP option development. He works on strategic accounts and major partner initiatives. Michael has contributed to benchmarks, case studies, and white papers highlighting the speed, quality, and massive scalability of the Oracle OLAP option.

Jameson White, Principal Applied Engineer, OLAP Server, Oracle Corporation, has worked as both an Applied Engineer and Product Manager for more than nine years in Oracle OLAP option development. He works directly with strategic customers, partners, and other development groups, giving special attention to the DBA aspects of the Oracle OLAP option. He also maintains a public blog and wiki.

 Oracle Press™

Oracle Essbase & Oracle OLAP: The Guide to Oracle's Multidimensional Solution

Michael Schrader

Mike Nader

Dave Collins

Mitch Campbell

Dan Vlamis

Chris Claterbos

Floyd Conrad

 McGraw Hill

New York   Chicago   San Francisco
Lisbon   London   Madrid   Mexico City   Milan
New Delhi   San Juan   Seoul   Singapore   Sydney   Toronto

The **McGraw·Hill** Companies

Cataloging-in-Publication Data is on file with the Library of Congress

McGraw-Hill books are available at special quantity discounts to use as premiums and sales promotions, or for use in corporate training programs. To contact a representative, please e-mail us at bulksales@mcgraw-hill.com.

Oracle Essbase & Oracle OLAP: The Guide to Oracle's Multidimensional Solution

1 2 3 4 5 6 7 8 9 0   DOC DOC   0 1 9

ISBN   978-0-07-162182-3
MHID   0-07-162182-2

Sponsoring Editor	**Technical Editors**	**Indexer**
Lisa McClain	Denis Desroches	Ted Laux
Editorial Supervisor	John Paredes	**Production Supervisor**
Patty Mon	Fred Richards	George Anderson
Project Manager	Michael Valianti	**Composition**
Harleen Chopra,	Jameson White	Glyph International
Glyph International	**Copy Editor**	**Illustration**
Acquisitions Coordinator	Marilyn Smith	Glyph International
Meghan Riley	**Proofreader**	**Art Director, Cover**
	Carol Shields	Jeff Weeks
		Cover Designer
		Pattie Lee

I dedicate this book to my father, Thomas Schrader. You are missed and always in our thoughts. I wish to thank my mother, Donna. And I wish to thank my wife, Donna, my two sons, Michael and Adam, and my daughter, Rachael, for all of their love and support. Thanks for all the insights on living.

—Michael Schrader

For my wife, Sally, and my two kids, Chris and Katherine. This is the book that kept me up late all those nights.

—Dan Vlamis

To my wife, Dawn, and my dear friend, Kathy Horton. I cannot thank you both enough for your help and support through this process.

"Innocence dwells with Wisdom, but never with Ignorance." (William Blake)

—Mike Nader

I dedicate this book to my loving and understanding wife, Joyce.

—Chris Claterbos

To my wife, Laurie; daughter, Grace; and son, Evan for their support and understanding through this effort. To Kathy Horton, my manager, my mentor, my friend. Thank you for motivating me to excel and for guiding me through this process. We could not have done it without you! Last, I would like to thank Jennifer Smith for showing me how to use my voice.

"Is someone getting the best, the best, the best, the best of you?" (Foo Fighters)

—Dave Collins

I would like to thank Kathy Horton for inspiring me to participate in writing this book. I would also like to thank Phil Vaughan for his patience during this process. I was told that I could thank my dog, but since I don't have one, I will thank my cat. So here it goes. Socks, thanks for keeping me company during those late nights, sitting between me and my laptop, and motivating me to finish on time.

—Floyd Conrad

Dedicated to my wife, Elizabeth; my son, Ethan; and my daughter, Grace

—Mitch Campbell

For Aaron and Zoë, thank you for your love and support.

—Jen Smith

Contents at a Glance

Contents

xiii

Foreword

e have seen tremendous consolidation in the high-technology industry in recent years. Mergers and acquisitions strengthen the product offerings of a company, but they also sometimes bring together products that, on the face of it, seem either to duplicate a solution or to present no possibility of working together.

In 2007, Oracle already owned a well-respected, multidimensional solution—Oracle OLAP—when Oracle's acquisition of Hyperion Solutions brought another leading multidimensional product—Essbase—into the Oracle fold. Oracle OLAP and Oracle Essbase address the same business need: to provide business analysts with the tools they need to analyze and report on shared data in a way that is meaningful to people in the line of business. Both products ensure that all stakeholders are working from the same set of data by pulling the shared data from data sources managed by the IT department. Yet even with this seeming duplication of purpose, Oracle is firmly committed to both products. Why?

For someone with a background in both Oracle OLAP and Oracle Essbase, the answer to this question is apparent. However, it soon became clear that the answer is not as obvious to those without knowledge of both products, both inside and outside Oracle. An explanation was in order, and we needed people with expert product experience to relay the message. That is the purpose of this book.

We are very pleased to have an expert team leading the writing effort. Michael Schrader has 30 years BI experience, specializing in Oracle BI solutions since 1987. He has an Oracle Essbase and Oracle OLAP background. He is the coauthor of *Oracle Data Warehousing* with Bonnie O'Neil, and has presented at numerous major conferences, including Collaborate, Oracle OpenWorld, and the Gartner Business Intelligence Summit.

The Oracle OLAP experts include Dan Vlamis and Chris Claterbos. Dan is the founder of Vlamis Software Solutions, which specializes in Oracle BI solutions such as Oracle OLAP and the Oracle Business Intelligence Suite. Both Dan and Chris are regular speakers at Collaborate and Oracle OpenWorld. They are also very active in the Oracle BI user groups.

The Oracle Essbase experts include Mike Nader, Dave Collins, Mitch Campbell, and Floyd Conrad. They are all Global Domain Experts for Essbase at Oracle. They are well known for their presentations at Collaborate, Oracle OpenWorld, and Oracle X-Week.

All of the contributors are the best of the best, and we are very fortunate to have them provide their expert insight.

This book will help you to understand the multidimensional solutions offered by Oracle. It is a valuable resource for anyone participating in the design and implementation of an OLAP solution from Oracle.

—John Kopcke
Senior Vice President, Business Intelligence and
Performance Management Oracle Corporation

Acknowledgments

This book is result of many thousands of hours of work by many talented people. I wish to express my gratitude to a few of them. First, I would like to acknowledge and thank Kathy Horton. Kathy managed a global team of domain experts that represent the BI and EPM product offering, including the Essbase authors. She was an inspiration and encouraged participation in this book project. Without Kathy's efforts, this book project would not have gotten off the ground. Secondly, I would like to acknowledge and thank our professional writer Jen Smith. She has been fantastic to work with, and her suggestions were great. Thirdly, I would like to acknowledge and thank our technical reviewers Denis Desroches, Fred Richards, Jameson White, and Michael Valianti. The book was significantly improved with their input. Fourthly, I would like to acknowledge and thank several material contributors including John Baker, Andy Lathrop, and Tim Tow. Thanks for the expert insights! Fifthly, I wish to acknowledge and thank the Oracle Press team, particularly Meghan Riley and Lisa McClain. Thanks for the patience. Finally, I would like to acknowledge and thank our author team members. They are an incredible group of highly skilled people. Thanks you to all who have helped us bring this book to a reality.

—Michael Schrader

Introduction

I f you are interested in multidimensional analysis and in introducing online analytical processing (OLAP) technology into your organization, this book is for you. As suggested by the title, the primary purpose of this book is to differentiate Oracle OLAP and Oracle Essbase, and help you choose the right product for your organization. However, while the focus is on Oracle products, you will also find general information about OLAP.

We explain what OLAP is and why it is important. Real-world case studies highlight Oracle products, but can also help you envision how OLAP in general enhances business intelligence in an organization. We introduce general OLAP concepts and design principles before showing how they map to Oracle products. Product-specific information includes architecture, application design, application building, and maintenance considerations. We also cover end-user analysis tools, reporting tools, and other front-end applications that can leverage OLAP data.

You do not need to have a technical background to understand the concepts we cover in this book. OLAP benefits everyone in the organization, and we try to make the information in this book accessible to all. Whether you work in the IT department or in the line of business, such as finance, sales, research, or marketing, you stand to gain a better understanding of OLAP concepts in general and Oracle's OLAP solutions in particular.

Because this book is intended for people in a wide variety of roles, including DBAs, architects, planners, business analysts, and potential consumers of OLAP results—from salespeople to CEOs to marketing managers—the level of detail in the book varies from high-level overview down to technical details. Most chapters begin with introductory material suitable for anyone, and then delve into technical product details.

For nontechnical people, we encourage you to focus on the introductory content in the chapters and skim or skip the more detailed sections. You should gain enough knowledge about OLAP to help you understand and contribute to the design and implementation of an OLAP system. For example, you will develop the vocabulary necessary to be able to communicate effectively with the project team handling the design and implementation details. You can also be an effective contributor on the user committee that determines OLAP reporting needs.

If you have a technical background, you will likely be most interested in the architecture, design, and implementation sections of the book. While you should not expect to be able to build a production-level OLAP system using this book alone, we do give you an overall picture of what you can do with Oracle's OLAP products, how to go about designing an OLAP system, and the steps you will go through to build your solution. We also provide some tips and recommendations for optimizing your implementation. When you are ready to begin your implementation, we encourage you to use the many resources available to you.

How to Use This Book

How you use this book depends on what you want to get out of it. The following list summarizes the learning goals for this book:

- Learn about OLAP technology.

- Discover which Oracle solution is right for your organization.

- Understand the overall process for designing and building an OLAP system.

- Learn about ways to analyze and report on OLAP data.

- Understand how you can leverage your OLAP investment.

- Expand your technical knowledge and expertise.

After you identify your goals, read the matching sections that follow. Each section tells you which chapters contain the information you need.

Learn About OLAP Technology

If your goal is to learn about OLAP technology and how you can use OLAP data, read Chapters 1 and 2. The first few sections of Chapter 1 explain how OLAP fits in with business intelligence implementations and describe OLAP technology. The case studies provide concrete examples of the value that Oracle's OLAP solutions bring to an organization. The first section of Chapter 2 describes the key concepts that underlie OLAP technology, and summarize how Oracle Essbase and Oracle OLAP implement those concepts.

Discover Which Oracle Solution Is Right for Your Organization

If you are trying to choose between Oracle Essbase and Oracle OLAP, the second part of Chapter 1 should help. It outlines the similarities and differences between the products, offers some case studies, and talks about using OLAP with a data warehouse. This entire chapter is also a good resource to share with others in your organization as you begin your implementation, so that they can understand the benefits OLAP brings to an organization and support your efforts. You may also be interested in the real-world examples presented in Chapter 9.

Understand the Steps to Design and Build an OLAP System

If your goal is to understand the steps involved in designing and building an OLAP system using one of Oracle's OLAP products, read Chapter 3 and then either Chapter 4 or Chapter 5, depending on which Oracle product you are considering implementing. Chapter 3 starts with general design principles, and then provides design advice for Oracle OLAP and Oracle Essbase. It also contains information about the architecture and components of each product. Chapter 4 walks through building an Oracle OLAP analytic workspace. Chapter 5 demonstrates how to build an Essbase database.

In both Chapters 4 and 5, we expand on product-specific implementation details introduced in Chapter 2. These chapters use a tutorial style to give you an overall sense of the process and provide a structure for introducing the product interfaces.

Learn About Ways to Analyze and Report on OLAP Data

Chapter 6 is concerned with the requirements of the business users that analyze and consume OLAP data. The chapter provides a framework for identifying who the end users are and what they need in terms of OLAP reports and ad hoc analysis capabilities. It also describes the type of reports that are available via web-based and desktop-based reporting.

Understand How You Can Leverage Your OLAP Investment

You can use other Oracle products as front-end tools for Oracle Essbase and Oracle OLAP. Chapter 7 offers an introduction to these tools.

Expand Your Technical Knowledge and Expertise

Database administrators may find Chapter 8 of some interest. It covers the care and maintenance of Oracle OLAP and Oracle Essbase.

Resources

If you decide to implement one of the Oracle products for OLAP, the following resources can help ensure your implementation is both smooth and successful:

- Product documentation
- Oracle University training courses
- Oracle consultants
- Product tutorials, wikis, and community groups on Oracle Technology Network

Conventions

Oracle OLAP and Oracle Essbase are both implementations of OLAP technology. Of course, the problem with writing a book where a product name includes the name of the technology is that we may appear to refer to a product when we actually mean the technology in general. Throughout this book, we use the following conventions:

- To refer to OLAP technology, we use *OLAP* or *OLAP technology*.
- To refer to OLAP components as a group, we use *OLAP system*.
- To refer to the product Oracle OLAP, we spell out *Oracle OLAP*.
- When something applies to both Oracle OLAP and Oracle Essbase, we use *Oracle's OLAP solutions* or *Oracle's OLAP products*.
- When talking about any OLAP product, we use *OLAP product*.

Throughout the book, our convention is to use the full product name at first mention, and then use an abbreviated form on subsequent occurrences when doing so will not cause confusion. Therefore, Oracle Essbase becomes Essbase, but Oracle Database and Oracle OLAP are not shortened.

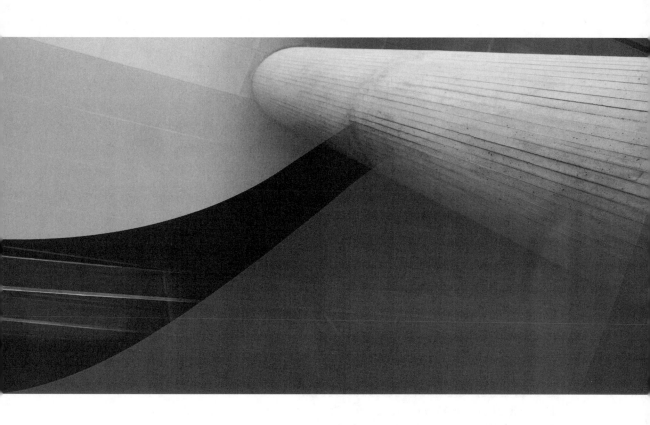

CHAPTER

1

Introduction to OLAP

Online analytical processing (OLAP) uses a multidimensional approach to organize and analyze business data. By storing data in highly optimized structures, businesses can very quickly explore the data and uncover important insights that would otherwise remain hidden. As a result, OLAP enables companies to achieve key organizational goals, including wide-ranging business intelligence.

We begin this chapter by defining OLAP within the larger context of business intelligence. Then we review the benefits you can expect to see by implementing OLAP technology in an organization. Next, we have an OLAP primer—a short introduction to what makes up an OLAP system and what kinds of OLAP implementations are possible. This foundation enables us to introduce Oracle's two OLAP solutions—Oracle OLAP and Oracle Essbase—i and review some case studies. The chapter ends with a section on architecting an OLAP solution, which compares and contrasts Oracle's two OLAP products and provides guidance on selecting the correct product for your organization.

OLAP as a Component of Business Intelligence

To explain how OLAP technology contributes to business intelligence (BI), we first need to define BI itself. BI means different things to different people. For some people, BI is only the data warehouse. Others see BI as the dashboards on their desktops. In this book, we define BI as all of the processes and technologies used to help businesses make better decisions.

BI includes the following:

- Enterprise performance management

- Data warehousing

- Business reporting, including dashboards and scorecards

- Predictive analytics and data mining

- OLAP

Together, these technologies support an organization's ability to create, maintain, analyze, and report accurate information about the business, and use that information for forward-facing activities such as budgeting and forecasting. The next sections define each of the technologies so that you can understand exactly what OLAP contributes to BI.

Enterprise Performance Management

Enterprise performance management (EPM) is a set of processes and related software that supports management excellence. EPM organizations are smart, agile, and aligned.

Smart organizations recognize that they must rationalize their analytical tools and data management systems to eliminate the noise and provide actionable insights to all the stakeholders of the enterprise.

Agile organizations are able to detect deviations between plans and execution quickly, find the root causes, and take fast corrective actions. They use best-of-breed technologies that offer advanced integration with operational systems, yet can be used easily with a company's existing architecture and information technology (IT) investments.

Aligned organizations address the needs of all stakeholders and share information through integrated systems and processes so that all stakeholders are working from the same set of facts—that is, the same data.

Data Warehousing

The objective of a data warehousing system is to provide business users with a time-based, integrated view of cross-functional data. To create a data warehouse, we start with data that may exist in different formats across several systems. We transform the data, cleanse it, and create an integrated view of the data.

Data warehousing provides historical data, as opposed to the current snapshot of data that can be found in an online transaction processing (OLTP) system. A data warehouse does not answer the question "What orders are shipping now?" but rather reporting questions such as "How many orders did we ship last month?" and analytical questions such as "When have we shipped orders the fastest?"

A data warehouse offers a central, reliable repository of historical business data that all stakeholders can use. End users can write queries to pull data from this single source of data, so that regardless of who asks the question, they will get consistent answers.

Business Reporting

Business reporting is about conveying information that is important to the organization and using that data to manage the business. Business reports have been around since the first data management systems were implemented.

The original medium of reports was paper documents. Today, many organizations implement business reports online through dashboards and scorecards. Business reports often require current data, and they can be widely distributed within an organization.

Predictive Analytics and Data Mining

Predictive analytics is concerned with examining historical data using statistical tools and techniques, such as regression or data mining, to forecast or predict future events and to determine the factors that best predict an event.

For example, using historical data, a company could forecast a customer's price point for a certain product. By determining each customer's profile, the company could manage its revenue stream better by charging different customers different prices. This would allow the company to increase revenue while maintaining customer satisfaction. After these models are developed, analysts can look for exceptions to the model for activities such as anomaly and fraud detection.

OLAP

OLAP is a technology that supports activities ranging from self-service reporting and analysis to purpose-built management applications such as planning and budgeting systems. What differentiates OLAP from regular business reporting is the analytics. In an OLAP application, metrics are often compared with a baseline, such as last year's numbers or the performance of the whole United States. Over the course of this book, we describe OLAP technology in general and Oracle's products for OLAP in particular.

The next two sections provide a foundation upon which you can begin to build up your understanding of OLAP technology and OLAP products. We describe the benefits of OLAP, and then provide some basic information about OLAP systems and implementations.

Why OLAP?

An effective OLAP solution solves problems for both business users and IT departments. For business users, it enables fast and intuitive access to centralized data and related calculations for the purposes of analysis and reporting. For IT, an OLAP solution enhances a data warehouse or other relational database with aggregate data and business calculations. In addition, by enabling business users to do their own analyses and reporting, OLAP systems reduce demands on IT resources.

OLAP offers five key benefits:

- Business-focused multidimensional data

- Business-focused calculations

- Trustworthy data and calculations

- Speed-of-thought analysis

- Flexible, self-service reporting

The next sections describe each of these benefits of OLAP.

Business-Focused Multidimensional Data

As mentioned in the first sentence of this chapter, OLAP uses a multidimensional approach to organize and analyze data. In a multidimensional approach, data is organized into *dimensions*, where a dimension reflects how business users typically think of the business. For example, business users may view their data by product, by market, and over time. Each of these is a dimension in an OLAP application. Note that business users instinctively refer to dimensions after prepositions such as *by* (by product/by market), *over* (over time), or *across* (across business units).

A dimension can be defined as a characteristic or an attribute of a data set. Each dimension contains members that share the common characteristic. The members are often organized hierarchically within the dimension. For example, Figure 1-1 contains a few dimensions and their members. The Time dimension, which represents a year, is divided into quarters, and each quarter into respective months. The Products dimension contains product groupings and then the individual products within each grouping. The Markets dimension demonstrates a division into geographic regions divided further into states.

The hierarchical aspect of the dimension represents the first option for aggregation. For example, Quarter 1 summarizes the data for its child members January, February, and March. Time summarizes the data for all four quarters in the year. The aggregations are inherent in the hierarchy. The metadata in an OLAP system contains the aggregation rules, freeing the application from needing to define these aggregation rules and ensuring that these rules are applied consistently for each report or analysis.

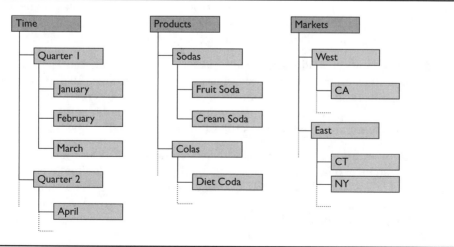

FIGURE 1-1.   *Sample dimensions with members*

We describe the multidimensional approach more fully in the next chapter. For now, it is enough to understand that OLAP organizes data in a multidimensional model that makes it easy for business users to understand the data and to use it in a business context, such as a budget.

Business-Focused Calculations

One reason OLAP systems are so fast is that they preaggregate values that would need to be computed on the fly in a traditional relational database system. The calculation engine handles aggregating data as well as business calculations. In an OLAP system, the analytic capabilities are independent from how the data is presented. The analytic calculations are centrally stored in the metadata for the system, not in each report.

Here are some examples of calculations available within an OLAP system:

- Aggregations, which simply roll up values based upon levels organized in hierarchies. For example, the application may roll up sales by week, month, quarter, and year.

- Time-series calculations with time intelligence, such as percent difference from last year, moving averages, and period-to-date values.

- Matrix or simple intradimensional calculations, such as share of parent or total, variances, or indexes. For those readers used to spreadsheets, this type of calculation replaces embedded spreadsheet formulas.

- Cross-dimensional or complex interdimensional calculations, such as index of expenses for current country to revenue for total United States. Someone using only spreadsheets would need to link spreadsheets and create formulas with values from different sheets to accomplish this type of calculation.

- Procedural calculations, in which specific calculation rules are defined and executed in a specific order. For example, allocating a shared expense, like advertising across products, as a percent of revenue contribution per product is a procedural calculation, requiring procedural logic to model and execute sophisticated business rules that accurately reflect the business.

- OLAP-aware calculations, with specialized functions such as ranking and hierarchical relationships. These calculations can include time intelligence and financial intelligence. For example, an OLAP-aware calculation would calculate inventory balances in which quarter 1 ending inventory is understood to be the ending inventory of March, not the sum of January, February, and March inventories.

- User-defined expressions, allowing a user to combine previously defined calculations using any operators and multidimensional functions.

Trustworthy Data and Calculations

When electronic spreadsheets, such as VisiCalc and Lotus 1-2-3, were released in the late 1970s and early 1980s, business analysts, who were already familiar with paper-based spreadsheets, embraced these new tools. Analysts would create spreadsheets starting from raw data and spend hours formatting and massaging the data into a form they could use. They would develop dozens to hundreds of these sheets. In turn, their organizations began to rely on an inordinate number of these manually produced spreadsheets for extremely important information.

Unfortunately, as soon as data starts living in spreadsheets, users start changing the data, entering new data, and creating calculations to augment what is already there. Soon, there are multiple definitions of something as basic as sales or profit. The resulting confusion gave rise to a phenomenon that came to be known colloquially as "spreadsheet hell." To get a sense of the depth of the problem caused by spreadsheet hell, consider the following scenario: There are ten people in a room, each with his own spreadsheet containing his own metrics, formulas, and numbers. None of the spreadsheets contains exactly the same data. It becomes exceedingly difficult, if not impossible, for management to make sound business decisions when no one can agree on the underlying facts.

The problem is not limited to just spreadsheets. Many organizations have multiple reporting systems, each with its own database. When data proliferates, it is difficult to ensure that the data is trustworthy.

OLAP systems centralize data and calculations, ensuring a single source of data for all end users. Some OLAP systems centralize all data in a multidimensional database. Others centralize some data in a multidimensional database and link to data stored relationally. Still other OLAP systems are embedded in a data warehouse, storing data multidimensionally within the database itself. Regardless of the implementation details, what is important is that OLAP systems ensure end users have access to consistently defined data and calculations to support BI.

Speed-of-Thought Analysis

Speed-of-thought analysis (also referred to as ad hoc analysis) means that analysts can pose queries and get immediate responses from the OLAP system. Not needing to wait for data means fewer interruptions in the analyst's train of thought. The analyst can immediately pose another query based on the results of the first query, then another query, and so on, leading the analyst on a journey of discovery. Fast response times, together with intuitive, multidimensional organization of data, enable an analyst to think of and explore relationships that otherwise might be missed.

For example, consider a company that experiences a sudden increase in the number of customer complaints concerning late product shipments. In investigating the issue, the analyst drills down into the financial cube and discovers that profits are at a record high. She then drills down on the average age of the company's payable invoices to discover that the average age is growing at a very high rate. Finally, the analyst drills down into inventories and discovers that raw materials are at low levels. From this analysis, she can draw the conclusion that the finance officer started paying invoices late, which improved short-term cash flow and profits, but now the company's vendors are upset and shipping later. Late shipments of raw materials translates into late products and an increasing number of related consumer complaints. Speed-of-thought analysis is a key component that enables this kind of drill-down investigative work across multiple functional areas.

OLAP systems respond much faster to end-user queries than do relational databases that do not capitalize on OLAP technology. Quick response times are possible because OLAP systems preaggregate data. Preaggregation means that there is no need for many time-consuming calculations when an end-user query is processed. In addition, OLAP systems are optimized for business calculations, so calculations take less time to execute.

OLAP systems make the analysis process easy for analysts by supporting tools they already use. For example, many OLAP systems support commercial spreadsheet tools such as Microsoft Excel or offer their own spreadsheet interface.

Flexible, Self-Service Reporting

The best report designers and builders usually come from within the business community itself because they know what is needed. Enabling these people to create their own reports is a hallmark of an OLAP system.

OLAP systems enable business users to query data and create reports using tools that are natural for them to use. Providing tools that are familiar to end users means that their learning curve is reduced, so they are more likely to use the system. In addition to commercial and custom spreadsheet applications, OLAP systems support other front-end reporting tools that are designed with business users in mind. For example, they include user-friendly tools that enable report designers to create and publish web-based dashboards and interactive reports using live OLAP data. The consumers of interactive reports are often able to customize their view of the data.

When business users can build their own reports, it reduces the reliance on IT resources for generating reports. Without an OLAP system, IT departments are often called upon to create a multitude of materialized views and specialized reports for business users on demand.

As with any application geared to business users, the front-end tools must be intuitive and flexible enough to be employed by casual users. That said, as with any new tool, people need to be trained on how to use these reporting facilities effectively. If end users deem the system too hard to use, they will not adopt it.

OLAP Primer

In this introduction to OLAP, we provide an overview of OLAP system components and implementations. In Chapter 2, we will identify and discuss underlying OLAP concepts and show how those concepts are used by Oracle OLAP and Essbase.

OLAP System Components

In describing the benefits of OLAP, we used the term *OLAP system*. An OLAP system is made up of the following four primary components:

- **Server**   The OLAP server hosts the multidimensional data storage and runs the calculation engine. An OLAP server can be a stand-alone server or embedded within a relational database. For example, Essbase can run on a stand-alone server. Oracle OLAP is contained within the Oracle Database. The latter part of this chapter describes similarities and differences between Essbase and Oracle OLAP.

- **Multidimensional storage**   OLAP data is stored multidimensionally in constructs often referred to as *cubes*. A cube is a useful concept for explaining multidimensionality. Dimensions (such as products, markets, and time) form the edges of the cube. Members from each dimension create intersections within the cube, each of which can potentially hold a data value. Depending on how an OLAP system is implemented, cubes can be stand-alone multidimensional databases or data objects within a relational database. We expand on the concepts of cubes, dimensions, and members in Chapter 2.

- **Calculation engine**   The OLAP engine handles aggregation of data and optimizes business calculations. Calculations are centrally stored in the metadata for the system, rather than in specific reports or applications. We talk more about calculations throughout this book.

- **Front-end analysis and reporting tools**   Front-end analysis and reporting tools communicate with the OLAP server and present multidimensional data to the end user. As mentioned earlier in this chapter, OLAP systems support user-friendly tools for analysis and reporting, including commercial and custom spreadsheet applications and functions for creating web-based dashboards and interactive reports. We describe OLAP reporting tools and processes in Chapter 6.

OLAP Types

If you have read about OLAP before picking up this book, you may have come across a description of the various types of OLAP implementations. Three main types of OLAP are available: multidimensional OLAP, relational OLAP, and hybrid OLAP. To help you understand where Oracle's OLAP solutions fit into this spectrum, we will briefly describe each type.

Multidimensional OLAP

With multidimensional OLAP (MOLAP), the data is stored in a multidimensional data store. Both Essbase and Oracle OLAP use MOLAP technology. Essbase stores data in a multidimensional database. Oracle OLAP cubes are multidimensional objects stored in the Oracle Database.

MOLAP cubes are automatically indexed based on the dimensions. Data can be located using offset addressing. To find a given value in a multidimensional array, a MOLAP product needs to use only multiplication and addition, and computers do those operations very fast. MOLAP technology is the best option for dense arrays, where most of the data cells in a cube contain a value. That said, both Essbase and Oracle OLAP have capabilities to manage sparse MOLAP cubes effectively. Figure 1-2 summarizes MOLAP cube advantages and challenges.

Relational OLAP

Relational OLAP (ROLAP) uses a traditional star/snowflake schema and relational data sources only. With ROLAP, data is neither aggregated nor manipulated. The data is stored in relational tables that can be queried by SQL.

ROLAP is ideal for lower density (sparse) cubes. ROLAP automatically provides all of the advantages of a relational database, such as high availability, replication, read consistent view of data, backup and recovery, parallel processing, and job scheduling.

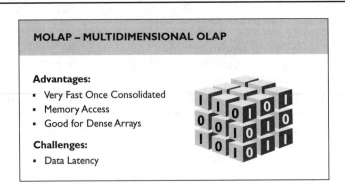

FIGURE 1-2. *MOLAP advantages and challenges*

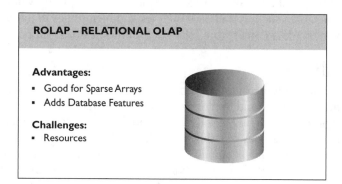

FIGURE 1-3.   *ROLAP advantages and challenges*

(Note that Oracle Database with Oracle OLAP offers these same advantages within a MOLAP structure.) Figure 1-3 summarizes the advantages and challenges of ROLAP.

Hybrid OLAP

With hybrid OLAP (HOLAP), the data is stored both in an OLAP data store and a relational database. For example, you may have summary-level data stored in the OLAP data store and detailed data stored in the relational database. You could then drill down from the OLAP data store to the detail stored in the relational database.

Today, most OLAP products support the hybrid architecture. Both Essbase and Oracle OLAP can be implemented in this fashion. Figure 1-4 summarizes the advantages and challenges of HOLAP.

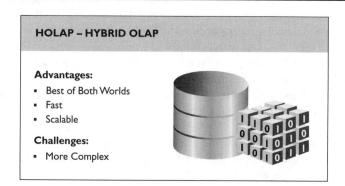

FIGURE 1-4.   *HOLAP advantages and challenges*

One new extension of HOLAP is called extended OLAP (XOLAP). With XOLAP, you can model metadata such as database outlines and hierarchies in the MOLAP product; however, the data comes from relational sources. Essbase supports XOLAP.

OLAP Products

There are many different types of OLAP products, each of which seeks to provide solutions to certain problems and to meet the needs of particular user communities. While all OLAP products share the ability to support business users with a highly interactive user experience, they can differ significantly in terms of that user experience, performance, analytic capabilities, target audiences, and architecture.

For example, some OLAP products provide a dimensional query model for data stored in relational tables in a way that makes it easier for users to define their own queries and navigate data interactively. Other OLAP products take a fundamentally different approach by tightly coupling data needed with the dimensional model for fast access to the data. This kind of OLAP product differs from one that also provides performance benefits and rich analytical capabilities, and is very different from an OLAP product that is designed to support, for example, a planning and budgeting application.

OLAP with a Data Warehouse

If you already have a data warehouse in place, you can leverage that investment by implementing an OLAP system within or alongside the data warehouse to support BI and performance management activities. Often, a finer level of granularity exists in the data warehouse than in the OLAP system. For example, many of today's implementations are HOLAP systems, where the data warehouse stores the detail data and the OLAP system stores summaries. The OLAP system has ways to allow a user to drill down to detailed data in the data warehouse.

When you implement a middle-tier OLAP system with a data warehouse, data flows from the data warehouse to the OLAP cubes. This is important because the data values in the cubes need to match those in the data warehouse. If you performed all of the data-integration steps for the OLAP system from the original data sources rather than the data warehouse, you would run the risk of the data warehouse and the OLAP environment having two slightly different versions of the data. This could lead to inaccurate analyses and errors.

When you implement a database-centric OLAP system, OLAP data is stored in cubes within the data warehouse itself. The cubes are data objects that can be treated like any other data objects. Connections between summary data and detailed data can be handled by joining a cube to a table.

SQL statements that normally would access a large fact table can be automatically rewritten to access cube-organized views. This greatly increases the performance of the system. Often, a single cube-organized materialized view can replace many table-based materialized views, easing maintenance of the data warehouse.

Typical OLAP Applications

OLAP has been used successfully in a wide variety of applications, including the following:

- Analyzing financial data

- Budgeting and planning

- Forecasting

- Replacing manual spreadsheets

- Accelerating a data warehouse

- Enhancing an enterprise resource planning (ERP) system

- Replacing custom SQL reports

This book includes cases studies—both in this chapter and in Chapter 9—that provide examples of these typical applications. The case studies are specific to either Oracle OLAP or Essbase.

Now that you have a basic understanding of OLAP, we can turn our attention to Oracle's product offerings. The rest of this chapter focuses on Oracle OLAP and Essbase.

Why Two OLAP Products from Oracle?

With the acquisition of Hyperion Solutions Corporation in 2007, Oracle now owns the two most capable OLAP products on the market: Essbase and Oracle OLAP. While both products fall within the OLAP category and have some similar capabilities, they are different in significant ways. One purpose of this book is to show how the products are the same and how they differ, so that you can choose the solution that best suits your environment.

Similarities Between Essbase and Oracle OLAP

Both Oracle OLAP and Essbase have the capability of storing data in OLAP cubes. As such, they share the following capabilities:

- Excellent performance for queries that require summary-level data

- Fast, incremental update of data sets, which is required to facilitate frequent data updates

- Rich calculation models that may be used to enrich analytic content

- A dimensional model that presents data in a form that is easy for business users to query and define analytic content

Because both Essbase and Oracle OLAP provide these core capabilities, it might seem like they are similar enough to be interchangeable. This is not the case. Each product focuses on delivering OLAP capabilities into different types of applications and for different classes of users.

Differences Between Essbase and Oracle OLAP

Essbase and Oracle OLAP are two of the leading OLAP solutions. However, the products have taken different paths based on the product strategies of Hyperion and Oracle and the roles that each product fulfills. From the mid-1990s to 2007, Hyperion focused on building solutions for the middle tier. Oracle spent the same period embedding an OLAP engine into its world-class database. Most of the differences between Essbase and Oracle OLAP derive from the fact that Essbase is a separate process, while Oracle OLAP is an option to the Oracle Database Enterprise Edition.

Essbase: Separate-Server OLAP

As noted, Essbase comes from a history of OLAP applications based in the middle tier. The strategy of Essbase centers on custom analytics and BI applications with a focus on EPM. This strategy addresses the what-if, modeling, and future-oriented questions that companies need answered today in order to see into the future.

Typically, Essbase applications are started and maintained by business analysts. The buyer is usually in the line of business. The typical end users are line-of-business users, such as analysts in the finance, marketing, and sales departments, who query and create data with Essbase tools and Oracle Hyperion applications. The line of business typically has a large degree of uncertainty and needs to understand a dynamic and changing environment.

Essbase is the OLAP server that provides an environment for rapidly developing custom analytic and EPM applications. The data management strategy allows Essbase to easily combine data from a wide variety of data sources, including the Oracle Database. Essbase is part of the Oracle Fusion Middleware architecture.

Oracle OLAP: Database-Centric OLAP

Oracle OLAP is available as an option to the Oracle Database Enterprise Edition. As an embedded component of the Oracle Database, Oracle OLAP benefits from the scalability, high availability, job scheduling, parallel processing, and security features inherent in the Oracle Database. With Oracle OLAP, all of the data resides in an Oracle database, governed by centralized data security and calculation rules.

An SQL interface to OLAP cubes allows SQL-based applications to query cubes within an Oracle database, and benefit from the performance and analytic content of the OLAP option. The primary data-access language for Oracle OLAP is SQL, making Oracle OLAP a natural choice for enhancing the performance and calculation capabilities of an existing Oracle data warehouse.

OLAP Business Case Studies

To get a sense of how the two Oracle OLAP solutions differ in a real-world setting, let's take a look at some case studies.

Essbase Case Studies

For the Essbase case studies, we examine a major airline and a major food processing company.

Airline Case Study

After the terrorist attacks of September 11, 2001, a major airline faced a crisis. Management needed to project cash flows in the face of extraordinary uncertainty about customer travel plans, fuel prices, new security regulations, and other variables in the wake of tragedy. The solution was implemented with alternative cash flow scenario models, capital spending plans, 15-month rolling forecasts, and "business cockpits" (multidimensional dashboards). The buyer was the vice president of the finance department, and the user community consisted of business users in finance, reservations, and ground operations.

Key to survival and success was determining how long cash balances of $1 billion would last based on immediately deferred capital spending, halted discretionary spending, and borrowing $400 million on an existing line of credit. The answer depended on return in revenues.

On September 11, Essbase enabled airline personnel to model many scenarios that provided the moral support, comfort level, and confidence for the many departments working hard to make it through that fateful day and the days that followed. Within five days, they were able to set up all scenario models, and they could forecast within 2 percent of outcome entirely in Essbase, providing top-to-bottom and bottom-to-top analysis capabilities.

Essbase performed very well. Queries that would have taken at least four hours to write, run, gather data for, enter on a spreadsheet, and analyze were instead accomplished in one minute with Essbase. Before Essbase, the finance department was spending 75 percent of its time accumulating data and 25 percent of its time analyzing. With Essbase, those ratios are now 10 percent and 90 percent, respectively.

Airline Case Study Summary

Business problem	Needed to project cash flow in the face of extraordinary uncertainty about customer travel plans, fuel prices, new security regulations, and other variables after 9/11
Solution	Alternative cash flow scenario models, capital spending plans, 15-month rolling forecasts, and "business cockpits" (multidimensional dashboards)
Buyer	VP of finance department
User community	Business users in finance, reservations, and ground operations

Food Processing Company Case Study

The food processing company is one of the world's largest providers of luncheon and deli meats. The company employs more than 1,000 people and distributes its products across all 50 states, as well as exporting to Mexico and Puerto Rico. It has three distribution centers in the United States, and sells its products through the largest grocery and mass merchandizing chains in the country.

The company had a requirement to do marketing lift analysis. For example, if the company launched a coupon campaign, the marketing managers needed to determine what the sales lift was by product. They wanted to know how the campaign affected sales over the life of the campaign, in addition to calculating the return on investment (ROI) of the campaign. They also needed to integrate data from a number of sources: third-party data, data from legacy systems, ERP data from JD Edwards (JDE), and data stored in multiple SQL Server databases. They evaluated a number of prepackaged solutions for marketing analysis and determined that their requirements were unique enough that a custom solution was required.

The food processing company implemented a custom solution of Essbase in less than two months and can now analyze its campaign performance effectively.

Food Processing Company Case Study Summary

Business problem	Visibility into marketing campaign effectiveness
Solution	Marketing analysis application that integrates internal data from JDE and SQL Server with external demographic feeds, calculates percentage lift of marketing promotions, and identifies advertising ROI by campaign
Buyer	Marketing department (also used in finance)
User community	Managed by marketing analysts; accessed by marketing and advertising managers

Oracle OLAP Case Studies

For the Oracle OLAP case studies, we present a major automotive manufacturer and a management consulting and research company.

Automotive Manufacturer Case Study

The challenge for the management of the automotive manufacturer was to analyze energy-consumption patterns within an automotive assembly plant, with the goal of rescheduling peak usage to coincide with times of day and with lower per-unit costs. The solution was to consolidate energy-meter readings in an Oracle data warehouse, including OLAP cubes utilized for time-series analysis. The buyer of Oracle OLAP was the IT department. The user community was the line-of-business users at product unit and cost center levels. They queried the Oracle data warehouse with the OLAP cube utilizing BusinessObjects Web Intelligence and Oracle Business Intelligence Spreadsheet Add-in.

The company faced the following challenges when approaching this problem:

- Enable automated and manual collection of detailed transactional data from the factory's many energy meters.

- Enable near real-time analysis of energy consumption, requiring frequent and rapid update of the data warehouse.

- Enable detailed analysis of past energy consumption.

The IT department, in consultation with the line-of-business users, implemented Oracle OLAP. They consolidated and centralized data sources using Oracle Database 10*g* and Oracle Warehouse Builder (OWB), enabling rapid data aggregation and near real-time analysis of energy usage. This allowed line-of-business users at the production unit and cost center levels to rapidly analyze data using Oracle OLAP, BusinessObjects Web Intelligence, and the BI Spreadsheet Add-In.

Automotive Manufacturer Case Study Summary

Business problem	Analyze energy-consumption patterns within an automotive assembly plant, with the goal of rescheduling peak usage to coincide with times of day with lower per-unit costs
Solution	Consolidate energy-meter readings in an Oracle data warehouse, using OLAP cubes for time-series analysis
Buyer	IT
User community	Line-of-business users at product unit and cost center levels, who query the Oracle data warehouse with OLAP cubes using BusinessObjects Web Intelligence and BI Spreadsheet Add-in

Management Consulting and Research Company Case Study

A management consulting and research company provides healthcare satisfaction metrics to thousands of healthcare providers, based on survey data from tens of thousands of patients per year. Because of the volume of data and privacy issues, the company requires a data infrastructure that is highly scalable, reliable, and secure. The data must be accessible to a wide variety of applications, including SQL-based BI applications.

This company's IT organization implemented an infrastructure that uses an Oracle data warehouse, including Oracle OLAP, to achieve a highly scalable and secure solution with time series and other analytic features. The goal was to gain the ability to support BI applications without replicating large amounts of data in specialized analytical databases.

The Oracle-based data infrastructure supports more than 1,000 concurrent users, without compromising performance, reliability, or security. The solution provides rapid response time for a custom SQL-based application, even for large documents that contain more than 20 thumbnail graphs and 20 cross tabulations per page (as many as 40 queries per page view).

Management Consulting and Research Company Case Study Summary

Business problem	Allow a large user community of third-party health providers to analyze healthcare satisfaction polling data
Solution	Consolidate healthcare satisfaction survey data in an Oracle data warehouse using OLAP cubes
	Custom SQL-based reporting application relies on the cube for required analytics and fast query response
Buyer	IT
User community	1,000+ concurrent third-party healthcare providers querying OLAP cubes

Architecting the Appropriate OLAP Solution

The case studies reveal how assessing an organization against a set of standard criteria can help determine the best OLAP solution for that environment. Here are five questions you can ask to help assess your own organizational needs in terms of those criteria:

- What is the purpose of the application?

- Who is the buyer of the application, and who will support it?

- Who are the end users, what needs do they have, and what tools will they use?

- How will the application acquire and manage data?

- Does a middle-tier or database OLAP architecture serve the organization best?

This section guides you in selecting the OLAP solution for your organization and describes the types of OLAP implementations that are available.

Choosing the Solution That Meets Your Needs

Table 1-1 compares and contrasts Essbase and Oracle OLAP based on the five criteria: purpose, buyer, typical end user, data management strategy, and architectural needs.

Better Together

Both Essbase and Oracle OLAP provide powerful OLAP solutions. They are not, however, mutually exclusive. When implemented together, they can form a complete OLAP solution.

Essbase provides a platform for EPM and pervasive BI. Oracle OLAP is a powerful enhancement to a data warehousing environment. Better together, the two OLAP solutions provide complementary benefits for a complete OLAP solution.

	Essbase	Oracle OLAP
Purpose	Custom analytic and BI applications with a focus on EPM; built and maintained by analysts	Improves the performance and analytic content of SQL-based BI applications
Buyer	Line of business	IT
Typical end users	Line-of-business users who query and create data with Essbase tools and OLAP applications	Users of SQL-based BI tools who query data in the database
Data management strategy	Combines data into a multidimensional database stored on disk and in RAM	Stores data in the Oracle Database
Architecture	OLAP in a server, part of Oracle Fusion Middleware	OLAP in the Oracle Database

TABLE 1-1. *Comparison of the Two Oracle OLAP Solutions*

Conclusion

Essbase and Oracle OLAP share common characteristics such as excellent query performance, fast update, rich analytic content, and a dimensional model. However, the products have different users and uses. Essbase is designed for line-of-business users and is focused on EPM applications. Oracle OLAP is part of the Oracle Database and is designed so that IT can support the needs of business users directly from the database or data warehouse. Implemented together, their capabilities provide a complete OLAP solution.

In the next chapter, we look at the concepts that underlie OLAP technology. We take the time to point out how Oracle OLAP and Essbase implement those concepts so that you have a foundation from which to approach the following chapters about designing and building Oracle OLAP and Essbase applications. We also present a history of each product to help you understand why the products approach general OLAP concepts differently.

References

Nader, Michael and Dave Collins. *Dare to OLAP*. Oracle Corporation, 2008.

Schrader, Michael, with William Endress and Fred Richards. *Understanding an OLAP Solution from Oracle*. Oracle Corporation, April 2008.

CHAPTER
2

OLAP Concepts
and History

hapter 1 introduced Essbase and Oracle OLAP, and showed how they both offer effective solutions for OLAP. The similarities between the products arise from a shared goal to provide business users with the technology they need to perform ad hoc analysis and to report on centralized data stored on a server. The differences between the two products stem primarily from who is responsible for (or "owns") the OLAP solution, how it is implemented and accessed, and where the OLAP data is stored.

Essbase is owned and managed, generally speaking, by line-of-business users in partnership with the IT group. Essbase uses a multidimensional database stored on disk and in RAM. In contrast, the organization's IT group typically owns Oracle OLAP, in partnership with line-of-business users. Oracle OLAP is a natural part of the Oracle Database, which means it can take advantage of other database features (such as security and access to data via SQL) and other options (such as Oracle Real Application Clusters). The similarities and differences are reflected in how each product implements OLAP concepts.

In this chapter, we introduce common OLAP concepts—such as multidimensionality, calculations, and ad hoc analysis—and show how the concepts are implemented in Essbase and Oracle OLAP. In subsequent chapters, we will build on this foundation, explaining product-specific implementations in more detail. We conclude this chapter with histories of Oracle OLAP and Essbase. The business problem each product was designed to solve and the evolution of each product help to explain the differences between the two products.

Common OLAP Themes

OLAP relies on a basic set of concepts. These concepts are shared between Oracle OLAP and Essbase. For the purposes of this book, we have organized the concepts into the following logical groupings:

- **Multidimensional view of information**   The concepts of a cube, dimensions, members, hierarchies, levels, attributes, measures, and aggregation

- **From data source to multidimensional data**   Data-related concepts such as transformation from transactional data sources to multidimensional cubes, dense and sparse cubes, partitions, slowly changing dimensions, user access to data, and write-back functionality

- **New results from existing data**   Advanced aggregation operators and calculated measures that are derived from data stored in multidimensional cubes

- **Ad hoc analysis**   Having a conversation with the data by using drill paths, pivoting dimensions, and manipulating data subsets

The following sections describe each group of concepts, including how Essbase and Oracle OLAP implement them. The goal here is to map the conceptual terms to particular features within each product so that you can begin to build up some product-specific vocabulary. Note that product-specific features are only briefly introduced here. They are described in more detail in the following chapters in the context in which the features are used.

Multidimensional View of Information

We defined the term OLAP in the first chapter, but you may also encounter another term that is used interchangeably: *multidimensional analysis. Multidimensional* means nothing more than thinking about a topic from more than one perspective. For example, consider your answers to the following questions:

- Where are you currently located?

- What day of the week is it?

- What are you doing right now?

You just performed your first piece of multidimensional analysis—analyzing location by time and task. In this example, location, time, and task are dimensions. Your specific answers to these questions—let's say head office, Monday, and reading—are members within the dimensions. In a multidimensional analysis, the dimensions can be thought of as forming the edges of a cube, with the names of the dimension members defining where you are on each edge.

A fundamental principle of OLAP systems is to optimize how data is stored so that it may be accessed as quickly as possible by the end user to support ad hoc analysis. Unlike transactional systems built with relational databases, or even data warehouses built on relational databases, OLAP systems provide highly optimized structures to store and aggregate data. The purpose of these systems is to precalculate measures that could possibly be used as part of the analysis. The precalculation happens when loading the data. A lot of the generic "overhead" used to store data in a relational database is omitted from OLAP cubes. The following discussion summarizes the concepts used to precalculate and efficiently store data so that access to the data is blazingly fast.

Cubes

We introduced the concept of a cube in Chapter 1. To recap, Figure 2-1 shows three dimensions, one on each axis of the cube. The intersection of members from each dimension has the potential to hold a value. The values represent a measure, which is sales in this case.

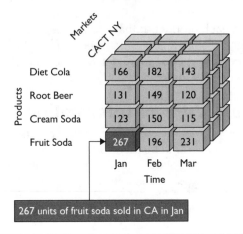

FIGURE 2-1. *Dimensions represented in an OLAP cube*

Fundamentally, Essbase and Oracle OLAP implement the concept of a multidimensional cube differently. Although Essbase applications can be made up of a series of interconnected cubes, they often store all data in a single cube that represents all possible combinations of all dimensions. Using the term *cube* in this context is a bit of a stretch, and sometimes the term *hypercube* is used to suggest the higher dimensionality. An Essbase cube is more accurately referred to as an Essbase *multidimensional database*, where the data is stored in a multidimensional structure rather than a relational structure, though the terms are often used interchangeably. In this chapter's discussion of generic OLAP concepts, we will continue to use the term *cube* to describe an Essbase database.

In Oracle OLAP, data is stored in cubes of varying dimensionality. Specifically, the data and the type of analysis required determine the number of dimensions represented in any given cube. For example, sales data may be broken down by four dimensions: region, time, channel, and product, but budgetary data may be broken down only by channel or region. With Oracle OLAP, you can specify the dimensions for each of the two cubes independently. A single cube is often loaded from a central fact table and the associated dimension tables. These cubes are presented as a star schema, and can be used as cube-organized materialized views in the larger relational database, which will be discussed in more detail in Chapters 3 and 4.

From a practical standpoint, the functionality that is exposed to the end user from either Essbase or Oracle OLAP is very similar. End users can interact with their data in an easy-to-understand, intuitive fashion. How the application is built and maintained relates to the core differences of the two products.

Dimensions, Hierarchies, and Members

As discussed in Chapter 1, a *dimension* is a collection of items that share some attribute or characteristic. You define dimensions for those attributes or characteristics that you want to report or analyze. Dimensions contain members such as January or February, which are often organized into one or more hierarchies.

The concept of a hierarchy is intuitive. Hierarchies are how human beings like to think of and categorize concepts. For example, if you have ever written an essay in school, you organized the information in a hierarchy.

1. Animals

    a. Dogs

        i. Labrador

        ii. Shepherd

        iii. Terrier

A typical dimension consists of one or more members, each of which may contain one or more hierarchies of members. Figure 2-2 shows partial dimension hierarchies for Time, Products, and Markets.

The relationships between members within a dimension define the dimension hierarchy. OLAP systems often use a genealogical model to explain the relationships among members, so we can talk about members having children, parents, siblings, ancestors, and descendants. In Figure 2-2, Sodas has two children (Fruit Soda and Cream Soda), one parent (Products), and at least one sibling (Colas).

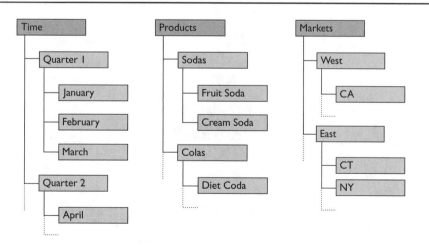

FIGURE 2-2.   *Dimension hierarchy*

Another way to talk about a member is by its location, or level, within a hierarchy. In Figure 2-2, the Time dimension has three levels: time (which corresponds to the year), quarters, and months. Members with no children are called *base-level members* or *leaf members*. In this Time dimension, the base-level members are the 12 months of the year.

When a hierarchy contains at least one base-level member at a different level than the other base-level members, it is called a *ragged hierarchy*. Ragged hierarchies are very common in OLAP systems, as they typically explain the complexity in the real world. For example, in Figure 2-3, the sales for a company are broken down by region of the country and then state for the United States, but only by a few provinces for Canada, and simply by country for Mexico. This type of hierarchy reflects that business people tend to think about the business in groups that are of a similar size. In the example in Figure 2-3, the company has sales that are approximately equal across the regions in the United States, within the selected provinces in Canada, and for the entire country of Mexico.

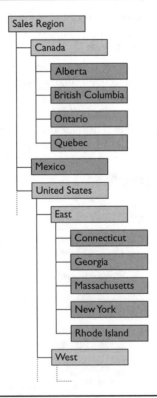

FIGURE 2-3. *A ragged hierarchy with leaf nodes highlighted*

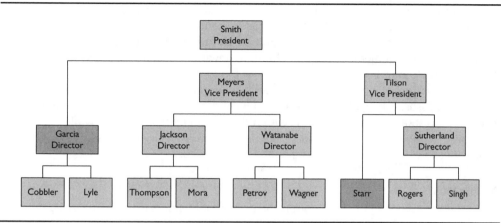

FIGURE 2-4. *Skip-level hierarchy with skip-through nodes highlighted*

When a hierarchy has at least one member whose parent is more than one level above it, the hierarchy is referred to as a *skip-level hierarchy*. For example, in Figure 2-4, the president, Smith, has vice presidents as well as a director reporting to him. The director, Garcia, skips through the vice president level. Another skip-level occurs in Tilson's reporting structure, where Tilson has a director (Sutherland) as well as a regular employee (Starr) reporting to her. Starr skips through the director level. Again, multidimensional systems make it easy to represent the real world in an intuitive manner.

Robust OLAP systems, including Oracle OLAP and Essbase, support ragged hierarchies and skip-level hierarchies.

NOTE
The homogenous use of a single dimension representing multiple levels is sometimes confusing to DBAs who are used to relational database concepts. Columns in a relational table can store only one type of item, such as a month or a year; they cannot store both types. In an OLAP application, to select just months, you simply ask for times at the month level.

Oracle OLAP and Essbase implement dimensions, hierarchies, and members in similar ways. They use the language of genealogy to describe member relationships. Both products also implement the concept of levels, but in different ways. In Oracle OLAP, you define and label levels in a hierarchy. You can also have value-based hierarchies, where the parent-child structure is in place, but specific levels are not identified—just the depth from the top. Essbase automatically identifies levels in two ways: levels and generations. Levels are numbered from bottom to top, where level 0 is a leaf member (a member with no children), level 1 is its parent, and so forth up the hierarchy. Generations are numbered from top to bottom, where generation 1 is the root of the dimension, generation 2 is all its children, and so forth down the hierarchies. Essbase also allows user-defined level names. In all cases, you can use levels to map source data to locations within dimension hierarchies. The walk-throughs in Chapters 4 and 5 provide more details on how to map data sources to dimensions.

Attributes

An inherent value of an OLAP system is the ability for business users to analyze data in a way that makes sense to them. We do this every day when we make a decision based on a variety of environmental and personal points of view. To that end, OLAP models have evolved to provide the ability to view data in a variety of ways.

One way to provide alternate views of the data is through user-defined attributes or groupings. An *attribute* is a tag or property assigned to a member. For example, you might tag some Market members as "Major Market," so that an end user can easily find and present all of the major markets in a report.

Oracle OLAP and Essbase approach user-defined attributes in the same way— that is, as tags assigned to members. Users can create as many different attribute tags as they need to suit their purposes. Attributes can be assigned to any dimension, and a member can have multiple attributes associated with it. There are no calculations inherent in attributes, but attributes can be used within calculations. In addition to user-defined attributes, Essbase also has a dimension type called an *attribute dimension*, which provides a way to create alternate hierarchies based on a characteristic of the members. For more information, see the related sections in Chapter 3.

Alternate Hierarchies

Another way to get alternate views of the data is to define more than one hierarchy for a dimension. Alternate hierarchies provide different ways to aggregate a dimension. For example, a Customer dimension may have a geographic hierarchy and a managerial hierarchy, as shown in Figure 2-5. If analysis is typically performed using one of these hierarchies (but not both at the same time!), this is best done with two hierarchies of the same dimension. OLAP products ensure that data is not counted more than once when using alternate hierarchies.

The products differ in their implementation of alternate hierarchies. In Oracle OLAP, each dimension has a current hierarchy that defines the current drill path

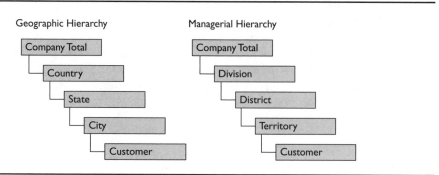

FIGURE 2-5. *Multiple hierarchies for a Customer dimension*

for the dimension. Users can select a hierarchy to use as their current hierarchy. Because users are working with only one hierarchy of a dimension at a time, there is little risk in counting the data multiple times. In Essbase, alternate hierarchies can be defined in two ways: by creating attribute dimensions and by creating hierarchies that contain shared members (pointers to members in the primary hierarchy). Users can drill through to different hierarchies as easily as drilling down from one level to the next. We define and discuss drill paths in the "Ad Hoc Analysis: Having a Conversation with Your Data" section later in this chapter.

Unique Versus Duplicate Members

A discussion about alternate hierarchies generally leads to another discussion—one concerning the concepts of unique and duplicate members. A duplicate member occurs when you use the same member name for more than one member.

For example, consider an OLAP system for a shipping company that has a dimension for Origin and another dimension for Destination. A customer in San Francisco could both send and receive packages from that location, which means that the customer would legitimately need to belong to both dimensions. Although the company could create unique names, a more elegant solution from the user perspective would be to allow the customer to exist in both dimensions, and use the context of the member within the hierarchy to provide the uniqueness. This approach to creating uniqueness is similar to that used in object-oriented programming, where the larger class defines the unique attributes of the member.

Essbase and Oracle OLAP support duplicate members. In Essbase, member names are assumed to be unique unless you enable support for duplicate members.

Duplicate members are made unique by prefixing the member name with its ancestors, up to and including the dimension name. Oracle OLAP, on the other hand, has no unified list of dimension values across all dimensions, so duplicate members across dimensions are not an issue. Oracle OLAP offers support for duplicate members within a dimension using surrogate keys. Support for surrogate keys is on by default. In Oracle OLAP, level names in a hierarchy are user-defined. Oracle OLAP makes the member name unique by prefixing the member name with the level name.

NOTE
In Essbase, working with a model that contains duplicates is more complex from a reporting perspective. In this book, assume that all examples are created using unique member names only.

Dimensions, hierarchies, members, levels, and attributes form the structure of a cube. The data comes from measures.

Measures and Values

Measures represent business data that is important for analysis, such as sales and cost of goods sold. Measure values are the data that fills the intersections in a cube. To be meaningful, a value must be defined in terms of all dimensions in the cube (hence the term *multidimensional analysis*). For example, in Figure 2-1, we determine the meaning of the highlighted sales value of 267 by examining the dimension members that form the intersection at that value, and so we understand that 267 units of soda were sold in California in January.

TIP
For those with a relational database data warehouse background, a measure is synonymous with a fact in a fact table. When a relational database provides the source data, unique key columns are often the dimensions and fact columns are often the measures.

Stored measures are values saved in the cube. *Calculated measures* are values derived from calculations based on stored measures and/or other calculated measures.

Oracle OLAP and Essbase have some key similarities in how they implement measures. Both products allow for stored measures and calculated measures (though

Essbase uses the terms *stored values* and *calculated values* instead). In each case, decisions must be made about the level of detail to include in the cube; for example, it may be more appropriate to provide summary-level data in a cube rather than detailed data.

The products also have differences in how measures are handled:

- With Oracle OLAP, you create multiple cubes of varying dimensionality, which means that understanding the context of a measure is straightforward. Measures are organized by their dimensions and typically include a Time dimension. In contrast, Essbase includes all dimensions in its multidimensional database, so querying and understanding the meaning of an individual measure can be more complex, because you need to think across more dimensions.

- Oracle OLAP has no internal representation of a "measures dimension" per se, and no hierarchy of measures, whereas Essbase has a dimension type for measures called *accounts.* What makes an accounts dimension special is that Essbase calculates the accounts dimension first. Other than that, it behaves exactly like any other dimension stored in the cube.

- With Essbase, any dimension can have calculated values, whereas with Oracle OLAP, calculated measures can be defined, but calculated values of other dimensions require special techniques called *models.* In Oracle OLAP 11*g* Release 1 and earlier, this is done in OLAP Worksheet via the OLAP Data Manipulation Language (DML). Models can be defined for any dimension by database administrators and will be covered later in this book.

Aggregation

OLAP systems leverage the concept of hierarchies for calculation purposes, providing default calculations simply by aggregating the values of the members up the hierarchy. Take the Time dimension in Figure 2-2, for example. Time has a value that represents the total of the values for each of the four quarters in the year. The quarter members get their value from the summation of the months within the quarter. This speeds the access to information and makes it easy for the OLAP system to find the values and present them to end users.

Both Essbase and Oracle OLAP implement the concept of aggregation. Aggregation, by default, is addition. You can turn off aggregation or change the operation from addition to some other operation. We discuss aggregation operators, as well as other ways to perform calculations, in more detail in the "New Results from Existing Data" section later in this chapter. With both Oracle OLAP and Essbase, aggregations can occur either in some batch process or on the fly as a user is querying the cube.

From Data Source to Multidimensional Data

In the previous section, we talked about measures as the data in the cube. All OLAP systems pull data into cubes from one or more data sources. An important part of both OLAP engines is how the data will be stored to optimize efficient access to respond to end-user queries. In this section, we discuss concepts related to data, including data sources, dense and sparse cubes, partitions, security of the data, and write-back to the cube.

Data Sources

A company's source data often comes from transactional systems, such as point-of-sale or customer relationship management (CRM) applications. To perform an OLAP analysis, source data needs to be made available to the OLAP engine. We use the phrase "made available" very deliberately, because depending on the type of OLAP implementation, data may or may not need to be moved into the OLAP engine.

Data Sources and OLAP Types   An OLAP engine stores and accesses data differently, depending on the type of OLAP implementation. As discussed in Chapter 1, the three main types of OLAP are multidimensional OLAP (MOLAP), relational OLAP (ROLAP), and hybrid OLAP (HOLAP), which store data as follows:

- With MOLAP, the engine stores data—often aggregated data—in a multidimensional structure.

- With ROLAP, data is stored in a relational source, and the OLAP engine generates dynamic SQL to extract the data for analytical processing at query time.

- With HOLAP, the engine stores some data in the OLAP engine and some data in a relational data source. Depending on the level of detail required for the query or analysis, the data may need to be accessed from one or both locations. For example, if you have a model that analyzes sales patterns across the United States, you might store data down to the city level in the OLAP structure, but leave granular data like zip (postal) codes in the relational structure. The decision to store data in one location or another is most often a factor of processing efficiency and query performance requirements.

Relational Database Schemas   When mapping a relational data source to a cube, OLAP products make use of the relational source's star or snowflake schema as a way to define dimensions and hierarchies.

As illustrated in Figure 2-6, a star dimensional model uses fact tables and a set of smaller dimension tables. The star dimensional model is a flat model that allows for

FIGURE 2-6. *Star model with one fact table and smaller dimension tables*

easier user access than third normal form. Dimension tables act much like foreign key tables or reference tables in an online transactional processing (OLTP) system. Fact tables have key values that relate to the dimension tables and fact columns, such as quantity.

A snowflake model is an extension of a star dimensional model, as illustrated in Figure 2-7. It normalizes and aggregates the dimensions in a star dimensional model. This has the effect of creating more tables and requires more SQL joins.

Both Oracle OLAP and Essbase have administrative applications that can read a star or snowflake schema and present the tables for selection in an OLAP cube.

Multidimensional Storage and Access

As noted in Chapter 1, speed-of-thought response time to queries is a hallmark of OLAP. The way OLAP engines store and retrieve data is necessarily different from a traditional, relational database-based, data warehouse approach. Before we visit OLAP solutions, let's explore how traditional data warehouses typically access data.

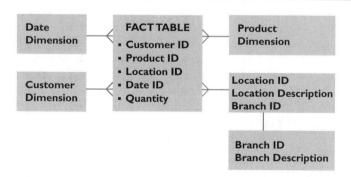

FIGURE 2-7. *Snowflake model*

Traditional Data Warehouse Approach—Bitmapped Indexes   Bitmapped indexes are important for data warehouses. Bitmapped indexes logically map each row with each distinct data value. Bitmapped indexes are generally chosen over a B-tree data structure for low-cardinality columns. Low cardinality is determined by dividing the number of distinct column values by the total number of rows. If the result is below 5 percent, the column has low cardinality. For example, a one million row table might have a State column that has only 50 distinct values. In this case, the State column has low cardinality, since 50 divided by 1 million is less than 5 percent.

A properly designed bitmapped index is approximately ten times smaller than a B-tree data structure. As these indexes must be stored as structures in the data warehouse and consume disk space storage, there is a constant tension between how much indexing is needed versus how much space is to be consumed and taken away from the data. Because of its much smaller size, a bitmapped index is ideal for traditional data warehouses.

An OLAP Approach—Arrays   At its most basic level, OLAP products store multidimensional data in arrays. Arrays provide a way of organizing OLAP data. Data is stored very efficiently, since the keys (dimension values) are kept separate from the data in the cube. OLAP dimensions are analogous to an array's subscripts. The dimensions serve as a sort of index to the array, and they provide fast access to the data. Data in arrays can be located with simple arithmetic.

In Oracle OLAP, the implementation of the array-based storage concept is more sophisticated than simple arithmetic, especially with respect to sparse data sets. For example, aggregate compression delivers very sophisticated algorithms for storing and retrieving data optimally. Oracle OLAP automatically manages retrieving data from disk when required and caching the data in memory as appropriate.

Essbase has two approaches to storing data: block storage and aggregate storage. For block storage, data is stored in an array. For aggregate storage, data is stored in tablespace—similar to a large array—as a collection of cells. We discuss the two types of storage models in more detail in Chapter 3.

Essbase handles data and requests for data using two primary structures: indexes and a data storage mechanism (array or cell). Whenever a data value is queried, loaded, or calculated, Essbase brings the specific data storage file into memory. To find the proper data, Essbase uses an index. All data values in the model are indexed. Essbase holds this index in RAM (in many cases), and each request first goes to the index to find the data location. Once identified, Essbase brings that data into RAM to perform the requested action. Both the data index and data files are compressed while on disk, and to a lesser degree, in RAM. The nature of the compression varies depending on the type of numeric data stored in the structure.

Dense and Sparse Cubes

Density is a ratio of the total number of cells in an OLAP cube that are populated with a value versus the total number of possible cells in the cube. The closer this ratio is to 1, the denser the OLAP cube; the further away from 1, the sparser the cube. For example, consider a cube that contains sales data by time by products by markets. If most of the products are sold in most of the markets over the year, then most of the cells contain data, and the cube is *dense*. If the opposite is true—most products are not sold in most markets—many of the cells are empty, and the cube is *sparse*.

Sparse cubes take more space than necessary to store because space is reserved for every cell, whether or not it has data in it. They may also take longer than necessary to calculate, because null data cells are considered for calculation along with values. OLAP systems use different approaches to address sparsity of data.

In Essbase, most cubes are inherently sparse because they contain all dimensions. Essbase handles sparsity in two ways, depending on which type of data storage is in use: block or aggregate. We will talk more about storage types later. For the moment, it is sufficient to know that, for block storage databases, Essbase requires that the administrator tag dimensions as dense or sparse at the outline level, so that it knows how to store the data. For example, a Time dimension is usually dense, while a Product dimension is often sparse. In aggregate storage databases, Essbase does not require the dense/sparse tag; it handles sparsity at the storage level.

In Oracle OLAP, the administrator defines a dimension as sparse. For all sparse dimensions, Oracle OLAP defines a special type of dimension called a *composite*. The composite holds only the combinations of the sparse dimensions that actually contain data. This composite is maintained automatically by Oracle OLAP and is integrated with its advanced compression algorithms for handling aggregate data. Composites are discussed in more detail in Chapter 3.

Partitions

Whenever a database handles volumes of data, the concept of data partitioning across multiple data storage becomes important. In a data warehouse environment, for example, partitioning allows huge tables to be broken up into a series of smaller tables with faster access, but the SQL application can query the series of smaller tables as if it were one big table. With partitioning, a data warehouse can expand to many hundreds of terabytes, while ensuring that results are returned in a reasonable amount of time. A partitioned architecture also enables you to drop a partition, which takes less than a second. If you do not partition, deleting old data could take a long time.

OLAP cubes can also benefit from partitioning data. By partitioning your data, you can break your data into more manageable chunks, but you are able to hide the complexity of this strategy from the application and end user. For example, you could partition a Time dimension so that historical data (say, older than five years) is kept in a separate partition, allowing faster access to data from more recent years. When implemented effectively, partitions help to ensure fast, reliable, and concurrent access to OLAP data.

Oracle OLAP and Essbase both offer partitioning strategies. Oracle OLAP allows you to define a dimension as a partitioning dimension. Generally, you identify a level (such as year) of the partitioning dimension, although more complex designs are possible. Cubes are physically separated into individual partitions for each year, but the partitioning scheme is transparent to applications that query or write to a cube. At query time, partition pruning occurs—meaning if you partition by year and ask for data for a single year, only one partition is accessed for the data. Partitions can be added and removed easily. We discuss partitioning Oracle OLAP cubes in Chapter 4.

In Essbase, you can think of a partition as a region of a cube that is shared with another cube. Partitions come in three types:

- *Replicated partitions* allow you to store data in different cubes and copy shared data from one cube to another.

- *Transparent partitions* enable users to navigate seamless from locally stored data to remotely stored data.

- *Linked partitions* provide a means of linking a cell in a cube to a different cube with potentially different dimensionality.

We discuss Essbase partitioning strategies in Chapter 3.

Slowly Changing Dimensions

Slowly changing dimensions are dimensions that change over time—sometimes a little, but sometimes (perhaps because of an acquisition) a lot. For example, consider a cube that tracks personnel data. The dimension that tracks employee names is a slowly changing dimension because it is possible for the names, in particular the surnames, to change. While you could simply overwrite the data, it may be important to track the changes.

Handling slowly changing data effectively is critical in any database. Data warehousing theory proposes methods for managing changing data that we can also apply to OLAP cubes:

- Type 1: Replace the value

- Type 2: Add a record with an effective start date and effective end date

- Type 3: Store the old value

- Type 6: A combination of Types 1, 2, and 3

Because slowly changing dimensions are so important, let's take some time to understand how each type works before we look at how Oracle OLAP and Essbase implement this concept. For this discussion, we will use the following example: Mary Smith marries Bob Jones and decides to change her name to Mary Jones.

Type 1   In Type 1, the column or attribute value is simply overwritten and the previous value is lost. In our example, a Type 1 methodology would just change the member dimension to update the last name from Smith to Jones. The fact that Mary was once Mary Smith is lost. For example, this data:

Key	First Name	Last Name
12345	Mary	Smith

becomes this data:

Key	First Name	Last Name
12345	Mary	Jones

Type 2   In Type 2, an additional record is created, as well as fields for the effective start date and the effective end date. In our example, a Type 2 methodology would add a new record for Mary Jones with the effective start date of today. The old record would have the effective end date updated with today's date. The fact that Mary was once Mary Smith is not lost.

Key	First Name	Last Name	Eff_Start	Eff_End
12345	Mary	Smith	1/18/1960	3/14/2006
45678	Mary	Jones	3/14/2006	

Type 3   In Type 3, an attribute is added to the record. In our example, a Type 3 change would add fields to the record to contain the old name. The old last name field would be set to Smith, and the current last name field would be changed to Jones.

Key	First Name	Last Name	Prior First Name	Prior Last Name
12345	Mary	Smith	Mary	Jones

Type 6   Type 6 combines Types 1, 2, and 3. Expanding on our example, let's say that Mary Smith was born on 1/18/1960. Mary Smith marries Bob Jones and

becomes Mary Jones on 3/14/2003. On 7/24/2005, Mary Jones divorces Bob Jones. On 9/17/2005, Mary Jones marries Mark Davis and chooses to take his last name.

Key	Current First Name	Current Last Name	Historical First Name	Historical Last Name	Eff_Start	Eff_End
12345	Mary	Smith	Mary	Smith	1/18/1960	

Key	Current First Name	Current Last Name	Historical First Name	Historical Last Name	Eff_Start	Eff_End
12345	Mary	Jones	Mary	Smith	1/18/1960	3/14/2003
45678	Mary	Jones	Mary	Smith	3/14/2003	

Key	Current First Name	Current Last Name	Historical First Name	Historical Last Name	Eff_Start	Eff_End
12345	Mary	Davis	Mary	Smith	1/18/1960	3/14/2003
45678	Mary	Davis	Mary	Jones	3/14/2003	7/24/2005
56789	Mary	Davis	Mary	Jones	9/17/2005	

This method gives us the most flexibility, but at the highest cost in terms of space and maintenance.

Oracle OLAP and Essbase Implementation   Both Oracle OLAP and Essbase support slowly changing dimensions. In Oracle OLAP, you can model slowly changing dimensions using attributes and measures. For example, to model the preceding example, you would simply map the key column to the dimension member. Type 1 will be handled automatically—when the dimension is maintained, the name will change. For Type 2 and Type 3, simply add attributes or measures for the Eff_Start and Eff_End and Prior First Name and Prior Last Name to allow the user to choose which dimension members to use for selection or display purposes. For Type 6, you can add attributes and measures for the historical names as well.

In Essbase, you can model slowly changing dimensions using user-defined attributes, aliases, alternate hierarchies created with shared members, or varying attributes. For example, to model the preceding example in a Type 1 scenario, you would simply change the name of the Mary Smith member to Mary Jones. For Type 3, you could use an alias, so that the member name remains unchanged, but you could use the new name for query and display purposes. If you need to track when the surname changed, as in a Type 2 scenario, a user-defined attribute or varying attribute may be more appropriate. Alternatively, if you are mapping a Type 2 or Type 6 approach directly from the relational source to an Essbase cube, you can load the columns into Essbase as usual, and then vary attributes across time on the Historical Last Name.

Security and User Access

The security of the data in OLAP systems is critical. Some organizations have all-or-nothing security procedures, meaning that you can either see the data or you cannot see the data. More often, various groups of users need access to specific portions of OLAP cubes. For example, maybe the Eastern region manager should have access to only the data for the Eastern region and all of the customers in the Eastern region. A robust OLAP system offers the ability to set user access for the cube, as well as at various levels in the cube, including dimensions and measures.

Oracle OLAP leverages Oracle Database user accounts, passwords, and security measures to protect data, using commands such as GRANT to control access to cubes, just like any other database object such as tables. In addition to this overall security, object security lets you grant and revoke access to dimensional objects using SQL. For data security, Analytic Workspace Manager (AWM) allows you to control access to sections of a cube at the cellular level, in a fashion similar to virtual private databases (VPDs), typically for each dimension.

Similar to Oracle OLAP, Essbase supports detailed user and group security. Essbase provides general security for cube access and administrative roles (such as the ability to provision users). Additionally, Essbase allows for a series of optional security levels on objects as well as data and metadata. From a data and metadata perspective, Essbase supports security down to the cell level.

Write-Back to the Cube to Build Scenarios

Write-back provides end users with the ability to change the values in the cube. End users can try out various scenarios (called *scenario playing*) by posing "what-if" type questions. For example, a business user might want to see what would happen if sales for a product or set of products increased by 5 percent. Many modeling and planning applications are based on scenario playing. When OLAP systems support scenario playing, system administrators assign write-back permission to authorized end users.

Essbase and Oracle OLAP support scenario playing and write-back via front-end applications. Essbase has write-back built in as a basic feature. Oracle OLAP provides the capability via the BI Spreadsheet Add-in, through the OLAP DML, or by using SQL to change the original source tables. For both products, administrators grant write access using the standard user access and security mechanisms for each product.

New Results from Existing Data

At the heart of an OLAP solution is the ability to perform quick and often complex calculations. In addition to the aggregation, OLAP engines contain hundreds of prepackaged calculation functions, ranging from a simple average function to the more complex allocation, return on investment (ROI), and trend functions. Many OLAP engines also provide the capability to define calculations based on standard mathematical operators.

Advanced Aggregation Operators

We have already discussed the concept of aggregation that is built in to the hierarchical structure of OLAP systems. Many OLAP products enable you to change what happens during the aggregation, either by preventing some values from rolling up where logically the results would not make sense or by changing addition to some other operation as a function of the underlying dimension or data.

Both Essbase and Oracle OLAP support additional aggregation operators, though the available operations are very different. In Essbase, they are called *consolidation operators*, and the set is limited to basic mathematical operations (addition, subtraction, multiplication, division, percentage, and do not consolidate). Oracle OLAP offers a different and larger set of aggregation operators, which are grouped as basic operators (such as sum and average), scaled and weighted operators (such as scaled sum and weighted average), and hierarchical operators (similar to the previous operations, but all children are taken into consideration, even if they do not contain data). In both products, when using different aggregation operators, the order of calculation becomes important and requires special attention.

Calculated Measures/Values

One powerful feature of the OLAP calculation engine is the ability to create and perform complex business calculations. The concept of a calculated measure is simple. The measures are derived from the values of other measures, including stored and other calculated measures in the current cube or other cubes. The calculated measures look the same as stored measures to the end users, which makes them easy for end users to use. As previously mentioned, OLAP engines can handle complex calculations very quickly, and it is often more efficient to allow the engine to calculate values at query time, rather than calculating and storing them.

Oracle OLAP and Essbase offer a wealth of predefined calculations and powerful expression languages, though they may differ in both the number and types of calculations available. The products also differ in how calculated measures/ values are created. Oracle OLAP has templates for calculating business measures. It has a rich library of dimension and hierarchical functions, and is syntactically similar to SQL analytic and window functions. Essbase allows you define calculated values by attaching formulas to members (for any dimension) and creating calculation scripts.

Ad Hoc Analysis: Having a Conversation with Your Data

A principal value of OLAP is that it is tangible. You get to interact with the data in a fashion that make sense to you, as opposed to looking at only static information in a report. Another way to think of it is that OLAP lets you have a conversation with your data. Ask a question based on the dimensions and hierarchies, and you get the answer in any visual format you desire. Interacting with an OLAP source in this fashion is often called *ad hoc analysis.*

In the real world, as you start to understand your business and ask questions of it, the first question often spawns a second set of questions. As you answer the second set, there can be third or fourth (or more) iterations of questions. Like a process of scientific discovery, asking a question and uncovering the answer will often spawn follow-up questions. OLAP is designed to support this line of inquiry.

It is important to draw a distinction here between end-user client tools and the capabilities of a centralized OLAP engine. The abilities described in this section are inherent to OLAP engines, and they are simply exposed to client tools as application programming interface (API) calls or query languages. There is no need for a client-side tool, for instance, to create the ability to drill down. Instead, the tool simply asks the engine for the members on the next level of the hierarchy. Front-end tools for Oracle OLAP and Essbase take advantage of these built-in capabilities in similar ways.

Drill Path

Drill paths determine what happens when a user navigates through data. Usually, the drill path correlates to the organization of the hierarchies. *Drilling down* (or *zooming in*) enables you to navigate to lower levels in hierarchy. For example, if you want to view data for a specific quarter rather than the data value for the whole year, you can drill down on the Year dimension to see quarter information directly below. *Drilling up* (also called *zooming out* or *rolling up*) lets you navigate to higher levels of the hierarchy by collapsing the current member tree. For example, as shown in Figure 2-8, if you drill down on Qtr1 to view data by months, you can drill up to see only the total Qtr1 member again. As you drill up, cardinalities shrink and the portion of the cube that is visible gets smaller.

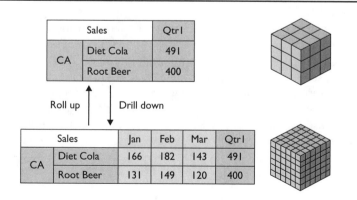

FIGURE 2-8. *Drilling down and rolling up values in a cube*

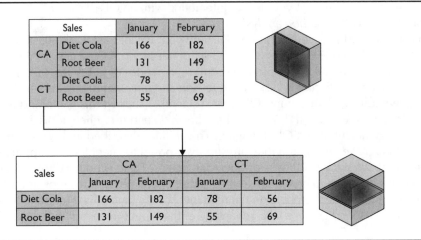

FIGURE 2-9. *Rotating the cube*

Pivot

Pivoting lets you change the orientation of a report. For example, you can move a dimension from a row to a column. Conceptually, pivoting can be thought of as rotating the cube to view analytic data from different perspectives. Figure 2-9 shows how you can change the visualization of sales data by pivoting the Markets dimension.

You can also use pivoting to move a dimension off the grid to the page. When a dimension is on the page, it acts as a report filter, filtering data visible on the current page by the selected member.

Slicing and Dicing Data

The ability to remove or retain subsets of members on a dimension is a hallmark of an OLAP reporting application. Often, the entire cube is enormous—much larger than can be effectively presented to the user at one time. The OLAP engine allows you to select a subset of data to be presented to the user, as shown in Figure 2-10.

Oracle OLAP implements slice and dice functionality using a powerful "selection" capability that allows you to determine which dimension values are to be displayed. Essbase uses the intuitive Keep Only action to focus on in a selected subset and the Remove Only action to remove the subset selected from the current view of data. While these differences are located in the front-end client tools, not

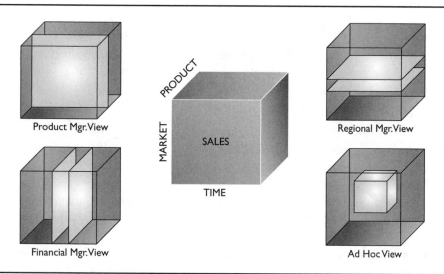

Product Mgr. View

Regional Mgr. View

Financial Mgr. View

Ad Hoc View

FIGURE 2-10.   *Slices of data in a cube*

the engines themselves, differences in the API calls for Oracle OLAP and Essbase influence the capabilities exposed to end users.

Summary of Common OLAP Themes

You should now have a better understanding of OLAP concepts in general and how Oracle OLAP and Essbase implement those concepts. Table 2-1 summarizes these OLAP concepts and maps them to the terms used by Oracle OLAP and Essbase. The concepts are listed in the order in which they were introduced in this chapter.

Each product offers full OLAP capabilities; only the implementations are different. Most of the differences in implementation stem from the different approaches taken by the products. The difference in approach is best understood within the context of the origins and evolution of the products. The next two sections summarize the history of Oracle OLAP and Essbase.

OLAP Concept	Oracle OLAP Terms	Essbase Terms
Cube	Cubes, cube-organized materialized views	Multidimensional database, cube
Dimension	Dimension	Dimension
Dimension member	Dimension member	Dimension member, shared member
Dimension hierarchy	Hierarchy, current hierarchy, level-based hierarchy, value-based hierarchy	Hierarchy, alternate hierarchy
Hierarchy level	Levels (user-defined), value-based hierarchy	Levels (automatic or user-defined), generations
Member relationships within a hierarchy	Ancestor, parent, sibling, child, descendant	Ancestor, parent, sibling, child, descendant
Attribute	Attribute	User-defined attribute (UDA), Attribute dimension
Alternate hierarchy	Hierarchy, current hierarchy, level-based hierarchy, value-based hierarchy	Alternate hierarchy, attribute dimension, hierarchy of shared members
Measure	Measure, stored measure	Data value, stored value, Accounts dimension type
Calculated measure	Calculated measure	Calculated value
Aggregation	Aggregation, aggregation operators	Consolidation, consolidation operators
Density and sparsity	Dense, sparse, compressed composites	Dense, sparse, block storage, aggregate storage
Drill	Drill up, drill down	Zoom out/drill up, zoom in/drill down
Pivot	Pivot	Pivot, point of view
Slice and dice	Selection capability	Keep Only and Remove Only

TABLE 2-1. *Mapping OLAP Concepts to Oracle OLAP and Essbase*

The History of Oracle OLAP

Oracle OLAP has a rich history extending back before the advent of relational databases. It grew out of a business need to represent business data in a form that could be easily analyzed. It has gone through several changes over the decades. This section reviews the history of Oracle OLAP, from its Express days to its current status as the multidimensional component of Oracle's flagship database, the Oracle OLAP option to Oracle Database Enterprise Edition.

Why a Multidimensional Database?

In the late 1960s, Jay Wurts, a student at Massachusetts Institute of Technology (MIT) was working on a project for his professor, John Little. When calculating how much should be spent on advertising for cookies, Wurts found that he spent most of his time wrestling with reformatting the data for his analysis, not on the statistical algorithms or the true data analysis. He realized that he needed some sort of computer-based analytical tool bench for supporting decision making. If the data model could be abstracted from the data itself, the system could be used for a wide array of projects, instead of starting from scratch each time.

Wurts found that once he had modeled the data in a multidimensional form, he was able to report the data in many different formats. By abstracting the data model from the data itself, his system could produce reports that were not part of the original specifications. The user could work with the data in an ad hoc fashion, asking questions that had not been formulated when developing the specifications, on data that was not even loaded when the system was first constructed. Wurts's system allowed users to interact with the data using meaningful names, such as regions, products, months, and so on. Enhancing the system to store numbers with more precision allowed the same engine to be used for financial analysis as well, opening up the software product to a new set of customers.

1960s to 1985—Glory Days of Mainframe Express

In the early 1970s, Wurts and others in the MIT community—including John Little, Glen Urban, and Len Lodish—formed the company Management Decision Systems (MDS) in Weston, Massachusetts, outside of Boston. They developed Wurts's original multidimensional engine into the product called Express. In the Express environment, arrays can be manipulated with a fourth-generation language (4GL) to conduct business analysis and build systems that help support business decisions, a class of applications then called decision support systems (DSSs). Eventually, this product would be called Mainframe Express.

Mainframe Express was delivered on the IBM VM/CMS, and then Primos platforms in the 1970s and 1980s. Over the years, advanced capabilities were added to Mainframe Express as it developed into a full-fledged decision-support calculation engine. These included advanced linear-programming capabilities, Box-Jenkins modeling, goal-seeking and a LIMIT command to scope down further commands in a session to subsets of the storage array, and embedded total dimensions for handling multiple levels of a hierarchy in a single structure. Built in this environment were applications such as EasyTrac, a general-purpose DSS application, and Easycast, a general-purpose forecasting product.

1985 to 1990—A New C-Based Engine

By the mid-1980s, it was time for Express to move to a more modern development environment. Originally written in the AED programming language, Express was rewritten in the C programming language, which was popular at that time. This allowed MDS to attract talented programmers to work on Express. It also allowed MDS to port Express to additional operating systems and hardware platforms, including the increasingly popular IBM PC.

At the same time, MDS recognized that it needed a more sophisticated method of storing data to deal with issues such as inserting new dimension values without needing to rewrite the entire array (a process called *shuffling*). This new engine was first delivered in 1986 on the MS-DOS operating system as pcEXPRESS version 1.0. As demand for larger databases grew, the limitations of the PC hardware became apparent. This new C-based engine was ported to several operating systems and servers, including VM/CMS, MVS/TSO, VMS, and several variations of UNIX. The product was called pcEXPRESS on the PC platform and Express MDB on other platforms.

Express became dominant in consumer packaged goods companies due to its flexible query capabilities and speed. Many of these companies were also customers of Information Resources, Inc. (IRI), a Chicago-based syndicated data company. IRI had been delivering its supermarket sales data in volumes of books called the *Marketing Fact Book*. By the mid-1980s, it was looking for a way to deliver its sales data in a new interactive manner. IRI wanted its users to be able to drill down on reports and make the experience of using the data more interactive. IRI purchased MDS in 1985, leaving the Express development staff in the Boston area.

Applications written in Express, especially those targeted to consumer packaged goods companies, became very important to IRI. Express was the underlying technology for EasyTrac, later named DataServer by IRI. In the first releases of EasyTrac/DataServer, pcEXPRESS was used as the front end, providing the ability to navigate through dimensions in a rich environment, and using Mainframe Express and then Express MDB to manage the data using a client/server model. DataServer would become the major delivery vehicle for IRI's new InfoScan data service, which replaced the *Marketing Fact Book*. Other applications were developed as well, most notably Financial Management System (FMS), a distributed budgeting and planning application.

Between versions 1.0 and 5.0, the pcEXPRESS/Express MDB engine eventually gained the same sophisticated capabilities as Mainframe Express, including self-ordering models that would intelligently figure out the order in which equations needed to be solved to calculate a model, and seasonally adjusted forecasting algorithms, such as Holt-Winters.

1990 to 1996—Express Goes GUI

pcEXPRESS was designed with a character-based user interface—80 characters by 25 lines. Data was presented in scrollable tables, and the keyboard was used for navigation. The end user could enter graphics mode to display graphs, but true interaction with graphs was limited. Express MDB had only a command-line interface. As personal computer hardware evolved to support graphical user interfaces (GUIs), users began demanding GUIs and the ability to use a mouse with applications. An Executive Information System (EIS) product was offered as a general-purpose tool for finance departments that operated entirely in graphics mode.

To address demands for a richer client interface, IRI started building applications with entirely separate GUIs using Visual Basic and C. Applications were rewritten in this object-oriented GUI environment. The two most successful applications included Financial Management System and SalesAnalyzer (successor to DataServer). Additional applications with analysis capabilities were developed using IRI's data, including SalesPartner, an expert system for fact-based selling; Coverstory, a tool for automatically producing board-room-ready presentations; and BrandPartner for fact-based marketing.

During these years, Express competed head-to-head with Essbase. Essbase touted its intuitive spreadsheet interface. Express touted its strong multicube storage model.

1995 to 1997—Oracle Buys and Markets Express

In 1995, IRI was looking for cash to retire debt and fund its international expansion. At the same time, Oracle Corporation wanted to augment the data warehouse capabilities in its relational database with OLAP technology. OLAP applications require a multidimensional view of the data, star schemas, and interrow joins for time comparisons and share calculations. Express seemed to fit the bill perfectly. Oracle ended up buying the Express product line and related applications, leaving IRI's syndicated data service with IRI. In effect, Oracle bought IRI's Boston-based products, applications, and development organization. DataServer and SalesAnalyzer were renamed to Oracle Sales Analyzer and sold as a very effective general-purpose performance analysis application. Financial Management System was renamed to Oracle Financial Analyzer (OFA) and sold as a very effective financial analysis and distributed budgeting application.

From 1995 to 1997, Oracle ran the Express products group as a separate group. In this time period, Express Server version 6.0 was delivered as a database service. As a database service, Express Server could deliver data to multiple sessions at once, address more memory, and scale much more than the previous platform would allow. Oracle also continued to enhance the Express platform. Oracle Express Objects (OEO) and its companion, Oracle Express Analyzer (OEA), were designed to allow developers to build applications using popular object-oriented techniques.

A new language, Express Basic (modeled after Microsoft's Visual Basic), was the host language for OEO and OEA, controlling events and the graphical presentation of data. Even the development of Express databases went graphical with the release of Express Administrator, the first graphical tool for developing Express databases.

Around this time, the World Wide Web became a dominant theme in user interfaces. A new API for building web-based applications called Express Web Agent was developed. This API was modeled after Oracle Web Agent and used an HTML template approach combined with Java applets to deliver very functional applications for running on a web server. The Java applets added higher-level objects like pivot table and charts. Programming in this environment leveraged the Express 4GL, the same language used to develop other Express-based applications.

1998 to 2001—Integrating Express into the Oracle Database

Oracle customers wanted their multidimensional data housed in the Oracle Database, not in the stand-alone Express Server. Oracle decided to start an ambitious project—the true integration of the Express engine directly into the Oracle Database. The C-based Express environment was absorbed into the Oracle kernel and was marketed as the Oracle OLAP option to the Oracle Database Enterprise Edition. This technically challenging project took several years and several releases to develop. The result is a true multidimensional engine embedded and integrated into the heart of the Oracle Database.

2002 to 2003—Oracle9*i* OLAP

In the first release of Oracle9*i* OLAP, OLAP data was still stored in a separate file with a .db extension. At first, Oracle OLAP could be used in ROLAP mode, with data stored in relational tables, or in MOLAP mode, with data stored in true arrays. Use of Oracle OLAP in ROLAP mode was met with limited success, with slow response times for cubes of any significant size.

In Oracle9*i* Database Release 2, Oracle capitalized on its new object technology in the database to store multidimensional data in a new *analytic workspace*—a binary large object (BLOB) inside an Oracle table. This allowed OLAP data to be managed, secured, and backed up just like other data in an Oracle database. The BLOB abstraction allowed the data to continue to be stored in arrays and to retain the true multidimensional characteristics from Express.

The application AWM allowed cube designers to create and maintain cubes. AWM provided a graphical environment for defining dimensions and variables, and for mapping to relational tables to source data. Since Oracle tables were the most likely source of data, AWM included a graphical interface for mapping source relational tables to multidimensional objects.

A new API, the Java OLAP API, was developed to give an interface to the multidimensional data. With the declining popularity of object-oriented programming environments, Oracle moved away from its OEO platform and focused its efforts on a new Java-oriented development environment, Business Intelligence Beans (BI Beans), which served as a more approachable programming interface to the Java OLAP API. BI Beans was delivered with Oracle's integrated development environment (IDE) for Java, JDeveloper. Oracle had no generic ad hoc reporting solution at the time, preferring to promote the development of custom applications using BI Beans and JDeveloper. Alternatively, customers could develop web-based applications using Oracle OLAP Web Agent, a web-based programming environment that was a simple port from Express Web Agent, but this environment was not widely promoted or deployed.

2004 to 2006—Oracle OLAP 10*g*

With the Oracle Database 10*g* release of OLAP, Oracle added more capabilities to the language and started the true integration work to bring the multidimensional metadata into the Oracle Database. Compression and dynamic models were added to the aggregation engine. A series of relational tables, the OLAP Catalog, allowed multidimensional objects to be exposed to relational applications. In Oracle Database 10*g* Release 2, Oracle truly had a platform on which relational applications could issue SQL against multidimensional objects. Again, Oracle turned to its object technology to expose multidimensional objects as a series of rows in a table, using the new function OLAP_TABLE. Oracle also released a plug-in for AWM that built views for accessing Oracle OLAP data using the OLAP_TABLE function. OLAP_TABLE enabled Oracle to establish SQL as the dominant method for accessing Oracle OLAP cubes.

While some companies developed their own custom applications using BI Beans, it became clear that Oracle needed its own ad hoc tool for accessing Oracle OLAP data. Oracle had a sample application that it delivered with BI Beans that some consulting companies developed into an ad hoc reporting tool, including Vlamis Software Solutions VSS Business Analyzer. Oracle used BI Beans to develop its own ad hoc tool for accessing Oracle OLAP cubes in 2004, extending its Discoverer product to include a sister product, Discoverer Plus OLAP. Web-based Discoverer Viewer was also extended to access Oracle OLAP data. At the time of this writing, Discoverer is now marketed as Oracle Business Intelligence Standard Edition. Using the same BI Beans technology, Oracle also released the BI Spreadsheet Add-in, which enabled access to Oracle OLAP cubes directly from Microsoft Excel.

In 2006, Oracle completed its acquisition of Siebel. Siebel had previously purchased nQuire and was using its ad hoc and dashboard tools to provide analytics in its popular CRM applications. Oracle quickly embraced the nQuire tools, branding them as Oracle Business Intelligence Enterprise Edition (OBIEE). At the time of this writing, OBIEE is Oracle's strategic platform for BI applications. As explained in Chapter 6, Oracle OLAP (and Essbase) data can be reported and analyzed using OBIEE. OBIEE 11*g* will include additional OLAP reporting and analysis capabilities.

2007 to 2009—Oracle OLAP 11*g*

With the release of Oracle Database 11*g*, Oracle took another major step in integrating multidimensional data into the relational engine and support for SQL access to Oracle OLAP cubes. Oracle's customers increasingly need the ability to store summary data from a data warehouse into summary tables.

In Oracle Database 11*g*, Oracle extended its materialized view logic to treat OLAP cubes as materialized views. The Oracle optimizer now knows about a "cube scan" operation that can greatly speed up SQL queries against fact tables by rewriting queries to run against cubes with summary data. Oracle created a new function, CUBE_VIEW, which directly reads the OLAP metadata to expose multidimensional data as relational views. Oracle OLAP 11*g* also automatically creates views to expose dimensions and cubes as relational views with a star schema. SQL-based applications can now access Oracle OLAP data and calculations as easily as selecting from a series of tables. In addition, dimensions, cubes, levels, hierarchies, and other OLAP metadata are now integrated into the Oracle dictionary. With this version, Oracle OLAP is truly integrated into the Oracle Database.

2009 and Beyond

Oracle OLAP is clearly influenced by its history. Over the years, the original Express 4GL language has been augmented considerably, yet still retains full application development and advanced calculation capabilities as the OLAP DML. The Oracle Database is now positioned as a rich analytic engine, with multidimensional data types, and SQL access to all of these calculations for analytical applications. In addition, a third party, Simba Technologies, has opened up access to Oracle OLAP cubes using the Multidimensional Expressions (MDX) query language from MDX-based tools such as Microsoft Excel. Oracle OLAP can be used as a calculation engine, or especially with cube-organized materialized views, as a sophisticated aggregation engine for a data warehouse.

The History of Essbase

Essbase was released in 1992 by Arbor Software. Like most successful products, Essbase was invented to address an urgent business need. It has endured and flourished because it fulfilled the need in the right way. We start our discussion of the history of Essbase by reviewing the original problems. Then we show how Essbase solved these problems using a multidimensional approach. Finally, we wrap up our discussion with a summary of important dates in Essbase history, ending with the acquisition of Hyperion Solutions (and Essbase) by Oracle.

Why Essbase?

Essbase was developed as a solution to the two main issues with electronic spreadsheets, called *spreadsheet hell* and *spread marts* by those who have experienced them. Both issues arise from the limitations of spreadsheets.

Spreadsheet Hell

As noted in Chapter 1, spreadsheet hell comes about as a side effect of the nature of spreadsheets themselves. Spreadsheets excel at capturing two dimensions. After all, spreadsheets are essentially a group of rows and columns. Figure 2-11 shows how two dimensions, Time and Measures, can be used to model a few data values in a spreadsheet.

In Figure 2-11, the row and column dimensions (Measures and Time) are used to track income and expense by month and quarter. The challenge is that organizations never model by just two dimensions. What if the company that owned this spreadsheet wanted to understand these values by market as well? The concept of a workbook containing multiple spreadsheets enabled analysts to include a third dimension by adding a new spreadsheet for each member in the dimension. Figure 2-12 shows how the company ends up with four additional spreadsheets (one for each region) when the Market dimension is included.

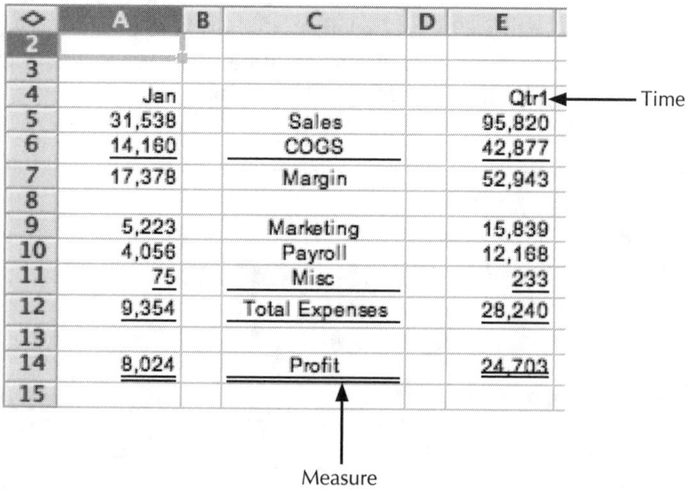

	A	B	C	D	E	
2						
3						
4	Jan				Qtr1	Time
5	31,538		Sales		95,820	
6	14,160		COGS		42,877	
7	17,378		Margin		52,943	
8						
9	5,223		Marketing		15,839	
10	4,056		Payroll		12,168	
11	75		Misc		233	
12	9,354		Total Expenses		28,240	
13						
14	8,024		Profit		24,703	
15						

Measure

FIGURE 2-11. *Two dimensions: Measures by Time*

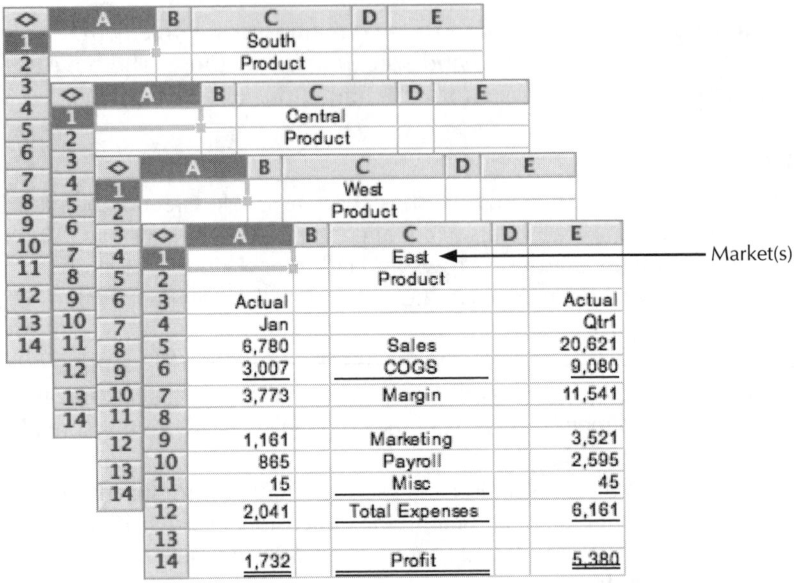

FIGURE 2-12. *Three dimensions: Measures by Time by Market*

You may be thinking that five spreadsheets (the original one plus the four regional spreadsheets) are not exactly a burden. But what if the company were to add products to the picture? Figure 2-13 shows what happens when the company adds five product groupings by the four geographic regions.

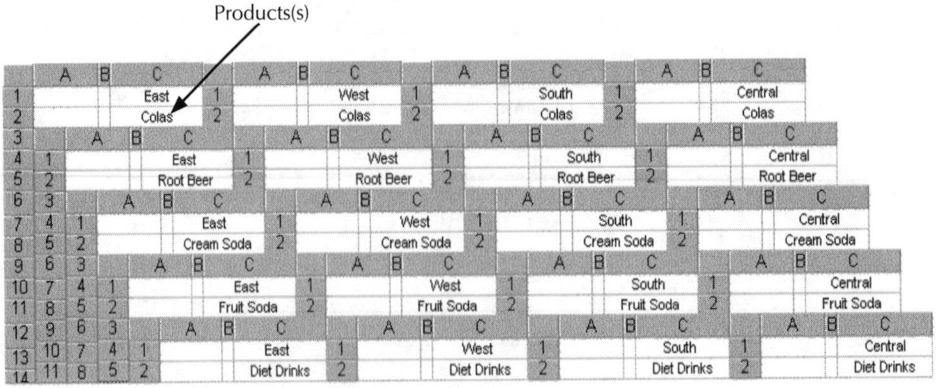

FIGURE 2-13. *Four dimensions: Measures by Time by Market by Product*

Dimension	Input Values	Aggregate Values	Total Number of Cells	Spreadsheet Representation
Time	12	5	17	Column
Measures	9	9	18	Row
Markets	20	5	25	Page
Products	14	5	19	Page
Scenarios	2	2	4	Page

TABLE 2-2. *Five Dimensions Represented in Spreadsheets*

In fact, most subject areas are analyzed by several dimensions, and this is where spreadsheets will typically bog down. As we move beyond four dimensions, it becomes increasingly difficult to represent the spreadsheets as images. To show five dimensions, we can use a table format. Table 2-2 represents five dimensions: the previous four plus a new one called Scenarios.

The Input Values column in Table 2-2 contains the number of cells that have a data value input for each dimension. For example, in the Time dimension, we have 12 months, hence the value 12 in the table. In the Aggregate Values column, we show how many aggregate values are associated with the dimension. Recall that a typical Time dimension represents a year with four quarters, where the value for each quarter is the sum of the months within the quarter, and the value for the year is the sum of the four quarters. Therefore, the dimension has five aggregate values (4 + 1). The total number of cells is the number of input values plus the number of aggregate values. In the last column, we identify where the dimension was represented in our original spreadsheet example. Recall that Time and Measures were the original column and row dimensions. Markets, Products, and Scenarios are what we call *page dimensions*. Each page dimension requires that a new spreadsheet be created for every member in the dimension.

On the surface, this example appears fairly simple. But let's do a bit of arithmetic. Beginning with the row and column dimensions, we multiply the number of members for Time and Measures (17 * 18) to arrive at 306 cells in a page. For the page dimensions, we multiply the members belonging to Markets, Products, and Scenarios (25 * 19 * 4) for a total of 1,900 spreadsheets. The result is 581,400 (306 * 1,900) data cells spread over 1,900 spreadsheets!

Spread Marts

Maintaining vital information across spreadsheets is often a tremendous challenge for organizations, large or small. For instance, if the definition of Total Expenses in the previous section's example were modified, the analyst would need to change each of the two calculations under January and Quarter 1 across all 1,900 spreadsheets. That is quite a lot of work and presents many potential sources for error.

Many IT people call data maintained in this fashion "spread marts," because the collection of spreadsheets often becomes a bit of a data mart, housing quite a lot of very important information. Unfortunately, that is where the "mart" comparison ends. A data mart is a collection of data available to many users, stored in a highly scalable database, along a specific subject area. In contrast, spreadsheets are personal productivity tools that allow users to model smaller amounts of data.

Essbase: A Multidimensional Solution

The inventors of Essbase decided to solve the dual problems of spreadsheet hell and spread marts by implementing a database and storing data in terms of dimensions. In fact, Essbase is an acronym for Extended Spread Sheet dataBase. Their idea was to create a database from a series of disconnected and often single-user-based files and use a spreadsheet tool like Lotus 1-2-3 or Microsoft Excel for query and report creation.

According to United States Patent 5,359,724, Essbase is defined as a "method and apparatus for storing and retrieving multi-dimensional data in computer memory." Essentially, this means that Essbase is a multidimensional database management system (MDBMS). Unlike a relational database management system (RDBMS), Essbase stores data much like a spreadsheet. However, where spreadsheets store values per the combination of just two dimensions (row and column), Essbase allows users to define the number of dimensions that are appropriate for the business case.

Returning to our example, Figure 2-1, shows the same dimensions—Measures by Products, Time, and Markets—represented as a cube. Each of the dimension members are combined to create a potential data cell that can contains a value. In other words, the combination of specific Product, Market, and Time members yields a value; for example, 267 units of fruit soda sold in California in January.

The great thing about an MDBMS is that you can select the dimensions you want, and the data cells and their relationships are created automatically. For example, you could query the database to create a report containing values for measures by time for a particular market and product, and using a specific scenario. Recall that, for our simple example, we calculated that you would need to create and save 1,900 spreadsheets to model these same five dimensions. Essbase allows you to create any of those 1,900 spreadsheets instantly, simply by querying the multidimensional database for the members you want to display in a spreadsheet.

1992 to 1994—Essbase Is Born

Essbase was patented on March 30, 1992. Though revolutionary at the time, initial releases of Essbase allowed for fairly small data sets to be stored in Essbase cubes. The cubes were stored on a server, and initially Lotus 1-2-3 and Microsoft Excel were the primary client-side query and reporting methods. A very rudimentary, script-based report writer was also included.

When first released, the Essbase Server was available only on OS/2. Windows and UNIX support followed shortly thereafter.

Application development and administration were achieved via a Windows-based studio called Essbase Application Manager. With the Application Manager's easy-to-use, drag-and-drop style interface, the power user could create applications without the help of IT. This represented an important major shift in application development.

1994 to 1998—APIs and the Essbase Web Gateway

The second half of the decade brought a host of improvements and innovation to Essbase. Arbor Software developers saw themselves as engineers of the best MDBMS available. Therefore, instead of creating proprietary reporting tools, the norm for RDBMS at the time, they created and nurtured a partner ecosystem. The approach was to open Essbase to other software developers. The mission was to ensure that Essbase could be integrated into just about anything that needed an MDBMS.

To achieve this mission, Arbor published a series of APIs, enabling both customers and partners to create complementary applications. Next, Arbor Software released the Essbase Web Gateway, a development environment that enabled developers to deliver browser-based applications on top of Essbase.

The Essbase Web Gateway was used to develop and deploy intranet- and Internet-based web-enabled applications for ad hoc analysis, management reporting, enterprise information systems, budgeting, and sales forecasting. Essbase and the Essbase Web Gateway enabled corporations to deliver OLAP applications directly from operational systems or within an overall data warehousing architecture.

1998 to 2003—New Reporting Options for Essbase

After Arbor Software merged with Hyperion Solutions in 1998, several new Hyperion-based reporting options appeared. Hyperion's approach to the software market was very different from Arbor's. After all, Hyperion was an applications vendor, rather than a software engineering company. This would cause some growing pains. The marriage eventually bore fruit, however, as Essbase was used to power some Hyperion applications, as well as to provide extensibility for many of Hyperion's other applications.

By 2002, Hyperion Solutions had evolved a business strategy to help companies better understand their performance. Hyperion, through thought leadership, created the term business performance management (BPM). Gartner later recognized BPM as a category of software called corporate performance management (CPM). Today we might know this better as enterprise performance management (EPM).

2003 to 2007—Aggregate Storage and Hybrid Architecture

When it first came out, Essbase had one storage type: block storage (BSO). BSO was relegated to a subset of multidimensional applications, due to size constraints. As such, Essbase was well positioned to assist in applications of a more financial nature. Additionally, spreadsheet problems were typically found in the finance department of an organization. This makes sense, as finance users use spreadsheets extensively.

During late 2003 and early 2004, developers undertook a project to create a new form of Essbase storage specifically designed to address applications requiring extensive dimensionality and small update windows. By increasing the amount of data and expanding the number of dimensions and members, Essbase could address a far wider range of applications. This new form of storage was eventually named aggregate storage (ASO). With ASO, most of the data limitations associated with BSO were addressed, so customers could create applications far outside the traditional realm of finance.

A third form of storage, called advanced relational access (ARA), was added with Essbase 9. ARA enabled a hybrid approach to OLAP using Essbase. Whereas BSO and ASO store all the data in their respective Essbase databases, ARA provides for the ability to link back to a relational database. Essentially, you can decide which information along a dimension was stored in the Essbase database versus what was left behind in the relational database. For example, you might drill down through a Time dimension from years to quarters to months. Then, when drilling down from months to days, Essbase queries the relational database and presents the data as though it had been in Essbase the whole time.

Actually, the aforementioned Essbase 9 had been renamed just as Essbase won an award. The new name was Hyperion System 9 BI+ Analytic Services. Over time, it became apparent that the user community preferred and continued to use the former name Essbase. And the recognition that Essbase achieved? *Information Age* magazine named Essbase as one of "The 10 Most Influential Innovations."

2007 to Present—Essbase Powers Oracle EPM and BI

July 2007 brought the legal entity merge of Hyperion Solutions into Oracle. Many companies "run" themselves via enterprise resource planning (ERP) systems such as Oracle or SAP. However, many of these same organizations used the Hyperion performance management applications to gather information from the ERP systems to provide information to management. So, it was logical for Oracle to join forces with such a complementary vendor. With Hyperion integrated into Oracle, a complete set of offerings would be available. In addition, Hyperion's BPM strategy was recognized by Gartner and, in turn, by Oracle.

Since the acquisition, Oracle has restored the Essbase brand and released Essbase versions 9.3.1 and 11.1.1. Essbase was core to the Hyperion acquisition by Oracle and has since become Oracle's strategic direction for EPM, powering Oracle Enterprise Performance Management System and functioning as a data source for OBIEE Plus. Although this arrangement was conceived of before the Hyperion acquisition, Oracle developers—backed by a host of Hyperion resources—made tremendous improvements to the integration. At present, Oracle is the leading source of performance management systems, per Gartner.

Conclusion

Oracle OLAP and Essbase both offer robust implementations of OLAP concepts. While the products diverge significantly in how they implement some concepts—for example, in their approaches to cubes, levels, and alternate hierarchies—they are remarkably similar in many other ways, including how they approach the concepts of dimensions, hierarchies, members, user-defined attributes, measures, and aggregation. The histories of each product shed some light on why the approaches to OLAP differ. Essbase grew out of the needs of the line of business, and so all relevant dimensions are available for analysis and calculation in an Essbase database. Oracle OLAP evolved from its origins as a mainframe application into an integrated OLAP solution for the Oracle Database. An Oracle OLAP cube serves to replace a set of single-level materialized views and to provide additional calculations.

An understanding of the history of the products also offers insight into how each fits into Oracle's BI and EPM architectures and possible future roadmaps. Oracle OLAP 11*g* represents the cumulation of years of work to integrate the Express engine fully into the Oracle Database, providing a truly unique partnership of data warehouse and OLAP capabilities. Oracle OLAP is focused on providing data to SQL-based front-end tools and dimensional tools using MDX such as Microsoft Excel as a natural extension to the Oracle Database. Essbase continues to provide a flexible, stand-alone OLAP server, as well as becoming the OLAP engine that powers the Oracle Enterprise Performance Management System suite of products. Both products can supply OLAP data to the front-end tools available with OBIEE Plus.

In the next chapter, we turn our attention to the general principles that guide the design of an OLAP solution, as well as product-specific design methodologies. We also present the architectures and components for Essbase and Oracle OLAP.

References

"Oracle Announces Next Generation of Open OLAP Technology." Oracle news release, January 8, 1996.

"Oracle Unveils the Industry's Most Comprehensive Solutions for Data Warehousing." Oracle news release, June 21, 1995.

Information Resources, Inc. Announces $100 Million Asset Sale and Technology Agreement with Oracle Corporation." IRI press release, June 12, 1995.

"Oracle Buys Enterprise Performance Management Leader Hyperion." Oracle news release, March 1, 2007.

CHAPTER
3

Design and Overall
Methodology

o begin to design an effective OLAP application, designers need a background in basic OLAP concepts, as well as knowledge of general OLAP design principles. Next, they need to learn the specifics of their selected OLAP product. Designers should know about the product's features, functionality, and restrictions, so that they can design an OLAP application that takes advantage of the strengths of the product while avoiding potential pitfalls. They should also understand the OLAP product's architecture and how that architecture fits into their existing infrastructure. Designers need to know about the capabilities of the product components that come out of the box—including the tools provided to make the process of designing and building an OLAP solution easier—as well as understand the front-end tools that may be available to support the analysis and reporting needs of business users.

Finally, the developer should work with end users to train them. Often, end users miss many nuances that truly make their lives easier in an attempt to "just get started." A training program should be implemented that starts with the basics, then allows users to get used to the system, then follows up with more advanced features that make tasks easier. Without this approach, end users often get frustrated and do not adopt the system. End-user adoption will be a critical component of the success or failure of the OLAP application.

In this chapter, we build on some of the OLAP concepts introduced in Chapter 2, showing how they affect the design process. We begin our discussion with some general design principles that are applicable to the design of any OLAP application. We then look at specific design issues for Oracle OLAP and Oracle Essbase. We conclude with a review of product architectures, product components, and compatible Oracle products for Essbase and Oracle OLAP.

General Design Principles

To reduce the concept of OLAP application design methodology into a few pages is a challenging exercise. As with developing most of types of applications, there are as many ways to design and build an OLAP application as there are OLAP consultants. The purpose of this chapter is to share general principles of successful methodologies.

NOTE
In this chapter, we use the general term OLAP application. For Essbase, the application is made up of one or more Essbase multidimensional databases. For Oracle OLAP, the application is an analytic workspace with multiple cubes and multidimensional objects.

A good application design methodology considers the following general principles:

- Design is an iterative process, requiring multiple releases of the application.

- User requirements must drive design.

- What is omitted from each release is as important as what goes in.

- Dimension types offer convenience for both the designer and end users.

- Data types improve data quality.

- Different uses require different views of the data.

- User access and security need to be planned in advance.

Applying these principles to the design of either an Essbase database or an Oracle OLAP analytic workspace will go a long way to ensuring the success of your project. In the following pages, we describe each of these general principles in more detail. Later in the chapter, when we introduce the design processes for Oracle OLAP and Oracle Essbase, we will expand on some of these principles and show how they apply to each product.

Design Is an Iterative Process

One of the most effective approaches to OLAP design is an iterative approach, which seeks feedback from users and incorporates that feedback into the application. Figure 3-1

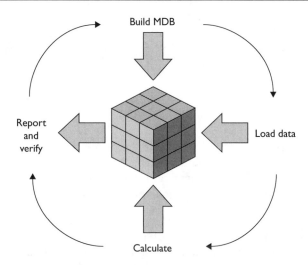

FIGURE 3-1. *Designing and building an OLAP application is an iterative process.*

shows a very simple diagram describing an iterative design and build process. While the diagram in Figure 3-1 was originally created with Essbase in mind, it applies just as well to Oracle OLAP and to OLAP design in general. Of course, the process may be more complex than this figure implies, requiring more than four steps.

There are three primary inputs for the design: the dimensions you identify and use, the source data you select, and the calculations you run. You need to consult with your user base while initially designing each input.

The output is a set of reports, which are used to validate the data and verify that the results match the expectations of business users. The results of the validation step feed back into the other steps of the process, allowing you to tweak your design and implementation to better suit your users.

With time and repetition, you will see incremental improvements to your OLAP application. This iterative process is a powerful way to ensure that your design actually does meet the needs of your users.

User Requirements Drive Design

We have said it before, and we will say it again throughout this book: OLAP applications are about the business user. While IT plays an important role in data management, business users—and their need for capabilities such as fast and easy reports, ad hoc analyses, and scenario modeling—will drive the implementation of an OLAP application. Ignoring this fundamental design principle will inevitably lead to dissatisfied users and the ultimate failure of the system to meet business needs.

With that in mind, the logical place to start the design process is with the tool most used by business users: reports. Long before you ever considered an OLAP system, users were creating reports. The reports might be in spreadsheets or some other reporting front end, but they exist. These reports will tell you a great deal about how to structure your OLAP model.

For example, consider the spreadsheet report shown in Figure 3-2. For the purposes of discovering the important design elements, the numbers are irrelevant. The labels and the delivery vehicle, however, tell us a great deal about the business. You just need to decode it.

When decoding a report, you need to channel your internal Sherlock Holmes. Looking at this report, we can deduce the following:

- There are six, possibly seven, required dimensions: Product (Colas), Region/ Market (East), Customer/Account (N.A. Strategic), Measures (row headers), Scenario (columns Actual, Budget, and Variance), and Time (may be two dimensions, see the next item for an explanation).

- For Time, we can see that the page header denotes fiscal years (FY10), and the column headers specify quarters (Qtr1 and Qtr2). This generally indicates that there is a cross-tab reporting requirement for time. *Cross-tab*

	A	B	C	D	E	F	G
1	Colas						
2	East						
3	FY10						
4	N.A. Strategic						
5							
6		Qtr1			Qtr2		
7		Actual	Budget	Variance	Actual	Budget	Variance
8	Sales	$6,303.00	$5,870.00	$ 433.00	$7,230.00	$6,760.00	$ 470.00
9	COGS	$2,164.00	$1,970.00	$(194.00)	$2,403.00	$2,190.00	$(213.00)
10	Margin	$4,139.00	$3,900.00	$ 239.00	$4,827.00	$4,570.00	$ 257.00
11	Marketing	$ 711.00	$ 570.00	$(141.00)	$ 794.00	$ 610.00	$(184.00)
12	Payroll	$ 660.00	$ 450.00	$(210.00)	$ 669.00	$ 480.00	$(189.00)
13	Misc	$ 10.00	–	$ (10.00)	$ 12.00	–	$ (12.00)
14	Total Expenses	$1,381.00	$1,020.00	$(361.00)	$1,475.00	$1,090.00	$(385.00)
15	Profit	$2,758.00	$2,880.00	$(122.00)	$3,352.00	$3,480.00	$(128.00)

FIGURE 3-2. *Design begins with reports.*

means using a dimension on both the row and column at once. This may or may not need to be done in two dimensions, depending on the tool and the business environment.

■ Variance calculations are required in the Scenario and Measures dimensions.

■ The sample report is a Microsoft Excel spreadsheet, which may indicate a preference for Excel as a reporting vehicle.

■ Report formatting might be a key concern in the delivery (see the previous item).

The point in reviewing existing reports is to start forming assumptions and questions for your end users. The end users will not tell you what dimensions they need. While your initial assumptions may not be correct, reviewing the elements the end users are currently using in their reports will be the best place to start your investigation for the design. You users will validate or invalidate your assumptions down the line.

What's Left Out Is as Important as What Goes In

What you leave out of an OLAP application is just as important as what you put into it. Creating a meaningful application is not about extensive dimensionality or volumes of data. It is not about tricky mathematics or an abundance of available metrics. At the end of the day, no matter how elegant a solution you create, the OLAP application will live and die on the perceptions of the users. Simplicity is often best. This advice does not mean that you cannot have a 30-dimension model.

In fact, we have seen a number of OLAP applications with many dimensions in production. It simply means that you should ensure that the dimensionality you build into your model is meaningful.

For example, consider the following dimensions used in an application whose purpose is to analyze profits: Time, Profit, Customers, Markets, and Weather. The dimensions that reference time, customers, and markets all make sense in respect to profit and in respect to each other. The dimension for weather seems a bit out of place. We are not arguing that weather can never have an impact on profits; depending on the products you sell, analyzing weather conditions may be important. Rather, we are suggesting that, in most cases, weather is not an indicator of profitability. If a dimension is irrelevant to the purpose for the database, omit it from the model. In this scenario, ask the end users to show how weather is being used in the current set of reports. If you hear "We think it would be nice to understand how weather impacts profits," gently push back on the request and suggest that it be added in the next release.

One best practice when building an OLAP application is to solve what is currently being manually analyzed by spreadsheets. After the first delivery of the application, it is very likely the end users will uncover other trends or hypothesize about other dimensions that may be relevant to the analysis. At that point, when the original problem is solved, you can begin a new iteration and consider extending the application to incorporate these other dimensions.

In addition, designers often add dimensions that really are simply extensions of other dimensions or not needed at all. For example, consider a model that has dimensions for Scenario, Project, Business Units, Time, and Accounts. On the surface, all of these dimensions seem to be relevant. However, you might discover that a given project is worked on by only one business unit. Figure 3-3 shows what a report might look like when Project and Unit dimensions are modeled separately in this situation. It can be difficult for users to find the data with this design. Practically speaking, if a project belongs to only one department, you could easily model Unit and Product as a single dimension, as shown in Figure 3-4.

January Actual Hours Worked						
	Project 1	Project 2	Project 3	Project 4	Project 5	Project 6
Unit 1	–	–	–	58	–	
Unit 2	–	31	–	–	–	40
Unit 3	–	–	28	–	13	
Unit 4	90	–	–	–	–	

FIGURE 3-3. *Project and Unit as separate dimensions results in many null cells.*

Actual	
Hours Worked	
	Jan
Project 4	58
Unit 1	58
Project 2	31
Project 6	40
Unit 2	71
Project 3	28
Project 5	13
Unit 3	41
Project 1	90
Unit 4	90

FIGURE 3-4.   *Project may be better modeled as a member of Unit.*

You can often spot irrelevant dimensions by considering the purpose of the application—the metrics. If your application is tracking customer profitability, then a dimension with employee numbers may not be relevant.

As a last note about dimensionality, remember that values in an OLAP cube must always be represented as an intersection of a member from all base dimensions. If you put 20 dimensions in your OLAP model, either your user must think across 20 dimensions or you must create a good template-reporting approach to make it easy for the users to focus on the dimensions that are important to them. Again, a step-wise rollout of dimensions to support additional functionality over the multiple releases of the OLAP application can ease this pain.

Dimension Types Offer Convenience

Dimension types provide the OLAP engine with a wealth of information about the dimensions, including metadata and inferences about how to process the data connected to the dimension. For example, dimensions of the time type have a sequential order (January is always before February), values that can be aggregated (rolled up), and members that can be compared to other members within the dimension (Quarter 1 versus Quarter 2). If you create a dimension as a time dimension, you can specify things such as time period ranges (January 2010 to May 2010), year-to-date values (January 2010 through May 2010 summed up), and year-over-year comparisons (January 2010 versus January 2009), and the OLAP engine will know how to store and calculate the data.

When designing your OLAP application, you should be aware of the built-in dimension types offered by the OLAP product and plan to take advantage of the convenience they offer. This can save time for the developer as well as the end users, because OLAP systems have built-in capabilities for certain dimension types. The dimension types for Oracle OLAP and Oracle Essbase are described in the product-specific design sections later in this chapter.

Data Types Improve Data Quality

Similar to dimension types, data types provide information about the data to the OLAP engine. Setting the appropriate data type for the data in your application can save space and execution time. Data types also help to ensure that only data with the appropriate data type is written back to the database. As with dimension types, you need to learn about the built-in data types offered by the OLAP product.

The most common data type in both Oracle OLAP and Oracle Essbase is the numeric type. Essbase stores numeric data in decimal format, occupying 8 bytes per cell of data. Oracle OLAP defaults to this data type, but can use any Oracle Database data type. Both products also offer a text data type, though with varying restrictions. The data types for Oracle OLAP and Oracle Essbase are described in more detail in the product-specific design sections later in this chapter.

Different Uses Require Different Views of the Data

Hierarchical dimensions provide one way of looking at data. Business users often want to look at their data in other ways as well. For example, different analyses call for different rollup structures. In addition, users require an efficient means for selecting specific dimension members for analyses and for summarizing dimension members in different ways.

During the design process, be on the lookout for user requirements that might indicate the need for alternate views of the data. Look at how your business is organized for additional clues on how to define alternate views. For example, the sales team may want to look at the data by sales representative and sales managers, and the product team may want to look at the same data, but by the company's product lines.

In general, there are two methods for repurposing members: attributes and alternate hierarchies, which were discussed in Chapter 2. Recall that an attribute is a tag assigned to a member. Its purpose is to aid an end user in finding that member without needing to navigate the dimensional hierarchies. Alternate hierarchies provide different ways to aggregate a dimension. Oracle OLAP and Oracle Essbase take a similar approach to user-defined attributes but differ in how they support alternate hierarchies. For more information, see the product-specific design sections later in this chapter.

User Access and Security Needs Planning

As noted in Chapter 2, in OLAP applications, user access rights are often defined on specific dimensions. For example, the Eastern region manager may require access to only the data for the Eastern region and all of the customers in the Eastern region.

While access rights are often considered after the first prototype of a system is built, they should be considered carefully in the design process, as often the data that drives security policies (such as which users map to the Eastern region) is not available in the source data. This data may need to be created and added.

When you design an OLAP application, you should be aware of your organization's policies and infrastructure for user authentication and user roles, as well as the security features included with the OLAP product. For more information, see the discussions of security in Chapters 4 and 5.

Allow Areas for Training and Testing

As mentioned at the beginning of this chapter, training end users is an important part of an OLAP project. You may want to include areas in your application design that are specifically designed for training purposes. Often, these areas can also be used for testing purposes. By incorporating these into your design, you will ease the job of those that are training people and testing the application.

Designing an Oracle OLAP Analytic Workspace

In this section, we discuss the features in Oracle OLAP that you should be aware of when designing analytic workspaces. The content here expands on the concepts introduced in Chapter 2 (where those concepts relate to design) and the general design principles discussed in the preceding section. For implementation details, see Chapter 4.

Determining Dimensions from User Requirements

As mentioned, user requirements must drive the design of Oracle OLAP cubes. This fact is often overlooked in Oracle OLAP design, as the data is sourced from relational tables or views. Often, these tables are part of a data warehouse with a well-defined structure. The structure of the source tables will be an important influence, but the ultimate structure of the OLAP cubes should be driven by user requirements, not the convenience of loading data from the data warehouse, because often the data warehouse design is not reflective of user requirements. Oracle OLAP cubes can be used solely for their cube-organized materialized views to accelerate performance of queries on data warehouses, but they offer much more.

Relating Oracle OLAP Data to a Star Dimensional Model

As mentioned in Chapter 2, OLAP data is often represented in relational tables as a star dimensional model. As shown in Figure 2-5, a central fact table contains the data, and dimension tables can be joined to the fact table to supply additional information about the dimensions. This is called a star model or a star schema because the dimension tables are often shown radiating from the central fact table, like a star. With OLAP data, each of the dimensions ends up being described in its own dimension table.

The star dimensional model is central to Oracle OLAP design. Data that is loaded into Oracle OLAP cubes and dimensions often comes from a star dimensional model. In this model, there is a one-to-one correspondence between a dimension and a dimension table. Likewise, there is a one-to-one correspondence between a cube and a fact table. As discussed in Chapter 4, the Oracle tool used to create and manage analytic workspaces, called Analytic Workspace Manager (AWM), is specifically designed to load Oracle OLAP cubes from star and snowflake dimensional models or from a collection of tables.

Oracle OLAP takes this relationship between star dimensional models and Oracle OLAP cubes even further by automatically creating a dimension view for each dimension and a cube view for each cube. These views can be queried just as if they were relational tables. This is the primary mechanism for querying Oracle OLAP data.

Many tools designed for reporting relational data are optimized for reporting against star models. By exposing cube data in a star schema, Oracle has made data in Oracle OLAP cubes accessible to reporting tools that can use SQL to access data.

As also discussed in Chapter 2, snowflake schemas are the same as stars, except there is a dimension table for each level of a dimension. In each level's dimension table, a column joins to the next higher level table. Snowflake schemas radiate out from the central fact table, hence the name snowflake schemas. Chapter 4 contains examples of loading from a star schema, a snowflake schema, and multiple tables.

Mapping Relational Data to Multidimensional Objects

In designing Oracle OLAP cubes, bear in mind that every object in your analytic workspace needs to be sourced from some relational table, view, or something that acts like a relational table, such as an external table or a gateway This enables access to many sources outside an Oracle database. You use AWM to define the mapping between relational columns and each multidimensional object, except calculated measures. Therefore, if you know you want to represent regions in your analytic workspace, you need some sort of column that gives a list of regions in some sort of table. Likewise, if you want to load cost data into your cube, and it cannot be calculated from other data already in the cube, you should have a column in a table or view that represents cost data.

Determining Dimensions of Cubes

Dimensions are the heart of an Oracle OLAP design; the dimensions you select affect performance and capabilities more than any other decisions. Often, the first clues as to what dimensions may exist in the data come from the star dimensional model. The list of dimension tables may indicate candidates for dimensions of a cube.

NOTE
As stated previously, user requirements should dictate the design of dimensions and cubes, but if you intend to use cubes simply as a method for accelerating queries, having the dimensions in the star schema dictate the dimension and cube design may be warranted.

As mentioned earlier in the "General Design Principles" section, you should become aware of the dimension-related features available with the product you are using before determining and designing dimensions. In this section, we describe Oracle OLAP dimension types, hierarchies, and attributes, which are all important considerations for dimensions that you may want to reuse across multiple cubes.

Dimension Types

Oracle OLAP offers two dimensions types: user and time. By default, Oracle OLAP dimensions are of type user. Most of your dimensions will be user dimensions.

Time dimensions are just like user dimensions, except they have special attributes (described in the "Attributes" section) and they support time-series calculations. If a dimension is continuous and contains time periods, and if users may want to create measures such as year to date or change from prior year, you should consider adding these special attributes to your dimension definition. Otherwise, you will not be able to create these special calculated measures. We describe the specifics of these special attributes in Chapter 4.

The list of measures (both ones that are loaded and those that are calculated) is sometimes represented as an additional measure dimension by some OLAP reporting tools. In the Oracle OLAP model, this is not a true dimension type. Rather, it is a list of measures, with little of the extra metadata associated with Oracle OLAP dimensions. Of course, you are free to design an Oracle OLAP cube with a single measure called Data or some other generic name dimensioned by a Measure dimension. The Oracle OLAP engine would not know anything special about this Measure dimension, but it would allow you to create hierarchies of measures, with drill-down paths and so forth.

Hierarchies

Dimensions can be a simple list of values. More often, however, dimensions have one or more hierarchies. Hierarchies give structure to a dimension, defining the aggregation from lower-level data to higher-level data and the drill path from higher-level data to lower-level data. You should usually include a top dimension value that represents all lowest-level dimension values aggregated together. Without this top dimension value, every time you view the data, it will be broken down by the dimension. A user may say, "I don't care about this dimension—sum it up for me please." This summation would need to be done by the end-user tool, eliminating one of the prime advantages of Oracle OLAP.

One notable exception to this rule is in time dimensions. Sometimes users never want to aggregate multiple years together. Still, be very careful with this lack of a requirement. Some in the user community may say they never want to aggregate multiple years together, but inevitably, someone will leave out the year selection and expect Oracle OLAP to add all of the years together. Without a top dimension value, Oracle OLAP cannot aggregate the data for all years. In addition, the top dimension value is often used in calculated measures, such as share measures (share of total for company).

Oracle OLAP hierarchies can be defined to be either level-based or value-based hierarchies. Often, the dimension tables that load the hierarchical information determine whether a given hierarchy is level-based or value-based.

Level-Based Hierarchies   In level-based hierarchies, each dimension value has a level associated with it. These levels typically have meaningful names, are ordered from most aggregate to least aggregate, and define the drill path for the dimension. For example, the levels of a time dimension may be Year, Month, Day. A dimension value is a year, a month, or a day. A given day belongs to only one month; a given month belongs to only one year.

End users can choose to view reports for a single level or for multiple levels, but typically with level-based hierarchies, users have a sense of the level at which they want to view the data. Star and snowflake dimension tables are presented as level-based hierarchies. Each column typically corresponds to a level.

Value-Based Hierarchies   In value-based hierarchies, each dimension value has a parent in that hierarchy. There is often no concept of a level in a value-based hierarchy. Users can drill from higher-level dimension values to the children of these higher-level values. With value-based hierarchies, a dimension table can list the values in a dimension, and a column defines the parent of each dimension value. Value-based hierarchies are often used in employee dimensions or in account and line item dimensions.

Additional Hierarchies   You can define as many hierarchies—either level-based or value-based—in a dimension as you need. Different user communities may want to look at dimensions differently. Some may prefer different rollup structures or ways of aggregating the data. Additional hierarchies allow you to meet the needs of these multiple communities or multiple uses within a community. You can have as many as you need to model your business. For example, you may introduce new hierarchies each year or to model a planned reorganization. Users operate with only one hierarchy at a time.

Often, combining two different ways of looking at the data into a single dimension is a good way of avoiding the explosion that occurs with multiple user communities. If one group wants to break out the data by state and another wants to break out the data by customer type, but no one ever wants to break out the data by state *and* customer type, it may make sense for a single Customer dimension to have a Type hierarchy and a State hierarchy. In contrast, if you were to include Customer, Type, and State as three separate dimensions, your aggregation time could be much greater, because Oracle OLAP would try to aggregate the data for every Type-State combination that could exist.

Attributes

Dimension attributes help users to find specific dimension values and provide information about those dimension values. They also supply multilingual descriptive values for dimension values. For example, suppose there is a list of 10,000 products for a user to sift through. How is that user to find the product of interest? Also, suppose you want to store the ending date of each time period so you can determine which time period precedes a given time period or sort time periods by ending date. Dimension attributes enable you to specify this information. Some attributes are automatically defined by the system (system-defined) and some are defined by the person creating the dimension (user-defined).

System-Defined Attributes   Oracle OLAP automatically defines the LONG_ DESCRIPTION and SHORT_DESCRIPTION attributes for each dimension. System-defined attributes are typically used by front-end tools to identify a given dimension value. Users can often search for text strings within these names. These attributes are dimensioned by an automatically generated language dimension to allow for names in multiple languages. Oracle OLAP does not require these description attributes, but some applications may need them.

For dimensions you identify as time dimensions, Oracle OLAP also creates the special attributes END_DATE and TIMESPAN. END_DATE contains the ending date of each time period. TIMESPAN contains the number of days in the time period. Oracle OLAP uses this information to calculate prior time periods and year-ago time periods. By using these attributes, Oracle OLAP cans support rich time-series calculations for just about any sort of time calendar, including fiscal calendars, promotional calendars, 13 periods per year, overlapping time periods, and more. If you do not populate these attributes, you will not be able to create time-based calculated measures. Bear this in mind when creating time dimension tables, because you will want to map to columns that contain this important metadata.

User-Defined Attributes You can create as many additional attributes on your dimensions as you want. Attributes are added to the Oracle database data dictionary. They are revealed as a column in dimension and hierarchy views. End users can use these attributes to find dimension values of interest.

For example, suppose you think that a user may want to create a report that displays sales for all products of a certain color. You could create an attribute called COLOR that enables users to select all of the products whose COLOR attribute is RED or WHITE. Attributes can be set for individual levels of a dimension or for all levels of a hierarchy, depending on whether that attribute applies to multiple levels.

Attributes are single-valued. For example, a product can be RED or WHITE, or even REDWHITE, but cannot be multiple values at once. Attributes are associated with a single dimension and are not tracked over time.

TIP
If you need to keep track of an attribute that changes over time, or varies by another dimension, you can define a cube with that information. For example, you may want to define a text Color measure that is dimensioned by Product and Time that defines the color of a product in a given month. This measure will generally occupy much more space than an attribute, because it is two dimensional. In addition, it will not benefit from having an index.

Attributes can be used together to find dimension values that meet certain criteria. This is especially handy for creating reports that need to select dimension values that should change as the data changes. If users were to select all the products that were red and white by selecting them from a list, when new red products were introduced, they would not be automatically added to the report. If a COLOR attribute were used instead, new red products would automatically appear on a report since the rule "select all RED products" is used. This technique is especially powerful when multiple attributes are used together, such as "select all RED or WHITE COLOR products or all VALENTINE THEME products."

When creating attributes, be sure to check the Index checkbox if you will be using the attribute in a filter, such as in a WHERE clause. It is faster to find all white products if there is an index of colors than to search sequentially through all products to see if the COLOR attribute is set to WHITE.

Designing Oracle OLAP Cubes

We discussed cubes in a general way in Chapter 2. This section focuses on the design considerations for Oracle OLAP cubes.

One of the great advantages of Oracle OLAP is the ability to define cubes to meet specific business requirements. These cubes can have varying dimensionality, and all share dimensions and reside in the same analytic workspace. If some of the data you want to represent varies by only three dimensions, create a cube with only three dimensions. If other data requires five dimensions, create a different cube with the five dimensions. By storing and calculating data for only the dimensions required for a certain analysis, you can save storage space, calculation time, and retrieval time.

Recall that cubes contain measures. If a measure is loaded from a fact table, it is a stored measure. You can also create calculated measures that are derived from other measures.

Stored Measures

Stored measures in Oracle OLAP are loaded directly from fact tables, views, or similar objects such as materialized views, external tables, or gateways. They are usually the columns in the fact table that are not keys. The precision and data type of these values determine the specific data type of your measures. Usually, these are the number data type, but Oracle OLAP can support cubes with decimal, shortdecimal (half the size of decimal), Boolean, date, and text measures. These stored measures are the source of all of the data in the cube. Examples are SALES, COSTS, and UNITS. All data is computed from the stored measures.

Stored measures can also be calculated from within a cube using OLAP DML code, such as a forecast. If a measure can be computed from one or more other measures, generally it is better to create a calculated measure and allow Oracle OLAP to calculate the value on the fly.

Calculated Measures

Calculated measures in Oracle OLAP are measures that can be calculated dynamically from stored measures and other calculated measures. Calculations include arithmetic calculations, such as ratios between two measures like DOLLARS_PER_UNIT and SALES_MINUS_RETURNS, as well as more sophisticated calculations. Often, calculations reference specific dimensions and hierarchies. A common calculation that includes dimensions is a share calculation such as DOLLAR_SHARE_OF_REGION, which represents the ratio of the dollars sold to a given customer divided by the dollars sold to the region to which that customer belongs. This calculation allows a user to determine how important this customer is to its region. Some calculations involve the Time dimension, such as DOLLARS_PERCENT_CHANGE_FROM_YEAR_AGO. We discuss specific forms of calculated measures in Chapter 4.

The key point here is that the calculations to compute these measures are performed at the time that the data is requested of the cube. Thus, calculated measures require no storage.

Models

Dimension calculation models provide an alternative to aggregations and allocations for calculating data for dimension members. Use models when no single rule, such as summing or averaging children, applies to how each dimension value is calculated. With a model, each member can be calculated using a unique equation.

Figure 3-5 shows an account financial model, which calculates three accounts from other accounts from other dimension values. The results of running this model

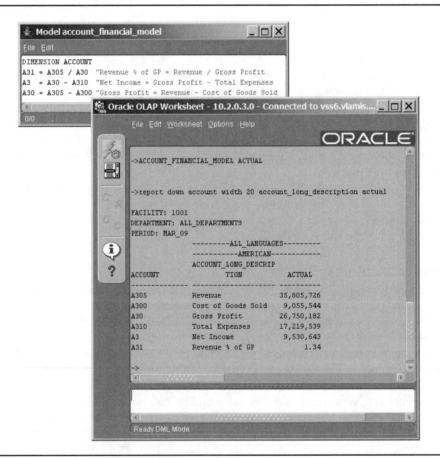

FIGURE 3-5. *A dimension calculation model*

are displayed in an Oracle OLAP Worksheet window. Notice that the values for Revenue % of GP, Net Income, and Gross Profit are calculated appropriately, even though the formula for Revenue % of GP uses Gross Profit before Gross Profit is defined. Oracle OLAP automatically computes the dependencies and solves the model in the proper order.

Models can be run after loading data, or you can have this run on the fly by attaching the model to an aggregation map. You use the OLAP DML language to enter your models.

Sparse and Dense Dimensions

We covered the concept of sparse and dense cubes in Chapter 2. When you define an Oracle OLAP cube, you specify which dimensions are sparse—in other words, which dimensions you expect to have a significant number of dimension value combinations for which there is no data present.

Oracle OLAP reserves space for every combination of dimension values that is defined as dense in a cube. For example, if you define a cube with 10,000 products and 1,000 geography values, and both dimensions are dense, you should expect Oracle OLAP to reserve space for 10,000,000 cells for each combination of any other dimensions of the cube. If, in reality, a given geography carries, say, only 2 percent of the detail product line, you should define these dimensions as sparse.

A couple of caveats are worth noting here. With hierarchical data, the sparsity of a cube often varies by level. As data is aggregated up a hierarchy, the data becomes denser. For example, while an individual store may carry a small fraction of a product line (sparse at low levels), at the total country level, most product categories have been sold at some point (dense at high levels).

For years, the general rule of thumb has been to define any dimension with less than 15 percent density as sparse, but to try to define as many dense dimensions as possible. Now, however, most Oracle OLAP cubes that we see are extremely sparse, and we recommend defining all dimensions as sparse. This is especially true for daily data. Define a dimension as dense only when you know that most combinations of sparse dimension values will have data for most values of that dimension. For example, if you are loading monthly sales data and you know that if a given store sells a product during any month, it is likely to sell at least some of that product most months, it may make sense to define the dimension as being dense.

After mapping a cube, you can run the Cube Storage Advisor from the Storage tab in AWM when defining a cube. This advisor analyzes your data and recommends which dimensions should be defined as sparse and dense. This is a great place to start if you are not intimately familiar with your data. Ultimately, the best way to determine which dimensions should be sparse or dense is to experiment using representative samples of your data.

Composites and Compressed Composites

As noted in the previous section, often your data is sparse. Oracle OLAP creates a special object like a dimension called a *composite*, which contains dimension values for each combination of sparse dimensions that exist in the data. In Figure 3-6, only 5 of the 16 possible combinations of Dim1 and Dim2 have data. If we define Dim1 and Dim2 as sparse dimensions when creating a cube, Oracle OLAP reserves only space for five cells, not the full 16. The work to create a composite is managed internally by the Oracle OLAP engine.

Often, certain dimension values have only one child. In this case, the data for the parent is the same as the data for the child, since the data for the parent is aggregated from only one child. With multiple dimensions and sparse data, the situation where only one child exists for a given parent cell is quite common. Before compressed composites, Oracle OLAP would store this data for the child level and again for the parent level. In Figure 3-7, Dim1 has a hierarchy with A being aggregated from B and C, B aggregated from D and E, and C from F and G. Dim2 is being aggregated horizontally with Q aggregated from R and S, R from T and U, and S from V and W.

As you can see, none of the dimension values have only one child, but given the sparsity in the data, certain values are replicated as we aggregate. The outlined values in the grid have only one child. With compressed composites, Oracle OLAP compresses these extra cells and points to the lower-level data, instead of taking up extra space. As the number of dimensions or sparsity increases, this ability to compress data can make a huge impact. We have seen cubes that have decreased their storage requirements (and solve times) by ten times because of compressed composites.

There is little overhead and no loss in functionality in using compression on composites. In general, you should choose to use compression.

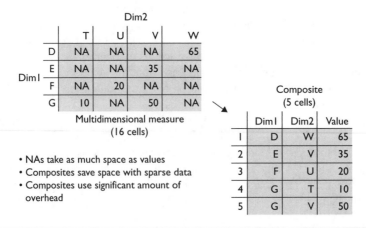

Dim2

Dim1		T	U	V	W
	D	NA	NA	NA	65
	E	NA	NA	35	NA
	F	NA	20	NA	NA
	G	10	NA	50	NA

Multidimensional measure
(16 cells)

- NAs take as much space as values
- Composites save space with sparse data
- Composites use significant amount of overhead

Composite
(5 cells)

	Dim1	Dim2	Value
1	D	W	65
2	E	V	35
3	F	U	20
4	G	T	10
5	G	V	50

FIGURE 3-6. *Composites list only the dimension combinations that contain a value.*

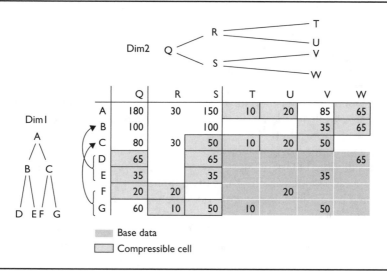

FIGURE 3-7. *Compression increases with multiple dimensions.*

Dimension Order

When listing dimensions in a cube, order is important. To optimize the performance of Oracle OLAP, list dense dimensions first, followed by sparse dimensions.

For dense dimensions, the first dimension listed is the one that varies the fastest, and the last dimension listed is the one that varies the slowest. For example, if Time is listed first and is a dense dimension, Time varies fastest when the data is stored on disk. This order is optimal for a trend graph of data that contains most of the time periods, because one disk access is likely to retrieve all of the months for whatever is being graphed, since all of the time periods are contiguously laid out on disk. However, this may not be optimal when loading data for the latest month, since the "latest month" for other dimension values are spread all over.

The order of sparse dimensions is less important than the order of dense dimensions, but still relevant. The rule of thumb is different for compressed and uncompressed cubes. If your cube is compressed (which in most cases, it should be), you should plan to list the sparse dimensions in ascending order based on the number of members in the dimensions. For uncompressed cubes, list sparse dimensions in descending order.

Aggregation

Data is typically loaded into OLAP cubes at the lowest level of a dimension, and then aggregated up hierarchies, but there are other possibilities as well. The default aggregation operator is Sum, but others are available. We discuss the aggregation operators in Chapter 4, when we show how to change the aggregation operator.

In addition to the aggregation operators, two other aggregation techniques are available to you: preaggregation and loading data at multiple levels.

Precomputing Aggregates Oracle OLAP always presents your data as if it were fully solved; that is, if you ask for the total sales for the entire year at the top of each dimension, Oracle OLAP computes aggregates from the data it has. Of course, if you have loaded 1 billion numbers and have not precomputed any aggregates ahead of time, it may take a while to add up all the numbers required for a given cell.

You can specify how much of the cube should be precomputed after loading data in the Aggregation tab when defining a cube. Determining how much you precompute is all about balancing the input/output (I/O) required to store and retrieve precomputed values against the CPU time it takes to compute values, both at build time and at run time. In general, the more you precompute, the faster your queries run, but the longer your builds run.

Cost-based aggregation allows Oracle OLAP to determine which aggregates should be precomputed based on the specific structure of the dimensions involved. You can specify a number from 0 to 100 (representing a relative scale, not a percentage) that defines whether the cube should be precomputed, and if so, how much of the cube. For example, suppose that Los Angeles has only 35 customers, and New York has 25,000 customers. With the cost-based aggregation method, Oracle OLAP is likely to choose to preaggregate New York and aggregate Los Angeles when queried, as illustrated in Figure 3-8. The cost-based aggregation method is a fine-tuned aggregation strategy that yields better build and query performance and should be used with compressed cubes in Oracle OLAP 11*g*. Cost-based aggregation is covered in more depth in Chapter 4.

NOTE
Cost-based aggregation is available in Oracle OLAP 11g and later.

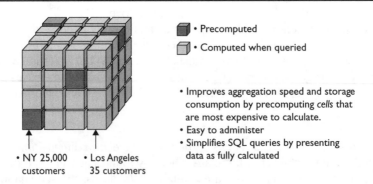

FIGURE 3-8. *Cost-based aggregation example*

In Oracle OLAP 10*g*, you can specify which levels of a dimension should be precomputed. You should generally precompute those levels that you expect to be accessed frequently. The default in Oracle OLAP 10*g* is to precompute every other level using a practice commonly called *skip-level aggregation*. Because every other level is already precomputed, only a few values must be aggregated at query time. Skip-level aggregation often represents a good balance between load performance and run-time performance.

Loading at Multiple Levels   Most Oracle OLAP implementations load data at a single lowest level and aggregate from that level, but other possibilities exist. For example, perhaps weeks can span multiple months, and you would like to view monthly and weekly data, but have no need for daily data in your cube. You could load data at the week level, and load data at the month level in two different hierarchies.

You may also want to load data at multiple levels because the data does not aggregate up the hierarchy—it has been computed outside Oracle OLAP, and there is no way to tell Oracle OLAP how to aggregate the data properly. In this case, you can load the data at multiple levels and tell Oracle OLAP not to calculate certain hierarchies.

Partitioning

Partitioning a cube allows you to break a cube into pieces for manageability, performance, and scalability reasons. Cube partitioning works just like table partitioning. Each partition of a cube can be processed independently and concurrently. Queries that can be satisfied by a single partition can be sped significantly, because Oracle can look at a much smaller set of rows, instead of an entire table. To help manage cubes, partitions are automatically added when required and can be easily dropped when no longer needed.

Partitioning becomes critical with large cubes and multiprocessor machines, because only one processor in Oracle OLAP can write to a given partition. If you want Oracle OLAP to use multiple processors in a write operation (such as loading or aggregating), you need to partition your cubes.

You set the partition on a dimension at a selected level within that dimension. For example, you can specify that you want Oracle OLAP to partition your Sales cube by the Year level of the Time dimension. This creates a separate partition for each year in your cube. If you load and aggregate eight years of data, Oracle OLAP can separate the task of loading and aggregating into eight different jobs: one for each processor. If you want to spread the work evenly among multiple processors, you should design your partitions to be of relatively equal sizes and ensure that in each load, you are processing multiple partitions. If you partition by month and are loading only the latest month, you will not be spreading out the load and aggregation work among multiple partitions. If your goal is to use multiple CPUs, consider partitioning by some other dimension, such as region of the country.

The Cube Partitioning Advisor can help you select the appropriate partitioning strategy by analyzing your fact tables. Run the Cube Partitioning Advisor from AWM after you map your cube, but before you load data. For more information, see Chapter 4 and the *Oracle OLAP User's Guide*. Specifics on how to partition cubes are discussed in Chapter 4.

Cube-Organized Materialized Views

As noted in Chapter 1, Oracle OLAP cubes are often used as materialized views. A bit of background is in order here. Materialized views save query time, since the data is precalculated when the view was materialized. When the Oracle optimizer creates the execution plan for a query, it can rewrite the query (or a block within the query) to a materialized view to improve performance.

NOTE
Cube-organized materialized views are available in Oracle OLAP 11g and later.

With Oracle OLAP, you can create cube-organized materialized views that improve performance on queries against fact tables. Some organizations implement Oracle OLAP for this single capability. Oracle OLAP can be deployed simply as a way to accelerate queries on a data warehouse. Applications do not need to be modified in any way; they simply query the fact tables, and queries are redirected to the cube-organized materialized views. Queries that once took hours now may take seconds!

The other major benefit of cube-organized materialized views is manageability. This type of view represents data at multiple levels of multiple dimensions. Traditional materialized views represent data at only a single level of each dimension, so a single cube-organized materialized view can replace many traditional materialized views. If you want to expose cubes as materialized views, bear in mind the following restrictions:

- All dimensions of the cube must have at least one level and one hierarchy. The Oracle Database requires not-null constraints on columns with dimension members. Ragged and skip-level hierarchies (discussed in Chapter 2) use nulls, so transform them by filling in these columns with the concatenation of the level name and the parent dimension value whenever there is a null value in the table.

- All dimensions of the cube must use the same aggregation operator, which is Sum, Min, or Max.

- The cube must be fully defined and mapped. For example, if the cube has five measures, all five must be mapped to the source tables.

- The detail tables must support dimension and rely constraints. If they have not been defined, then use the Relational Schema Advisor to generate a script that defines them on the detail tables.

- The cube must be compressed.

- The cube can be enriched with calculated measures, but it cannot support more advanced analytics in a cube script.

AWM enforces these rules and tells you if a cube can be used as a materialized view. The mechanics of enabling cubes to be used as materialized views are covered in Chapter 4.

You can refresh cubes used as cube-organized materialized views using the same mechanisms as relational materialized views. You will find that the DBMS_MVIEW.REFRESH syntax for refreshing cube-organized materialized views is the same as refreshing relational materialized views. This makes cubes more transparent as a mechanism for storing materialized views. Cube-organized materialized views can also be updated incrementally. For example, if you modify data for only the latest month, Oracle OLAP is smart enough to modify only the current month's data and any values that are aggregated from the current month. Designing your update process to capitalize on this capability can speed your update time significantly.

Summary of the Oracle OLAP Design Process

You must take into account many factors when designing an Oracle OLAP analytic workspace. Of paramount importance is how users are planning to use the cubes. Also important is the structure of the source data, although this can often be changed by loading from views that transform tables while data is being loaded. You also need to consider how users find dimension values—the need for run-time calculated measures, aggregations, and partitioning strategies.

The design of Oracle OLAP analytic workspaces offers a great deal of flexibility. Much of this information will be clearer after we walk through building an Oracle OLAP analytic workspace in Chapter 4. To master these concepts, however, requires practicing the art of designing Oracle OLAP analytic workspaces.

Designing an Essbase Database

Earlier in this chapter, we covered general principles for designing effective OLAP applications. In this section, we expand on those general principles as they apply to the process of designing an Essbase database.

Who Designs Essbase Databases?

As mentioned in Chapter 1, Essbase is often "owned" by line-of-business users, rather than by IT departments. Essbase databases are therefore designed and built either by an Oracle solutions consultant contracted by the line of business or by a business user within the organization itself.

A good candidate for an internal Essbase designer/administrator is someone we call the *power business user*. You can recognize the power business user in your own organization by the types of activities this employee is currently performing, such as engineering multispreadsheet analyses and creating Microsoft Access applications with macros. Our experience shows that with appropriate training, in-house Essbase designers/administrators are very effective, because they are intimately familiar with the organization's data and needs.

As previously mentioned, designing any OLAP database begins with analyzing existing reports and the data sources that feed those reports. From the reports, you can deduce dimensions and select the dimensions to include in our OLAP model. The Essbase-specific part of the design methodology begins when you create an outline of the model in Essbase. You then validate a label outline with the business users and incorporate feedback. You enhance the label outline with dimension types, data types, and alternate hierarchies. Finally, you decide which type of data storage best suits the model that you have created.

Identifying Data Sources

A common question when first starting to design an Essbase database is "Where do I get my source data and metadata?" A complementary question is "What data sources are supported by Essbase?" Essbase supports the following data sources:

- Flat files (text)

- Spreadsheets (xls)

- Singular relational sources

- Star/snowflake schema

- Extract, transform, and load (ETL) process output (such as from Informatica or Oracle Data Integrator Enterprise Edition)

- API-based data streaming

In short, Essbase is data source-agnostic. If you can provide data output from a system, it can be input into an Essbase database.

Source data and metadata depend on the specific type of analysis the users want to perform and the types of systems in which that information is stored. Many companies have an extensive data warehouse and build Essbase databases directly off the warehouse. Just as many companies store data in a plurality of formats (flat file extracts, data warehouse, departmental relation models, and so on) and build Essbase databases from these federated sources. The source data and metadata for your specific Essbase database vary based on the specifics of your deployment environment. From a design perspective, it is important to remember that regardless of its source, data can be consolidated into an Essbase database for reporting and analysis.

Defining the Outline

With the results of the reports analysis in hand, the next step is to create the OLAP model. In Essbase, the design process moves online via one of the console tools: Essbase Studio console, Administration Services console, or Integration Services console. The tool you choose depends on your data source. Essbase Studio can be used for most data sources, while each of the other tools is more specialized. For more information, see the "Essbase Architecture and Components" section later in this chapter.

In the console tool, you map the data sources and model the dimensions and their hierarchies. The outcome of this process is the Essbase outline. In Chapter 5, we walk you through the process of mapping the data source in Essbase Studio. For the rest of this section, we will focus on developing a deeper understanding of how Essbase works by defining the outline in terms of reports and calculations.

The Essbase outline is, quite simply, a collection of dimensions. It is the fundamental reporting and mathematical structure of your OLAP model. You can view the outlines for all Essbase databases in the Administration Services console. Figure 3-9 shows a sample outline.

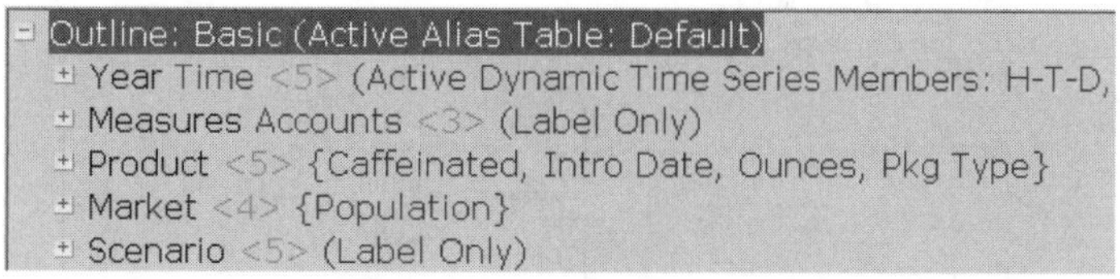

Outline: Basic (Active Alias Table: Default)
  ⊞ Year Time <5> (Active Dynamic Time Series Members: H-T-D,
  ⊞ Measures Accounts <3> (Label Only)
  ⊞ Product <5> {Caffeinated, Intro Date, Ounces, Pkg Type}
  ⊞ Market <4> {Population}
  ⊞ Scenario <5> (Label Only)

FIGURE 3-9. *Sample Essbase outline*

FIGURE 3-10. *Sample report based on the dimensions in the preceding outline*

Any piece of numeric data provided by this Essbase database is in respect to all dimensions. For example, if you queried the database for sales for the East region in January, the resulting report might look like the spreadsheet in Figure 3-10.

Notice that the dimensions not specified in our query (Product and Scenario) are shown on the point of view (POV). Essbase must represent data in respect to all base dimensions. While we asked for sales in the East for January, we got this result for all products and all scenarios (in this case equivalent to actual). Whenever you get data from, or send data to Essbase, you must represent a member from every dimension. It is possible that a tool might abstract the display and hide the POV dimensions; nonetheless, if they are not on the grid, they are implied in the result Essbase returns.

The requirement of representing all dimensions is only one way in which the outline dictates the reporting structure. When you refresh an empty spreadsheet in either Oracle Hyperion Smart View for Office or the Oracle Essbase Spreadsheet Add-in, the resulting report is populated with a default retrieval, which is made up of the top of all dimensions and a value, if one exists at that intersection. Figure 3-11 shows a sample report.

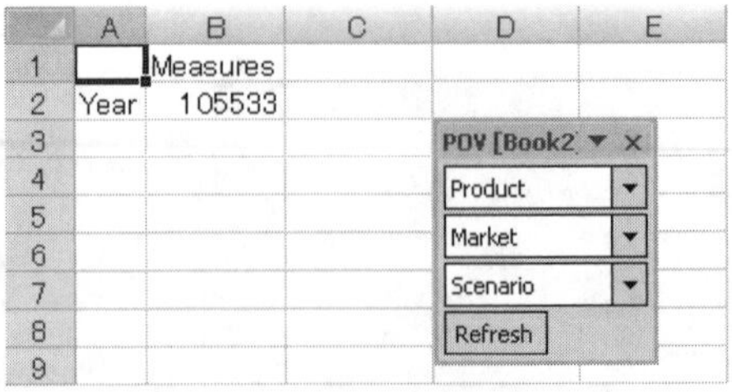

FIGURE 3-11. *Default data retrieval shows the top level of all dimensions and a value.*

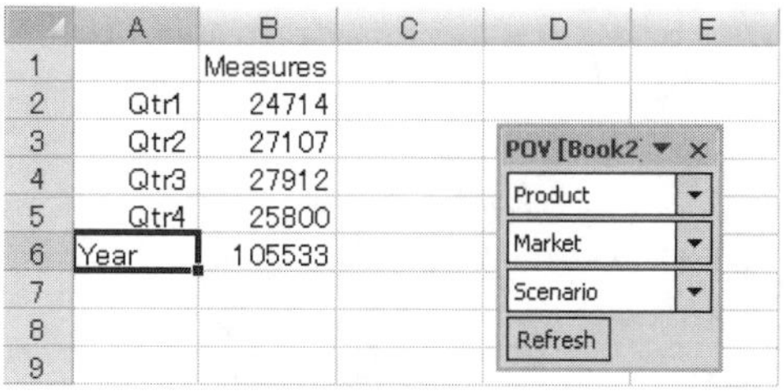

FIGURE 3-12. *Drilling down on a dimension in a report reveals the dimension members.*

In this case, the outline dictates dimensional positioning. The first dimension in the outline (Year) is placed in the row, and the second dimension (Measures) is placed on the column. The remaining dimensions are placed on the POV toolbar in the order in which they appear in the outline.

When we drill into the Year dimension, we see the quarters in the year, as shown in Figure 3-12. Figure 3-13 shows the outline that supports the report in Figure 3-12. Notice that the order of the quarters is the same.

We understand the logic inherent in ordering the quarters sequentially. Essbase, however, lets you order them in any manner you desire. If you were to place Qtr1 in between Qtr3 and Qtr4 in the outline, it would affect all reports drilling into that dimension, as shown in Figure 3-14. This affects the default display order only. Essbase still knows that the prior quarter for Qtr 4 is Qtr 3, because Essbase has time intelligence built in. It is important to know that time-series and other calculations would adjust automatically to work with the new structure.

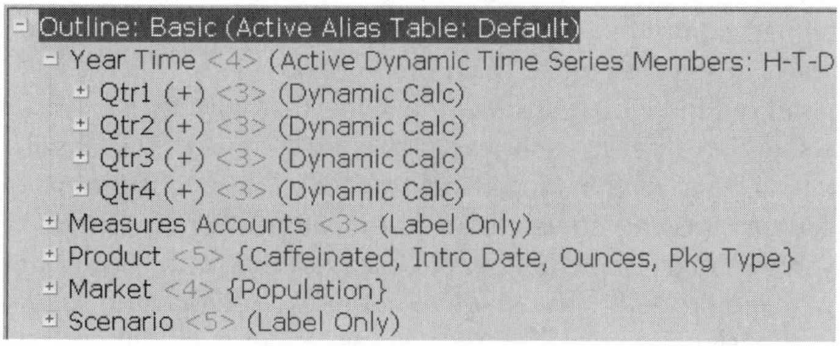

FIGURE 3-13. *The outline controls the order in which members are displayed in reports.*

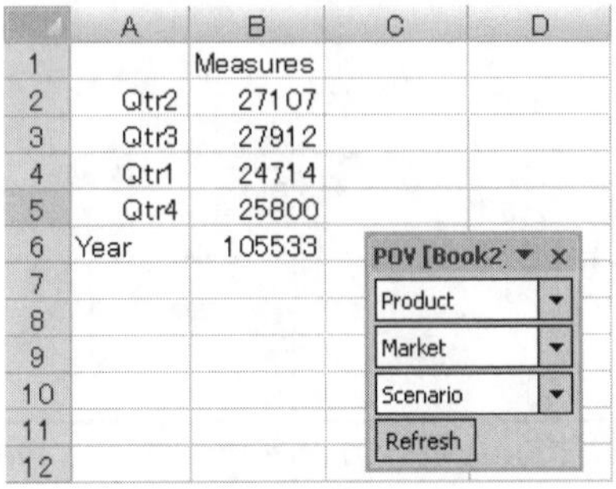

FIGURE 3-14. *Changing the order in the outline changes the order in the report.*

The outline also controls dimensional math—that is, the aggregation behavior inherent in the hierarchical structure. In Figure 3-13, you can see plus signs (+) to the right of each quarter. These are called *consolidation operators* or *unary operators.* In this case, we add the quarters together to derive the value for Year. Essbase also offers built-in time intelligence capabilities. These are discussed in the "Essbase Dimension Types" section later in this chapter.

Design methodology extends beyond the concept of the outline. When building an Essbase database, you must consider data sources and flow, available RAM, user load requirements, and a myriad of other factors. Having said that, the outline is the engine that drives everything in the database. When creating the outline, some thought needs to be given to the order of dimensions (for retrieval), the hierarchy of members (for aggregation), and the order of members at each level (for display purposes).

Validating the Outline with Business Users

The design of the outline is intended to serve the needs of the business user. A common approach to engaging users is to present them with a label-based outline. This lets the designers communicate their understanding of the business requirements and allows the users to see the outline in common terms.

In a label-based outline, you first show the levels that will be defined. You then pick one or two sample values at each level, showing sample drill paths. This helps users relate to the abstract level names, using some well-known values as examples of each level. You can incorporate feedback from this review to improve the outline.

Figure 3-15 shows an example of a label-based outline, with hierarchies for two dimensions: Entity and Products. The first tree under each dimension shows the drill path using general business names. The second tree under each dimension shows a practical example from the data set.

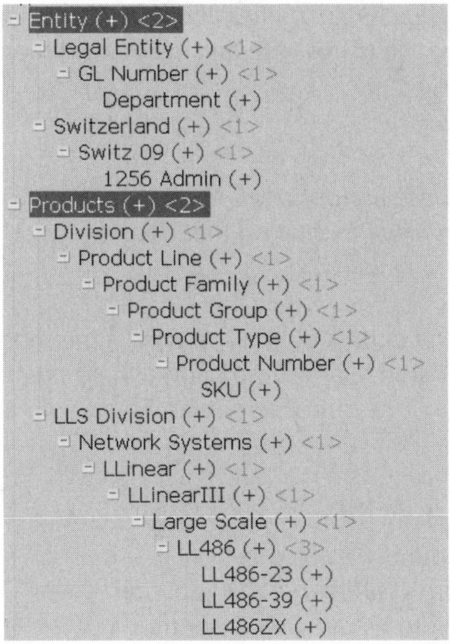

```
Entity (+) <2>
   Legal Entity (+) <1>
      GL Number (+) <1>
         Department (+)
   Switzerland (+) <1>
      Switz 09 (+) <1>
         1256 Admin (+)
Products (+) <2>
   Division (+) <1>
      Product Line (+) <1>
         Product Family (+) <1>
            Product Group (+) <1>
               Product Type (+) <1>
                  Product Number (+) <1>
                     SKU (+)
   LLS Division (+) <1>
      Network Systems (+) <1>
         LLinear (+) <1>
            LLinearIII (+) <1>
               Large Scale (+) <1>
                  LL486 (+) <3>
                     LL486-23 (+)
                     LL486-39 (+)
                     LL486ZX (+)
```

FIGURE 3-15.   *A sample label-based outline*

Enhancing the Outline

Determining the dimensional structures in an outline is key to overall success. However, you also need to consider the following items:

- Dimension types

- Data types

- Alternate views of the data

Remember that design is an iterative process. After enhancing the outline, be sure to validate the changes with business users.

Essbase Dimension Types

By default, dimensions in Essbase have no dimension type (they are tagged as "none"). Untyped dimensions are often called *business view dimensions*, because they reflect how you view your business. For example, dimensions like Products, Customers, and Regions are common business view dimensions.

Dimension types enhance the analysis you can do across the standard dimensions. Dimension types offer specialized capabilities and have a considerable impact on the design of the model. Essbase calculates time and accounts dimensions before other dimensions.

NOTE
Dimension types in Essbase are optional. It is, however, rare to find an implementation that does not use one or more dimension types.

Accounts Dimension   The accounts dimension type is the most widely used. Applying this tag to a dimension lets Essbase know where the majority of the calculations will occur. Only one dimension in an Essbase database can be tagged as an accounts dimension.

NOTE
The use of the term accounts *can be a bit misleading. Many people assume that this is a chart of accounts or explicitly financial. This is not the case. Essbase is (at the core) a calculator. While it does contain many functions that are financial in nature, it contains just as many that are statistical or analytical.*

The accounts dimension type provides specialized functionality across the members in the selected dimension. Two key capabilities are expense reporting and time balancing.

Expense reporting flips the sign on variance calculations involving expenses. For example, if you have a variance calculation that is Actual-Budget, then you could get a report that looks like this:

	Actual	Budget	Variance
Sales	100	120	−20
COGS (Expense Reporting)	100	120	20

Notice that the same calculation derives differently. For Sales, a variance against the budget shows as negative. However, for Cost of Sales (COGS), the variance is in your favor, so it derives as positive. The expense reporting tag handles that logic for you. There is no need to account for it in the logic of the database.

Time balancing specifies how values derive across time. For example, consider Sales and Opening Inventory over time:

	January	**February**	**March**	**Quarter 1**
Sales	100	120	150	370
Opening Inventory (Time Balance First)	50	75	93	50

For Sales, the value at Quarter 1 is derived using straightforward aggregation—it is the sum of the months in the quarter. Opening Inventory, on the other hand, requires that the value at Quarter 1 be the same as the value at the beginning of the time period—in this case, the value for January. Essbase provides these time-balance capabilities for the accounts dimension:

- Time Balance First (TB First), which uses the first value in time period

- Time Balance Last (TB Last), which uses the last value in a time period

- Time Balance Average (TB Average), which uses the average values across a time period

- Flow, which lets values flow across years (for example cash on hand)

As the name of the feature implies, time balancing requires a time dimension.

Time Dimension   Essbase has a time dimension type for managing time. The specific capabilities of this dimension type vary depending on the nature of your deployment, but in general, time dimensions provide date-differencing and time-aware calculations and selections, as well as period-to-date reporting.

Essbase recognizes that January 21, 2008, is a greater overall value compared to January 25, 2007. Essbase provides the ability to count the number of seconds, hours, days, weeks, quarters, months, and years in between those dates. Additionally, Essbase can easily perform parallel period analysis by letting you select comparative time periods. For example, if you want to look at the third day of each week across the year, you can perform simple selections to bring these periods onto a report.

Essbase also lets you provide time-to-date values in reports. For example, you can ask for a sales-to-date summary for May, and Essbase totals the values from January to April as well as May and presents the total (see Figure 3-16). Alternatively, you can ask for sales-to-date values for the quarter, and Essbase adds values for April and May.

	A	B	C	D	E	F
1		East	West	South	Central	Market
2	Jan	6780	11891	3976	10346	31538
3	Feb	6920	12108	4082	10503	32069
4	Mar	6921	12180	4055	10563	32213
5	Qtr1	20621	36179	12113	31412	95820
6	Qtr2	22449	38161	12602	33056	101679
7	Q-T-D(May)	14554	25011	8261	21780	66591

FIGURE 3-16.   *Sales-to-date summary for the quarter as of May*

There are two variations of the time dimension type: the standard time dimension and a date-time dimension. Both types provide the preceding features, but specific capabilities may vary depending on the time dimension variation. For more information, see the Essbase Database Administrators Guide.

Attribute Dimension and Base Dimension   Attribute dimensions provide the ability to group members by characteristics. For example, you might have an attribute dimension that groups products by package type or by introduction date. Attribute dimensions are listed at the bottom of a database outline, as shown in Figure 3-17, and identified with the Attribute tag.

Attribute dimensions are assigned to base dimensions. *Base dimension* simply means any dimension that is not an attribute dimension. In a block storage model, an attribute can be assigned to only a sparse base dimension; in an aggregate storage model, any dimension can be assigned attributes.

In an outline, the attribute dimensions for a given base dimension are listed in braces ({}) next to the base dimension name. For example, in Figure 3-17, the Product dimension has four attribute dimensions assigned to it: Caffeinated, Intro Date, Ounces, and Pkg Type.

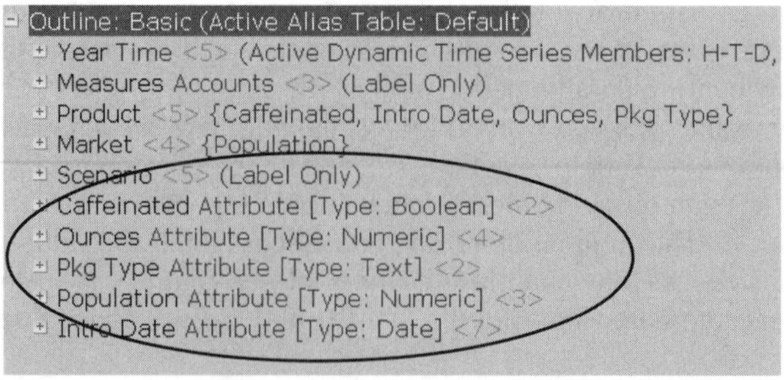

Outline: Basic (Active Alias Table: Default)
 + Year Time <5> (Active Dynamic Time Series Members: H-T-D,
 + Measures Accounts <3> (Label Only)
 + Product <5> {Caffeinated, Intro Date, Ounces, Pkg Type}
 + Market <4> {Population}
 + Scenario <5> (Label Only)
 + Caffeinated Attribute [Type: Boolean] <2>
 + Ounces Attribute [Type: Numeric] <4>
 + Pkg Type Attribute [Type: Text] <2>
 + Population Attribute [Type: Numeric] <3>
 + Intro Date Attribute [Type: Date] <7>

FIGURE 3-17.   *Attribute dimensions*

		Qtr1		
		Margin	Total Expenses	Profit
Bottle	100-30	1694	1101	593
	200-10	5388	3691	1697
	200-20	5343	2380	2963
	200-30	2499	1346	1153
	200-40	1518	610	908
	300-10	5926	3382	2544
	300-20	1897	1207	690
	400-10	4949	2111	2838
	400-20	4375	2092	2283
	400-30	1506	1622	−116
	Product	35095	19542	15553
Can	100-10	8915	3808	5107
	100-20	3780	2421	1359
	300-30	5164	2469	2695
	Product	17859	8698	9161
Pkg Type	Product	52954	28240	24714

FIGURE 3-18.   *Pkg Type attribute dimension assigned to rows*

You can use attribute dimensions in a report on any axis and navigate through them like any other dimension. In Figure 3-18, the Pkg Type attribute dimension is assigned to rows and is expanded to show its children: Bottle and Can.

If you zoom in on a level 0 attribute member, Essbase traverses the base dimension and brings back all members with an assigned attribute. For instance, in Figure 3-18, products 100-10, 100-20, and 300-30 are packaged in cans. The ability to navigate through the bottom of an attribute dimension and into the base dimension hierarchy is an advantage attribute dimensions have over shared members (pointers to existing members).

Another advantage of attribute dimensions is that you can assign them to a different axis than the base dimension (often called a cross-tab report) as shown in Figure 3-19.

		Bottle	Can	Pkg Type
Margin	Caffeine Free Cola	1694	--	1694
	Old Fashioned	5388	--	5388
	Diet Root Beer	5343	--	5343
	Sasparilla	2499	--	2499
	Birch Beer	1518	--	1518
	Dark Cream	5926	--	5926
	Vanilla Cream	1897	--	1897
	Grape	4949	--	4949
	Orange	4375	--	4375
	Strawberry	1506	--	1506
	Cola	--	8915	8915
	Diet Cola	--	3780	3780
	Diet Cream	--	5164	5164

FIGURE 3-19.   *Attribute dimensions can be assigned to a different axis than the base dimension.*

You can also take advantage of built-in calculations for attribute dimensions. By default, Essbase sums values for attribute dimensions dynamically (derived at query time, not stored). You can ask Essbase to derive the values in a variety of ways:

■ Sum

■ Count

■ Minimum (Min)

■ Maximum (Max)

■ Average (Avg)

Sum is the default. To select a different representation, you enter the keyword (shown in parentheses in the preceding list) in the spreadsheet (see Figure 3-20). Note that you can enable alternate keywords as desired. This might be to match other languages or just to use preferred terms.

Because attribute values are derived dynamically, there are performance considerations when implementing alternate data views in this fashion. For more information, see the "Optimizing Essbase" section in Chapter 8.

Attributes can be of five types: text, date, Boolean, numeric, or linked value. The linked value attribute is a special attribute type reserved for Essbase. Linked value attributes are created automatically when building a date-time dimension type. They allow for the cross-tab reporting of time. Each time period is categorized by its characteristics in relationship to the other members in the time dimension. For example, a day might have an attribute that denotes that it is the third day of the week, twenty-third day of the month, and a Tuesday. The specific linked value attributes that are created are based on the selections you make when creating the date-time dimension.

		Sum		Count		Avg		Min		Max	
		Bottle	Can	Bottle	Can	Bottle	Can	Bottle	Can	Bottle	Can
Margin	Caffeine Free Cola	1694	--	1	--	1694	--	1694	--	1694	--
	Old Fashioned	5388	--	1	--	5388	--	5388	--	5388	--
	Diet Root Beer	5343	--	1	--	5343	--	5343	--	5343	--
	Sasparilla	2499	--	1	--	2499	--	2499	--	2499	--
	Birch Beer	1518	--	1	--	1518	--	1518	--	1518	--
	Dark Cream	5926	--	1	--	5926	--	5926	--	5926	--
	Vanilla Cream	1897	--	1	--	1897	--	1897	--	1897	--
	Grape	4949	--	1	--	4949	--	4949	--	4949	--
	Orange	4375	--	1	--	4375	--	4375	--	4375	--
	Strawberry	1506	--	1	--	1506	--	1506	--	1506	--
	Cola	--	8915	--	1	--	8915	--	8915	--	8915
	Diet Cola	--	3780	--	1	--	3780	--	3780	--	3780
	Diet Cream	--	5164	--	1	--	5164	--	5164	--	5164

FIGURE 3-20. *Built-in calculations for attribute dimensions are easy to use.*

Depending on the attribute type, you can leverage the member's attribute values for further analysis. For example, if you wanted to derive profit per ounce, you could divide the total profit for a product SKU by its numeric ounces value. Essbase provides functions to let you query a member's attribute values.

Attribute dimensions are one way to provide alternate hierarchies. You can also use shared members to create an alternate hierarchy, or you can use user-defined attributes to group members differently. For more information, see the "Alternate Views of the Data" section a little later in this chapter.

In addition, any attribute association can be defined to vary across other dimensions. For example, the product manager for a product may vary across the additional dimensions of geography and time.

Essbase Data Types (Typed Measures)

Historically, Essbase was limited to storing only numbers. However, with more recent releases, Essbase has expanded its capabilities to store not only numeric data but also text and dates. From a design perspective, the capabilities that these data types provide either expand historical capabilities or serve to make specific types of analysis easier.

Numeric Measures   The numeric data type is the default data type for Essbase. By default, all metrics are stored as doubles. Before version 11.*x* of Essbase, the numeric data type was the only storage format for data within an Essbase database.

Text Measures   In Essbase, the text data type is associated with a text list. The text list takes a list of user-defined text tags that can be assigned to a measure or to any other member in any dimension. For example, you might have a metric to track customer satisfaction based on a scale from 1 to 3. Instead of showing the numerals 1, 2, and 3 in a report, you can show High, Medium, and Low. Additionally, you can alter a value at a given intersection and use the write-back capabilities of Essbase to submit an updated satisfaction rating to the database.

Figure 3-21 shows how a text list looks in Smart View. In this tool, you can select text values from a drop-down list associated with a data cell. Regardless of the front-end reporting tool, Essbase provides the text tag so the reporting display is consistent.

	Sales	Package Type
Cola	40013.2	Bottle
Diet Cola	12640.6	Can
Caffeine Free Cola	6281.6	Can
Colas	58935.4	Bottle
		Can
		Invalid

FIGURE 3-21.   *In Oracle Hyperion Smart View for Office, text values are shown in a drop-down list for the selected data cell.*

Smart View is able to leverage some of the user interface capabilities of Microsoft Excel to provide additional functionality.

You can also do math across the text values. Internally, Essbase understands these strings as numbers. So, for example, you can take an average of customer satisfaction across a given region.

Thinking more about the database design, you might consider using text measures instead of attributes in some cases. For example, Figure 3-21 shows how a product is packaged in the data grid instead of using attributes as row or column headers. Leveraging text in this fashion lets you show how a product is packaged differently from region to region. Essentially, this accommodates the requirement of showing many-to-many relationships. When designing the analytical database, do not forget the reports. If there is a reporting requirement to show data (text included) in this fashion, then you should consider the use of textual data.

Date Measures Similar to text data, you can display date values in an Essbase report. This is done by specifying that a given member (generally a measure) is of type date. You can then specify the date format (*MM-DD-YY, YYYY-DD-MM*, and so on) for the output. Figure 3-22 shows an example of using a date type instead of, say, an attribute dimension for introduction date. Essbase understands the numeric value of the date, so you can easily perform date-differencing calculations (such as day's sales outstanding).

Alternate Views of the Data

In Chapter 2, we discussed how there is more than one way to look at data, and we introduced the general concepts of alternate hierarchies and user-defined attributes. In Essbase, you can create alternate hierarchies using shared members or attribute dimensions. You can also specify user-defined attributes. When designing your Essbase database, you need to make decisions about how to implement alternate

	Sales Program Intro Date	Sales Program Term Date	Deviation from Average Life Span
All Merchandise	October 22, 2004	December 16, 2004	-22
Digital Cameras	April 6, 2004	July 25, 2004	-77
Camcorders	October 18, 2004	December 31, 2004	-41
Photo Printers	September 6, 2004	September 24, 2005	-18
Handhelds	June 17, 2005	November 6, 2005 / November 24, 2005	-174
Memory	April 6, 2004	February 24, 2006	-27
Other Accessories	May 13, 2005	March 23, 2006	-174
Boomboxes	May 2, 2006	May 12, 2006	-23
Radios	June 24, 2006	June 4, 2006 / August 1, 2006	28
Direct View	December 23, 2005	March 5, 2006	-38

FIGURE 3-22. *Sample report with date measures*

views of the data. This section presents all three options, and then gives you some advice for choosing the most suitable option for your application.

Alternate Hierarchies Using Shared Members   A *shared member* is a pointer to an existing member. This means that you can include a member in more than one dimension hierarchy while ensuring that the Essbase database does not store the member more than once. For example, Figure 3-23 shows an alternate hierarchy contained in the Sample Basic outline.

The Diet hierarchy contains a list of members representing the diet soda. We know the members are shared members because the tag Shared Member appears beside the member name. The actual members reside under Colas, Root Beer, and Cream Soda, respectively. The values of the shared members aggregate to the Diet member, thereby representing an alternate reporting structure and mathematical total within the Product dimension. Using this technique, you can minimize data storage (and disk space requirements), but still provide a broad range of reporting capabilities.

Alternate Hierarchies Using Attribute Dimensions   We discussed the attribute dimension approach to alternate hierarchies earlier, in the "Attribute Dimension and Base Dimension" section. Attribute dimensions have restrictions on when and how you can use them. Some of the restrictions are apparent in Table 3-1, which compares the alternate view methods. One restriction that is not obvious from the table is that attribute dimensions can be applied to only sparse dimensions in a block storage database. For more information about attributes and attribute dimensions, see the Oracle Essbase *Database Administrator's Guide.*

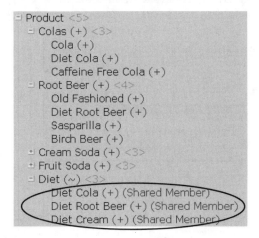

FIGURE 3-23.   *Alternate hierarchies can be created using shared members.*

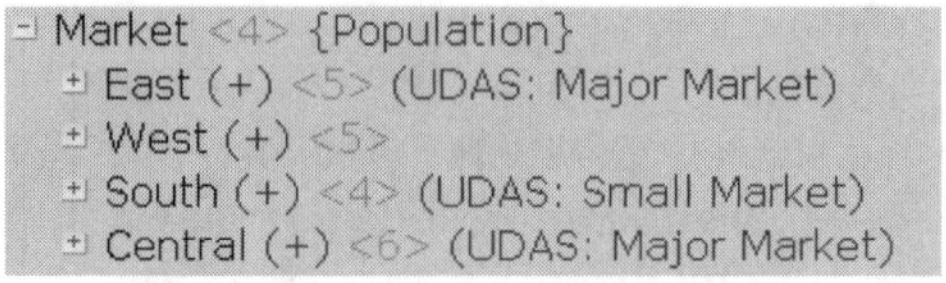

Market <4> {Population}
East (+) <5> (UDAS: Major Market)
West (+) <5>
South (+) <4> (UDAS: Small Market)
Central (+) <6> (UDAS: Major Market)

FIGURE 3-24. *User-defined attributes are identified with the UDA tag.*

User-Defined Attributes Recall that user-defined attributes are text tags that make it easier to find and display members in alternate ways. In Essbase, you can define as many tags as you need and associate those tags with members in any dimension and at any level. In the outline, members with attributes have an UDA tag followed by the attribute text, as shown in Figure 3-24.

When querying against an Essbase database, you can select members based on their user-defined attributes and bring them into the sheet. You use a member selector, such as that shown in Figure 3-25, to filter results by user-defined attributes.

Member Selection
Dimension
Market
Use Descriptions
Dynamic Time Series Members
Active Members:
Filter
UDA
Members
Market
East
West
South
Central
Filter Arguments
Filter:
UDA
Arguments
Top Dimension or Member
Market
UDA
Major Market
Small Market
New Market
Help
OK
Cancel
Help
OK
Cancel

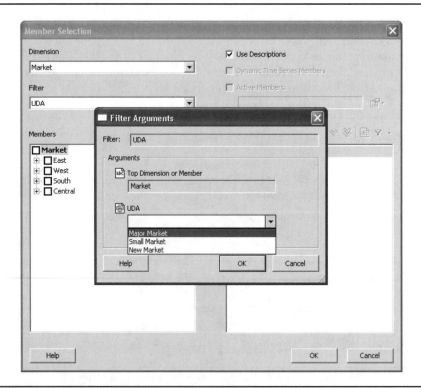

FIGURE 3-25. *User-defined attributes let you filter your results.*

Unlike attribute dimensions, user-defined attributes do not provide any additional capabilities such as attribute calculations or cross-tab capabilities. They can, however, be assigned to any dimension, and a single member (such as New York, for the example in Figure 3-24) can have multiple user-defined attributes from the same category—neither of these apply with attribute dimensions. For example, if you have an attribute dimension for package type (bottles or cans), then you can assign a given product (such as Cola) the attribute of bottle or can, not both. Conversely, you could assign both if they were user-defined attributes.

Comparing Alternate View Methods   It is almost inevitable that users will want to view data via multiple methods. You need to consider which technique to use to meet your users' needs. While there are no absolutes for choosing one method over another, Table 3-1 provides some guidance for making this choice.

Whichever way you choose to implement alternate views of the data, doing so means that you will be meeting a critical need of your end users to see and calculate data in a variety of ways.

Varying Attributes

Varying attributes can be thought of as an extension of the attribute capability. They are neither a dimension type nor a data type, but have elements of each to enable you to store data associations that change over other dimensions. Varying attributes let you vary information in one dimension by up to four additional dimensions. For example, if you classify employees by marital status or number of dependents, you can vary this over time. If an employee has no dependents in January, but has twins in April, you can classify data correctly in each time period.

	Shared Members	Attributes	User-Defined Attributes
Drill-down capability	X	X	
Work across dense and sparse dimensions	X		X
Many-to-many relationships	X		X
Additional dynamic calculations		X	
Cross-tab reporting		X	

TABLE 3-1.   *Comparison of Features Supported by the Alternate View Techniques*

Manager	Category	Jan	Feb	Mar	Apr	May	Months Jun	Jul	Aug	Sep	Oct	Nov	Dec
Vlad	Colas	8,314	8,327	8,407	8,685	8,265	8,172	7,595	7,478	6,849	7,303	8,220	8,772
	Root Beer	8,716	8,960	8,951	8,969	9,071							
	Cream Soda							9,318	9,163	8,169	8,276	8,157	8,589
Igor	Root Beer						9,361	9,463	9,538	8,941	9,192	8,942	8,982
	Cream Soda	7,874	8,046	8,077	8,367	8,517	8,852						
	Fruit Soda	6,634	6,736	6,778	6,896	7,141	7,318	7,440	7,520	7,119	6,997	6,652	6,999

FIGURE 3-26.   *Varying attributes let you model slowly changing dimensions.*

You can vary information across up to four independent dimensions. Using our package type attribute as an example, you could vary the packaging over time and geography, as shown in Figure 3-26.

There are no special client requirements to query a varying attribute. The structure is modeled into the database, and users simply query the information like any other Essbase data. However, using Smart View, it is possible to produce alternate views of the data based upon specific attribute associations, for example, view the data as it would have been if all associations were as specified in March.

Choosing a Data Storage Model

A key decision in design is the type of model you choose. When we talk about Essbase model types, we are not talking about the classifications of OLAP (MOLAP, HOLAP, ROLAP, and XOLAP). Rather, we are referring to the two storage types available within Essbase: aggregate storage and block storage.

Often, the model type is a direct result of user or analytic requirements. Other times, either Essbase model type can meet the requirements, and the choice is simply a matter of performance and maintenance considerations.

Block Storage

Block storage is the historical storage methodology in Essbase. Databases using this storage method hold data in small linear arrays, called *blocks.* The exact architecture of the blocks is determined by dense and sparse dimensions, which are discussed in detail in Chapter 8. The easiest way to think about a block storage model is by looking at a spreadsheet like the one in Figure 3-27. For the sake of this discussion, assume that the entire block structure is represented on this spreadsheet.

For every intersection where a piece of data exists, Essbase creates a block. Using our example, every block in the database contains all the members under Year and all of the members under Profit. Essbase also creates a block for every intersection of Product, Market, and the scenario (Actual, Budget, and so forth) where there is numeric data. For example, if you have a sale for product 100-10 in New York for the Actual scenario, one block is created. If you then put in a value in

	A	B	C	D	E	F	G	H	I	J	K
1		Sales	COGS	Margin	Marketing	Payroll	Misc	Total Expenses	Profit		
2	Jan	31549	14160	17389	5223	4056	75	9354	8035		
3	Feb	32069	14307	17762	5289	4056	71	9416	8346		
4	Mar	32213	14410	17803	5327	4056	87	9470	8333		
5	Qtr1	95831	42877	52954	15839	12168	233	28240	24714		
6	Apr	32917	14675	18242	5421	4081	96	9598	8644		
7	May	33674	15056	18618	5530	4081	78	9689	8929		
8	Jun	35088	15631	19457	5765	4081	77	9923	9534		
9	Qtr2	101679	45362	56317	16716	12243	251	29210	27107		
10	Jul	36134	16122	20012	5985	4056	93	10134	9878		
11	Aug	36008	16272	19736	6046	4056	89	10191	9545		
12	Sep	33073	14949	18124	5491	4056	88	9635	8489		
13	Qtr3	105215	47343	57872	17522	12168	270	29960	27912		
14	Oct	32828	14642	18186	5388	4056	89	9533	8653		
15	Nov	31971	14205	17766	5263	4056	80	9399	8367		
16	Dec	33342	14907	18435	5509	4056	90	9655	8780		
17	Qtr4	98141	43754	54387	16160	12168	259	28587	25800		
18	Year	400866	179336	221530	66237	48747	1013	115997	105533		

POV [Book1]
Product
Market
Actual
Refresh

FIGURE 3-27.   *Block storage saves data in blocks of memory.*

for same product and market in the Budget scenario, a new block is created. And if you sell product 100-10 in Boston in the Actual scenario, this is another block.

All blocks have the same time periods and same accounts. The specific numeric values will most likely be different. Essbase preallocates the space for data storage. Whenever you query values from or submit values to the database, the specific block or blocks need to be brought into memory.

In general, block storage supports a smaller number of dimensions and overall members. For example, if there are 10,000 members in the Market dimension and 1,000 products, this represents 10,000,000 blocks (assuming every product has data for every market). But even though the overall dimensionality, members, and data tend to be smaller for block storage databases, these databases do not need to be small. We have worked with many block storage databases that have millions of members and hundreds of gigabytes of input data.

Block storage databases have the following functional advantages:

■ **Upper-level input**   You can input a total charge at an upper level, such as the dimension level, and then use an allocation method to push those values down to the members. For example, you can input a total charge at all markets and at all products and allocate the values down to individual product SKUs in individual cities. Upper-level inputs are particularly useful in situations where you want to do target budgeting or perform allocations such as a corporate overhead charge.

■ **Preaggregated values** You can have Essbase precalculate every intersection. This means that query times (assuming the data request volume is synonymous) from request to request are consistent. In practice, however, many intersections of a block storage database are left to calculate dynamically at retrieval time. Total time period values, such as the total at Quarter 1, are often dynamically calculated as an overall efficiency practice.

■ **Period-to-date reporting** Period-to-date reporting capabilities come out of the box with block storage databases.

■ **Procedural calculations** You have complete control over calculation behavior, down to the cellular level. If you need to model a complex calculation process, such as a goal-seeking calculation, you can control the process in detail with a calculation script.

Aggregate Storage

Aggregate storage databases store and manage data very differently from block storage databases. Instead of storing data in arrays (blocks), aggregate storage databases work with cells. In a block storage database, if you query a single value from a block, the entire structure comes into memory on the server. In an aggregate storage database, the same data that we used in the block storage example is represented as 136 data cells. Now if you query a single value, only that value is retrieved.

Because data structures are not preallocated, aggregate storage database can handle very expanded dimensionality and a lot more data. For instance, we have worked with models containing more than 10 million customers in a single dimension, as well as those with multiple millions of members per dimension in many dimensions.

With aggregate storage databases, data is loaded at level 0, and all upper-level members (for example, East) and member formulas are derived dynamically. To optimize retrieval performance, you can run an aggregation process on the database to build stored values at some upper-level intersections. After loading data, Essbase analyzes the source data and builds aggregates to optimize those queries that will take the longest to resolve based on the structure of the database. You can also have Essbase monitor the query patterns of your user base, and then build aggregations to serve your specific queries better. Essentially, the model is self-learning. Detailed information on tuning aggregate storage databases is provided in Chapter 8.

In general, aggregate storage models are ideal for aggregating large data sets (also called *rack and stack applications*). While you can do complex mathematics in aggregate storage models, all formulas are derived dynamically. A formula that is overly complex can affect performance. Although there are usually numerous ways to optimize processing in aggregate storage databases so that complex formulas do not have a large impact on performance, the dynamic nature of such formulas should be taken into consideration.

Aggregate storage databases provide the following advantages:

■ **Dimension, member, and data scale**   It is common to see aggregate storage databases with many millions members, with large dimensionality (20 or more dimensions), and being sourced with hundreds of gigabytes of data. In many cases, databases that could not be built in block storage work without difficulty in aggregate storage mode.

■ **Load and aggregation speed**   The smaller, cell-based structures tend to load more rapidly than blocks. Additionally, because you are not aggregating large portions of the database, but rather strategic points, the data is available to your users with less system downtime. Running an aggregation process, while recommended for performance reasons, is optional. Because all upper-level values are dynamic, the values at upper levels calculate on retrieval immediately after loading data.

■ **Smaller disk footprint**   Following the logic in the previous point, the overall structure of an aggregate storage database is smaller. A smaller structure coupled with a smaller aggregation footprint can lead to a disk footprint significantly smaller than that of a block storage database.

Selecting an Appropriate Data Storage Model

From an end-user perspective, querying an aggregate or block storage database is exactly the same. The nuances between the storage types are purely a deployment decision on the part of the Essbase database designer. At no point should an end user need to know how the data is handled within the database. Instead, you choose the model type based on the user requirements.

For example, we worked with a client who needed a six-dimensional model built with hundreds of gigabytes of input data. The company did not need any member formulas—the database was a series of simple aggregations and ratios. Our initial thought was to use aggregate storage. However, this company buys data, so the totals (for example, East) are not equal to the sum of the details (such as the children of East). In this case, we needed to load data at all levels in the database, which functionally is provided only by the block storage model. In addition, the company also had a ten-dimensional model that covered product SKU level information across 1.9 million customers. For this product database, we loaded level 0 data into an aggregate storage model. Your requirements may not always be so cut and dry. It is important to consider the attributes of each model type carefully, and especially the user requirements, before building the database.

User Requirements	Block Storage	Aggregate Storage
Level 0 write-back	X	X
Upper-level write-back	X	
Procedural calculations	X	
Large dimensionality		X
Large input data sets		X
Hybrid/XOLAP deployment	X	X
Using attributes across all dimensions		X

TABLE 3-2. *Comparing Block and Aggregate Storage*

Table 3-2 compares block storage and aggregate storage models based on user requirements. If both models can address the use requirement equally well, both columns are marked. If one is better at meeting the requirement, then it is selected, but this does not necessarily mean that the user requirement cannot be met by the other model (as shown by the example in the preceding paragraph, where we use block storage for a large input data set). For a list of current restrictions, see the Oracle Essbase *Database Administrator's Guide*.

Considering Partition Strategies

In Chapter 1, we talked about the importance of partitions in the data warehouse world, and mentioned how OLAP systems face some of the same challenges with respect to partitioning data. In Essbase, you can design applications with or without partitions, depending on the needs of your organization and the technical challenges of your environment.

Up until now, we have assumed that we are working with one Essbase database. As you will see, there are some very good reasons to implement multiple Essbase databases connected via partitions. To implement multiple databases, you need to create multiple Essbase applications. An Essbase application is essentially a container for an Essbase database and all the rules, reports, and metadata associated with that database. It is a best practice to have one database per application, though technically speaking, you could have more than one. Partitions allow you to manage and traverse data across multiple Essbase databases (and applications) seamlessly.

This section summarizes when you might want to partition data and outlines the types of partitions that are available. For more information, including guidelines, restrictions, and case studies, see the Oracle Essbase *Database Administrator's Guide*.

Reasons to Partition Data

You may want to partition your data for any of the following reasons:

- **Differing dimensionality** Different planning systems require different dimensionality. For example, you may want to budget costs for personnel, but that detail is unnecessary in a sales-focused application. You can create two applications and link them with a partition.

- **Currency conversion** This is a special case of differing dimensionality. Essbase has built-in features for creating a currency database and managing currency conversions.

- **Redundancy** You may want to have multiple copies of the same data available. For example, if your end users are reporting that they need to wait for access to a database, you can replicate the data to other databases and spread user access among the databases.

- **Regional versions** Remote offices may suffer from poor network response times, or they may need access when the master database is offline, so a local copy of the database is required.

- **Local control over local data** When a centrally administered database goes down, it affects everyone—local and remote. It may be preferable for remote offices to have control over their own data in local databases, with shared access to corporate data stored centrally.

- **Security** Not everyone needs to have access to all data. For example, personnel information is highly sensitive. This information can be safeguarded by maintaining the data separately and carefully controlling access to parts of the data via partitions. Although Essbase allows full security control within a database (to the individual cell level, if required), sometimes it can be easier to administer at the database level, or you may want different administrators for each database.

- **Differing data storage** Some data may be best stored in an aggregate storage database, while other data may be best handled in a block storage database. For example, an aggregate storage database can support write-back only to level 0. You might implement a block storage partition to handle changes to higher-level data for scenario playing or top-level adjustments. Additionally, you may wish to present a mix of stored data (aggregate storage or block storage), that is loaded daily, together with dynamic data from the data warehouse using an XOLAP database.

- **Long timelines**   If you have (or plan to have) decades of data, you may want to store historical data separately, while retaining the ability to drill down into historical data from the current data.

- **Regional batch windows**   If you have a composite database with data from multiple regions or business areas across different time zones, it may make sense to create different databases for each region and partition them together for presentation purposes.

Types of Partitions

Before we launch into a description of each of the partition types, let's start by defining some terminology. Figure 3-28 shows two multidimensional databases connected by a mapped partition. The *source database* is the primary database, which contains the stored multidimensional data. The *target database* is the secondary database—the one to which you copy or map stored data defined by a partition. Any given database can function as both a source database and a target database simultaneously. The *partition area* is the region of data to be shared. A *partition cell* identifies the cell used in linked partitions.

Essbase offers three types of partitions: replicated, transparent, and linked. You can use different partition types within the same database, with some documented restrictions.

Replicated Partition   With a *replicated partition*, Essbase copies data in the partition from the source database to the target database. The databases must share a similar dimensionality, and you need to map the dimensions, members, and attributes within the partition to the target database. As shown in Figure 3-29, a target database can be made up entirely from data copied from multiple source databases. For example, imagine that each of the source databases belong to a sales region. The summary data from each source database is partitioned and replicated to the target database,

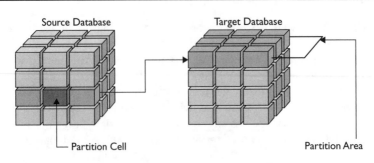

FIGURE 3-28.   *Partition terminology*

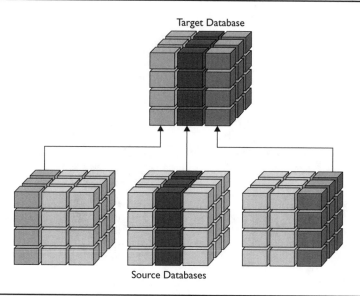

Target Database

Source Databases

FIGURE 3-29. *Replicated partitions copy data to another database.*

which is used by head office to analyze sales. The target database can also contain its own data, as well as additional data coming from other partitions.

The replicated data in the target database reflects the state of the data at the time the region was copied. The administrator updates partitions on a regular schedule, either by recopying the entire partition or by updating changed values. Periodic updates mean that at any given point in time, end users accessing the target database may be working with data that is not up-to-the-minute current. This may or may not be of concern. In many scenarios, such as analyzing past performance (for a month, quarter, or year for example), the data does not need to be up-to-date.

Transparent Partition   If you do need up-to-the-minute data, a *transparent partition* may be more suitable. A transparent partition opens a window from the target database to the source database, as illustrated in Figure 3-30. End users can access data in the partition without the need to copy the data to the target database. As with replicated partitions, the source and target databases must share similar dimensionality, and you need to map the dimensions, members, and attributes in the partition to the target database.

End users query their target database as usual. Essbase retrieves data from the source database as required and presents it to the user as if it were part of the target database. If a user updates data that lives in the source database, the update is

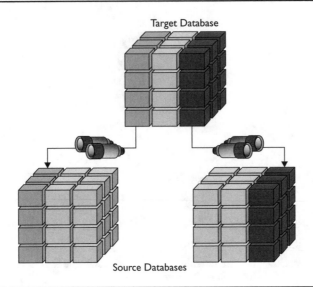

FIGURE 3-30. *Transparent partitions connect databases.*

written back to the source database. Calculations may be faster because they are distributed across multiple databases (and potentially multiple computers and/or processors).

While transparent partitions have clear advantages, they may also cause higher network traffic as Essbase retrieves data from the source database, which may be on a different server. If the number of retrievals becomes excessive, end users may experience slower response times. Implement transparent partitions using the documented guidelines to avoid this and other performance-related issues.

Linked Partition A *linked partition* is not so much a partition as a drill path associated with a data cell. As illustrated in Figure 3-31, the partition cell enables users to drill across from the target database to the source database. The target and source databases can have different dimensionality. The partition cell can be a single cell or a group of cells.

When an end user drills down on a partition cell in Excel, a new grid is created based on the data in the source database. Linked partitions are supported in Excel with Spreadsheet Add-in. Not all front-end reporting tools implement linked partition functionality, so check the documentation for any tools you use before implementing linked partitions. Finally, be sure to set user access separately for each database to ensure the security of the data. You do not want an end user linking to another database and having unrestricted access to potentially sensitive data.

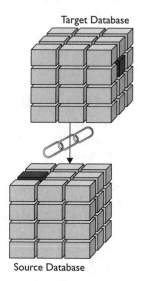

FIGURE 3-31. *Linked partitions enable drill-across to a database with different dimensionality.*

Designing an OLAP Solution with Partitions

Partitions are the tools that can take you from a single, stand-alone database to a distributed Essbase solution tailored to meet your business needs and technical environment. When designing a distributed database model, you can use the following approaches:

- In a *top-down approach*, your primary database contains all your data, and the data is copied or mapped to other databases. For example, you could use this approach to create redundant or regional versions of a central database.

- A *bottom-up approach* takes data from a set of databases and presents that data together. Figure 3-29, which illustrates replicated partitions, shows a bottom-up approach: regional data is stored locally, and summary data goes to a target database at head office.

- For an *attribute-driven approach*, you create a partition that contains data for members that share the same user-defined attributes and map or copy that partition to a target database under a base dimension.

You can use the different partition types and strategies together to create a model that meets the unique needs of your organization. Bear in mind, however, that a distributed Essbase model adds layers of complexity to an OLAP solution. You need a solid understanding of each of the partition types and how they can be used together before beginning the design process.

Summary of the Essbase Design Process

Essbase is an independent OLAP solution that lets organizations extend their analytic and reporting in environments by providing large data scale, exemplary performance, and centralized control over metadata definitions and calculations. The driving factors in an Essbase deployment are the reporting requirements of the end user. While it is important to have a fundamental grounding in OLAP modeling, it is equally important to talk to the line-of-business users being served by the analytic system. In general, this drives most decisions, ranging from alternate hierarchy requirements, to data partitioning, to storage type.

After gaining the understanding of the overall reporting and analytics requirements, it is important to consider the built-in capabilities Essbase provides. Attribute dimensions, user-defined attributes, and shared members (for example) provide an array of capabilities without driving complex design or maintenance. In that same spirit, dimension types, built-in time-series calculations, and expense reporting capabilities can often serve to simplify the model and provide a greater level of user satisfaction. In short, do not forget to consider the out-of-box capabilities that Essbase provides.

In the next section, we look at the architecture of Oracle OLAP and Oracle Essbase and introduce the components for each product.

OLAP Architectures

Your choice of an OLAP product from Oracle depends in part on your current IT infrastructure. If you are running an Oracle database as a data warehouse, the obvious solution is to add the Oracle OLAP option to your data warehouse. If you have an Oracle database as one source of data or if your organization has only non-Oracle data sources, your choice will depend on the criteria discussed in Chapter 1: purpose, buyer, typical end user, data management strategy, and architecture. Knowing how Oracle OLAP and Oracle Essbase are architected and understanding their components will help you choose the correct product for your needs.

Oracle OLAP Architecture and Components

Oracle OLAP is a feature of the Oracle Database. This section describes how Oracle OLAP fits in with the Oracle Database, and then describes the Oracle OLAP components.

Oracle OLAP Architecture

Oracle OLAP has a simple architecture, as depicted in Figure 3-32. Oracle OLAP is a licensed option to the Oracle Database Enterprise Edition. As such, Oracle OLAP applications benefit from other features of Oracle Database, including scalability, reliability, security, backup and recovery, and manageability.

Client Tier Oracle delivers multiple tools to work with Oracle OLAP, but fundamentally, Oracle OLAP is part of the Oracle Database. While AWM is the main client tool that manages objects in Oracle OLAP, you can also use Oracle Warehouse Builder (OWB) to build cubes. From an architectural standpoint, client tools communicate directly with the Oracle Database, typically using Oracle Call Interface (OCI), Java Database Connectivity (JDBC), or Open Database Connectivity (ODBC), in the same way as other Oracle Database tools. You can query OLAP cubes using SQL, PL/SQL, or the Multidimensional Expressions (MDX) language (via a driver available from Simba Technologies). Any tool that can query an Oracle database can query Oracle OLAP.

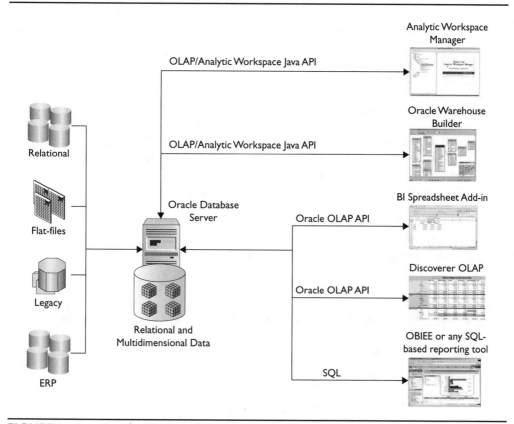

FIGURE 3-32. *Oracle OLAP architecture*

Database Tier Oracle OLAP is in the kernel of the Oracle Database, part of oracle.exe, that is running when you are running the database. Because of this, there is no such thing as running Oracle OLAP without running the Oracle Database or starting it separately. OLAP is always installed when you install the Enterprise Edition of the Oracle Database. You can choose to disable the OLAP option, but it is on by default.

At the heart of Oracle OLAP are analytic workspaces. Think of analytic workspaces as containers for multidimensional structures (cubes) in a relational database. Analytic workspaces are stored as binary large objects (BLOBs) in one or more rows in relational tables. An Oracle BLOB provides a convenient way to store binary data in a table. The BLOB provides this mechanism and is the magic that allows Oracle to store true multidimensional data in a system built around relational data. The analytic workspaces are stored in tablespaces and data files just like any other data in an Oracle database.

OLAP DML The OLAP DML is a rich, dimensionally aware 4GL procedural programming language that can be used to enhance the analytic content of the Oracle OLAP cube. As described in Chapter 2, this language is the same as that was used in Oracle OLAP's predecessor, Express, but it has been enhanced with many new commands. Using the OLAP DML, you can design advanced custom measures and user-defined functions, and write programs that perform calculations, assign data to stored measures, or flow data from one cube to another.

As a dimensionally aware language, the OLAP DML makes it easy to navigate and refer to data in a dimensional model. For example, the OLAP DML has hundreds of analytic functions and understands how to loop over dimensions and reference dimensional and hierarchical data. As a procedural programming language, it includes the ability to write programs and functions, looping, if/then/else, local variables, and other standard programming constructs.

You do not need to use the OLAP DML to design or query a cube, but it is a powerful tool that is available to add analytic content and to manipulate cubes. The OLAP DML is especially helpful if you are upgrading from Express.

SQL Interface to Multidimensional Data Types The primary method for accessing Oracle OLAP data is through SQL. With Oracle OLAP 11g and beyond, any time you create dimensions or cubes using API calls or using AWM, views are automatically created that present a star schema for your OLAP cubes. You access your data using standard SQL against these views. If you want to bypass these views, you can use the CUBE_TABLE function that was introduced in Oracle OLAP 11g, which takes advantage of the metadata stored in the Oracle database, as in the following command:

```
select * from table(cube_table('global.units_cube'));
```

NOTE
For Oracle OLAP 10g and earlier, the `OLAP_TABLE`
function translates between Oracle OLAP objects in
analytic workspaces and views accessible from SQL.

The syntax for `OLAP_TABLE` has a great deal of flexibility, and it is documented in the *Oracle OLAP DML Reference*. `OLAP_TABLE` is still available in Oracle OLAP, but it is generally simpler to use `CUBE_TABLE` or the built-in views with Oracle OLAP 11*g*.

OLAP API   The OLAP API is a Java-based programming interface for OLAP applications, used to query OLAP objects. This API is quite extensive. Oracle Business Intelligence Beans (BI Beans) uses the API and provides an easier to use way of accessing the power in the OLAP API. BI Beans is available with Oracle JDeveloper.

A portion of the OLAP API (called the Analytic Workspace Java API in Oracle OLAP 10*g*) supports the creation and maintenance of analytic workspaces in Java. It provides a programmatic method for defining a logical dimensional data model and instantiating that model in an analytic workspace. AWM uses this API to create and modify analytic workspaces.

System Views with OLAP Metadata   In Oracle OLAP 11*g*, tables and views with information about analytic workspaces were added to the system catalog, in the SYS schema. These views can be queried to obtain information about the Oracle OLAP data available on your instance. This allows applications to find cube metadata, such as the list of cubes, measures, dimensions, hierarchies, attributes, and their definitions and interrelationships. For example, in the same way that ALL_TABLES provides information about all of the tables, the view ALL_CUBE_DIMENSIONS provides information about all of the cube dimensions.

Client Applications for Managing Oracle OLAP
AWM is the administrative tool used to design and manage Oracle cubes. This application is installed when the Oracle Database 11*g* client tools are installed, and it is generally available under the Integrated Management Tools menu choice, but it can be installed separately as well.

Analytic Workspace Manager   AWM is used to create and manage analytic workspaces. It enables you to develop a logical dimensional model, map logical objects to data sources, and load and aggregate the data.

Generally, there is a new release of AWM for each new release of Oracle OLAP; AWM is enhanced to present new features of Oracle OLAP with each release. You should always use the version of AWM that matches the version of Oracle OLAP you are using.

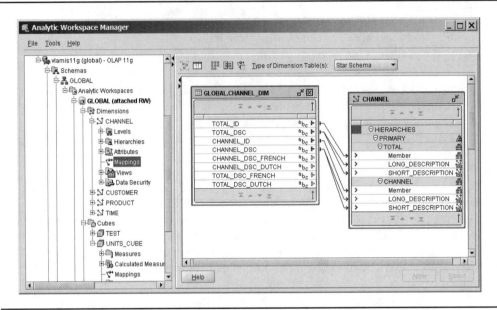

FIGURE 3-33. *Using Analytic Workspace Manager*

AWM is a Java application and runs anywhere Java runs. Figure 3-33 shows a typical use for AWM to map the CHANNEL_DIM table to the CHANNEL dimension.

Oracle OLAP Worksheet   Oracle OLAP Worksheet, launched from AWM, is the command-line interface to Oracle cubes and dimensions. Using the OLAP DML, OLAP Worksheet can be used to view data; create new functions and programs; define and maintain forecasts; and add dimension calculation models, allocations, and other analytic enhancements to the cube. It serves as the primary mechanism for entering and viewing output for OLAP DML commands. The complete OLAP DML reference is available from OLAP Worksheet's help system.

Figure 3-34 shows the result of entering some typical OLAP DML commands in the lower portion of the OLAP Worksheet window.

Oracle Warehouse Builder   OWB can also be used for generating Oracle OLAP cubes. With OWB, the building of dimensions and cubes is integrated into the entire ETL process, including transforming tables and views for use with Oracle OLAP. It provides a central application for building and managing data warehouses based on relational and multidimensional data.

Currently, OWB 11*g* supports building 10*g*-mode analytic workspaces on Oracle Database 10*g* and 11*g*. The next release of OWB 11*g* (Release 2) is expected to

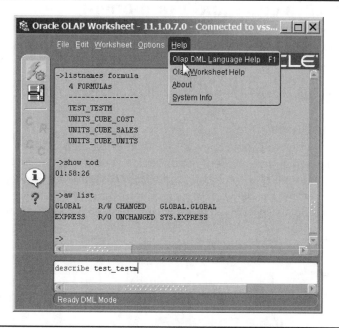

FIGURE 3-34. *OLAP DML commands and result in the Oracle OLAP Worksheet window*

support building 11*g* dimensions and cubes. For the purposes of this book, we will use AWM to build analytic workspaces, dimensions, and cubes in an Oracle Database 11*g* database.

OX OX is a freeware tool developed by several Oracle consultants. It is made freely available with no support. It serves as an alternative way to present an OLAP DML command line with some useful features not available in OLAP Worksheet. You can access it from the Oracle OLAP Downloads web page.

Support for MDX Using an MDX provider developed by Simba Technologies, applications can also query Oracle OLAP cubes using MDX. For example, Microsoft Excel can query data directly from cubes using the MDX provider in the same way that Excel connects to Microsoft Analysis Services.

Support for SQL-Based Tools Because Oracle OLAP data is exposed via SQL views, any front end that uses SQL to access data can be used to present data from Oracle OLAP. An example of such a tool is Oracle's own Application Express, as well as many third-party tools.

Essbase Architecture and Components

As a storage-independent OLAP solution, Essbase can be implemented in an existing IT environment with no modification or disruption to the systems containing your source data. The data for an Essbase database can come from one or more data sources simultaneously. The following sections describe the architecture for a typical Essbase implementation, as well as the core and optional components.

Essbase Architecture

Figure 3-35 shows a high-level overview of a typical Essbase installation. As you can see, the implementation is broken into three tiers: client, middle, and database. The client tier contains all of the end user and design components. The middle tier is a web services tier that sits between users (end users and administrators) and the Essbase server. The database tier contains one or more Essbase servers. Additionally,

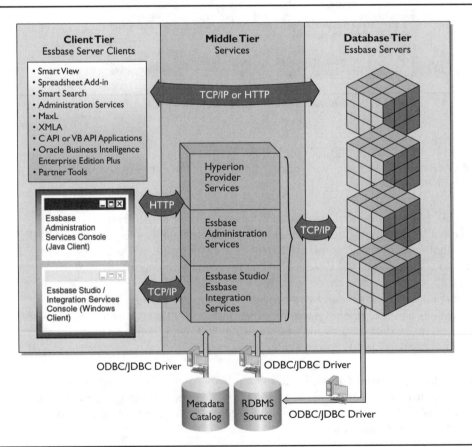

FIGURE 3-35. *A typical Essbase architecture*

a relational database may contain a metadata catalog and may provide source data for the Essbase databases. Let's start with a high-level look at each of the tiers.

Client Tier   The client tier includes the front-end options for Essbase. Analysts may use either Smart View or the Spreadsheet Add-in to retrieve and analyze data and to create ad hoc reports in Microsoft Excel. Smart View is the next generation of the Spreadsheet Add-in, offering integration with Microsoft Word and PowerPoint, as well as Excel.

Administrators use the consoles for Oracle Essbase Administration Services, Essbase Integration Services, and Essbase Studio to model and manage Essbase databases.

MaxL is a language used by developers to provide command scripts used for scheduled processes. XML for Analysis (XMLA) is a query language. There are several command-line and API options available as well, such as C and Visual Basic. Oracle offers a comprehensive set of query and reporting tools called Oracle Business Intelligence Suite Enterprise Edition Plus (OBIEE Plus). In addition, several Oracle partners have created custom applications integrated with Essbase.

Middle Tier   In the middle tier, three services form a layer between the data sources and the Essbase Server. Whether these three services are installed on individual servers is a matter of design. They are able to exist on a single server and have been configured as such for smaller implementations.

Smart View requires a middle-tier component called Oracle Hyperion Provider Services. When a user issues a request using Smart View, it flows through Provider Services. We will discuss the advantages of such an approach later in this chapter.

The Administration Services Server is used to manage users and user security, server options, applications, databases, and database objects. When building a cube from a data source, the Administration Services Server supports reading from a single relational table or a flat file.

The third possibility in a typical installation can be either Essbase Studio or Integration Services. Neither of these services is required. Rather, both tools support cube building from a data warehouse with a star or snowflake schema. Essbase Studio, however, is the next generation of Integration Services and is the tool of choice for a new Essbase implementation. Essbase Studio can also be used instead of Administration Services to build cubes from a single relational table or a flat file, with the added benefit that it generates all the data-load rules automatically.

Database Tier   The database tier is where you find the Essbase Servers. These servers are responsible for storing, calculating, and serving data to the various components as needed. In many respects, the Essbase Server is the heart of the implementation. Historically, it brokered all of the transactions and was responsible for the tasks now available through the middle tier.

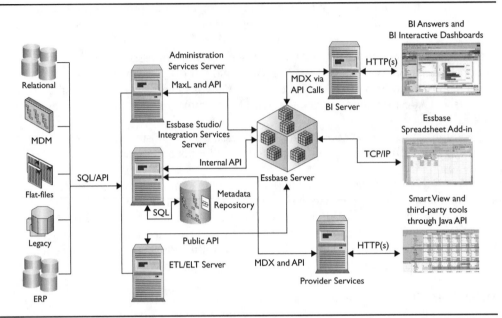

FIGURE 3-36. *Types of communication protocols and query methods used with Essbase*

Relational Database Sources Below the middle tier are two relational sources: the Metadata Catalog and the RDBMS source. The Metadata Catalog is required by Administration Services, Integration Services, and Essbase Studio. The RDBMS source represents the original data sources that provide data to the Essbase databases in the Essbase Server. Essbase does not require data be placed in a relational structure before loading. In fact, data can also come from legacy systems, enterprise resource planning (ERP) systems, data warehouses, and flat files.

We have reviewed a typical architecture and some additional front-end components. Note that few components are required to simply build an Essbase database, load data, and create reports. A little later in this chapter, we will discuss these core components. For now, we turn our attention to how the components in a typical architecture talk to one another.

Communication Protocols and Query Methods We omitted the communication protocols and query methods from the preceding discussion to be able to focus on the tiers. Figure 3-36 identifies the protocols and query methods.

Generally speaking, if a client-tier component needs the ability to communicate through a firewall it uses HTTP(s); otherwise, it uses TCP/IP. The query method varies by component. Table 3-3 summarizes the client-tier components.

Component	Protocol	Query Method
Smart View	HTTP(s) to Provider Services	MDX
Essbase Spreadsheet Add-in	TCP/IP to the Essbase Server	API
Administration Services Console	TCP/IP to Administration Services Server	MaxL and API
Essbase Studio Console	TCP/IP to Essbase Studio Server	API
Integration Services Console	TCP/IP to Integration Services Server	API
BI Answers and BI Interactive Dashboards via browser	HTTP(s) to BI Server using a browser	MDX

TABLE 3-3. *Client-Tier Communication Protocols and Query Methods*

All the middle-tier components use TCP/IP to connect to the Essbase Server. The query method varies by component. Table 3-4 summarizes the middle-tier components.

In the database tier, the Essbase server uses TCP/IP to communicate with other components. The query method varies by component. The Essbase Server uses the protocols and components listed previously. The ETL components, such as the Oracle Data Integrator Enterprise Edition, use TCP/IP to the Essbase Server and query through the API to Essbase via prebuilt adapters.

Component	Protocol	Query Method
Provider Services	TCP/IP to the Essbase Server	MDX via API
Administration Services Server	TCP/IP to the Essbase Server	MaxL and API to Essbase; SQL or API to data sources (SQL interface leverages ODBC drivers)
Essbase Studio Server	TCP/IP to the Essbase Server	Internal API to Essbase; SQL via JDBC or API to data sources
Integration Services Server	TCP/IP to the Essbase Server	Internal API to Essbase; SQL via ODBC or API to data sources
BI Server	TCP/IP to the Essbase Server	N/A

TABLE 3-4. *Middle-Tier Communication Protocols and Query Methods*

As you can see from Figure 3-36, a typical implementation connects an Essbase Server to your data sources and to front-end applications. Your implementation will depend on what you currently have in place and the Essbase capabilities you want to use. To help you in your assessment, we break out the core components of an Essbase installation and explain what they do. Then we discuss the other components and products that are available for Essbase under four categories: administrator and developer tools, data-integration tools, end-user applications, and additional Oracle components.

Core Components

Essbase has five core components: the Essbase Server, Administration Services, Spreadsheet Add-in, Smart View (Fusion Edition), and Provider Services. With only these components, you can create an Essbase database, connect to data sources, populate the database with data, retrieve and analyze data, and create ad hoc reports. In this case, the only reporting options are Smart View or Spreadsheet Add-in. All data loads are done through the Data Prep Editor inside Administration Services, and security is handled internally on the Essbase Server. Figure 3-37 shows how the core components relate to one another.

In this section, we touch briefly on each of the core components.

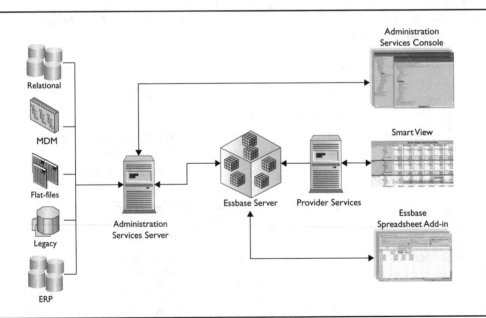

FIGURE 3-37. *Essbase core components*

The Essbase Server   The Essbase Server is at the heart of an Essbase implementation. It is a powerful multidimensional database that offers two kinds of storage options (block and aggregate), an extendable library of functions to define business logic, and a powerful calculation engine. As suggested by Figure 3-37, an Essbase Server can host multiple Essbase databases. Moreover, while only one Essbase Server is pictured in the figure, it is possible to run multiple instances of Essbase Servers at the same time. Essbase Servers are managed using Administration Services.

Oracle Essbase Administration Services (Server and Console)   Administration Services is the gateway to your Essbase server. Database and system administrators use Administration Services to manage users and user security, server options, applications, databases, and database objects. It supports cube-building tasks, such as data modeling and loading data, for single relational tables and flat files.

TIP
For cube-building tasks, you can choose to use Essbase Studio. You will still need Administration Services for security and server options.

The Administration Services console provides a graphical user interface (GUI) to the Administration Services Server. For example, from the Administration Services Console, a database administrator can create an Essbase database, design a database outline containing dimensions and members, create rules that transform source data to matching fields in the new database, load data from a single relational table or a flat file, and create and run calculations scripts. The Administration Service Server does the actual work.

Oracle Essbase Spreadsheet Add-in   Spreadsheet Add-in is a software program that merges seamlessly with Microsoft Excel. With the Spreadsheet Add-in installed, your analysts have menus, toolbars, and keyboard shortcuts for Essbase within Excel. Analysts can connect to an instance of an Essbase server, retrieve data, analyze data, and create ad hoc reports. For analyzing the data, they can pivot the point of view, drill down to show more detail, roll up to show less detail, remove or retain subsets of data, format data, and calculate data. With the appropriate security permissions, they can edit the data and write back to the database.

The next generation of the Spreadsheet Add-in is Smart View, Fusion Edition.

Oracle Hyperion Smart View for Office, Fusion Edition   Smart View is a web-deployed, thin-client program that is embedded in Microsoft Office applications—Excel, Word, PowerPoint, and (if Word is the e-mail editor) Outlook. Within Excel, Smart View provides similar functionality to the Spreadsheet Add-in, but improves upon the Spreadsheet Add-in with an intuitive, customizable user interface.

With Word and PowerPoint, analysts can connect to a database, copy a data point from an Excel spreadsheet to a document or slide, refresh the data, and display the data in charts or graphs. Imagine having documents and slides with data that you can refresh on demand! Analysts can even add content to Outlook e-mail messages if Word is set as the e-mail editor.

Smart View supports not only data coming from Essbase, but also data from OBIEE (and hence, Oracle OLAP) and Oracle Hyperion Planning, and content from Oracle Hyperion Financial Management, Oracle Enterprise Performance Management System, and Hyperion Financial Reporting and Hyperion Web Analysis. This means that you can collate information from multiple sources in one report.

Smart View is part of Oracle Hyperion Foundation Services, which ships with Oracle Essbase. Smart View requires Provider Services.

Oracle Hyperion Provider Services   Provider Services is a set of services that connects end-user applications to data sources. There are three services: the Smart View provider, a Java API provider, and an XMLA API provider. Provider Services also enables high availability, clustering, load balancing, and failover services for Essbase Servers, bringing enterprise-level performance and reliability to Essbase and performance management applications. Figure 3-38 shows which services are used by the various applications and data sources.

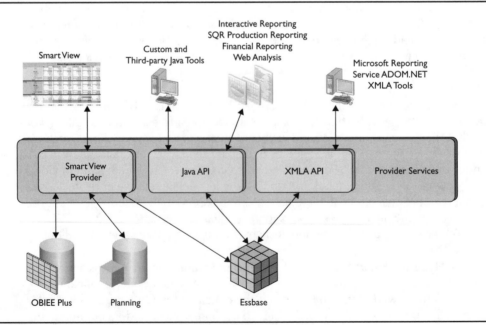

FIGURE 3-38.   *Provider Services connects end-user applications to data sources.*

NOTE
If you are currently using Smart View with Planning or OBIEE Plus, you already have Provider Services in your architecture.

Additional Administrator and Developer Components and Tools

The components and tools described in this section ship with Oracle Essbase. They include Essbase Studio, Integration Services, and command and query languages.

Oracle Essbase Studio (Server and Console)   Oracle Essbase Studio combines the cube-building functionality previously provided in Integration Services and Administration Services into a single environment. Essbase Studio supports modeling for all the different types of data sources from which Essbase applications are typically built. The Essbase Studio Console provides an easy way to perform tasks related to data modeling, cube design, and construction of analytic applications. A command-line language is also available.

Essbase Studio supports MOLAP, HOLAP, and XOLAP architectures. For the hybrid architectures, Essbase Studio supports several drill-through options: relational databases, OBIEE Plus, URLs, custom SQL, Oracle Hyperion Financial Data Quality Management, and Java methods. Drill-through functionality is supported from data cells and member cells and is dynamically linked to cubes with matching metadata context. Figure 3-39 shows the drill-through functionality.

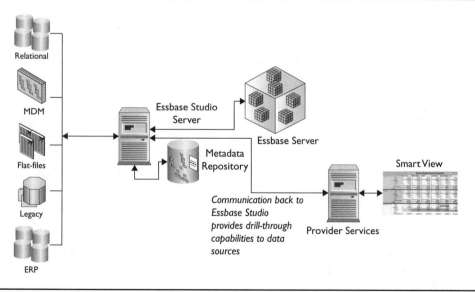

FIGURE 3-39.   *Essbase Studio enables drill-through from data cells through Essbase to data sources.*

A common metadata repository, or catalog, captures all metadata related to all Essbase applications built in the enterprise and allows the reuse of metadata at the lowest level of granularity. The catalog gives Essbase Studio knowledge of the common metadata that is shared across the various applications enterprise-wide. For example, you can model a customer dimension once, and then leverage it across a series of Essbase databases. Essbase Studio also supports lineage tracking through a rich graphical view of the metadata relationships, allowing users to follow application lineages to their metadata components and through to the data sources from which they were sourced.

How does Essbase Studio compare with Integration Services? Essbase Studio is the next generation of Integration Services, incorporating all the functionality of Integration Services plus the cube-building functionality from Administration Services, and adding a wizard-driven interface. It provides the ability to connect to data sources via JDBC or ODBC, rather than just ODBC. Essbase Studio automates some work that used to be done manually, including automatically creating joins between tables and autogenerating data-load rules. In Essbase Studio, database administrators create minischemas instead of OLAP models. Essbase Studio provides greater flexibility in designing and reusing hierarchies across metaoutlines, because the hierarchies have been separated from the metaoutline. Finally, Essbase Studio separates the grouping of hierarchies and their relationships from the metaoutline by organizing metadata elements, such as measures and hierarchies into a cube schema. For more information, see the New Features guide for Oracle Essbase Studio 11.1.1.

Essbase Studio is a component of Oracle Essbase. Essbase Studio requires Hyperion Shared Services for user management and security.

Oracle Essbase Integration Services (Server and Console)   Oracle Essbase Integration Services is the predecessor to Essbase Studio. For new Essbase implementations, you should choose Essbase Studio. If you have an existing Essbase implementation, your organization may be already using Integration Services. This section is for you.

Integration Services offers a set of scalable data-integration services and graphical tools to create multidimensional Essbase databases from SQL-based relational sources and data warehouses. Its services enable drill-through access from summary-level data in an Essbase database to detailed data in relational databases and/or data warehouses (HOLAP architecture) via ODBC connections. Built on a flexible, multitier architecture, Integration Services easily scales to accommodate changing requirements, and delivers scalability, performance, and reliability.

The Integration Services Console is a GUI in which database administrators can create a logical OLAP analysis model from the tables, views, and columns of relational databases and/or data warehouses. They can use the OLAP model to create a metaoutline containing the structure and rules required to generate an

Essbase database outline, and then use the metaoutline to create and populate an Essbase multidimensional database.

Integration Services Server does the actual work of extracting data from the data sources, performing the operations specified in the associated metaoutline, and loading the data into an Essbase database. It uses the information in an OLAP Metadata Catalog to extract dimensions and members. This catalog is a relational schema containing: metadata describing the nature, source, location, and type of data to retrieve; metadata describing information required to generate Essbase outlines; and OLAP models and metaoutlines. You can create multiple OLAP Metadata Catalogs to store models and metaoutlines.

Integration Services is a component of Oracle Essbase.

Essbase Command and Query Languages   MDX is a query language specification for OLAP data sources. MDX is the most commonly used multidimensional expression language today. The Essbase version of MDX includes an ever-growing list of functions developed specifically for Essbase. Because of this, MDX for Essbase is also called MaxL MDX and is technically a subset of MaxL. However, MaxL MDX and MaxL Data Definition Language (DDL) have little in common syntactically. MaxL MDX is used in Essbase to query both block and aggregate storage databases, and for outline member formulas in aggregate storage outlines.

Data definition means structural control of a database system, including operations like creation, deletion, and updating of users, applications, databases, and database objects. Statements in MaxL DDL include verbs like CREATE, ALTER, DROP, GRANT, and DISPLAY. Comments begin with /* and end with */.

MaxL is used to create repeatable processes. For instance, suppose that each month, you need to load the most current data. The following is an example MaxL script from the Essbase Bootcamp course:

```
/* CREATE PROCESS LOG AND LOGIN TO SERVER */
spool on to "$arborpath\\salesrisk_log.txt";
login $1 $2 on 'localhost';
/* Activate  Bigcorp Sales database */
alter system load application 'Bigcorp';
alter application 'Bigcorp' load database 'Sales';
/* Load data files                          */
import database 'Bigcorp'.'Sales' data from server text data_file
'SalesRisk.txt'
  using server rules_file 'SlsRisk' on error write to acterr;
/* CLOSE OUT PROCESS LOG AND EXIT */
spool off;
exit;
```

For queries, Essbase supports MaxL MDX through the C API, Java API, MaxL interface, and XMLA API.

In many ways, MaxL MDX is comparable to Essbase report scripts. MaxL MDX and report scripts are both capable of performing similar member selection and calculation functions, but report scripts also include a set of report-formatting options to control how results are represented. On the other hand, the focus of a MaxL MDX query is analytical data retrieval, with the underlying API handling the resulting data structures.

```
SELECT {Jan, Feb, Mar} ON ROWS,
{[Net Sales], [Cost of Sales]} ON COLUMNS
FROM [HyptekAS].[HyptekAS]
WHERE ([North America], FY06)
```

Additionally, MDX is the core calculation functionality for Essbase aggregate storage applications.

Closely associated with MDX is XMLA, the most recent attempt at a standardized API in the OLAP and BI space. XMLA is a standard that allows client applications to talk to multidimensional or OLAP data sources. The communication of messages back and forth is done using the HTTP, SOAP, and XML web standards. The query language used is MDX. XMLA has already gained broad support, including from companies like Oracle, Microsoft, SAP, and SAS.

ESSCMD is a legacy command-line interface that performs operations interactively or through a batch or script file. Developers should avoid ESSCMD, as MaxL was introduced as a replacement with the release of Essbase 6.5.

Data-Integration Tools

If your data source is a data warehouse or transactional system, you may want to include a data-integration tool in your Essbase implementation. Data-integration tools fall into three categories: ETL; extract, load, and transform (ELT); and application-based solutions.

Oracle provides many options in the realm of data-integration tools, depending on the source and usage requirements. In this section, we introduce tools for data integration. These tools are available separately; they do not ship with Oracle Essbase. For more information, see the Oracle web site.

Oracle Data Integrator Enterprise Edition   Oracle Data Integrator Enterprise Edition (ODI) delivers unique next-generation ELT technology that improves performance and reduces data-integration costs, even across heterogeneous systems. Unlike conventional ETL tools, ODI offers the productivity of a declarative design approach, as well as the benefits of an active integration platform for seamless batch and real-time integration.

In addition, hot-pluggable Knowledge Modules provide modularity, flexibility, and extensibility. Oracle provides Essbase-aware Knowledge Modules, allowing developers to create an end-to-end integration from transaction systems to an enterprise data warehouse to Essbase. ODI also supports the rest of the Oracle Enterprise Performance Management System.

For many organizations, a standards-based approach is important, if not critical. To that end, ODI may be used as an approach to Essbase integration. With ODI, you can import both data values and dimensional information.

Hyperion Data Integration Management Adapters   If your organization has adopted Informatica PowerCenter, a third-party ETL tool, as a standard, rather than ODI, Hyperion Data Integration Management (DIM) may be appropriate. Simply stated, DIM is a collection of adapters that Oracle created to support the use of Informatica PowerCenter with Essbase and the rest of the Oracle Enterprise Performance Management System.

Like ODI, DIM allows you to import both data values and dimensional information.

Oracle Hyperion Financial Data Quality Management, Fusion Edition   Another form of data integration is provided via Oracle Hyperion Financial Data Quality Management (FDM). Its data-preparation server can ease integrating and validating financial data from any of your source systems. Like ODI and DIM, FDM includes prepackaged adapters for Essbase and the rest of the Oracle Enterprise Performance Management System.

Unlike ODI and DIM, which are more IT-centric, FDM is a packaged solution for business users that helps develop standardized financial data management processes using a web-based guided workflow user interface. FDM does not provide dimension integration. Rather, with FDM, users validate, map and move data from source systems to Essbase or the target application.

Other Oracle Components for Use with Essbase

In this section, we introduce you to other components that can be used with Essbase: Oracle Hyperion Data Relationship Management, Shared Services, Smart Search, and other Oracle Enterprise Performance Management System applications.

Oracle Hyperion Data Relationship Management, Fusion Edition   Generally speaking, the dimensional information used by products such as Essbase might be referred to as master data. Oracle Hyperion Data Relationship Management, previously known as Hyperion Master Data Management, provides organizations with a solution to build consistency within master data assets despite endless changes within the underlying transactional and analytical systems. Specifically, Data Relationship Management provides a master data management solution built to enable dimension management.

In essence, Data Relationship Management is an application managed by IT and used by business users to do the following:

- Create an enterprise view of analytical dimensions, reporting structures, performance measures, and their related attributes and hierarchies.

- Construct departmental perspectives that bear referential integrity and consistency.

- Provide validations and business rules that enforce enterprise governance policies.

- Synchronize master data with downstream processes.

Often, Data Relationship Management is implemented alongside FDM, as they complement each other; the latter specializes in data values, and the former provides dimension management.

Hyperion Shared Services   Shared Services provides a single sign-on (SSO) service, not only for Essbase and its components, but for all Oracle Enterprise Performance Management System products. SSO promotes an uninterrupted workflow when moving between Essbase components and/or Oracle Enterprise Performance Management System products. Shared Services can be linked with your existing corporate repository—for example, a Lightweight Directory Access Protocol (LDAP) server to authenticate users. Administrators can create user roles and groups to define which products end users can use and the level of access they have to the product. Together, user authentication and role-based authorization provide a secure environment.

Shared Services is part of Oracle Hyperion Foundation Services, which ships with Oracle Essbase. It is required for managing users in Essbase Studio.

Oracle Hyperion Smart Search   Smart Search was originally designed for use with Google OneBox for Enterprise Google Search Appliance. The thought was to allow a user to search the company's internal data using business terms. As such, the OneBox appliance first creates an index of all dimension information for all deployed Essbase databases. Then people can use their browser to query the dimensions via Google. For example, you could type in "fourth-quarter cost of goods sold" and Smart Search would find related items. The found items are presented much like any other Google search results—as a list of content sorted by relevance. If you click a link, the associated data is presented in Excel using Smart View.

Smart Search now supports Oracle Secure Enterprise Search as well as Google OneBox. Smart Search is a component of Oracle Essbase.

Oracle Enterprise Performance Management System Applications   Two of the applications in Oracle Enterprise Performance Management System use Essbase as a database and calculation engine: Planning and Oracle Hyperion Profitability and Cost Management. If you have either of these products installed, then you have the core components of Essbase already installed. For more information, see Chapter 7.

End-User Tools

End users are the consumers of OLAP data. End users include people at all levels in an organization and in many departments. The needs of end users will differ depending on roles and responsibilities. A financial analyst needs more investigative capabilities than say a CEO, who is likely more interested in seeing results presented in a dashboard report. OBIEE and OBIEE Plus provide the tools you need to satisfy the diverse reporting needs of your organization. In addition, many third-party vendors offer tools that are compatible with Essbase or Oracle OLAP. Alternatively, you can use Java to create custom end-user applications, as discussed in Chapter 7.

Oracle Business Intelligence Suite Enterprise Edition Plus

Oracle OLAP and Oracle Essbase both support two key components of OBIEE: BI Interactive Dashboards and BI Answers, which provide a key pairing for delivering a world-class dashboard solution. BI Interactive Dashboards provides a personalized, role-based, 100 percent thin client web browser interface for important trends and key performance indicators, including gauges, charts, summary reports, and even condition-based guided analytics. BI Answers is a 100 percent thin client ad hoc reporting and analysis solution that is fully integrated with BI Interactive Dashboards and BI Publisher. End users can quickly create their own reports and then drill through, analyze, visualize, and embed the results in their own personalized dashboard.

Because BI Interactive Dashboards and BI Answers sit directly on Oracle BI Server, they provide two unique capabilities:

- You can create federated queries that cross the bounds of relational and multidimensional data.

- You can provide a single definition for a metric (such as profit) and reuse that consistent definition across all your reports.

For more information, see Chapter 6, which covers reporting OLAP results.

OBIEE Plus extends OBIEE by bundling Hyperion analysis and reporting applications for use with Essbase: Web Analysis, Financial Reporting, Interactive Reporting, and SQR Production Reporting. Two of these products—Web Analysis and Financial Reporting—are particularly useful for sharing Essbase data throughout

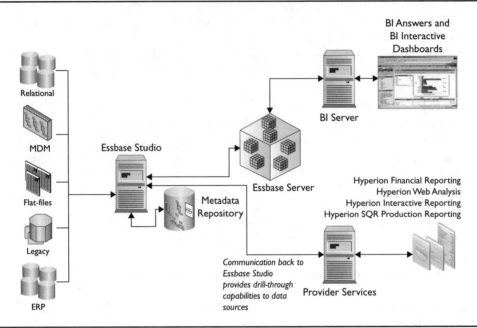

FIGURE 3-40. *Oracle Business Intelligence Suite Enterprise Edition Plus applications*

the organization. Figure 3-40 shows how these front-end applications fit into an Essbase implementation. Note that the BI Server pictured here could just as easily be hooked up to an Oracle database to retrieve Oracle OLAP data.

Web Analysis is a powerful, intuitive, web-based interface that delivers interactive analytics to everyone in the enterprise. It is a purpose-built interface for ad hoc analysis and executive reporting systems. Web Analysis provides a broad range of flexible, easy-to-use display types, including grids, charts, pin boards, traffic lighting, and personalization. Users have complete control over layouts, formatting, fonts, and colors, as well as a flexible array of output options enabling wide distribution via print, HTML web pages, PDF, and online viewing. Web Analysis facilitates access to multidimensional data sources as well as Oracle Enterprise Performance Management System applications. It supports drill-through to relational sources, including drill-through to URL.

Financial Reporting, Fusion Edition, is the application-intelligent structured reporting solution for Essbase applications. It is a powerful tool that lets you graphically design and present your analytic data. You can use the Financial Reporting Windows client interface to design traditional financial reports (such as cash management reports and balance sheets) and nontraditional reports. Finished reports can be routed to a printer and viewed on the Web through a browser.

You can also use Hyperion Interactive Reporting and Hyperion SQR Production Reporting. For more information, see Chapter 6.

Third-Party Applications

Oracle partners and other vendors offer their own front ends for Essbase and Oracle OLAP. For example, for Essbase, Applied OLAP offers an enhanced spreadsheet-style interface called Dodeca, which integrates Oracle applications and non-Oracle applications on the desktop. For Oracle OLAP, Collaborative Consulting, Inc. has developed the ClearView add-in for Microsoft Excel that enables users to view and write back to Oracle OLAP cubes. It has sophisticated "spreading tools" for writing back to Oracle OLAP cubes and also tracks changes. For more information, see Chapter 6.

Conclusion

OLAP design requires a foundation in basic OLAP concepts and general OLAP design principles, as well as an understanding of the architecture, features, functionality, and restrictions of the selected OLAP product. Designers need to give more importance to end-user requirements than to the structure of the data source. OLAP products from Oracle offer effective ways to restructure and enhance data to meet user requirements, such as adding aggregate and calculated data or combining data from multiple sources.

Both Oracle OLAP and Oracle Essbase have architectures that fit easily into existing infrastructures. Oracle OLAP is an option to the Oracle Database, while Essbase is an independent OLAP database that can augment existing systems. The products are full featured and offer next-generation administration tools to making building and maintaining cubes as easy as possible.

The next two chapters provide an overview of the steps needed to build an Oracle OLAP analytical workspace and an Essbase database, respectively. The intention is to provide an overview of the build processes, rather than building a working Oracle OLAP analytical workspace or Essbase database. The procedures and sample data also allow us to introduce the user interfaces of some of the build/administration tools within a logical flow.

References

Alexander, Lisa. *Hyperion System 9 BI+ Essbase Analytics Bootcamp Student Guide.* Hyperion Solutions Corporation, 2007.

Collins, Dave. "Hyperion 7.x New Features." Presentation. Hyperion Solutions, 2004.

EPM Information Development Team. *Oracle Essbase Database Administrator's Guide, Release 11.1.1.* Oracle Corporation, 2008.

EPM Information Development Team. *Oracle Essbase Studio New Features, Release 11.1.1.* Oracle Corporation, 2008.

EPM Information Development Team. *Oracle Hyperion Provider Services Administration Guide, Release 11.1.1.* Oracle Corporation, 2008.

Nader, Michael and Dave Collins. *Dare to OLAP.* Oracle Corporation, 2008.

Oracle Corporation. *Oracle OLAP User's Guide 11g Release 1 (11.1).* Oracle Corporation, 2008.

CHAPTER
4

Building an Oracle OLAP
Analytic Workspace

he previous chapter focused on designing OLAP applications. In this chapter, we walk you through the steps required to build an Oracle OLAP analytic workspace. Recall that an Oracle OLAP analytic workspace contains a collection of dimensions and a collection of cubes, where any given cube contains only the dimensions required to describe the measures in that cube. The analytic workspace also holds other multidimensional objects, such as folders and programs, that are required for an OLAP analysis.

The chapter starts with an overview of the components and files used in the demonstration. During the demonstration, we walk you through how to prepare data, create an analytic workspace, create and populate dimensions, and create and populate cubes. Along the way, we will expand on the work begun in Chapters 2 and 3 and provide more details about the Oracle OLAP implementation of a variety of OLAP concepts. After the demonstration, we highlight how to use calculated measures to create business-savvy calculations. We end this chapter with a few advanced topics, including cube-organized materialized views and security.

Oracle OLAP Demonstration Overview

Our goal for this demonstration is to provide an overall workflow and some best practices to get you started with Oracle OLAP. You can use the same workflow to build both simple and complex OLAP models. This walk-through is for demonstration purposes only. Before building an analytic workspace for a production environment, see the *Oracle OLAP User's Guide* and the *Oracle OLAP DML Reference*.

In this demonstration, we create an analytic workspace using a four-step process:

- Prepare the data.

- Create an analytic workspace.

- Create and populate dimensions.

- Create and populate cubes.

After we show how to create a cube with dimensions and some simple calculations, we discuss adding more advanced calculations and operations to dimensions and cubes.

NOTE
Unless otherwise specified, the instructions and screen captures in this chapter reflect Oracle OLAP 11g and Oracle Database 11g running in a UNIX-based environment. For those using Oracle OLAP 10g, we point out where version 11g is different from version 10g. For instructions for other operating systems, see the Oracle OLAP documentation set.

In the architecture diagrams for Oracle OLAP presented in Chapter 3, we introduced the key components involved in the building process. These components, circled on Figure 4-1, are OWB and AWM.

OWB is a general-purpose warehouse construction and extract, transform, and load (ETL) tool that has the ability to build and maintain OLAP objects, as well as all

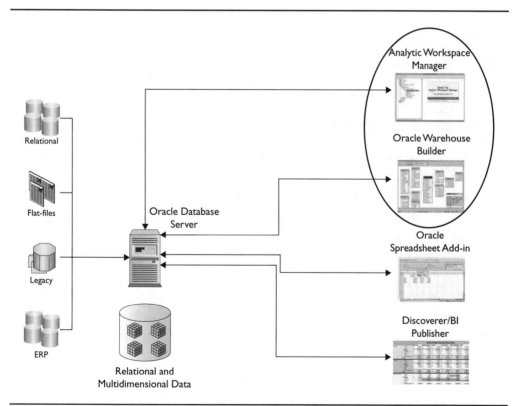

FIGURE 4-1. *You can build analytic workspaces using the administration tools.*

the other warehouse components. AWM focuses solely on the construction and maintenance of OLAP objects. Both tools are written in Java and use the Java API for Oracle OLAP to perform a bulk of the work. For this chapter's example, we use AWM. If you want to use OWB, you will find the processes and concepts to be similar, although the user interface is different.

The examples and screen captures used in this chapter are based on the OLAPTRAIN OLAP demo data. You can download the sample data from the Oracle Press web site.

From Source to Cubes with Analytic Workspace Manager

In this section, we describe how to use AWM to build an analytic workspace and the objects contained within. After an overview of AWM, we walk you through the four steps required to build and populate OLAP cubes, as noted in the previous section.

Getting Started with Analytic Workspace Manager

The first time you start AWM, you are asked to create a database connection. AWM uses either SQL*Net or JDBC to connect to an Oracle database. You will need to know the host, port, and service ID (SID) for the database or the TNS Alias created to connect to the database. Your Oracle Database Administrator can supply this information. After you connect to the database, you are prompted to log in to the database. If you like, you can configure your AWM environment at this time. The following sections describe the steps to get started with AWM.

Creating a Database Connection and Logging In

1. To launch AWM, do one of the following:

   - On Windows-based systems, click Start | All Programs | Oracle – OraClient Home1 | Integrated Management Tools – OLAP Analytic Workspace Manager.

   - On UNIX-based systems, open a prompt and run the following shell script:

   ```
   $ORACLE_HOME/bin/awm.sh
   ```

2. If this is the first time you have opened AWM, you are prompted to define a database connection.

3. Enter a description to identify the server.

4. If you want to use SQL*Net, specify the TNS Alias for the server. Otherwise, specify the host, port, and SID, separated by colons. Then click Create.

5. The following image is for illustrative purposes only; do not copy these values.

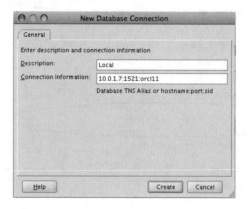

6. Right-click the connection and select Connect Database.

7. When prompted, specify the user name and password that you use to connect to the database. For this example, we are using the OLAPTRAIN schema with a password of **oracle**.

8. After you are connected, you will be presented with a list of schemas to which you have access. Select the schema that will contain the new analytic workspace. Expand a schema tree to see what, if any, analytic workspaces exist in those schemas.

Configuring Analytic Workspace Manager

You can configure AWM to suit your environment and preferences. The configuration settings affect the way that AWM behaves. To set your configuration preferences, select Tools | Configuration. We recommend setting the following options:

- **Template directory**   Specify where you want template files stored.

- **Enable plugins**   Select this option to install plug-ins automatically.

■ **Plugin directory**   Specify where you want the plug-ins located.

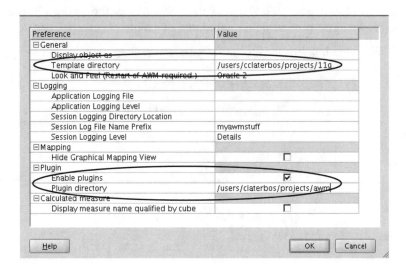

Preference	Value
⊟General	
Display object as	
Template directory	/users/cclaterbos/projects/11g
Look and Feel (Restart of AWM required.)	Oracle 2
⊟Logging	
Application Logging File	
Application Logging Level	
Session Logging Directory Location	
Session Log File Name Prefix	myawmstuff
Session Logging Level	Details
⊟Mapping	
Hide Graphical Mapping View	☐
⊟Plugin	
Enable plugins	☑
Plugin directory	/users/claterbos/projects/awm
⊟Calculated measure	
Display measure name qualified by cube	☐

| Help | | OK | Cancel |

You can specify other options as desired. For descriptions of the options, click Help.

NOTE
If you are building 10g mode AWs with either Oracle Database 10g or Oracle Database 11g in 10g mode, and you want to use SQL to access cubes, you need to obtain and install the plug-in that enables the generation of SQL views. You can download the plug-in from the Oracle Technology Network (OTN) web site under Oracle OLAP. In Oracle OLAP 11g connected in 11g mode, SQL views are generated automatically.

Setting Read-Only Access on Analytic Workspaces

Before we get started building the analytic workspace, here is one more helpful tip. Normally, when you attach an analytic workspace, it comes up read-write. This behavior can be changed by modifying the awm.properties file. By adding a setting, you can have AWM prompt you for how to open the analytic workspace. This will give you the option to attach the workspace as read-only, which is useful when you want to explore an analytic workspace without the danger of inadvertently modifying it.

To make this modification, follow these steps:

1. Go to the directory where the AWM program is started, usually Oracle Home/olap/awm.

2. Open the awm.properties file.

3. Insert the following command in the list of settings:

    ```
    aw.model.show.attach=y
    ```

    Your file should look like similar to this:

    ```
    _awm.object.display=
    _aw.model.show.attach=y
    olap_dml_log.log_results=y
    awm.hide.map.graphical=n
    awm.plugin_dirname=/
    ```

4. Save and close the file.

The next time you attach an analytic workspace, you will be prompted to choose how you want to open it: Read Only, Read Write, or Read Write Exclusive. If you want to save your work, do not select Read Only.

Preparing the Data

Before we jump into building the OLAP analytic workspace, we need to start with some data. In this demonstration, we are working with a relational fact table that contains daily sales data for a computer sales company. The fact table has four lookup tables, as shown in Figure 4-2.

In Figure 4-2, the All level is represented explicitly in the source data. This single value represents the top of the hierarchy and it is repeated in every data row. In Oracle OLAP 11*g*, you do not need to include it and can enjoy some space savings by leaving it out. Version 11*g* also provides the ability to enter equations in the mapping panel, so that you can calculate source values on the fly from other data without physically storing it. This gives a mechanism for handling missing values. Many reporting tools, including OBIEE, require an All level for user-defined dimensions, so it is a good idea to include this level where possible.

Oracle OLAP uses Oracle tables, views, and materialized views as the primary data sources. These data sources can be represented as a star schema (as in Figure 4-2) or a snowflake schema (as in Figure 4-3), as parent-child relations, or as a collection of tables and views. You can also use flat files as data sources, however, the flat files need to be represented by external tables or loaded into tables via an ETL process. It is possible to use gateways to non-Oracle data as well.

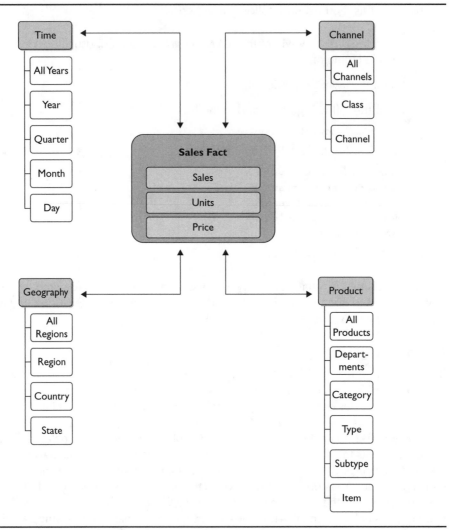

FIGURE 4-2. *Demonstration data in a star schema*

TIP

If a dimension has skip-level or ragged hierarchies, consider using a snowflake schema to represent the data source. AWM automatically handles the relationships between levels in a snowflake schema.

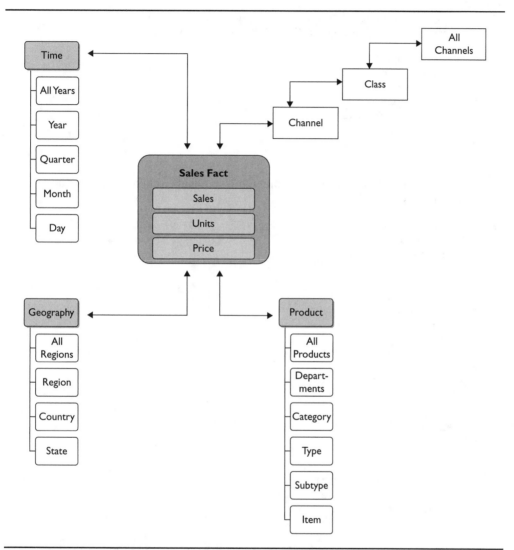

FIGURE 4-3. *Demonstration data in snowflake schema*

When preparing the dimension table or view, you need to ensure that each member has a key value and description. If you are using a star schema, the dimension sources must have the full parentage in each row. With a snowflake schema, where each level of a dimension is in a separate source table or view, you need to provide an additional column for the parent key of that level. Here is an example of a star schema table for a CHANNEL dimension:

```
create table channel
    (all_channels_key number,
     all_channel_name varchar2(20),
     class_key number,
     class_name varchar2(20),
     channel_key number,
     channel_name varchar2(20)
)
```

In addition, the following is an example of the snowflake schema tables for a CHANNEL dimension:

```
create table  all_channels
    (all_channels_key number,
     all_channel_name varchar2(20))

create table channel_class
    (all_channels_key number,
     class_key number,
     class_name varchar2(20)
     constraint "CH_ALL_FK"
      foreign key ("ALL_CHANNELS_KEY")
      references all_channels
      ("ALL_CHANNELS_KEY") enable
)
create table channel
    (class_key number,
     channel_key number,
     channel_name varchar2(20),
     constraint "CH_CLASS_FK"
      foreign key ("CLASS_KEY")
      references channel_class
      ("CLASS_KEY") enable
)
```

As you can see, the snowflake tables represent the same data as the star table. The same data is spread across three tables linked with parent keys. To support skip and ragged levels, the parent keys can be any parent key above the child level in any table.

Lastly, a parent-child table represents a value-based hierarchy with columns for the member key, parent key, and member description.

Creating an Analytic Workspace

Now we are ready to create an analytic workspace that will hold our OLAP dimensions and cubes. Before we get started, let's review some best practices for creating workspaces and naming the metadata used within the workspace.

Best Practices

Following the advice in this section will help you to create cubes that are easy to understand and use. The naming conventions that we suggest ensure that the generated column names in your views are easy to read, and reduce the chances that generated column names will be truncated to fit within the limits for a column name in the Oracle Database. These naming conventions also make it easier and quicker to map to the columns in AWM, because the screens are less cluttered with long object names.

The following guidelines have proven effective in many Oracle OLAP implementations:

- If possible, create the analytic workspace in its own schema. This helps with security and backing up the analytic workspaces. For more information, see Chapter 8.

- Store the workspaces in a separate tablespace from the relational data. In most cases, you should turn off logging during maintenance to reduce the size of the IO and redo buffers.

- Create simple, meaningful names and avoid the use of the underscore character (_), especially when naming dimensions, hierarchies, levels, and attributes.

- Keep names as short as possible for dimensions, levels, hierarchies, and attributes. In Oracle OLAP 11*g*, the dimension level creation tool limits the length of level names to 30 characters.

- Dimension names must be unique within an analytic workspace, but level and attribute names do not need to be unique. You can use the same level name, such as TOTAL or ALL, in more than one dimension. The same is true for attributes.

- Do not put the dimension name in level or attribute names. CLASS is fine to represent PRODUCT_CLASS.

- Do not be too cryptic in your naming standard (for example, do not use just the first two characters of the dimension names in the cube as the name of the cube). This may make sense initially, but it can be very hard to read and find the objects later.

Object Type	Instead Of	Use	Suggested Character Length	Recommended Character Length
Dimensions	COMPUTER_PRODUCT_DIM	PROD	3–6	< 12
Levels	PRODUCT_CATEGORY	CAT	3–6	< 15
Hierarchies	FISCAL_CALENDAR_HIERARCHY	FISCAL	4–10	< 16
Attributes	PRODUCT_COLOR_ATTRIBUTE	COLOR	3–8	< 16
Cubes	TI_PR_GE_CH or SALES_CUBE	SALES	6–12	< 20

TABLE 4-1.   *Suggested Naming Conventions*

■ Do not try to make names too descriptive (for example, avoid putting "DIM" in the name of everything that is a dimension or "ATT" into the name of all the attributes). Adding prefixes makes names too long and harder to read. The database knows which objects are which, and you can query the analytic workspace if needed. For example, to find the names of all the dimensions in an analytic workspace, you can use a simple SQL command like the following:

```
select * from all_cube_dimensions
```

■ Avoid using plurals in the names of objects where appropriate. For example, name a dimension PRODUCT instead of PRODUCTS.

Table 4-1 suggests some possible names for common object types and provides guidelines for the number of characters to use for each type of object.

To illustrate the importance of naming your objects appropriately, Figure 4-4 shows two implementations of the same CUSTOMER dimension. The dimension on the right side implements the preceding best practice guidelines.

Figure 4-5 shows the same dimensions in a different view. Notice that in this view, some column names have been truncated due to the maximum length of column names in the database. For the poor names, the truncation makes things even more unreadable.

Here is an example of a SELECT statement to retrieve data from the poor naming convention:

```
select
all_company_customers_di,sales_districts_long_des,sales_managers_long_desc,
customer_sales_represent,sales_customers_long_des
from company_customers_dim_mai_view
```

In addition, the following is an example of a `SELECT` statement using the recommending naming conventions:

```
select
all_customers_long_descr,district_long_descriptio,managers_long_description,
sales_rep_long_descripti,customer_long_descriptio
from customer_standard_view
```

As you can see, the shorter names make for easier `SELECT` statements, which are also easier to read and may actually run faster.

NOTE
Long and short description attributes are created automatically. You can change them if shorter names are desired.

Creating the New Analytic Workspace

Analytic workspaces can become very big, and the maintenance of the analytic workspaces is very disk-intensive. If your analytic workspace will be large, we recommend that you create a separate tablespace to store the analytic workspace. Depending on the update frequency and the size of each update, it may be appropriate to disable logging on this tablespace.

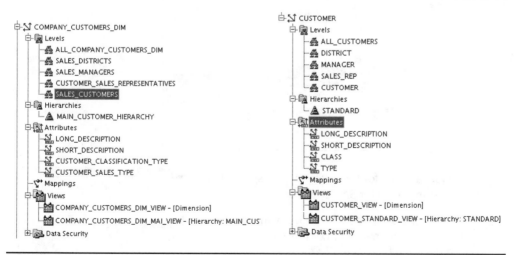

FIGURE 4-4. *Names are easier to read when you follow best practices*

Column Name	Data Type	Column Name	Data Type
DIM_KEY	VARCHAR2(100 BYTE)	DIM_KEY	VARCHAR2(100 BYTE)
LEVEL_NAME	VARCHAR2(30 BYTE)	LEVEL_NAME	VARCHAR2(30 BYTE)
LONG_DESCRIPTION	VARCHAR2(60 BYTE)	LONG_DESCRIPTION	VARCHAR2(60 BYTE)
SHORT_DESCRIPTION	VARCHAR2(60 BYTE)	SHORT_DESCRIPTION	VARCHAR2(60 BYTE)
ALL_COMPANY_CUSTOMERS_DI	VARCHAR2(60 BYTE)	ALL_CUSTOMERS_LONG_DESCR	VARCHAR2(60 BYTE)
ALL_COMPANY_CUSTOMERS__1	VARCHAR2(60 BYTE)	ALL_CUSTOMERS_SHORT_DESC	VARCHAR2(60 BYTE)
SALES_DISTRICTS_LONG_DES	VARCHAR2(60 BYTE)	DISTRICT_LONG_DESCRIPTIO	VARCHAR2(60 BYTE)
SALES_DISTRICTS_SHORT_DE	VARCHAR2(60 BYTE)	DISTRICT_SHORT_DESCRIPTI	VARCHAR2(60 BYTE)
SALES_MANAGERS_LONG_DESC	VARCHAR2(60 BYTE)	MANAGER_LONG_DESCRIPTION	VARCHAR2(60 BYTE)
SALES_MANAGERS_SHORT_DES	VARCHAR2(60 BYTE)	MANAGER_SHORT_DESCRIPTIO	VARCHAR2(60 BYTE)
CUSTOMER_SALES_REPRESENT	VARCHAR2(60 BYTE)	SALES_REP_LONG_DESCRIPTI	VARCHAR2(60 BYTE)
CUSTOMER_CLASSIFICATION_	VARCHAR2(60 BYTE)	SALES_REP_SHORT_DESCRIPT	VARCHAR2(60 BYTE)
CUSTOMER_SALES_TYPE	VARCHAR2(60 BYTE)	CLASS	VARCHAR2(60 BYTE)
SALES_CUSTOMERS_LONG_DES	VARCHAR2(60 BYTE)	TYPE	VARCHAR2(60 BYTE)
SALES_CUSTOMERS_SHORT_DE	VARCHAR2(60 BYTE)	CUSTOMER_LONG_DESCRIPTIO	VARCHAR2(60 BYTE)
SALES_CUSTOMERS_CUSTOMER	VARCHAR2(60 BYTE)	CUSTOMER_SHORT_DESCRIPTI	VARCHAR2(60 BYTE)
SALES_CUSTOMERS_CUSTOM_1	VARCHAR2(60 BYTE)	CUSTOMER_CLASS	VARCHAR2(60 BYTE)
PARENT	VARCHAR2(100 BYTE)	CUSTOMER_TYPE	VARCHAR2(60 BYTE)
DEPTH	NUMBER	PARENT	VARCHAR2(100 BYTE)
ALL_COMPANY_CUSTOMERS__2	VARCHAR2(100 BYTE)	DEPTH	NUMBER
SALES_DISTRICTS	VARCHAR2(100 BYTE)	ALL_CUSTOMERS	VARCHAR2(100 BYTE)
SALES_MANAGERS	VARCHAR2(100 BYTE)	DISTRICT	VARCHAR2(100 BYTE)
CUSTOMER_SALES_REPRESE_1	VARCHAR2(100 BYTE)	MANAGER	VARCHAR2(100 BYTE)
SALES_CUSTOMERS	VARCHAR2(100 BYTE)	SALES_REP	VARCHAR2(100 BYTE)
		CUSTOMER	VARCHAR2(100 BYTE)

FIGURE 4-5. *Truncation can cause readability issues.*

To create an analytic workspace:

1. In AWM, right-click Analytic Workspaces and select Create Analytic Workspace.

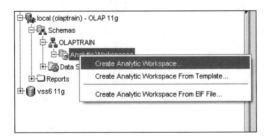

2. Specify a name for the analytic workspace. For this example, enter **SALESTRACK**.

3. Select the tablespace where you want to store the analytic workspace. For this example, use the default tablespace.

4. Click Create. The analytic workspace is created and displayed in the main AWM window.

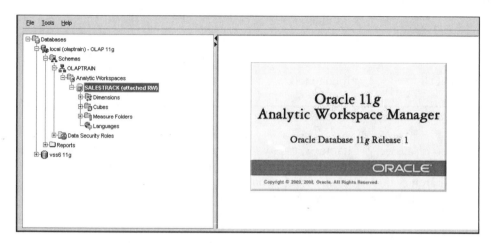

The next step is to create the dimensions for the cubes.

Creating and Populating Dimensions

You can create your dimensions in any order. AWM will list them in alphabetical order once they are created. Remember that dimensions are created once in the analytic workspace and are reused in the cubes. Dimensions require a default hierarchy and may contain more than one hierarchy. You need to create all dimensions for a cube before you can create the cube itself. The process consists of the following steps:

■ Create the dimensions.

■ Optionally, define summary levels (not required for value-based hierarchies).

■ Organize dimension levels into hierarchies.

■ Map to a data source.

■ Load the dimensions.

As you may recall from Chapter 3, Oracle OLAP has two basic types of dimensions: user-defined and time. User-defined dimensions represent a majority of the dimensions used by the cubes. Time dimensions are specialized dimensions that have additional characteristics that allow for time-series analysis. If the application or the cube does not require time-series analysis, you do not need to create a time dimension.

Incoming Member Key	Level	Assigned Key
DIRECT	Channel	CHANNEL_DIRECT
NA	Class	CLASS_NA
NA	Channel	CHANNEL_NA
ALL_CHANNELS	All channels	ALL_CHANNELS_ALL_CHANNELS

TABLE 4-2. *Assigned Keys When Generate Surrogate Keys Is Selected*

As also discussed in Chapter 3, the two types of hierarchies are level-based and value-based. Level-based hierarchies, the default, require at least one level. Value-based hierarchies do not require levels; you simply give the hierarchy a name and select the Value Based Hierarchy option in AWM.

Oracle OLAP requires that all keys for a dimension be unique across all levels and hierarchies within that dimension. They do not need to be unique across all dimensions; for example, you can have a customer 1001 and a product 1001. If they are not unique within a dimension, the data loader will not load the dimension members during the maintenance process.

When you create a dimension, you specify how you want Oracle OLAP to handle duplicate members by selecting either the Generate Surrogate Keys option or the Use Keys from Data Source option. As a safety measure, AWM defaults to Generate Surrogate Keys, which means that Oracle OLAP adds the level name as a prefix to all incoming member names to ensure uniqueness across levels. For example, Table 4-2 shows the assigned keys for the members in the CHANNEL dimension.

Surrogate keys are especially helpful if you are not sure that your members are unique across levels. As you can see, there were nonunique NA members in the preceding example. Prefixes create large key values, which can increase the size of the analytic workspace. However, the increase in size due to surrogate keys is very slight, because the dimension members are only stored once (unlike with tables, where the impact on storage is larger because the key repeats for each row in the table). Surrogate keys can also make querying the data via the OLAP command language and possibly SQL map more complex, because you may need to know the level name.

NOTE
Keys must be unique within a level. For example, you are not allowed to have a city with the key KC that is a child of Missouri if there is a separate city with the key KC that is a child of Kansas. In this case, surrogate keys do not help you, because the key for each city KC would be assigned the key CITY_KC; Oracle OLAP would not be able to differentiate these when loading the data.

Creating Dimensions

Now let's build the dimensions. In this demonstration, we are creating the four dimensions shown in our original star schema (shown in Figure 4-2): CHANNEL, PRODUCT, GEOGRAPHY, and TIME.

To build dimensions:

1. Right-click Dimension and select Create Dimension. The Create Dimension dialog box has four tabs where you can enter information for a dimension. However, you do not need to enter information on all the tabs at the time the dimension is first created.

2. On the General tab, specify the name of the dimension. In this case, enter **CHANNEL**. As you type, the Short Label, Long Label, and Description fields are filled in automatically. The name is created in uppercase characters. The name cannot contain spaces or special characters. Underscores are permitted, though it is a best practice to avoid them where possible. If you use an underscore in the Name field, the underscore is converted to a space in the label and description fields. If desired, edit the labels and description for the dimension.

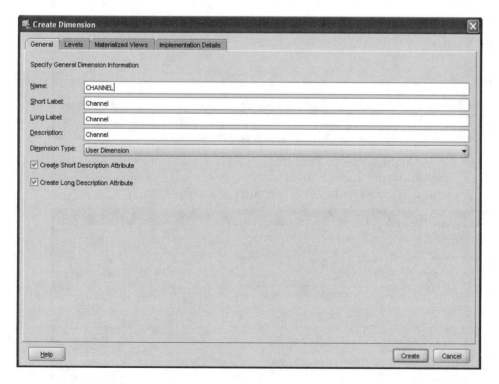

NOTE
In Oracle OLAP 10g, the Levels and Materialized Views tabs are not part of the Create Dimension dialog box, and this information is entered separately.

3. On the Levels tab, enter **ALL_CHANNELS**, **CLASS**, and **CHANNEL**. If desired, edit the labels and description for the level.

TIP
While not required, you can avoid confusion later by entering the levels in a top-down order that reflects the parent-child relationships between members, as shown in the following illustration.

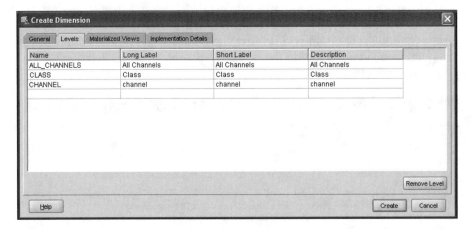

4. On the Implementation Details tab, if you are sure that the data source contains no duplicate member names (keys), select Use Keys from Data Source. The data for this demonstration uses unique keys.

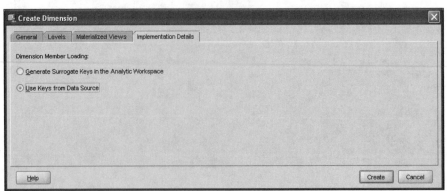

5. Click Create to generate the CHANNEL dimension.

6. Repeat this process to create the following dimensions and levels:

Dimension Name	Level Names
TIME	All Years
	Year
	Quarter
	Month
	Day
PRODUCT	All Products
	Department
	Category
	Type
	Subtype
	Item
GEOGRAPHY	All Regions
	Region
	Country
	State

Creating Hierarchies

For this demonstration, we create four level-based hierarchies: one for each of the dimensions. While there is no functional limit to the number of hierarchies in a dimension, you can have only one default hierarchy in each dimension. You can use any name you want for hierarchies, but it is a good idea to establish a naming convention for the default hierarchies, such as STANDARD or DEFAULT.

NOTE
By default, when you create a new hierarchy, it is a level-based hierarchy. It is also set as the default hierarchy. If you have more than one hierarchy in a dimension, you need to choose one of them to be the default hierarchy.

If you did not create levels in the previous procedure (for example, you are using Oracle OLAP 10g) or if you want to add new levels, create the levels now.

1. For the CHANNEL dimension, right-click Levels and select Create Level.

2. Specify the name for the level and fill in short label, long label, and description. Then click Create.

3. Repeat this procedure to add the rest of the levels for this dimension and the rest of the dimensions.

   You are now ready to create the default dimension hierarchies.

1. For the CHANNEL dimension, right-click Hierarchy and select Create Hierarchy.

2. Enter the name of the hierarchy. For this example, you may want to use the default name: STANDARD. If desired, change the autogenerated labels and description.

3. Select the levels to include in the hierarchy from the Available Levels list and add them to the Selected Levels list. If necessary, change the order of the levels in the Selected Levels list so that the list reflects the desired top-down hierarchy order (and by extension, the desired drill path).

TIP
If you created the levels in a top-down order, you will not need to change the order here.

Create Hierarchy

General

Specify General Hierarchy Information

Name: STANDARD

Short Label: Standard

Long Label: Standard

Description: Standard

☑ Set as Default Hierarchy

⦿ Level Based Hierarchy   ○ Value Based Hierarchy

Define the levels for this hierarchy by moving levels from the Available list to the selected list. The order of levels in the Selected list reflect the order of the levels (highest to lowest) in the hierarchy.

Available Levels:

Selected Levels (Highest to Lowest):

ALL_CHANNELS
CLASS
CHANNEL

Help   Create   Cancel

4. Click Create to create the default hierarchy for the CHANNEL dimension.

5. Repeat this procedure to create default hierarchies for the other dimensions, as follows:

Dimension Name	Default Hierarchy Name	Level Names/Order
TIME	STANDARD	All Years Year Quarter Month Day
PRODUCT	STANDARD	All Products Department Category Type Subtype Item
GEOGRAPHY	STANDARD	All Regions Region Country State

Create Attributes

Attributes are used in two ways: to display as dimension member labels, and to use in calculations and when selecting data. For user-defined dimensions, AWM automatically creates the attributes LONG_DESCRIPTION and SHORT_DESCRIPTION. These attributes represent the dimension member labels. These labels can be used by the front end to display a long or short descriptive label for the dimension. The name of the attribute can be changed, but the attribute type should not be changed. You can also create user-defined attributes.

In this example, we create a user-defined attribute called TYPE that can be used in calculations and when selecting data. We define the name, labels, and description, but Oracle OLAP sets the attribute type.

To create the TYPE attribute:

1. Right-click Attributes and select Create Attribute.

2. Specify a name for the attribute. For this example, enter **TYPE**. The labels and description are filled in automatically. If desired, modify the labels and description. By default, the new attribute will be included in SQL views (not available in Oracle OLAP 10*g*). In addition, an index is created to improve the performance of attribute-based queries. You can choose not to create an index by deselecting the Index option.

3. Associate the attribute with levels by selecting the levels in the Apply Attributes To area. For this example, select CHANNEL.

NOTE
The data source will need an attribute value for each level selected here.

4. Click Create to create the TYPE attribute.

Repeat this procedure to create additional attributes as desired.

Mapping Dimensions

As we described previously, we have source data for the dimension contained in either a table or a view. We must now tell AWM how to relate this source data to the dimension levels. This is done through a process called *mapping*.

There are three basic steps to mapping dimensions:

■ Choose the mapping type.

■ Choose the data source.

■ Map the source columns to the dimension members and attributes.

The mapping tool supports mapping standard star schemas, snowflake schemas, and source collections. This section covers the two basic types of mappings: star schema and snowflake schema.

Mapping Dimensions Using a Star Schema   In the following procedure, we map the demonstration data to dimension members and attributes using a star schema. After the procedure, we discuss the differences that would occur if we selected a snowflake schema instead.

To map to a star schema:

1. Click Mappings to display the mapping panel. The window shows a list of available schemas, and the mapping panel displays the dimensions to be mapped. By default, Star Schema is selected as the type of the dimension table, and Oracle OLAP 11*g* displays information in a table mapping view. Version 10*g* defaults to the graphical mapping view. You can switch between views in either version. In 11*g*, if you use expressions in the mapping, you will not be able to go back to the graphical mapping. The following illustration shows the graphical mapping view in version 11*g*.

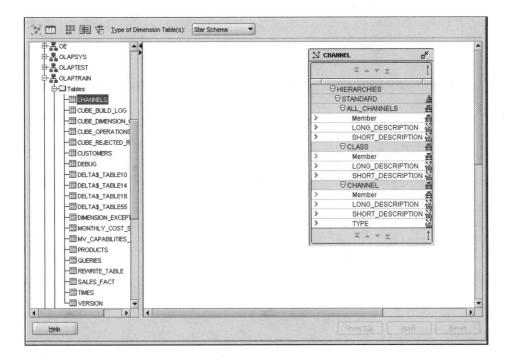

2. In the schema list, find the table or view, and either drag it over to the mapping panel or double-click it. For this example, double-click the CHANNELS table.

3. If desired, you can now hide the schema list so there is more room to map to the dimension by shrinking the schema pane or clicking on the shrink icon on the divider.

4. Map table columns to dimension members by dragging and dropping the column name to the appropriate dimensional object. Key columns are mapped to level members. Name columns are mapped to the description attributes.

NOTE
If there is only one description column for each level in the source, map the column to both attributes. It is important that all levels and attributes be mapped, especially if you plan to use cube-organized materialized views, as discussed in the "Working with Cube-Organized Materialized Views" section later in this chapter.

For this example, create the following mappings:

OLAPTRAIN.CHANNELS Column	CHANNEL Dimension	CHANNEL Members/ Attributes
CLASS_KEY	CLASS	Member
CLASS_NAME	CLASS	LONG_DESCRIPTION SHORT_DESCRIPTION
CHANNEL_KEY	CHANNEL	Member
CHANNEL_NAME	CHANNEL	LONG_DESCRIPTION SHORT_DESCRIPTION
CHANNEL_TYPE	CHANNEL	TYPE

The following illustration shows what the resulting mapping looks like in the graphical view.

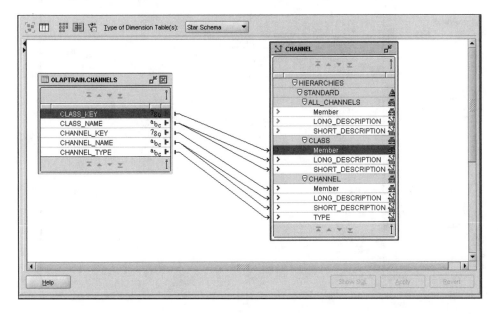

You may have noticed that we did not map columns to the All Channels level. In Oracle OLAP 11*g*, we do not need to have these columns because it has the same value for every row. You can choose to add custom values, as shown in the following steps.

5. To add values, switch to the table mapping view by clicking the Table Map button in the toolbar.

6. Under ALL_CHANNELS, specify **'ALL_CHANNELS'** to the right of Member. The long and short descriptions are filled in automatically. Click Apply to add the value.

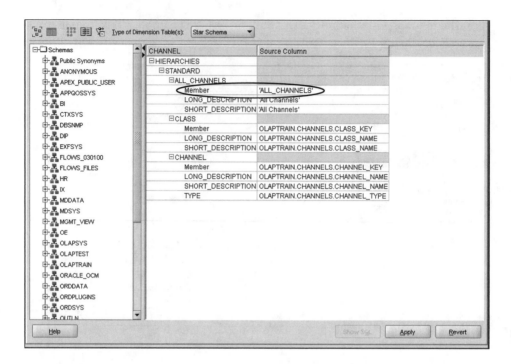

Here, we assigned a literal string as a value for the dimension member. However, you can also concatenate columns (name||title), apply functions (upper(name)), or create more complex SQL expressions. Also, we specified only text in this example, but you can also specify equations. We will explore the use of equations in later examples.

NOTE
In Oracle OLAP 10g, it is not possible to enter text or equations here; the source table or view must contain these values. You may need to create and populate the necessary columns in the source or define a view that contains the necessary columns.

Understanding the Differences for a Snowflake Schema   Snowflake schema mapping is used when the relational schema is a snowflake or when the data has ragged or skip-level hierarchies. The information required for a value-based hierarchy is the same as for a snowflake mapping. The source must contain columns for a parent, child, and description.

To change to a snowflake schema, select Snowflake Schema from the Type of Dimension Table(s) drop-down list. In Figure 4-6, there are two hierarchies: Region

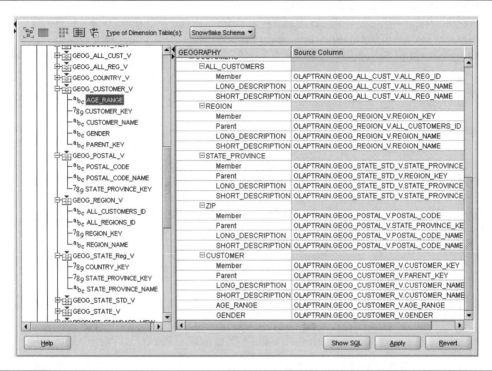

FIGURE 4-6. *GEOGRAPHY dimension mapped as a snowflake schema*

and Customer. The Zip level (above Customer) is a skip-level hierarchy because not all customers have a ZIP code. When a ZIP code is not provided for a member, the parent key for that member is the State key. This ensures that all the customers will roll up to State and above. When drilling down on a State, both ZIP codes and customers that are children of that state will be shown.

Notice that every level in the mapping has a different source (in this case, views) specified with parent, member, and name fields. If a dimension has more than one hierarchy, the sources can have additional parent keys. For example, GEOG_REGION_V has two keys—ALL_REGIONS_ID and ALL_CUSTOMERS_ID—to reflect its inclusion in the Region and Customer hierarchies, respectively. You will also notice that there are sources for the All levels. This is required for Oracle OLAP 10*g*, but in version 11*g*, they can be replaced with a text literal similar to the one we used for the CHANNEL dimension.

In the case of a value-based hierarchy, the mapping screen requires only the parent and member keys.

Understanding Time Dimensions

A time dimension is a specialized dimension that is similar to a user-defined dimension, except that the time dimension must be level-based, and you need to specify two additional attributes for each level:

- END_DATE, which represents the end date of a period and must be of type date

- TIMESPAN, which is a number representing the number of days in the period

Time dimensions generally have multiple hierarchies to handle items such as calendar year and fiscal year. In addition, if weeks and months are modeled, you need two separate hierarchies if weeks can cross months. It is very simple to support a 4-5-4 calendar, where weeks easily fit within months and quarters. Figure 4-7 shows the additional attributes.

NOTE
If you never want to be able to combine all years together (display the sum of all years), you do not need to have an All level. In some reporting tools, such as OBIEE, the All level is desired even for time.

You will need to provide the attributes for all of the levels. If these fields are not populated, or populated incorrectly, errors will result when performing a time-series analysis. If the required data is not present in the time sources, you can specify equations for the missing information. For example, in Figure 4-8, we specify an equation for the END_DATE attribute.

NOTE
In Oracle OLAP 10g, the easiest way to provide data not present in the time table is by using a view.

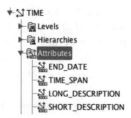

FIGURE 4-7. *Time dimension with four attributes*

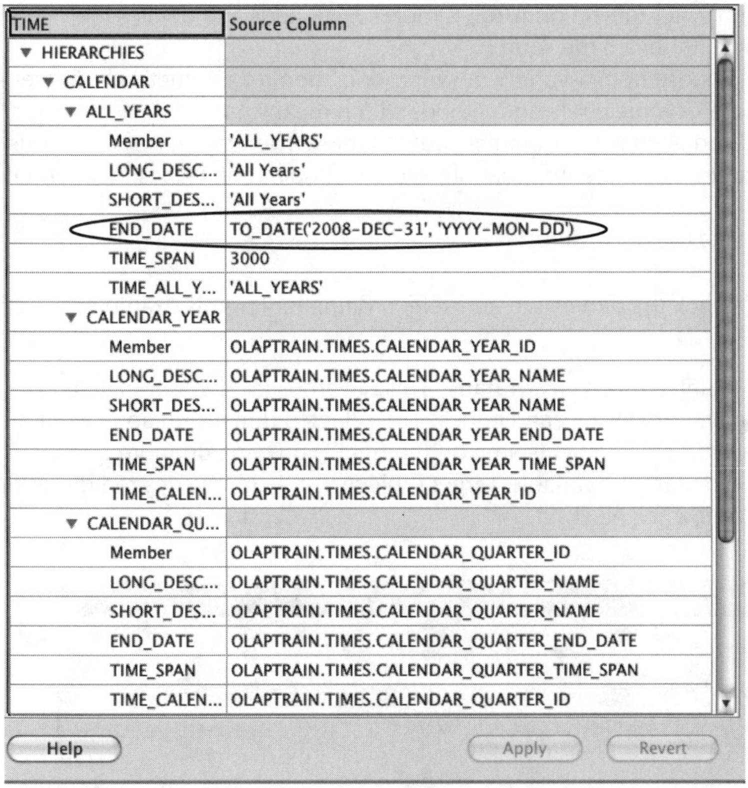

TIME	Source Column
▼ HIERARCHIES	
▼ CALENDAR	
▼ ALL_YEARS	
Member	'ALL_YEARS'
LONG_DESC...	'All Years'
SHORT_DES...	'All Years'
END_DATE	TO_DATE('2008–DEC–31', 'YYYY–MON–DD')
TIME_SPAN	3000
TIME_ALL_Y...	'ALL_YEARS'
▼ CALENDAR_YEAR	
Member	OLAPTRAIN.TIMES.CALENDAR_YEAR_ID
LONG_DESC...	OLAPTRAIN.TIMES.CALENDAR_YEAR_NAME
SHORT_DES...	OLAPTRAIN.TIMES.CALENDAR_YEAR_NAME
END_DATE	OLAPTRAIN.TIMES.CALENDAR_YEAR_END_DATE
TIME_SPAN	OLAPTRAIN.TIMES.CALENDAR_YEAR_TIME_SPAN
TIME_CALEN...	OLAPTRAIN.TIMES.CALENDAR_YEAR_ID
▼ CALENDAR_QU...	
Member	OLAPTRAIN.TIMES.CALENDAR_QUARTER_ID
LONG_DESC...	OLAPTRAIN.TIMES.CALENDAR_QUARTER_NAME
SHORT_DES...	OLAPTRAIN.TIMES.CALENDAR_QUARTER_NAME
END_DATE	OLAPTRAIN.TIMES.CALENDAR_QUARTER_END_DATE
TIME_SPAN	OLAPTRAIN.TIMES.CALENDAR_QUARTER_TIME_SPAN
TIME_CALEN...	OLAPTRAIN.TIMES.CALENDAR_QUARTER_ID

Help		Apply	Revert

FIGURE 4-8. *A fully mapped time dimension with an equation for END_DATE*

As you can see, the values for the ALL_YEARS attributes were created manually using constants or function calls. This All level is occasionally required by some front-end tools, like OBIEE, where a total level with only one member must be provided. The All level allows for the proper reporting of summary data when a time dimension member is not part of the query. An All level is not always required and can be added later if required.

Populating Dimensions

After the dimensions have been defined, the next step is to populate the dimensions with data. You will need to set a synchronization policy, to control whether and how to synchronize the dimension with the source. If synchronization is set to off,

Oracle OLAP retains members that are specified in the dimension, but not in the source. When synchronization is on, Oracle OLAP adds and deletes members from the dimensions to match the source.

You can choose from a variety of synchronization refresh methods. Dimensions usually use the Complete refresh method, which means that all data is cleared, and then loaded and aggregated from the source tables. The other refresh methods are used with cubes. For more information, see the "Populating Cubes" section later in this chapter.

To populate the dimensions:

1. Right-click the dimension and select Maintain. For this example, select CHANNEL.

2. The Maintenance Wizard starts. This wizard is used to populate and maintain dimensions and cubes. The selected dimension appears in the Selected Target Objects area on the right. You can add more dimensions as needed from Available Target Objects list. With the desired dimensions selected, click Next.

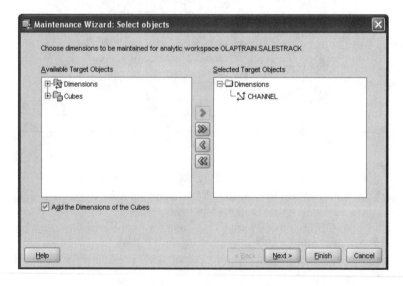

3. Specify the synchronization option and the refresh method. For this example, choose Yes and Complete. Then click Next.

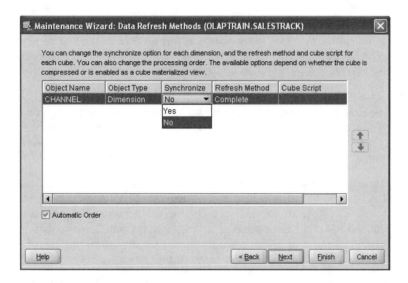

4. Set the processing options as follows, and then click Next to continue.

- **Atomic Refresh** If you want all updates to the dimensions (and cubes) committed to the database as a single transaction rather than individual transactions, select Atomic Refresh. For this example, select this option.

- **Refresh After Errors** If you want Oracle OLAP to stop processing individual transactions when an error occurs, select Refresh After Errors. For this example, deselect this option.

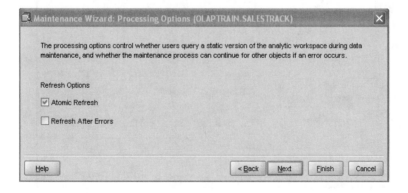

TIP
If Refresh After Errors is selected, the Atomic Refresh option should be deselected so that if an error occurs, processing is stopped.

5. Set when and how to update the dimension:

■ **Run maintenance task immediately in this session**   If the maintenance process runs quickly and does not need multiple processors, select this option. For this example, deselect this option.

■ **Submit the maintenance task to the Oracle Job Queue**   If the process requires multiple processors or runs a long time, you need to submit as a batch job. Select this option and choose whether to run it immediately or at a specified date and time. For this example, select this option and select Run immediately.

■ **Maximum number of parallel processes**   If you are maintaining a cube that has been partitioned, you can also set the number of parallel processors to use. Only partitioned cubes can be run using the parallel processing capabilities of the database. Dimensions and nonpartitioned cubes are always maintained using one processor, regardless of the number of processors selected. This is discussed further when we build cubes,

■ **Save maintenance task to script**   If you want to save this maintenance process as a SQL script that can be run from a PL/SQL process or from an external batch process such as cron, select this option and specify (or browse to) a file. For this example, select this option and specify a file name.

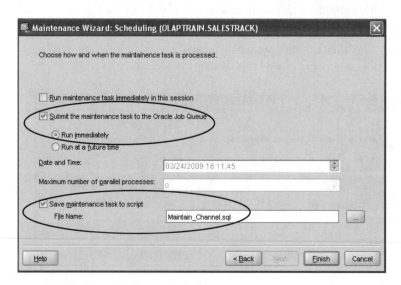

6. Click Finish to populate the CHANNEL dimension. Because we chose to run the process immediately, the process begins and the dimension is populated with data. When the process ends, the Build Log dialog box is displayed. It shows the run statistics and can show the number of members processed

during the run. The build log is beneficial for discovering errors and tracking how long it takes to load the rows from dimension and fact tables.

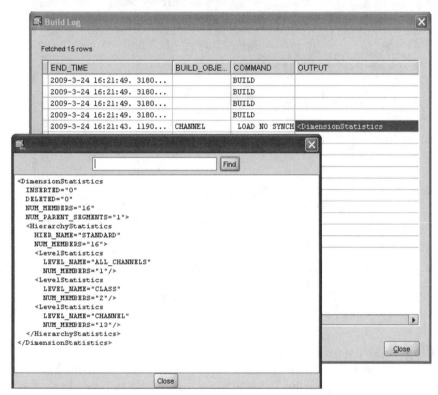

7. Repeat this procedure to populate the PRODUCT, GEOGRAPHY, and TIME dimensions.

This completes the dimension creation portion of the demonstration. However, there are two related topics—templates and security—that we will cover here before moving on to creating a cube.

Saving Dimensions as XML Templates
You can save the dimensions as XML templates. Templates serve as a backup of the workspace definitions and make it easy to move objects from one schema or database to another. When you select the Save as Template option, you can select a location and specify a file name for the XML file, as shown in Figure 4-9. You can also save analytic workspaces, cubes, and even calculated measures as templates using the same dialog box. The XML file stored on the local file system contains only the structure, and not the data for the OLAP object.

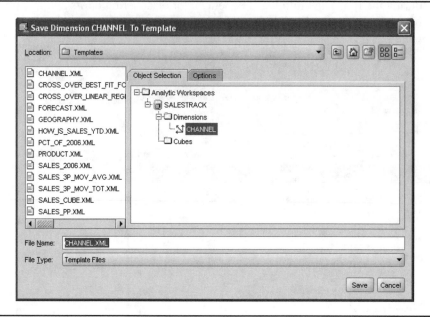

FIGURE 4-9. *Saving the CHANNEL dimension as a template*

Setting Security on Dimensions

In Oracle OLAP 11*g*, you can control security of OLAP objects. In the case of dimensions, you can grant the ability to select, update, delete, and alter a dimension to a role or database user using the Set Object Security dialog box, as shown in Figure 4-10. You can open the dialog box from the dimension context menu.

Creating and Populating Cubes

Now that we have created, mapped, and populated our dimensions, we can use those dimensions to create a cube. In this part of the demonstration, we start by reviewing some key concepts related to cubes. Then we complete the following steps:

- Build a cube using the Create Cube wizard.

- Create measures (stored and calculated).

- Map the cube.

- Populate the cube.

We end with a discussion of cube scripts.

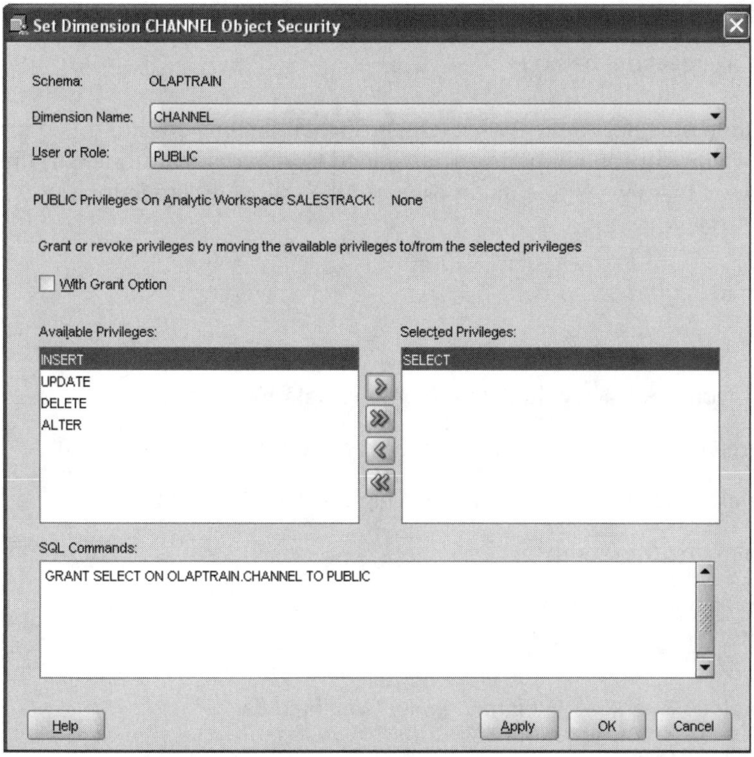

FIGURE 4-10. *Setting security on the CHANNEL dimension*

Understanding Oracle OLAP Cubes

In this section, we discuss aggregation policies, partitions, and storage for Oracle OLAP cubes. In Oracle OLAP, cubes can be defined as compressed or uncompressed. If the cube is to use compression, then there are some additional restrictions. Compressed cubes must use the same aggregation types for the dimensions and all stored measures in the cube must be the same data type. If you want the measures in the cube to have different data types or aggregation methods, then you must either define a different cube to hold them or use an uncompressed cube.

Aggregation Policies   Aggregation policies include the following information:

- Aggregation operators for each dimension

- The order in which to aggregate dimensions

- Whether or not any given dimension or hierarchy should be loaded and aggregated
- The aggregation method

Aggregation operators define what happens when dimensions are rolled up. By default, the values for sibling members are added together and attributed to their common parent member. You can choose from the following predefined aggregation operators:

- Sum (default)
- Average
- First Non-NA Data Value / Last Non-NA Data Value
- Hierarchical Average / First Member / Last Member
- Hierarchical Weighted Average / Weighted First / Weighted Last
- Minimum / Maximum
- Non Additive (do not summarize)
- Scaled Sum
- Weighted Average / Weighted First / Weighted Last
- Weighted Sum

If you use an aggregation operator other than Sum, the order in which the dimensions are aggregated can make a difference in the results. It is important that aggregations occur in the order specified. When aggregating across multiple dimensions, you must keep in mind that numbers may not appear to add up the way you look at two-dimensional spreadsheets. This is especially true when aggregation types are different for each dimension. Be aware of this when you start reviewing the results. It may be necessary to change the order of aggregation to achieve the desired results.

By default, all dimensions and hierarchies are loaded and aggregated. In some cases, it may not be required, or desired, to load and aggregate all the dimension hierarchies. Some hierarchies may be used only for loading the data, while other hierarchies are used for aggregation. Restricting the aggregation to only the required dimensions and hierarchies can improve load and aggregation performance of the cube. However, this can also mean that those levels that are not aggregated will be calculated on the fly, which can affect query performance.

A good example of the use of multiple hierarchies is having one hierarchy that is used to load and aggregate the data, and another hierarchy that is used for navigational purposes and may not be used for aggregation. This allows for displaying only levels that are needed to fulfill a business requirement, although the data is still loaded into the cube.

There are two aggregation methods: cost-based aggregation and level-based aggregation. With cost-based aggregation, you can precompute none, some, or all data by specifying a value between 0 and 100. Note that although the scale goes to 100, this value is *not* a percentage of the cube being precomputed; rather, it is a relative scale—the designers could have just as easily picked 0 to 200. Using a setting of 0 means do nothing to optimize the aggregation of the cube. This represents a low cost for the build, but it is not usually very useful for queries. A setting of 1 causes the cube composite to be built, but none of the measure values are precomputed. Unless the cube is small (like what-if type cubes), you should always choose a value of 1or higher. Values between 2 and 100 precompute progressively more of the measure values. A good starting point is 20. A value of 50 is on the high side.

In cases where cost-based aggregation is not going to be used or if the cubes are uncompressed and level-based aggregation is used, you will need to select which levels should be solved and stored. The default setting is to use skip-level aggregation, which aggregates and stores data at only every other level. This conserves space and still provides reasonable performance. It is also a good practice to select those levels that are most commonly viewed by the end users.

 NOTE
Only level-based aggregation is available in
Oracle OLAP 10g.

Partitions   If a cube is small and loads quickly, it may not be necessary to define a partition. However, most real-world cubes can benefit from partitioning. Partitioning can be used for life-cycle management, where you can partition by time, allowing for old time periods to be dropped from the cube as new periods are added.

The most common use of partitioning is to improve load and query performance. Without partitioning, you are restricted to the processing power of a single processor. Partitioning enables you to spread data loads and other cube maintenance tasks across multiple processors, which means that the cube can take advantage of parallel processing and complete tasks faster.

Each cube can be partitioned by only one dimension, so it is important to select the correct dimension and level. While there is only one partition specification for a cube, there are still multiple partitions. A cube partitioned by quarter over two years will still have eight partitions for the eight quarters plus a total partition. The number of partitions is maintained automatically, like table-based interval partitioning.

When selecting a dimension for partitioning, you need to choose one that has a level-based hierarchy, because you will need to specify a level along which to partition. It is a good idea to select an upper level within a dimension. Do not choose the top level, as this would not provide any practical advantage. This level should have a number that will divide the data as evenly as possible, so that the aggregation can be spread as evenly as possible across as many processors or processes as would be appropriate for the hardware utilized.

A good dimension to consider partitioning on is a time dimension. When you partition using a time dimension, you are generally loading and using more than one partition, which means that you can take advantage of parallel processing. The Month or Quarter levels are both suitable candidates for partitioning. For example, if the data contains 24 months (eight quarters) of data, you could partition at the Quarter level and split the load process across up to eight processors.

There are reasons to choose other dimensions instead of time. For example, suppose that after the initial data load, you choose to refresh the cube data only for the current month. Because the data is for a single month, you will be using only one partition (the one assigned to that Month or Quarter), which in turns means you will be using only one processor (the processor assigned to that partition). In this case, you should consider a different dimension and level, such as geographical region or product division, where the incremental changes to data will be spread across multiple partitions. It may take some trial runs to determine the best partition to use for the particular data in the cube and refresh methodology used.

You may also consider using partitioning to improve query performance. If a query can be satisfied within a partition, only that partition is accessed, thereby reducing the amount of the cube that is queried. This is known as *partitioning pruning*.

Before we wrap our discussion of partitions, it is important to understand the relationship between partitioning and the cost-based aggregation method. When you partition a cube, Oracle OLAP creates cost-based aggregation settings for both the bottom and top partitions. The bottom partition includes all the members of the partitioned dimension, up to and including the partition level. For example, if you partition on Quarter, the bottom partition includes the Day through Quarter levels (as well as values from the other dimensions). The top partition includes the levels above the partition dimension, such as Year and All Years.

The top partition can be very large. For example, it could include all years by all other dimension values. Therefore, any significant preaggregation of the top partition can be expensive—great amount of data in a single partition, which often gets bogged down in input to and output from the cube. A good rule of thumb is to partition at as high a level as possible, and set the top partition cost-based aggregation parameter to 0 (no preaggregation) or 1 (minimal preaggregation).

NOTE
It is not important to partition at a low level to isolate refreshes. A cube is aggregated incrementally within a partition during a refresh (unless the data is cleared out first). Partitioning has more to do with parallel processing and keeping data in memory to reduce cube access.

In Oracle OLAP 11*g*, you can run the Cube Partitioning Advisor (located on the Partitioning tab of the Create Cube dialog box) to help you decide how to partition the cube. You need to fully define and map the cube before you can run this advisor.

Cube Storage   You have a fair amount of control over how Oracle OLAP cubes are stored. You can choose whether or not the cube is compressed, the order and sparsity of the dimensions, and the base data type of the cube.

Cubes can be defined as compressed or uncompressed. Oracle OLAP compresses cubes by default. As described in Chapter 3, most cubes are very sparse, and compression helps to save disk space and data load time. All stored measures in a compressed cube must be of the same data type, and all dimensions in a compressed cube must use the same aggregation operator. If you need more flexibility, you must either define a different cube to hold the nonconforming stored measures and dimensions or use an uncompressed cube. By default, compressed cubes use the cost-based aggregation method. Level-based aggregation is the default aggregation method for uncompressed cubes.

You can identify dimensions as sparse or dense. A composite is created to contain combinations of all sparse dimension members for which there is data. By default, time is considered dense, because if data exists for one time dimension member, it likely exists for multiple time dimension members. This may not be the case for all cubes. It may be that all dimensions in a given cube are sparse, and all dimensions will be contained in the composite. The order of dimensions is important only for uncompressed cubes and has no effect on compressed cubes. For uncompressed cubes, all dimensions identified as sparse must be grouped together.

All cubes have a default data type. If you are creating a cube to be used as a materialized view for query rewrite (see the "Working with Cube-Organized Materialized Views" section later in this chapter), you should ensure that the cube uses the same data type as the source data. For uncompressed cubes, the measures will inherit the cube data type, but you can specify a different data type for each measure. Depending on the data type chosen, you can also define the data precision (number of significant digits), scale (number of decimal places), and the maximum number of bytes (for text data types).

Each cube, whether compressed or uncompressed, has at least one composite. Unpartitioned cubes always have only one composite. A partitioned, compressed cube always has a composite for each partition. With partitioned, uncompressed cubes, you have the choice between a single (global) composite and multiple composites.

In Oracle OLAP 11*g*, you can run the Cube Storage Advisor (located on the Storage tab of the Create Cube dialog box) to help you select storage parameters. You need to create the cube before you can run the advisor. The Cube Storage Advisor will examine the data and suggest storage options appropriate for your data.

Creating a Cube

Now we use the Create Cube wizard to specify dimensions for the new cube, aggregation policies, partitions, and storage policies.

To create a cube:

1. Select Create Cube from the Cube selection menu.

2. Specify a name for the cube. The labels and description are filled in automatically. If desired, edit the labels and description.

3. Select dimensions for this cube from the Available Dimensions list and add them to the Selected Dimensions list. For this example, the cube has four dimensions: TIME, CHANNEL, PRODUCT, and GEOGRAPHY. Generally speaking, we recommend placing the dense dimension first, if there is one, followed by the user-defined dimensions, in order from fewest members to most members. By default, AWM puts TIME first, because this dimension is usually dense. But that is not always the case and can certainly be changed.

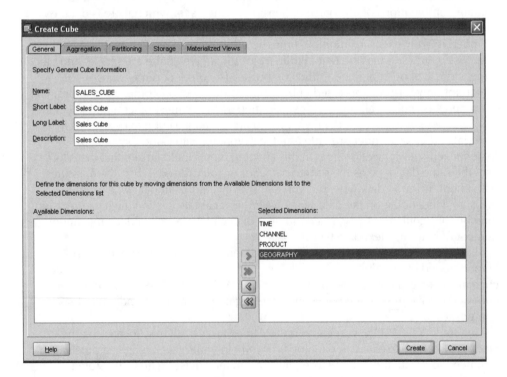

4. Select the Aggregation tab. The Rules subtab should be selected. The default dimension order, aggregation operators, and hierarchy settings are suitable for this example.

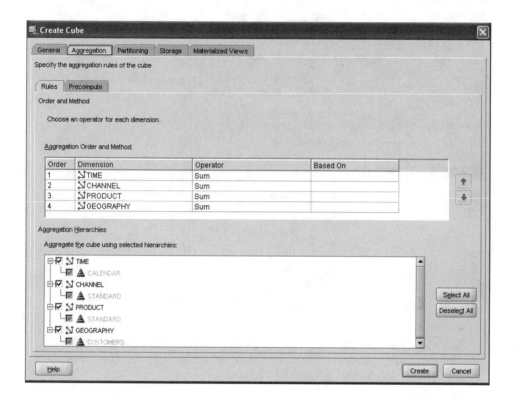

5. Select the Precompute tab. Because the cube is compressed, the default aggregation method is cost-based aggregation. The cube is not partitioned, so only the bottom partition value is used. The default bottom partition value is 20, but we changed it to 35 because it is a more reasonable value for the demonstration data set. Even if a cube is partitioned, we generally leave the top partition value at its default value of 0, as explained in the previous section.

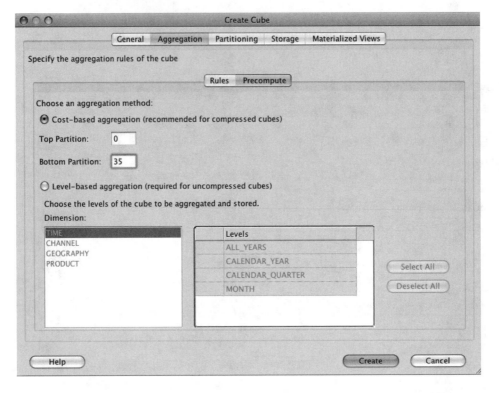

6. Select the Partitioning tab. By default, cubes are not partitioned. For this demonstration, we will create a partition. Select the Partition cube checkbox and specify the following partition details:

- **Dimension**   TIME

- **Hierarchy**   CALENDAR

- **Level**   CALENDER_QUARTER

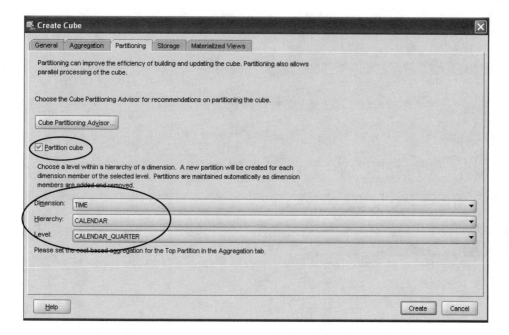

7. Select the Storage tab. By default, all cubes are compressed. You can change
    this cube to an uncompressed cube by deselecting the Use compression
    option. We will leave it compressed for this example. The TIME dimension
    is dense by default. Change it to sparse by selecting the checkbox in the
    Sparse column in the TIME dimension row. Now the TIME dimension will
    be included in the composite with all the other dimensions. For our data set,
    this approach loads faster.

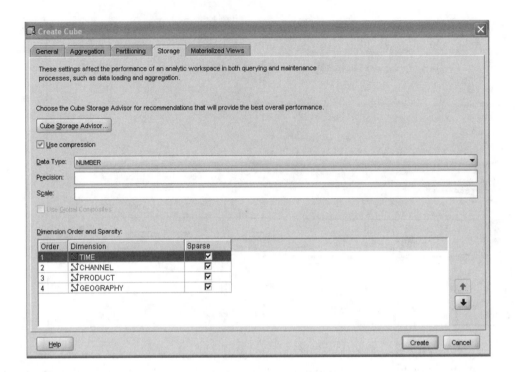

CAUTION
Once a cube has been defined as compressed or uncompressed, it cannot be changed.

8. Click Create to generate the new cube.

After the cube is created, you can return to the Storage tab of the Create Cube dialog box and run the Cube Storage Advisor. It will recommend storage parameters for the cube. After you have defined and mapped measures, you can use the Materialized Views tab, as discussed in the "Working with Cube-Organized Materialized Views" section later in this chapter.

Creating Measures

Recall that in its basic form, a cube is a collection of measures that have the same dimensionality. Oracle OLAP cubes contain two types of measures: stored measures and calculated measures. Stored measures are values saved in the cube. The values are either loaded from a data source or calculated and stored using a program. Calculated measures are defined by calculations or formulas. The calculated measures are not stored in the database, but rather calculated on the fly when requested by the application or an end-user query.

Many traditional data warehouses simply publish basic measures, such as sales, cost, and quantity. Most of these measures are considered stored measures because they come from the fact table. End users can do very little with this basic data. Both business and financial communities usually want to see information like sales compared to the same time last year, rate of growth of sales, and actual sales versus forecast. This means that end users are actually more interested in calculated measures derived from the base data.

Calculated measures are one of the most powerful features of OLAP. While it is fairly easy to do some of these calculations in spreadsheets and other reporting tools, these calculations can be a major performance drain, and the calculations reside only in the reporting repository, limiting access to and use of the measures. Furthermore, many calculated measures, such as time-series analysis, are very hard to compute outside the database.

AWM provides a wizard to help define many common types of business calculations. These are divided into four functional categories of calculations:

Basic,

Advanced,

Prior/Future Comparisons, and

Time Frame.

In addition, Oracle OLAP has an expression language that allows for building just about any calculation desired. The following calculations are available in Oracle OLAP 11*g*:

Addition	Share
Subtraction	Rank
Division	Parallel Period
Percent Difference	Diff from Parallel Period
Index	% Diff from Parallel Period
Prior Period	Moving Total
Diff from Prior Period	Moving Average
Percent Diff from Prior Period	Moving Maximum
Future Period	Moving Minimum
Diff from Future Period	Cumulative Total
Period to Date	Cumulative Average
Period to Date Period Ago	Cumulative Maximum
Percent Diff from Future Period	Cumulative Minimum
Diff from Period to Date Period Ago	User Defined Expression
% Diff from Period to Date Period Ago	

NOTE
Oracle OLAP 10g uses a calculation wizard for specifying calculated measures and can use the OLAP DML. Some calculations are not available in Oracle OLAP 10g.

In order to create a calculated measure, you must first have stored measures, so we begin by creating stored measures.

Creating Stored Measures   For compressed cubes, creating a stored measure is as simple as opening the Create Measures dialog box and specifying a name for the measure. For uncompressed cubes, however, you can choose to override the cube-level aggregation policy and set one for the measure. The Aggregation tab in the Create Measure dialog box is identical to the same tab in the Create Cube dialog box.
  To create a stored measure:

1. Right-click Measures and select Create Measure.

2. Specify a name for the measure. For this example, enter **SALES**. The labels and description are filled in automatically. If the cube is compressed, which it is by default, and for this example, you do not need to supply any other information.

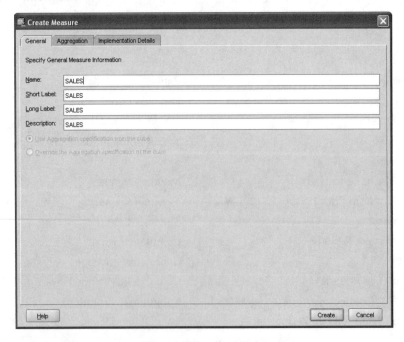

3. Click Create to create the SALES measure.

Creating Calculated Measures   For this demonstration, we create a calculated measure for profit, where the formula for profit is sales minus costs. To create this calculated measure, follow these steps:

1. Right-click Measures and select Create Calculated Measure.

2. Specify a name for the measure. For this example, enter **PROFIT**. The labels and description are filled in automatically.

3. Select the type of calculation from Calculation Type drop-down list. For this example, select Subtraction.

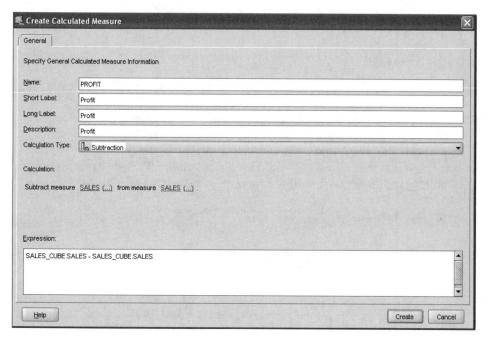

4. Under Calculation, click the first SALES measure to view a list of measures, and then select COSTS.

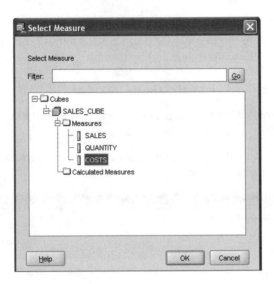

5. Click OK to create the SALES measure. Under Calculation, SALES changes to COSTS. You do not need to change the second SALES measure, because profit is sales minus costs. Notice that the syntax for the calculation is displayed in the Expression field. The syntax is helpful when you want to build complex expressions that cannot be handled by the wizard.

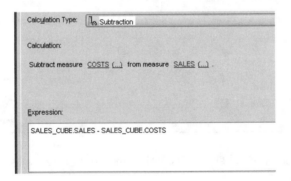

Mapping Cubes
The mapping of cubes is similar to the mapping of dimensions, but generally much simpler.

Creating Joins from Fact Tables   For this demonstration, we set join conditions that map data from the fact table for a summary level above the level contained in the fact table. The sample data has a fact table that has data at the day level, but the

TIME dimension starts at month. The TIMES table contains the day data, as well as the month ID. We join the TIMES table with the fact table to get the month key.

NOTE
Join conditions are not available in Oracle OLAP 10g. You need to create a view to accomplish the same task.

To create a join condition:

1. Click Mappings under the cube. The right panel displays the cube-mapping panel.

NOTE
In Oracle OLAP 11g, the default mapping type is table view. In Oracle OLAP 10g, the graphical mapping view is the default.

2. While in the table view, drag the MONTH key from the TIMES table to the MONTH level source, and then drag the TIMES DAY_KEY to the Join Condition field.

3. Drag the DAY_KEY from the SALES_FACT table to the Join Condition field. The join condition appears as OLAPTRAIN.SALES_FACT.DAY_KEY = OLAPTRAIN.TIMES.DAY_KEY.

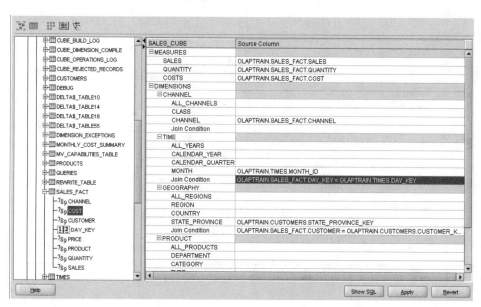

NOTE
Notice that the cube-mapping panel in our example contains a similar join condition in the GEOGRAPHY dimension, using the CUSTOMERS table.

When the data is loaded, the load processor will perform a join and summary operation on the data from the fact table and load the results.

Loading Data from Multiple Tables   You can load data from multiple tables into the same cube, but only if you do not use materialized views. This is done using the graphical mapping view. You place both sources on the panel, and drag and drop the keys from the fact tables to the associated targets. Oracle OLAP is not able to do any joining for this type of mapping.

Figure 4-11 shows an example of this type of mapping. This example includes an additional time hierarchy called Week that rolls up the data from week to year. This requires loading the data at the Week level as well as Month level. Two views were created to provide data at these levels. The views were then mapped to the appropriate levels of the TIME dimension.

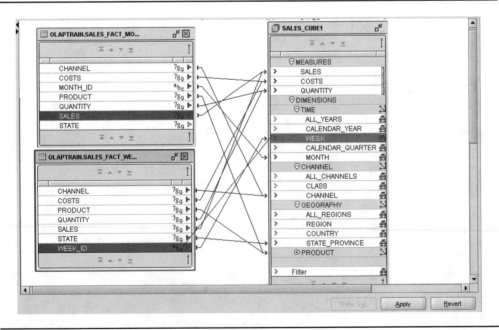

FIGURE 4-11.   *Mapping from multiple sources*

You might ask, "Why not just load the data at the Day level and then roll up the data to the respective hierarchies?" This is definitely possible, but it would add an additional level in the TIME dimension and 365 members per year. Such a high number of members can have a dramatic impact on space requirements. If there is a need to report data at the daily level, add the extra level to the dimension. Otherwise, save the resources for something that is required.

One nice feature of the mapping tool is the ability to view the table data while you are in the mapping panel. You can use it to verify that there is data in the source or to validate that the correct source and columns are being used. To view the data, right-click the source and select View Data. The first 1,000 rows of the source will be displayed in a tabular format, as shown in Figure 4-12.

Populating Cubes

You can populate a cube using the same Maintenance Wizard that you use with dimensions. When you select a cube to maintain, you see the cube and all the

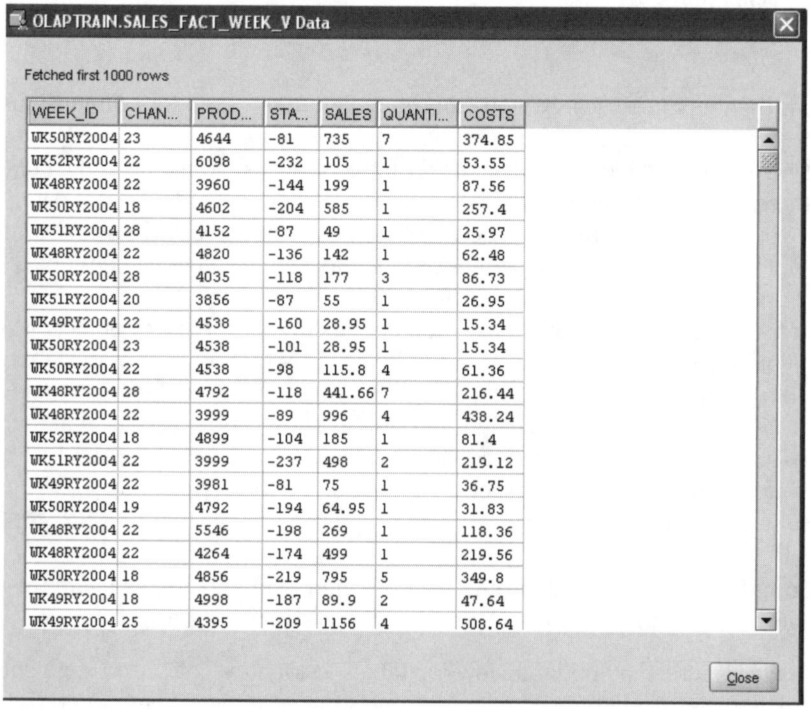

OLAPTRAIN.SALES_FACT_WEEK_V Data

Fetched first 1000 rows

WEEK_ID	CHAN...	PROD...	STA...	SALES	QUANTI...	COSTS
WK50RY2004	23	4644	-81	735	7	374.85
WK52RY2004	22	6098	-232	105	1	53.55
WK48RY2004	22	3960	-144	199	1	87.56
WK50RY2004	18	4602	-204	585	1	257.4
WK51RY2004	28	4152	-87	49	1	25.97
WK48RY2004	22	4820	-136	142	1	62.48
WK50RY2004	28	4035	-118	177	3	86.73
WK51RY2004	20	3856	-87	55	1	26.95
WK49RY2004	22	4538	-160	28.95	1	15.34
WK50RY2004	23	4538	-101	28.95	1	15.34
WK50RY2004	22	4538	-98	115.8	4	61.36
WK48RY2004	28	4792	-118	441.66	7	216.44
WK48RY2004	22	3999	-89	996	4	438.24
WK52RY2004	18	4899	-104	185	1	81.4
WK51RY2004	22	3999	-237	498	2	219.12
WK49RY2004	22	3981	-81	75	1	36.75
WK50RY2004	19	4792	-194	64.95	1	31.83
WK48RY2004	22	5546	-198	269	1	118.36
WK48RY2004	22	4264	-174	499	1	219.56
WK50RY2004	18	4856	-219	795	5	349.8
WK49RY2004	18	4998	-187	89.9	2	47.64
WK49RY2004	25	4395	-209	1156	4	508.64

Close

FIGURE 4-12. *Source data view*

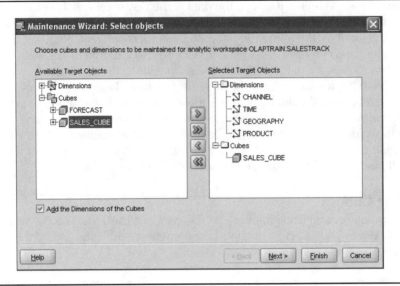

FIGURE 4-13. *Maintaining a cube*

dimensions that the cube uses. As you can see in Figure 4-13, all four dimensions, along with the cube, are selected automatically.

It is generally a good idea to update the dimensions at the same time as the cube, because there are often changes to dimensions if there are changes to the fact data. However, you can remove any dimensions you do not want to maintain with the cube. If you do not want to maintain any dimensions, deselect the Add the Dimensions of the Cubes option before you move the cube over to the target objects.

The Refresh Methods page will now include the cube in the list of objects. With the cube, you have the option to choose a cube script, which is a series of steps required to maintain a cube. For example, a script might load the data, calculate a forecast, and aggregate the data. The cube script list shows the scripts available for this cube. Cube-organized materialized views always use the SYS_DEFAULT script. For more information, see the next section on creating cube scripts.

The cube refresh methods are:

- **Complete**   Clear all data from the cube, then load and aggregate all the data from the source tables. All cubes can use this method.

- **Fast**   Use the materialized view log tables to identify, load, and aggregate only the new and changed data from the source tables. Cubes defined as a fast refresh or a materialized view can use this method.

- **Force**   Use the Fast method if possible; otherwise, use the Complete method.

- **Partition Change Tracking**   Clear, load, and aggregate only the values from an altered partition in the source tables.

- **Fast Solve**   Load all the detail data from the source tables, then aggregate only the new values. Compressed cubes and cube materialized views can use this method.

NOTE
Some of the cube refresh options in Oracle OLAP 11g are not available in Oracle OLAP 10g.

The remaining pages are the same as those for maintaining dimensions. On the last page, Scheduling, for this cube, you may want to choose to run in batch mode, because the sample data has been partitioned. Running in batch mode allows you to set the amount of parallelism and run on more than one processor. Figure 4-14 shows that two processes will be used. This number can be set from 1 to the maximum number of processors accessible to the database instance. In cases where there are other processes running on the server and there are more than two processors, it is often wise to set the number to be equal to the number of processors minus 1 to reserve a processor for other processes. You can also set this batch process to run at a later time or date.

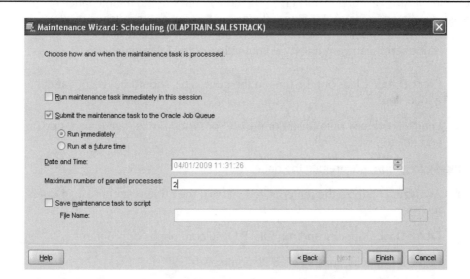

FIGURE 4-14.   *Scheduling maintenance on multiple processors*

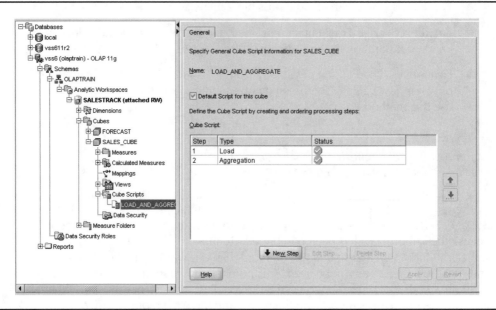

FIGURE 4-15. *Creating a cube script*

Creating Cube Scripts

In Oracle OLAP 11*g*, cube scripts give you more control of the maintenance process. As shown in Figure 4-15, you define each script as a sequence of steps. You determine the order in which these steps are to be executed.

A cube script can contain any combination of the following actions:

- **Clear Data** Clear out the data in the cube. This should not be put after a load step!

- **Load** Load new data (insert or update) or synchronize data (insert, update, and delete).

- **Aggregation** Aggregate the data.

- **Analyze** Analyze the materialized views if the cube is set for use in query rewrite.

- **OLAP DML** Specify and run OLAP DML commands or programs.

- **PL/SQL** Specify and run PL/SQL commands.

Cube scripts open up many ways to customize the loading, calculation, and aggregation of the cube data. In the past, external OLAP DML and PL/SQL programs did much of this work. Now you can integrate custom maintenance tasks in the system processes.

NOTE
Cube scripts are not available in Oracle OLAP 10g.

The Maintenance Wizard and refresh materialized views execute the default cube script when refreshing a cube. The default cube script is named SYS_DEFAULT, and it includes load and aggregation steps. The script is displayed in the navigation tree only after you define a second cube script. During the Maintenance Wizard process, you can explicitly choose which script you want to execute during the load.
To create a cube script:

1. Expand the folder for a cube, right-click Cube Scripts and select Create Cube Script. The Create Cube Script dialog box is displayed.

2. Fill in the information on the General tab.

3. To create a new step, choose the type of step you want to create.

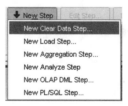

4. Complete all tabs associated with the step, and then click Create. The new step is listed on the General tab.

5. Create additional steps as desired. You can edit, delete, or reorder the steps at any time. Remember that if you are performing calculations and aggregations, your data must be loaded first, so be careful how you order your steps.

6. Click Create to generate the script. The new cube script is displayed as an object in the Cube Scripts folder.

We will revisit cube scripts in the "Creating Advanced Cubes for Typical Business Purposes" section later in this chapter.

Summary of the Cube-Building Process

For this demonstration, we completed the following major steps:

1. Prepare the data.

2. Create an analytic workspace.

3. Create and populate dimensions.

4. Create and populate a cube.

An analytic workspace generally contains a set of cubes, so in a real-world environment, steps 3 and 4 would be repeated to create the rest of the cubes.

Next, we take a more in depth look at the types of calculated measures that are available to you.

Adding Business-Savvy Calculations to Cubes

This section describes how to create the following business calculations:

■ Share calculation

■ Percent different prior period or parallel period calculation

■ Moving average calculation

■ Custom calculated measures

We also review how to modify and manage calculated measures.

Creating a Share Calculation

A very useful calculation is the calculation of share. A *share* is a dimension member's contribution compared to another member (a baseline), where this baseline is often a parent or ancestor at a level.

You create a share calculation through the Share template, shown in Figure 4-16. The most common use of the Share template is to express the share as a percent of total or percent of parent in the chosen hierarchy. You can also select a dimension member to be used as the baseline of the calculation. This is useful if you want to compare members of the dimension in question to a specific benchmark or model member, such as an established market leading product, flagship store, or key competitor.

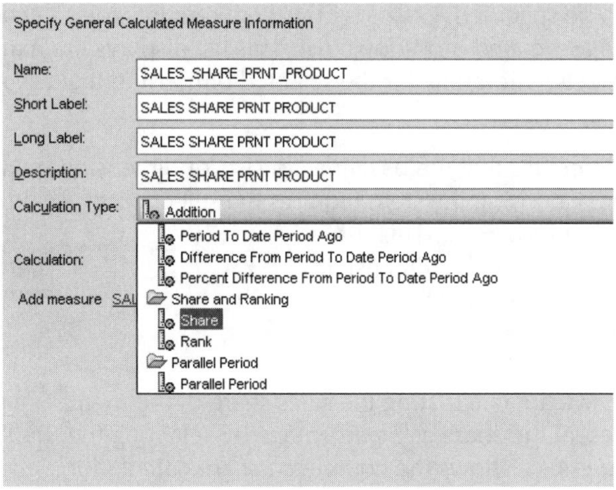

Specify General Calculated Measure Information

Name: SALES_SHARE_PRNT_PRODUCT

Short Label: SALES SHARE PRNT PRODUCT

Long Label: SALES SHARE PRNT PRODUCT

Description: SALES SHARE PRNT PRODUCT

Calculation Type: Addition

Calculation:
    Period To Date Period Ago
    Difference From Period To Date Period Ago
    Percent Difference From Period To Date Period Ago

Add measure SAL   Share and Ranking
    Share
    Rank
   Parallel Period
    Parallel Period

FIGURE 4-16. *Creating a share calculation*

After you select the Share template, you are prompted for the components for the calculation. From here, you fill in values for the various parameters:

- **Share of measure**   A measure or calculated measure (SALES in this example).

- **In**   The hierarchy to be used while calculating the share for the selected dimension (if more than one hierarchy exists in the chosen dimension).

- **Of the**   The dimension for which the share is to be calculated (PRODUCT in this example).

- **As a ratio of**   The dimension member to be used as a baseline to calculate the share.

When calculating a ratio, select one of the following choices (the first three are disabled for a dimension that does not have any hierarchies):

- **Top of hierarchy**   Specifies that the baseline consist of the total of all items on the level that is associated with the current member (that is, the item for which the share is being calculated).

- **Member's parent**   Specifies that the baseline consist of the total on the level of the parent for the current member (that is, the item for which the share is being calculated).

■ **Member's ancestors at level**   Specifies that the baseline consist of the total of a level to be specified. Choosing this item requires the selection of a value in the associated drop-down list. This list displays the names of levels from the selected hierarchy for the selected dimension that are available for calculating the share.

■ **Member**   Specifies that the baseline consists of dimension member to be specified. Choosing this item requires the selection of a value in the associated drop-down list. This list displays the names of the dimension members that are available for calculating the share.

PRODUCT	dimension as a ratio of	top of hierarchy .
		top of hierarchy
		member's parent
		member's ancestors at level
		member

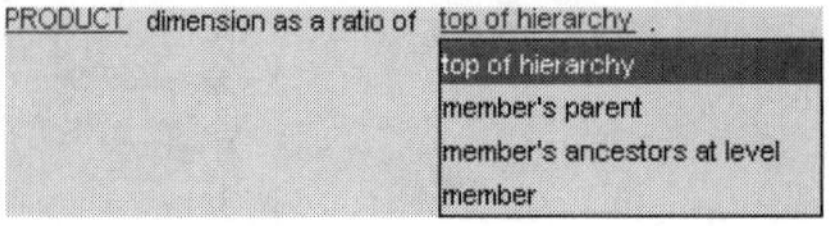

In this example, we are calculating the sales share of the member's parent. You can choose to represent the share as a percentage by selecting the Multiply Result by 100 option. Figure 4-17 shows the completed share calculation.

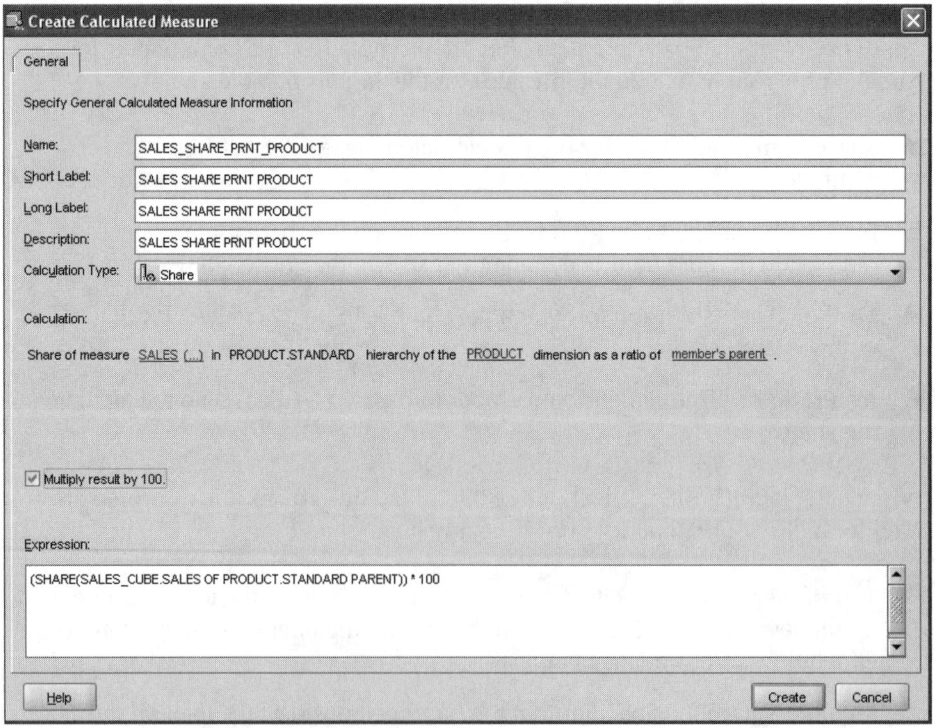

FIGURE 4-17.   *The completed share calculation*

	SALES	SALES SHARE TOT PROD	SALES SHARE PRNT PRODUCT
All Products	138,960,159.40	100.00%	100.00%
Computers	112,123,808.09	80.69%	80.69%
Total Personal Computers	91,680,172.61	65.98%	81.77%
PDAs	93,239.61	0.07%	0.08%
All Computer Furniture	72,577.20	0.05%	0.06%
Computer Printers and Supplies	18,339,588.07	13.20%	16.36%
Total Server Computers	1,938,230.60	1.39%	1.73%
Cameras and Camcorders	10,572,098.22	7.61%	7.61%
Cameras and Accessories	6,056,792.62	4.36%	57.29%
Camcorders and Accessories	4,515,305.60	3.25%	42.71%
Portable Music and Video	16,264,253.09	11.70%	11.70%

FIGURE 4-18. *Sample share report*

It may be necessary to create multiple calculated measures using the same Share template to provide different results, such as shown in Figure 4-18. The report in Figure 4-18 is showing the SALES base measure and two share calculations: share of product total and share of product parent level. Notice how the SALES SHARE TOT PROD and SALES SHARE PRNT PRODUCT measures return the appropriate results as you drill down the product hierarchy.

Creating a Percent Different Prior or Parallel Period Calculation

Using the Percent Difference from Prior Period template, you can create a calculated measure that indicates growth or decline of a measure over time. This calculation template is found in the Prior/Future Time Period calculation type folder. This template accepts the following inputs:

- **For measure** Select a measure or a dimension member for which you want to calculate the percentage difference from the prior period.

- **In** If there is more than one time dimension, you can select the one you want to use. Otherwise, the default time dimension is used.

- **And** Select the hierarchy for the specified dimension.

- **Number of periods ago** Enter a specified number of periods ago, for each level (such as Year, Quarter, or Month).

A sample measure is shown in Figure 4-19.

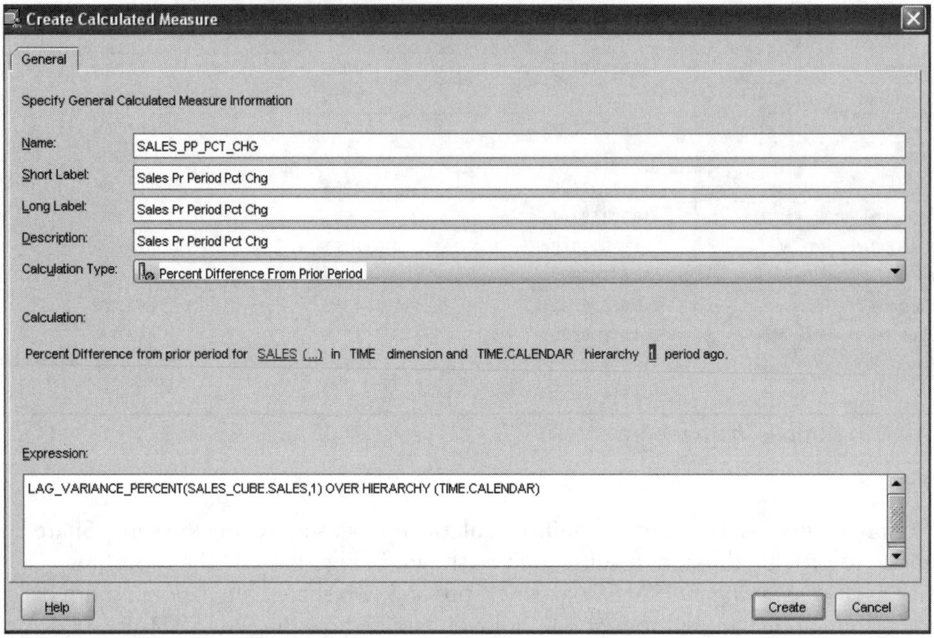

FIGURE 4-19. *Creating a percent difference prior period calculation*

A similar, but more complex, calculation is the percent difference between the current time period and a prior parallel period, such as prior year. To do this calculation, we need to use the parallel period calculation not the prior period calculation. To perform this calculation, you provide the following inputs:

- **From**   Select either Parallel period or Parallel period closest.

- **For measure**   Select a measure or a dimension member for which you want to calculate the percentage difference from the parallel period.

- **In**   If there is more than one time dimension, select the desired dimension from the list box. Otherwise, the default time dimension is used.

- **Number of periods**   Enter a number of periods ago.

- **Ago**   Select the level to use as a basis.

- **From**   Select either beginning to ending of period or ending to beginning of period.

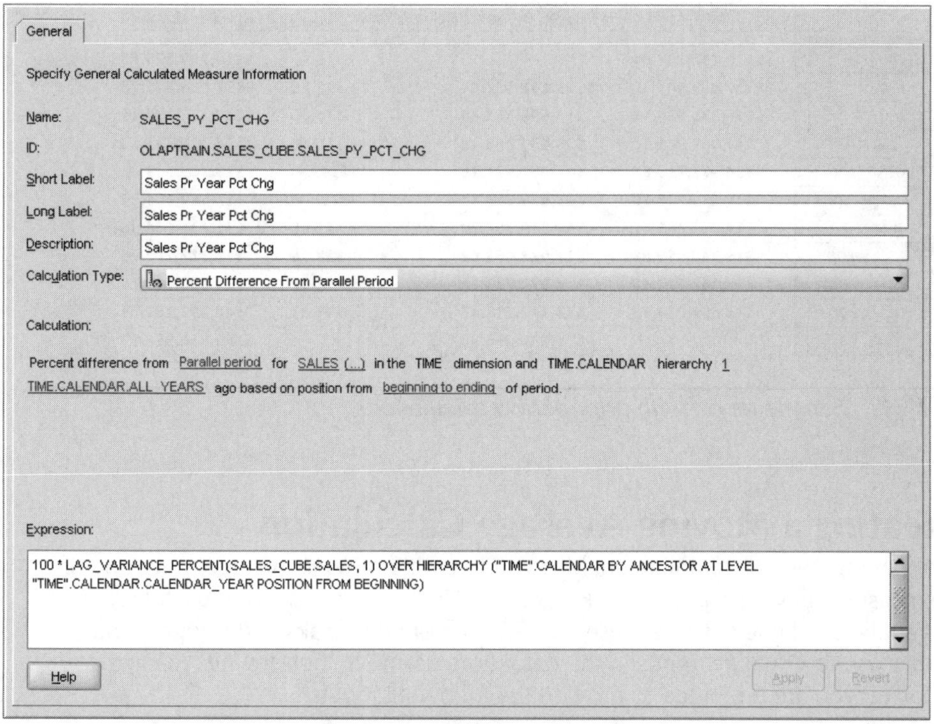

FIGURE 4-20.   *Creating a percent difference from parallel period calculation*

A sample percent difference from parallel period calculation is shown in Figure 4-20.

Figure 4-21 shows a report that contains calculations of a number of alternative percentage differences from prior periods. All the measures automatically handle the situation in which the user needs to drill down into the time dimension and look at time periods at different levels. A single calculated measure in the analytic workspace can be used at any level of time, by any query tool, including SQL tools.

Note the following from Figure 4-21:

■   The Sales Pr Period calculation works at all levels of time, and shows the value for the previous time period at the same level.

■   The Sales Pr Period Pct Chg calculation works at all levels of time, and compares each time period with the previous period at the same level.

■   Similar calculations can be easily generated for costs, quantity, and profit measures.

	Sales	Sales Pr Period	Sales Pr Period Pct Chg	Sales 3 Per Mov Avg
► CY2005	$119,132,107.04			$137,889,875.78
► CY2006	$137,698,563.40	$119,132,107.04	$15.58	$137,889,875.78
▼ CY2007	$156,838,956.90	$137,698,563.40	$13.90	$147,268,760.15
► Q1–CY2007	$41,067,921.16	$38,430,388.10	$6.86	$38,153,315.10
▼ Q2–CY2007	$34,972,733.68	$41,067,921.16	($14.84)	$39,209,739.22
Apr–2007	$10,839,708.20	$15,383,284.53	($29.54)	$12,589,004.55
May–2007	$11,022,065.62	$10,839,708.20	$1.68	$11,736,564.96
Jun–2007	$13,110,959.86	$11,022,065.62	$18.95	$12,317,779.26
► Q3–CY2007	$38,142,217.48	$34,972,733.68	$9.06	$38,590,345.25
► Q4–CY2007	$42,656,084.58	$38,142,217.48	$11.83	$40,399,151.03
► CY2008		$156,838,956.90		$156,838,956.90

FIGURE 4-21. *Sample report with prior period calculations*

Creating a Moving Average Calculation

The Moving Average template enables you to create moving averages over any of the measures in your analytic workspace. Moving averages are very useful when you analyze volatile data, because they smooth out the peaks and troughs, and enable you to visualize trends in the data more easily. In the Moving Average template, you are prompted to provide the following inputs:

■ **Measure** Select the measure for which you want to calculate a moving average.

■ **Over time in** If there is more than one time dimension, select the desired dimension from the list box. Otherwise, the TIME dimension and the default hierarchy will be used. This is the case for our demonstration.

■ **Include preceding** Enter the number of periods preceding the given time period to be included in the moving average calculation.

■ **Include following** Enter the number of periods following the given time period to be included in the moving average calculation.

■ **Within** The choices here are level, parent, ancestor at level, Gregorian year, Gregorian week, Gregorian month, and Gregorian quarter.

For example, let's say you want to create a calculation that represents the moving average of sales for the last three months. When displaying this value for

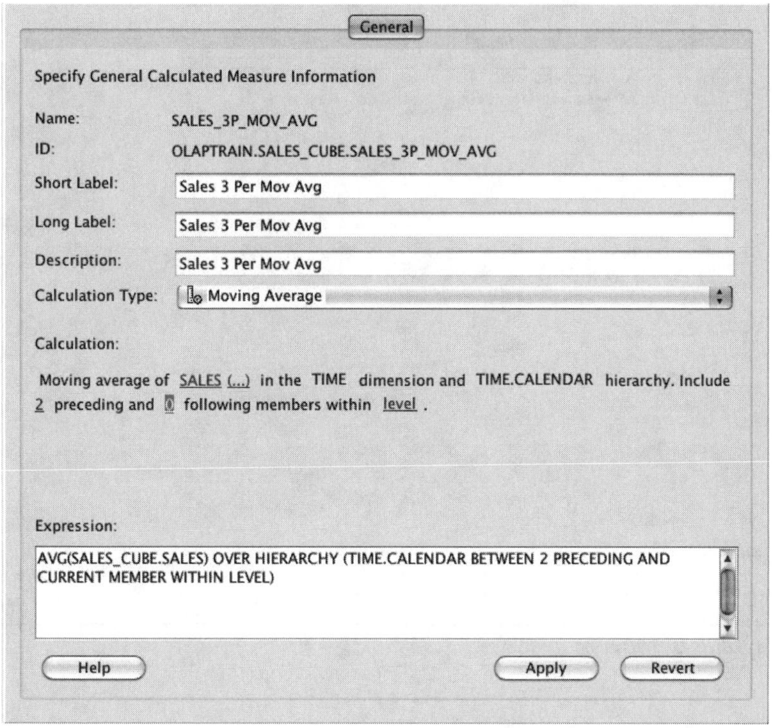

General

Specify General Calculated Measure Information

Name: SALES_3P_MOV_AVG

ID: OLAPTRAIN.SALES_CUBE.SALES_3P_MOV_AVG

Short Label: Sales 3 Per Mov Avg

Long Label: Sales 3 Per Mov Avg

Description: Sales 3 Per Mov Avg

Calculation Type: Moving Average

Calculation:

Moving average of SALES (...) in the TIME dimension and TIME.CALENDAR hierarchy. Include 2 preceding and 0 following members within level .

Expression:

AVG(SALES_CUBE.SALES) OVER HIERARCHY (TIME.CALENDAR BETWEEN 2 PRECEDING AND CURRENT MEMBER WITHIN LEVEL)

Help   Apply   Revert

FIGURE 4-22. *Creating a moving average calculation*

March, this would average January, February, and March. When displaying this value for April, this would average February, March, and April. Figure 4-22 shows how this calculation is structured in the Moving Average template.

NOTE
Similar templates are available for creating moving total, moving maximum, and moving minimum calculations.

Figure 4-23 shows a combination graph reflecting the sample moving average calculation. The fluctuating line is sales, and the smoother line is the three-month average.

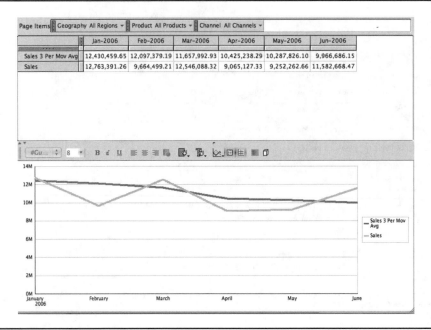

FIGURE 4-23. *Graph of moving average*

Creating Custom Calculated Measures

Using the Expression template, you can build just about any calculation desired.
You can use this template to simply take action on more than one measure or to
create very complex calculations. Oracle OLAP has a very powerful calculation
engine that supports a huge library of functions:

- Numeric

- Time series

- Text

- Financial

- Statistical

- Date and time

- Aggregation

- Data type conversion

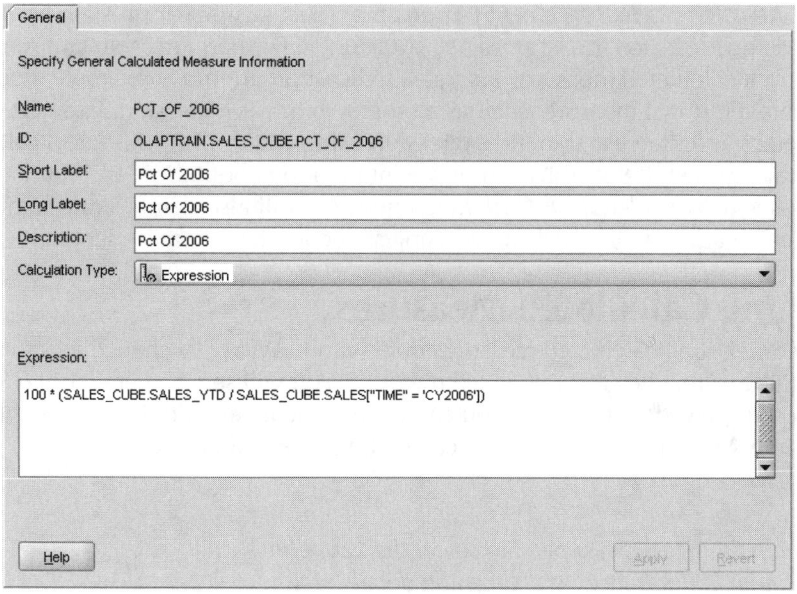

FIGURE 4-24. *Expression for sales percent of 2006*

Any these functions can be used to create a custom calculated measure, and can be used in a procedural function or program.

A simple custom calculation would be to produce a measure that is the percent of sales for 2006, such as sales year to date divided by total sales for 2006. As shown in Figure 4-24, the expression would look like this:

```
100 * (SALES_CUBE.SALES_YTD / SALES_CUBE.SALES["TIME" = 'CY2006'])
```

Note that this expression uses an existing calculated measure for SALES_YTD, and then uses what is called a qualified data reference to find the sales for 2006. (Qualified data reference syntax is discussed in the "Using OLAP DML" section later in this chapter.)

You can also edit the expression and define your own calculations using any expression you care to enter as shown in Figure 4-25.

FIGURE 4-25. *Editing an expression*

You can also use OLAP DML in the expression. For example, you could use an `OLAP_DML_EXPRESSION('function',datatype)` form such as `('lag(sales,1,time,nostatus)', NUMBER)`. Furthermore, you can run programs in a calculated measure, such as a forecast program. For example, you could create a forecast measure, such as a crossover linear regression, in an OLAP DML program and then use it in the expression using `OLAP_DML_EXPRESSION ('program_name', NUMBER)`. For more information about these various functions, see the *Oracle OLAP DML Reference*. We will also demonstrate some complex calculations in the "Advanced Topics" section later in this chapter.

Managing Calculated Measures

You can edit existing calculated measures from within AWM. To change a calculated measure, click the calculated measure. You will see the general information displayed on the right. You can change the labels and description, but not the name. You can also change the calculation type and the expression.

NOTE
In Oracle OLAP 10g, you need to select the Launch Calculation Editor button to change the details of a calculated measure. Note that you can change the details, but not the type, of the measure.

As you have seen, calculated measures are part of the cubes, but occasionally cubes need to be changed, such as by modifying their dimensionality or data type. These changes require that the cube be deleted. There are two ways to delete a cube but keep the calculated measures:

■ Save the calculated measures to XML templates.

■ Edit the XML definition for the cube.

Saving calculated measures to XML files is always a good idea because this creates a backup of the definition. Once the cube is dropped and rebuilt, you can simply import the calculated measures. However, you can save only one measure per XML template, which is fine if you create the XML template when you define the calculated measure, but not practical if you have many calculated measures in a cube and then decide to save them all to XML templates.

Editing the XML is not something we would normally recommend, but it is possible to move calculated measures from one template file to another using a text editor such as Notepad. Assuming that you do not change the dimensionality, you can cut and paste the XML. The calculated measures are all defined at the bottom of the XML definition file. Each measure is contained in a single block of XML code, using the tag `DerivedMeasure`. Copy all the `DerivedMeasure` blocks to your new cube XML template and reload that template to restore all your calculated measures. This work-around works in Oracle OLAP 10*g* Release 2 and later.

Advanced Topics

In this section, we cover the following advanced topics:

- Managing workspaces with Oracle OLAP Worksheet

- Working with cube-organized materialized views

- Managing security of cubes and dimensions

- Creating advanced cubes for typical business purposes

- Using SQL with OLAP

Managing Workspaces with OLAP Worksheet

Oracle OLAP Worksheet provides full use of the OLAP DML for users who need to manage the contents of an object or execute a program. It opens in a separate window from the AWM console. As shown in Figure 4-26, OLAP Worksheet provides menus, a toolbar, an input pane for OLAP DML commands on the bottom, and an output pane on the top. You can access the OLAP DML documentation through the Help menu.

In Figure 4-26, the output pane shows that the SALESTRACK workspace is attached with read/write access in both OLAP Worksheet (as shown by the `AW LIST` command) and AWM. The two applications share the same session, so whatever you do in OLAP Worksheet affects AWM as well. Changing the status or closing the workspace may have consequences on commands that you issue in AWM.

TIP
Use the `AW LIST` command to check which workspaces are attached and in which order, because many OLAP DML commands—like `LISTNAMES` and `DEFINE`—operate on only the first workspace.

OLAP Worksheet is an interactive environment for working with analytic workspaces, similar to SQL*Plus Worksheet. In addition to providing easy access to

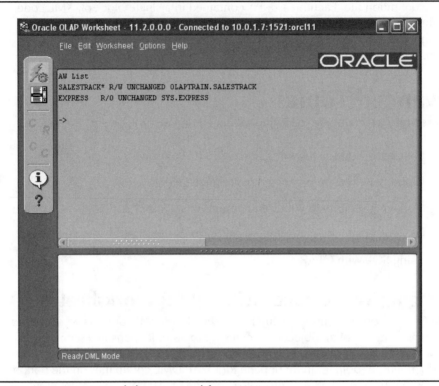

FIGURE 4-26. *OLAP Worksheet opened from AWM*

the OLAP DML, OLAP Worksheet enables you to perform sophisticated business analyses, such as modeling, forecasting, and allocation. You can switch between two different modes: one for working with analytic workspaces in the OLAP DML language and the other for working with relational tables and views in SQL.

You can use OLAP Worksheet to perform the following tasks:

- Connect to an analytic workspace.

- Execute most OLAP DML commands.

- Create and populate data objects.

- Create, modify, compile, and execute DML programs.

- Execute SQL statements.

To open OLAP Worksheet from AWM, after you have connected to your database and opened an analytic workspace, place your cursor on the analytic workspace or an object within the analytic workspace and select Tools | OLAP Worksheet. To execute an OLAP DML command, type it in the input pane at the bottom of the window. For example, to view the list of attached analytic workspaces, issue the command AW LIST.

Using the Editor in OLAP Worksheet

You can use the built-in editor in OLAP Worksheet to change the content of a program, model, or aggregation map. You cannot use the editor to change the contents of a dimension, variable, relation, value set, or other data containers.

To change a program, issue the following command to open the program in the editor window:

```
EDIT program_name
```

For example, enter EDIT ONATTACH to open the ONATTACH program, which is shown in Figure 4-27. The object type PROGRAM is the default type, so you do not need to specify it. You must specify the other object types. For example, to edit an aggregation map, you would issue a command such as EDIT AGGMAP units_cube_aggmap.

In the editor, type the OLAP DML commands that you want in the program. When you are finished editing the program, save it and close the editor. The status bar at the bottom of the window will tell you if there have been changes that have not been saved.

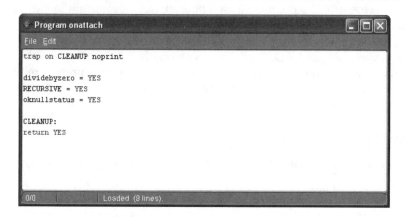

FIGURE 4-27.   *Opening a program in the OLAP Worksheet editor*

To execute the program, issue this command:

```
CALL program_name
```

To issue SQL commands, you need to select SQL Mode from the Options menu. To resume issuing OLAP DML commands, clear the SQL Mode selection.

Using OLAP DML

The ability to manipulate data directly using a stored procedure language is key to developing sophisticated OLAP-based applications. We have previously shown how to do this by creating calculated measures. These calculations use the OLAP stored procedure language, OLAP DML. As you have seen, the custom expression option available for calculated measures allows for entry of a complete OLAP DML script or program.

NOTE
The OLAP DML is very much like PL/SQL. In fact over the years, Oracle has included many of the same functions and features of SQL in the OLAP DML.

The OLAP DML language is the same language as the Express language mentioned in Chapter 2. There have been many enhancements to the language (mostly new commands and functions), but the language is the same. Originally, entire applications were written in this language, so all of the capabilities that you would expect in a modern computer language are there. Today, most applications use other technology to display the data, so generally, commands that generate output (such as the REPORT command) are not used, but they are still in the language.

OLAP DML programs contain a series of OLAP DML statements and reside in an analytic workspace. An OLAP DML program is an object in the analytic workspace, just like a dimension or variable. In order to change or run a program, you must first attach the analytic workspace that contains the program.

The OLAP DML language is used for multiple purposes:

- Specify a data expression.

- Manipulate OLAP data with commands (potentially in a batch process).

- Diagnose problems.

- Load data.

Function	Description
TOTAL	Sum data
MOVINGTOTAL	Calculate a total of a series of time periods
COUNT	Count the number of instances that meet a Boolean condition
MEDIAN	Calculate a median of a series of numbers
NPV	Calculate the net present value of a series of cash-flow values
SQRT	Return the square root of a number
ABS	Calculate the absolute value
DECODE	Decode a value (just as in PL/SQL)
LOG	Calculate the natural logarithm
RANK	Calculate the rank of values
ROUND	Round a number to a specified number of digits
SIN	Calculate the sine of an angle expression
JOINCHARS	Concatenate multiple strings
FINDCHARS	Search a string for a substring
UPCASE	Convert a string to uppercase

TABLE 4-3. *Some OLAP DML Data-Manipulation, Numeric, and Text Functions*

Using OLAP DML for Expressions   BI applications often need to calculate data. This data can often be calculated on the fly, at run time. The OLAP DML operates as a sophisticated expression language, much like MDX.

Many functions are built in to the OLAP DML, including those specifically designed to manipulate multidimensional data, as well as numeric and text functions. Table 4-3 lists some common OLAP DML functions.

In addition, there are functions to convert from one data type to another, time manipulation functions, database information functions, statistical functions, and more. These functions, along with operators such as + (plus), - (minus), * (multiply), / (divide), ** (exponent), and others provide the ability to calculate many business calculations as simple expressions. Expressions can also refer to programs that calculate a return value, allowing you to create your own functions. For a complete list of functions, see the *Oracle OLAP DML Reference* online documentation or the OLAP Worksheet Help.

OLAP DML expressions automatically have "dimensionality." If the SALES measure is dimensioned by PROD, GEOG, and TIME, the expression SALES*2 (multiple sales by the constant 2) is likewise dimensioned by PROD, GEOG, and TIME. Oracle OLAP always knows the dimensionality of an expression and will loop over the dimensionality in most situations, so no explicit FOR loop is necessary.

Using QDRs to Change the Dimensionality of an OLAP Expression If you wish to work with only a single dimension value, you can limit your expression using syntax called a *qualified data reference* (QDR). This syntax removes a dimension from the dimensionality of an expression. For example, the expression SALES(GEOGRAPHY 'US') *qualifies* the GEOGRAPHY dimension to the single value 'US'. The expression is dimensioned by the remaining dimensions of SALES, namely PRODUCT and TIME.

QDRs are often used in expressions when calculating a share. For example, the expression SALES / SALES(GEOGRAPHY 'US') calculates the sales share of the United States. Because the numerator (SALES) is not qualified in any way, this will work for any geography value.

The expression SALES(GEOGRAPHY 'US') specifies a single geography dimension value. The literal expression 'US' can be replaced with another variable, such as TOPCOUNTRY, which can be set to different values depending on the region of interest.

If instead of a single scalar value, you use another dimensioned expression, the dimensions of the reference are added to the other dimensions of the qualified expression. For example, suppose the top region needed to depend on the sales channel of interest. TOPCOUNTRY could be dimensioned by CHANNEL and have a different value for each CHANNEL. In that case, the expression SALES(GEOGRAPHY TOPCOUNTRY) would be dimensioned by PRODUCT, TIME, and CHANNEL. The qualification of the GEOGRAPHY dimension removes that dimension from the expression; the reference to TOPCOUNTRY, which is dimensioned by CHANNEL, adds the dimension CHANNEL to the overall expression.

This ability to remove and add dimensions using QDRs is used often to transform and manipulate Oracle OLAP data. Note that this expression language allows for combining data from multiple measures, cubes, and dimensions.

Manipulating OLAP Data with Commands If you wish to store the result of an expression permanently in a database, you can use an assignment statement to assign this expression to a variable. Usually, this can be calculated on the fly, eliminating the need to use disk space to store results permanently. Other commands are specifically designed to manipulate data, such as the following:

- AGGREGATE and ALLOCATE, which aggregate data up and down a series of hierarchies, respectively

- FORECAST and REGRESS and commands beginning with FC for advanced forecasting

- FILEREAD and OUTFILE and other file reading and writing commands

- EXPORT and IMPORT for moving data between workspaces or database instances

- Commands to directly access the Oracle relational data

- Commands to create or execute Models

- And many more commands

The OLAP DML language also contains standard control structures such as FOR loops, WHILE loops, SWITCH statements, and IF-THEN-ELSE statements. You can also trap for error conditions, and transfer control to an error procedure to handle anticipated and unanticipated error conditions (such as division by zero). Options are available to control behavior of certain conditions.

TIP
One option in particular can be very handy: If you set DIVIDEBYZERO to yes, Oracle OLAP will return an NA when you attempt to divide a number by zero, instead of producing an error.

The OLAP DML language has more than 100 commands. Some of the more common include:

- DEFINE, to create new objects

- DESCRIBE, to obtain the definition of an object

- LISTNAMES, to list all of the objects in an analytic workspace

- SHOW, to display the contents of an expression

- REPORT, to produce a formatted report of a series of expressions

- LIMIT, to control the current status of dimensions

- AW, to attach or detach an analytic workspace, or to list the attached analytic workspaces

See the *Oracle OLAP DML Reference* for more information about the OLAP DML commands.

Persistent Status Within a Session   Dimensions in Oracle OLAP sessions have a "status" associated with them. This is persistent throughout a given user session. You can think of dimension status as a sort of persistent SQL WHERE clause. Session status allows you to focus a series of OLAP DML statements on certain dimension values. All subsequent statements that are executed apply to only those values in current status until the status is reset to something else. For example, suppose you execute the following commands:

```
limit prod to all
limit geog to 'US'
limit time to '2007' to '2009'
limit time add descendants
sales = na
limit geog to 'CANADA'
sales = 100
```

Sales will be set to the special value na (not available) for all products, for just the geographic region US and for the time periods 2007 to 2009, and all values that are descendants of those time periods (typically quarters and months in 2007, 2008, and 2009). Sales for Canada for the same time periods will be set to 100. Note that no FOR loop is necessary—Oracle OLAP loops over all dimension values for sales currently in status. This status is automatically reset to ALL at the beginning of every session.

Wrong assumptions about the status of key dimensions are a common source of bugs and performance problems in Oracle OLAP applications. When operating on the data, be sure to limit to the minimum status necessary to perform a given task. For example, if you need to calculate only the average price for certain products, limit the Product dimension to only the products in question.

TIP
A powerful DML is at the core of the Oracle OLAP environment. This language expands Oracle OLAP to be an analysis environment, instead of simply a reporting environment. This section only introduces the concept of the Oracle OLAP DML. To become more familiar with all the features of the language, download and read the Oracle OLAP DML Reference.

Working with Cube-Organized Materialized Views

With query rewrite, Oracle can automatically convert a SQL query into a more efficient SQL query. The Oracle query engine can direct a query to take advantage of materialized views or, as in Oracle OLAP 11*g*, a cube-organized materialized view from an analytic workspace cube. Oracle's optimizer is intelligent enough to take advantage of preexisting summaries instead of reading all the detail records and summarizing them again. The end users do not know a transformation has occurred. The end users would only notice the improvement in performance.

Oracle's optimizer examines the query to determine if the SQL query can be rewritten for improved performance. If Oracle's optimizer determines it cannot improve the results, it performs the original plan by accessing the detail table rows and summarizing them.

Originally, Oracle had a rules-based optimizer that used a heuristic approach. In other words, the optimizer followed a series of rules. For example, one of the top rules was for the optimizer to utilize a unique index over any other access method. The rules-based optimizer would not care about other particulars of the situation, such as the number of rows in the table or whether the index was fragmented; it would simply follow the rule, even if the change actually resulted in poorer performance.

For Oracle8*i*, Oracle created a cost-based optimizer. A cost-based optimizer uses statistics on the objects, such as tables and indexes, to determine the best execution plan to return the results of the query. For example, if a table has very few rows in it, the cost-based optimizer may choose to perform a full table scan as opposed to an index scan. Normally, a full table scan would be more expensive; however, the expense of a full table scan depends on the size of the table.

In Oracle OLAP 11*g*, the cost-based optimizer takes into account cube-organized materialized views for query rewrite. If the cost-based optimizer thinks that the query will perform faster using OLAP cubes, the query will be rewritten to use OLAP cubes.

Setting Up for Cube-Organized Materialized Views

Each Oracle database has a set of parameters used to configure the database. For example, these parameters establish how much memory is allocated or whether to allow query rewrite. The following sections describe the two parameters that need to be set— QUERY_REWRITE_ENABLED and QUERY_REWRITE_INTERGRITY— and how to enable a cube for query rewriting.

Setting the QUERY_REWRITE_ENABLED Parameter The QUERY_REWRITE_ ENABLED database parameter controls the query rewrite feature for the database. It has three settings: TRUE, FALSE, and FORCE. Query rewrite is enabled on TRUE or FORCE, and disabled on FALSE. If set to FORCE, this parameter forces the optimizer to utilize the rewritten queries, even when the cost of the original query is lower.

The following example enables the query rewrite feature on the database:

```
query_rewrite_enabled = true;
```

You can override the database setting with the `ALTER SESSION` command:

```
alter session set query_rewrite_enabled = true;
```

Enabling Query Rewrite for Cube   With Oracle OLAP 11*g*, it is very easy to enable query rewrite on the cube-organized materialized view. You just need to check a box in AWM, as follows:

1. In AWM, select the cube.

2. Select the Materialized View tab.

3. Select Enable Materialized View Refresh on the Cube.

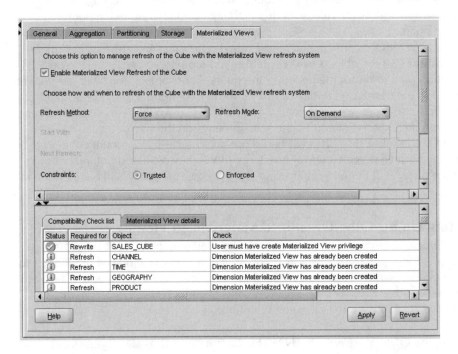

4. If desired, set the Refresh Method and Refresh Mode options.

Enabling materialized view refresh of the cube also enables the dimensions associated with the cube. Once this refresh is enabled, it is not possible to make changes to the cube or dimension structures, such as adding levels or hierarchies. If changes are necessary, you must first disable materialized views. Then you can make the changes and re-enable materialized views.

Setting the QUERY_REWRITE_INTEGRITY Parameter   The QUERY_REWRITE_
INTEGRITY parameter has three settings:

- **ENFORCED**   This is the default value. The optimizer will utilize the query
  rewrite feature only if the summary data represents the current detail values.
  For example, if the source fact table has been changed since the cube was
  loaded, the optimizer will not rewrite the query. The materialized view cube
  must be current, and no changes can have occurred to the detail tables
  since the last refresh of the materialized view cube.

- **TRUSTED**   With the TRUSTED value, the optimizer assumes that the
  relationships with foreign keys constraints are correct. It also trusts that
  declared, but not enabled, primary keys or unique keys are valid. With
  this setting, data integrity is assumed (not checked with the database
  constraints); therefore, there may be some invalid data.

- **STALE_TOLERATED**   With STALE_TOLERATED, the optimizer can
  rewrite queries even though the summary data may not be current. This
  setting has the risk that the summary data does not reflect the detailed data
  in the database. For example, detail data has been loaded with new rows;
  however, the materialized view cube has not yet been refreshed to reflect
  the current changes.

To set the parameter at the database level, use the following syntax:

```
query_rewrite_integrity = enforced;
```

In addition to setting QUERY_REWRITE_INTEGRITY at the database level, you
can set the level of query rewrite for a session. This allows users to set this
parameter to meet their needs, as in the following example:

```
alter session set query_rewrite_integrity = stale_tolerated;
```

Verifying Query Rewrite Occurred

If the query rewrite happens automatically, how do you check to see if the query
rewrite worked? You can run an explain plan to see the execution plan.

The easiest way to run an explain plan is to run the query in SQL Developer,
press F6, and examine the results in the Explain tab. Figure 4-28 shows the SQL
Developer results.

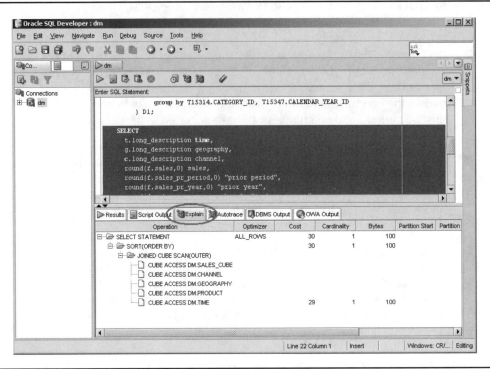

FIGURE 4-28. *Sample execution plan in SQL Developer*

Managing Security of Cubes and Dimensions

With Oracle OLAP 11*g*, Oracle has now brought an additional security option to OLAP. In the past, access control needed to be provided through the use of OLAP DML programs, was difficult to set up, and was not user-friendly. AWM 11*g* includes the capability to control access to OLAP data. This is fully compatible with the virtual private database (VPD) features in the Oracle Database. Oracle VPD enforces security, to a fine level of granularity, directly on database tables, views, or synonyms. Because you attach security policies directly to these database objects, and the policies are applied automatically whenever a user accesses data, there is no way to bypass security. With VPDs, you are able to control users' access to data related to them only, and prevent them from accessing data they are not authorized to see.

Setting Basic Security

You can grant access to users and roles on a particular analytic workspace, just as you can grant access to other database objects such as tables and views. These privileges are SELECT, ALTER, INSERT, and UPDATE. Granting these accesses to the analytic workspace does not grant these privileges to dimensions or cubes within an analytic workspace; these permissions must be granted separated. It is possible to grant basic access using SQL or using AWM.

The following shows an example of granting privileges. These SQL commands enable user Scott to query the Units cube. They give Scott SELECT privileges on the Global analytic workspace, the cube, and all of its dimensions. Scott also gets privileges on the dimension views, so that he can query the dimension attributes for formatted reports. Notice that we are using standard database GRANTS, which are familiar to all DBAs and users of the Oracle Database.

```
/* Grant privileges on the analytic workspace */
grant select on olaptrain.aw$salestrack to scott;
/* Grant privileges on the cube */
grant select on olaptrain.sales_cube to scott;
/* Grant privileges on the dimensions */
grant select on olaptrain.channel to scott;
grant select on olaptrain.geography to scott;
grant select on olaptrain.product to scott;
grant select on olaptrain.time to scott;
/* Grant privileges on the cube, dimension, and hierarchy views */
grant select on olaptrain.sales_cube_view to scott;
grant select on olaptrain.channel_view to scott;
grant select on olaptrain.channel_primary_view to scott;
grant select on olaptrain.geography_view to scott;
grant select on olaptrain.customer_shipments_view to scott;
grant select on olaptrain.customer_segments_view to scott;
grant select on olaptrain.product_view to scott;
grant select on olaptrain.product_primary_view to scott;
grant select on olaptrain.time_view to scott;
grant select on olaptrain.time_calendar_view to scott;
/* grant privileges to materialized views using query rewrite */
grant global query rewrite to scott;
```

Different types of privileges can be granted to users and roles individually for dimensions and cubes. For example, you may want a user to see only the Sales cube and not the Forecast cube. This is considered object-level security, which is set using the Object Security wizard in AWM, as shown in Figure 4-29.

Setting Finer-Grain Security

Data security policies enable you to grant users and roles privileges on specific dimension members. For example, you might restrict district sales managers to the data for just their own districts instead of all geographic areas. While it is possible to set security at the dimension and cube levels, it is not recommended to set this policy only at the cube level. Setting security on the cube level can cause confusion

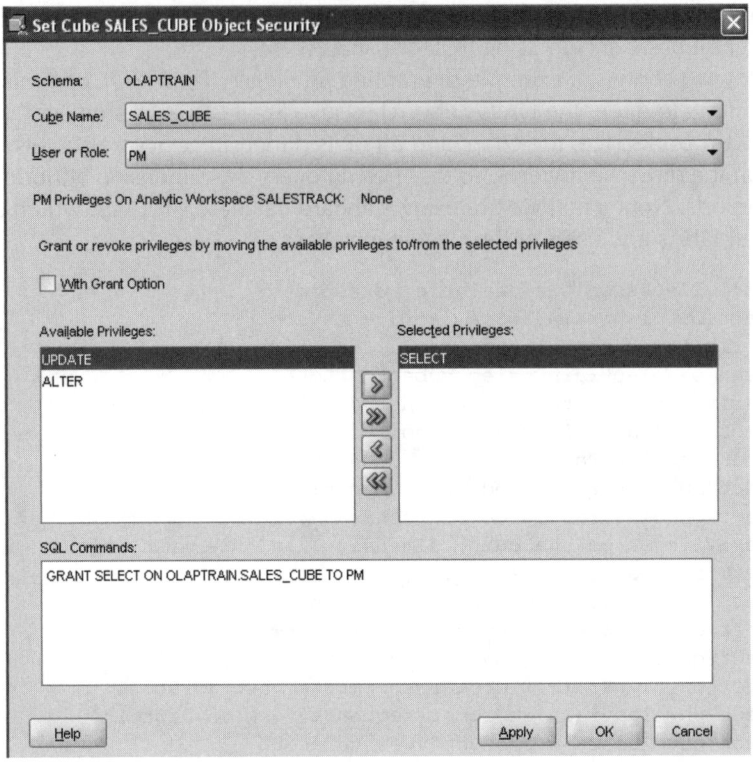

FIGURE 4-29.   *Setting object-level security*

for end users; they will be able to choose a dimension member that they are not permitted to see, but the cube will not report that data.

The data security policy on a dimension extends to all cubes within that dimension. You do not need to re-create the policy for each cube. When you create a data security policy on a cube, you select the members for each dimension of the cube. The policy applies to only that cube. When you create data security policies on both dimensions and cubes, users have privileges on the most narrowly defined portion of the data, where the policies overlap.

As soon as you create a data security policy, all other users are automatically denied access. AWM creates a default policy that grants all privileges to the owner. Otherwise, the owner would not be able to access any data.

Set these policies using AWM by selecting the Data Security option under the dimension or cube that will have the policy. Name the policy, and then add a user

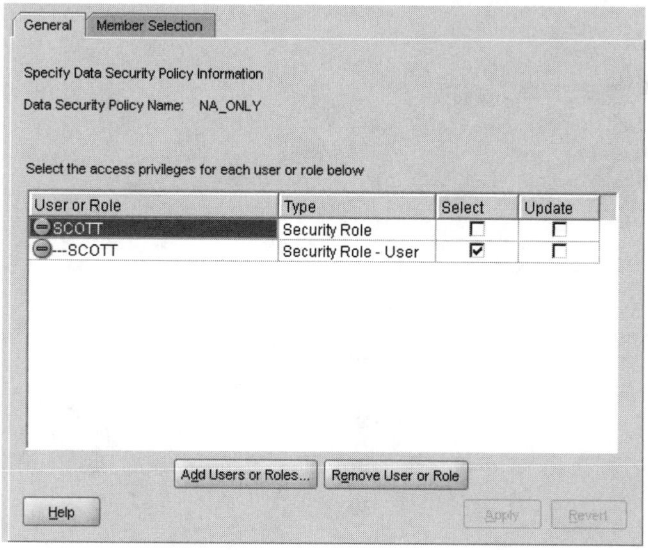

FIGURE 4-30. *Creating a data security policy*

or role. In the example in Figure 4-30, we have added the user Scott to a new policy called NA_ONLY (NorthAmericaOnly).

Next, use the Member Selection tab to choose the dimension members that will be visible to this user. In this case, we want to limit the Geography to only North America and the members below it. Using the selector, choose Geography and then select North America to appear in the selected panel, as shown in Figure 4-31. Since we do not want to restrict access on any of the other dimensions, we leave them alone. If you look at the condition expression, you will note that the statement WHERE 1 = 1 for all other dimensions. Clicking Create will create this policy, and it will be applied. The next time Scott logs on, he will have access to view the data in the Sales cube, but only for data from North America. This applies to looking at the data via AWM as well as using the SQL views, assuming Scott has access to the views.

Creating Advanced Cubes for Typical Business Purposes

Oracle OLAP has the flexibility and power to handle a wide range of analytical needs. The previous sections have addressed how to work with typical star and snowflake multidimensional models. This section addresses how some more complex problems can be handled using Oracle OLAP. As an example, we show how you can use advanced forecasting techniques to compute additional cube-based measures.

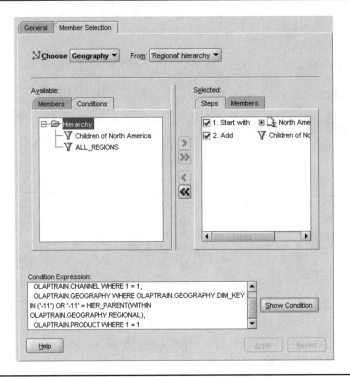

FIGURE 4-31. *Selecting data security members*

A close examination of the OLAP DML guide shows that several forecasting and statistical analysis functions are provided in the OLAP engine. The forecasting engine supports basic forecasting, as well as advanced forecasting using the Geneva Forecasting engine, acquired from Roadmap Technologies. OLAP DML supports simple linear regressions, several nonlinear regression methods, single exponential smoothing, double exponential smoothing, and the Holt-Winters method. The OLAP engine also can decide the best fit for your data based on past performance.

For our forecasting program example, the following commands are used to calculate a forecast:

■ FCOPEN, to open a forecast full table scan

■ FCSET, to specify the options of the forecast

■ FCEXEC, to execute the forecast

■ FCQUERY, to retrieve information and characteristics about the forecast

■ FCCLOSE, to close a forecast

The following is an example forecast:

```
"Set forecast parameters for 'best fit'
fcset _handle approach 'APPAUTO' periodicity 12 histperiods 36
"Execute the forecast
"save seasonal and seasonal smoothed into the variables just defined
fcexec _handle time time into forecast_best -
        seasonal forecast_seasonal -
        smseasonal forecast_smseasonal backcast -
        sales_cube_sales
```

We can use this in a program written in OLAP DML to calculate the forecast and store the results back to the cube so that it can be viewed like any other stored variable.

OLAP DML programs are very similar to PL/SQL scripts. The program Load_Forecast, shown in Figure 4-32, defines variables and then calls the FCEXEC function to compute the forecast and place it in the variable MyForecast.

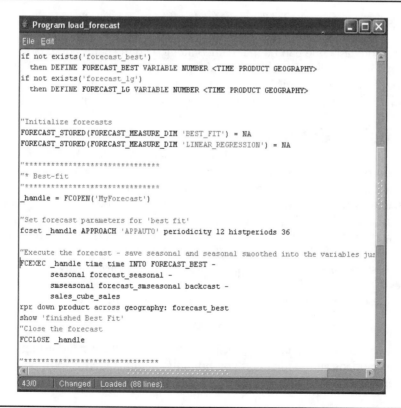

FIGURE 4-32.   *Forecast program*

The execution of the forecast takes less than a minute to run for the entire cube. This program can be executed from a SQL or PL/SQL call, or can be incorporated into the maintenance routine of the Forecast cube, using cube scripts.

NOTE
The full code for the forecasting program is available as part of the OLAPTRAIN demo.

As mentioned earlier in the chapter, it is possible to have custom steps in Oracle OLAP 11*g* cube scripts. In this case, we can add an OLAP DML command step to the LOAD_AND_AGGREGATE cube script for the Forecast cube by doing the following:

1. Select the LOAD_AND_AGGREGATE script.

2. Delete the existing Load step.

3. Add a new step (OLAP Command).

4. Save the step and reorder the steps so that this new step is the first step.

Now the Forecast cube can be maintained along with the Sales cube. However, when the maintenance is performed, this cube must be maintained after the Sales cube has been maintained. This is because the data needed for the forecast is in the Sales cube, and it must be present before the forecasting program is run.

Using SQL with OLAP

One of the most useful features introduced with Oracle OLAP is the ability to use SQL queries to access the multidimensional calculation engine and multidimensional data. This single feature dramatically increases the reach and applicability of OLAP to a vast range of BI query and reporting tools, as well as SQL-based custom applications. Many more applications and reporting tools can now benefit from the superior performance, scalability, and functionality of a first-class multidimensional server contained within the Oracle Database. The bottom line is that applications that can connect to an Oracle database instance and execute simple SQL can benefit from analytic workspaces.

Follow these recommendations to gain the maximum benefit from OLAP SQL views:

■ Always build your analytic workspaces to Oracle OLAP standard form. This happens automatically if you build them with AWM, OWB, or the supplied API.

■ If you are using Oracle OLAP 10*g*, use the View Generator plug-in for AWM 10*g* to build your 10*g* views. If you are using Oracle OLAP 11*g*, leverage the automatically generated views.

If you follow this advice, you will save much of time on your project and increase your ability to support the application in the future.

The plug-in for AWM 10*g* Release 2 is free shareware and can be downloaded from the Oracle Technology Network (OTN) web site. The plug-in adds a simple wizard within AWM. As you follow the steps in the wizard, you choose the measures and other items you need, and then the wizard creates the views for you. The wizard stores the biggest lump of syntax—the `limitmap` parameter, which describes which analytic workspace objects show up in what columns in your view—inside the analytic workspace itself, in a multiline text variable/measure.

In Oracle Database 11*g*, `OLAP_TABLE()` is still available for you to use. It is sometimes suitable for your needs, as it has many very clever hooks by which you can trigger various OLAP actions whenever a user selects from the view. For most cases, however, the new `CUBE_TABLE()` function added in Oracle Database 11*g* is recommended. `CUBE_TABLE()` views are what AWM 11*g* automatically creates for you when defining the objects inside the analytic workspace. Assuming that you have a valid standard form analytic workspace, such as you might build in AWM 11*g*, `CUBE_TABLE()` is much easier to use than `OLAP_TABLE()`. For example, the entire syntax required to create a dimension view for a specified hierarchy of that dimension in an analytic workspace is as follows:

```
create or replace force view mydim_myhier_view as
select * from table( cube_table('MYSCHEMA.MYDIM;MYHIER') );
```

Remember that AWM 11*g* already does this for you. All you need to know about your analytic workspace is the name of the hierarchy (`MYHIER`), dimension (`MYDIM`), and schema that the analytic workspace is built in (`MYSCHEMA`). All the object mappings that you need to tell `OLAP_TABLE` about, in the `limitmap` parameter, are automatically done as a result of improvements in the Oracle Database 11*g* data dictionary. The data dictionary is now fully aware of all the OLAP objects created by AWM, OWB, and the OLAP API.

AWM 11*g* creates the necessary view for each dimension and cube in the analytic workspace. Figure 4-33 shows the view information (from AWM) for the Sales cube view.

Notice that the dimensions and measures are shown in the view. The dimensions have only one column for each dimension, which represents the dimension member or key. There is one row for each member in the cube that has data, for all levels of all dimensions of the cube. This data can either be stored or not stored. The data that is not stored is aggregated on the fly when the data is retrieved from the view. The cube view can be joined with the dimension views in queries to produce data at any

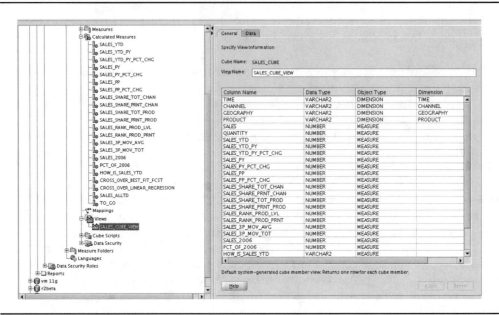

FIGURE 4-33. *Sample cube view*

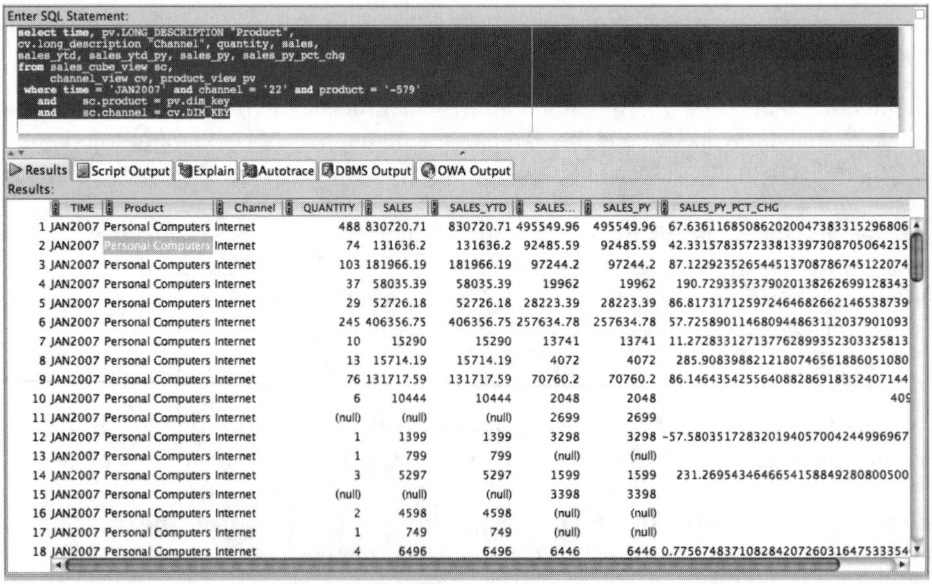

FIGURE 4-34. *Example of selecting data from a cube*

desired aggregation level. The data can be used in any SQL-based query tool, just like any other relational data.

A simple SELECT statement such as the one shown in Figure 4-34 on the preceding page yields results from the cube rapidly. The performance of the SELECT statement is not significantly affected by the complexity of the calculations, unlike a similar SELECT from relational tables. Remember that many of these measures are calculated on the fly, and yet the SELECT performance is still excellent.

Conclusion

Oracle OLAP is a logical extension of the Oracle Database that increases the power of the database. The Oracle OLAP environment provides a great deal of flexibility in building multidimensional applications. We have shown how easy it is to take relational data and build simple but powerful OLAP cubes that can greatly improve the ability to provide rapid answers to end-user questions. By using the built-in features of AWM, or by extending it with the functionality of OLAP DML, you can take those simple solutions and extend them into complex applications that can solve just about any BI problem.

If you keep in mind Oracle OLAP's strengths and take into account what it is going through to service your requests, you can create more efficient applications. As is true with any computer environment, having an understanding of what the software is doing at a lower level helps to enhance database design and performance.

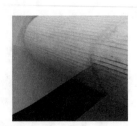

CHAPTER
5

Building Your
Essbase Database

hapter 3 introduced potential architectures for Essbase implementations, components of the overall solution (both required and optional), and fundamental design methodology. Now we present a hands-on demonstration of how to build an Essbase database.

The chapter starts with an overview of the components and files used in the demonstration. During the demonstration, we walk you through how to build and deploy an Essbase database using Oracle Essbase Studio. Then we talk about how to calculate the database and validate the data in the database using reports. After the demonstration, we discuss some Essbase features you can take advantage of, such as custom load rules and member calculations. The chapter ends with examples of automating the build and load processes.

Demonstration Overview

Our goal for this demonstration is to show you the overall process for building, deploying, calculating, and validating an Essbase database. By the end of the demonstration, you will be able to deploy a simple database, and you will have a foundation from which to explore more advanced topics.

NOTE
Unless otherwise specified, the term database *in this chapter refers to an Essbase multidimensional database. In the Essbase Studio console, an Essbase database is also called a* cube.

In this demonstration, we build an Essbase database in five steps:

- Map the data source.

- Model the data source.

- Build dimensions (hierarchies).

- Model the Essbase database.

- Deploy the Essbase database.

After building the Essbase database, we will calculate it and show you how to validate it. Along the way, we will discuss related aspects of an Essbase database.

NOTE
The instructions and screen captures in this chapter reflect a Windows-based environment. For instructions for UNIX-based systems, see the Oracle Essbase documentation set.

This demonstration is for illustrative purposes only. There are a many ways to build an Essbase database. The specific methodology you use will depend on your data sources, the data-integration components that are available to you, the versions of your software, and your overall comfort level with Essbase.

While there are external aspects of building a database, such as extract, transform, and load (ETL) processes, the components discussed are those that are provided out of the box with Essbase. As indicated in Figure 5-1, the following components are required for this demonstration:

■ Essbase server

■ Essbase Administration Services server and console

■ Essbase Studio server and console

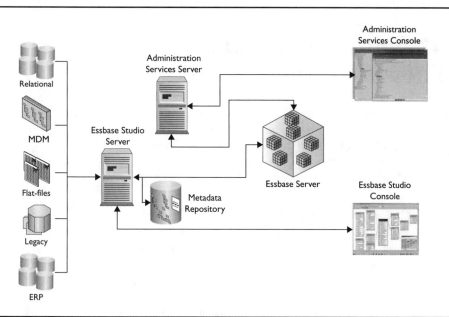

FIGURE 5-1. *Essbase architecture used for the demonstration*

Because we use a relational database as the data source in this example, we had a choice of build tools for this demonstration: Essbase Studio, Integration Services, or Administration Services. Both Essbase Studio and Integration Services are much faster to deploy against this type of data source than Administration Services. We selected Essbase Studio because it is likely to replace Integration Services in the future, as discussed in Chapter 3.

Essbase Studio also provides a significant advantage over Integration Services, in that it generates data-load rules—the underlying files used to build and update a database—automatically. Essbase Studio provides a graphical means to generate load rules. Instead of needing to map each individual field and select a variety of specific settings, you can accomplish these tasks using simple drag-and-drop actions. In short, Essbase Studio simplifies the process of creating dimensions and building a database. At the end of the process, Essbase Studio not only builds the Essbase database, but it also places the load rules it generates into the database directory for use in batch processes.

If you intend to follow the steps in this chapter's example, you need to create the relational database to be used as a data source. First, you need a working installation of one of the following relational databases: Oracle Database, SQL Server, Teradata, or DB2. You then run the SQL scripts that ship with Essbase Studio to create all of the tables, data, and metadata in the relational database. The SQL scripts are located in the sqlscripts subdirectory of your Essbase Studio installation. The sample relational database is called TBC (for The Beverage Company).

From Source to Database with Essbase Studio

In this section, we demonstrate an efficient method for building and deploying an Essbase database using Essbase Studio. We start with an overview of the Essbase Studio console. We then walk through the steps required to build and deploy an Essbase database, as outlined in the previous section. Then we will take a quick look at one of the generated load rules, summarize the building process, and calculate and validate the completed database.

Overview of Essbase Studio

Introduced in version 11.x of Essbase, Essbase Studio represents a much simplified methodology for creating Essbase databases compared to previous methods. While it is always possible to create a complete model using load rules created manually in Administration Services, Essbase Studio provides distinct advantages:

- Greater reusability of metadata (including dimensions) and data across analytic applications without requiring the user to model twice

- Lineage tracking of a database and its parts (dimensions, members, and so on), which allows administrators to perform impact analysis of changes to underlying data sources and elements on analytic applications

- Unification of database-building processes, regardless of the data source type

- Enhanced ability to drill through from Essbase to supporting data sources

- Simplification of federated data source environments

- Ease of integration into existing batch processes

To start the Essbase Studio server on a Windows-based system, if the server was installed as a service, open the Windows Services management console and start the service named Hyperion Essbase Studio Service. Otherwise, from the Windows taskbar, select Start | Programs | Oracle EPM System | Essbase | Essbase Studio | Start Server. The server starts in the foreground after a few seconds.

NOTE
On a Windows system, the display may show error messages as the Essbase Studio server tries to load drivers that are not installed. For example, you will see an error message if you do not have the MySQL driver installed. The messages are a normal part of the Essbase Studio startup process. They will not interfere with the server's operation.

To start the Essbase Studio console, select Start | Programs | Oracle EPM System | Essbase | Essbase Studio | Essbase Studio Console. When prompted, enter your user name and password, and then click OK.

As shown in Figure 5-2, the Essbase Studio console contains three distinct areas:

- **Metadata Navigator**   The left panel contains all analytic objects created based on the data sources and database schemas that are selected in the Data Sources panel on the right. These include (but are not limited to) hierarchies, cube schema, drill-through reports, and metadata elements (which are used to create hierarchies).

- **Work Area**   In the central panel, you can edit objects selected in the Metadata Navigator or the Source Navigator.

- **Source Navigator**   The right panel lists data sources and data source internal mappings (minischemas). You can add, delete, and edit data source connections in this area. You can also add tables from an existing source, modify joins, and edit or create a minischema.

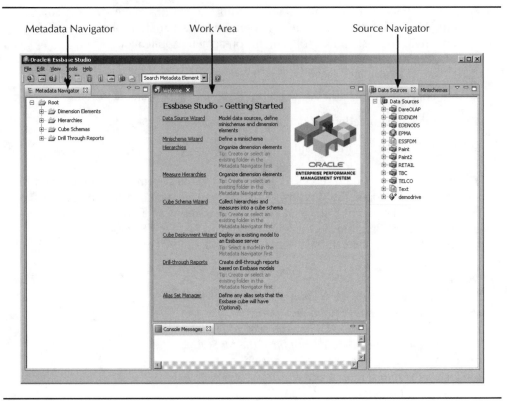

FIGURE 5-2. *The Essbase Studio Console*

Mapping Data Sources

At the time of publication, Essbase Studio supports the use of data from any of the following sources for an Essbase database (a JDBC driver is required for each source):

- Oracle Database
- OBIEE
- Oracle Enterprise Performance Management Architect
- Microsoft SQL Server
- IBM DB2

- Teradata databases

- Sun Microsystems MySQL

- Delimited text files

NOTE
*Microsoft Excel cannot be used directly as a data
source for an Essbase database. The data must first
be saved to a delimited text file (a comma-separated
values, or CSV, file).*

As noted earlier, for this demonstration, we use a relational database as a data
source. Therefore, while the following procedures are generalized, the examples
and screen captures represent a relational database as a data source.

Follow these steps to map a relational data source from the Essbase Studio
console:

1. In the Source Navigator, select the Data Sources tab.

2. Right-click the Data Source root node and select New | Data Source.

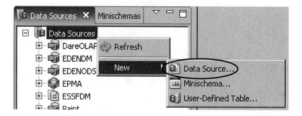

3. The Connection Wizard starts. Specify the parameters—database type, server
    name, database SID, and so on—applicable to your local environment and
    data source. In the both the Connection Name and Database Name fields,
    enter **TBC** for this example. Then click Next to continue. The following
    image is for illustrative purposes only; do not copy these values.

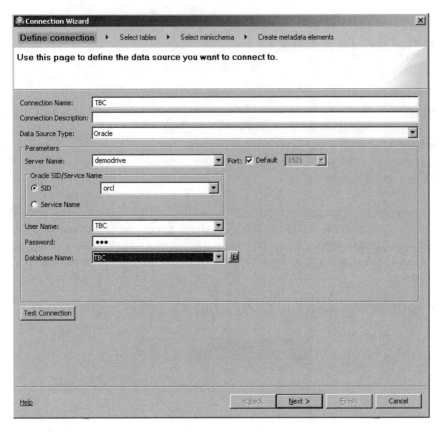

4. On the Select Tables page, select the following tables, and then click the Add button:

- TBC.Family

- TBC.Market

- TBC.Measures

- TBC.Population

- TBC.Product

- TBC.ProductDim

- TBC.Region

- TBC.Sales

- TBC.Scenario

- TBC.Supplier

5. Click Finish. In the Source Navigator, the database is added to the Data Sources tree.

6. If necessary, expand the Data Sources root node to see the new data source. Then expand the TBC database tree to view the tables in the database.

7. Expand one of the table trees to view the columns in the table.

8. Right-click the Family table and select View Sample Data. A sample set of records from the table is displayed. Note that the column headings match the column names in the table.

	FAMILYID	FAMILY	FAMILY_ALIAS	INTRODATE
1	1.0	100	Colas	Mon Mar 25 00:00:...
2	2.0	200	Root Beer	Wed Sep 27 00:00:...
3	3.0	300	Cream Soda	Wed Jun 26 00:00:...
4	4.0	400	Fruit Soda	Tue Oct 01 00:00:0...

9. Close the Sample - Family tab by clicking the X icon beside the tab name.

Modeling the Data Source

In a sense, modeling the data source is optional. The reason we model the data source is so that we can load data from a relational source. Therefore, if you want to build an outline from the relational source *without* loading data, you can skip this step. However, you will need to create custom load rules to load data into the database later. For more information, see the "Creating Custom Load Rules" section later in this chapter. For this demonstration, we will model the data source and let Essbase Studio do the work of generating the load rule files.

NOTE
If data is stored in flat files, the wizard used to map the data source does the modeling automatically. This step is not required.

Minischema Basics

You model a relational source by creating an Essbase Studio minischema. In the minischema, you create the join relationships between tables. The minischema does not contain hierarchy information; it simply provides the mappings so that Essbase Studio can traverse the data source. The following are other important points regarding minischemas:

- Text files can be added to a minischema for logical grouping only. They cannot be joined to other text files or relational tables.

- Essbase Studio supports the use of multiple fact tables in the minischema.

- There is no requirement to have a fact table for hierarchy creation or Essbase database deployment. To that end, you can use columns from a relational source to build the model without a minischema, and use a flat file to load the data.

Creating a Minischema from a Relational Source

Follow these steps to create the minischema for this example:

1. In the Source Navigator, select the Minischemas tab.

2. Right-click the Minischemas root node and select New | Minischema.

3. Specify a name for the minischema and, optionally, a description of its purpose. For this example, enter the name **SalesAnalysis**. You do not need to enter a description. Then click Next.

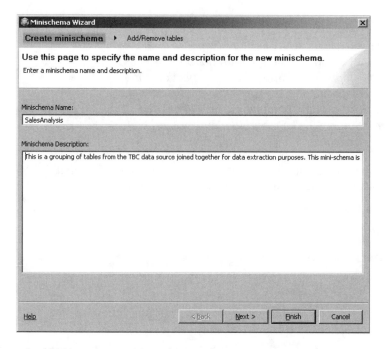

4. On the Add/Remove Tables page, ensure TBC is selected and add all tables to the minischema.

5. Click Finish. The tables in the database are laid out in the schema viewer.

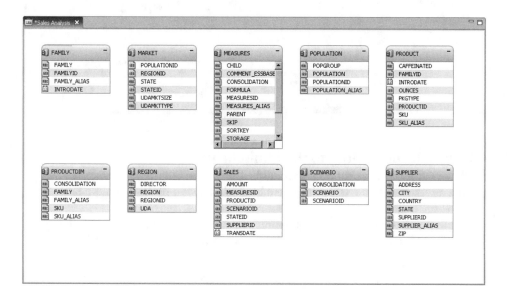

6. Right-click in the schema viewer and select Add Joins by Inspection.

CAUTION
While the Add Joins by Inspection option is selected here for simplicity, adding joins by inspection can potentially create numerous repetitive joins between tables. For a production database, it is generally better to inspect the keys and foreign keys and build the joins manually.

7. In the Create Joins by Inspection dialog box, select Select all Items, and then click OK. Like columns across tables are joined.

8. Right-click in the schema viewer and select Layout Schema to view the current schema.

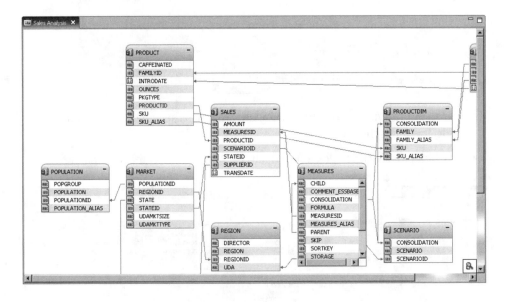

Adding a Recursive Join to the Minischema

Now we will modify the schema to include a recursive join for the Measures table. Adding a recursive join lets us do parent/child dimension builds from the table.

1. Right-click the Measures table and select Add Join. The Properties dialog box appears. Here, you can edit the properties of a minischema join.

2. Select the Measures table from the second drop-down list.

3. In the Column area, click in the first cell and select CHILD from the drop-down list.

4. Click in the cell to the right and select PARENT from the drop-down list.

TIP
Alternatively, in the Measures table (in the schema viewer), you can select PARENT and drag and drop it on top of CHILD.

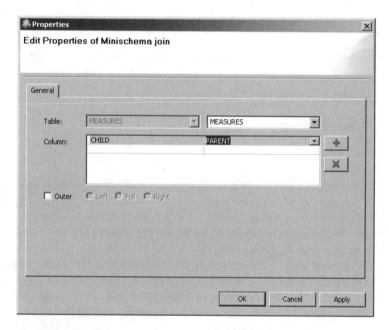

5. Click OK to add the join.

6. Save the changes to the SalesAnalysis minischema and close it.

Building Dimensions (Hierarchies)

When using other Essbase components, we use the term *hierarchy* to refer to a specific portion of a dimension. In Essbase Studio, hierarchy *means* dimension. Therefore, this section focuses on building the dimensions—in other words, creating the hierarchies—for our database. Hierarchies are built using metadata elements, such as column names in a relational source and fields in a text file.

In this demonstration, we begin by creating a folder structure in the Metadata Navigator. The folder structure enables us to organize the elements for the new database, including metadata elements and hierarchies. You can create as many folders and subfolders as desired to organize your deployment. You can add folders at any time, but we recommend that you organize the metadata elements before creating hierarchies, because it simplifies the process.

A metadata element is anything that you can use to create an analytical model. A metadata element in Essbase Studio is any of the following:

- Relational column (based on the source or user defined)

- Field from a text file

- User-defined element (such as a variance that does not exist in the relational source)

- Hierarchy

- Drill-through report

- Cube schema

Hierarchies are built by dragging and dropping metadata elements into the hierarchy. In Chapter 2, we talked about dimensions organized from top to bottom (generations), from bottom to top (levels), or in a recursive fashion (parent/child). Essbase Studio removes the necessity to think about a dimension build in this way. Instead, you drag and drop the sources for each level either from the Metadata Navigator (the easiest way) or directly from the Data Sources tab in the Source Navigator. The term *level* is used here in a very generic sense, in that there is no requirement to understand the concepts of levels, generations, parents, or children. You can create custom members, hierarchies, attributes, and alternate hierarchies in the same fashion. At any point during the process, you can see a full preview of the resulting hierarchy.

NOTE
The hierarchy corresponds to the Essbase outline discussed in the "Designing an Essbase Database" section in Chapter 3. If you like, you can use the Administration Services console to view and edit the hierarchy in the Outline Editor.

Creating a Folder Structure in the Metadata Navigator

To create a folder structure, follow these steps:

1. In the Metadata Navigator, right-click the Root folder and select New | Folder.

2. In the Properties dialog box, name the folder **SalesAnalysis**, and then click OK.

3. Create the following additional folders under the SalesAnalysis folder: **Dimension Elements**, **Hierarchies**, **Cube Schemas**, and **Drill Through Reports**.

Selecting Metadata Elements

Follow these steps to add metadata elements to the Dimension Elements folder:

1. In the Source Navigator, select the Data Sources tab.

2. Expand the Market table.

3. Drag STATE from the Source Navigator to the Metadata Navigator, and drop it in the Dimension Elements folder.

4. In the Source Navigator, expand the Region table and drag REGION to the Dimension Elements folder.

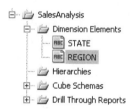

5. Repeat the process to add the following columns to the Dimension Elements folder:

Table Name	Column Name
ProductDim	FAMILY
Product	SKU
	CAFFEINATED
	OUNCES
	PKGTYPE
Region	DIRECTOR

Creating Hierarchies

Follow these steps to create the hierarchies for this example:

1. In the Metadata Navigator, right-click the Hierarchies folder and select New | Hierarchy.

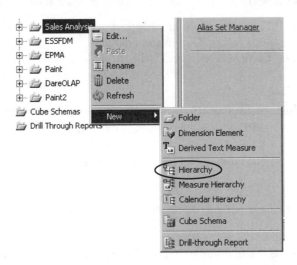

2. Specify a name for the hierarchy. For this example, enter **Product**.

3. Drag FAMILY from the Dimension Elements folder and drop it in the first empty cell in the data table.

4. Drag SKU from the Dimension Elements folder and drop it *on top of* the FAMILY entry in the first cell. SKU becomes a child of FAMILY.

5. Add the following columns to the Product hierarchy at the specified level:

Hierarchy Name	First Level	Second Level
Product	OUNCES	SKU
Product	PKG TYPE	SKU
Product	CAFFEINATED	SKU

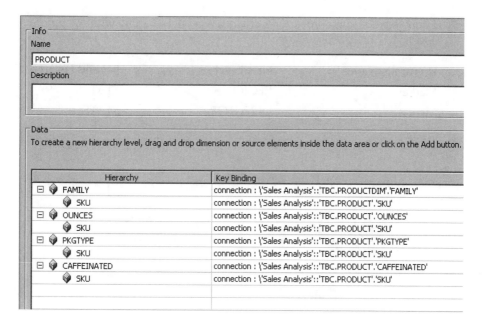

6. Click Save and Preview. The Product hierarchy is displayed in a tree format.

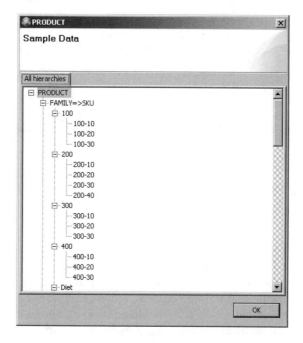

7. Following the same procedure, create a Market hierarchy with the following levels:

Hierarchy Name	First Level	Second Level
Market	REGION	STATE
Market	DIRECTOR	STATE

8. Click Save and Preview. The Market hierarchy is displayed.

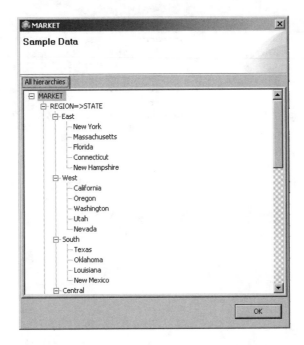

9. Create the following additional hierarchies and levels:

Hierarchy Name	First Level	Second Level
Accounts	PARENT	CHILD
Scenario	SCENARIO	N/A

Building a Time Dimension

Our demonstration requires a time dimension, but our data source does not enumerate year, quarter, and month columns. However, it does contain a column with a date-time stamp. Through a simple wizard, Essbase Studio can extract the individual date elements from a single record to create the time dimension.

TIP
If your data source contains columns or fields for years, quarters, months, weeks, days, and so forth, you can build a time dimension in the same fashion as you would any other hierarchy.

1. In the Metadata Navigator, right-click the Dimension Elements folder and select New | Dimension Element. The Properties dialog box is displayed.

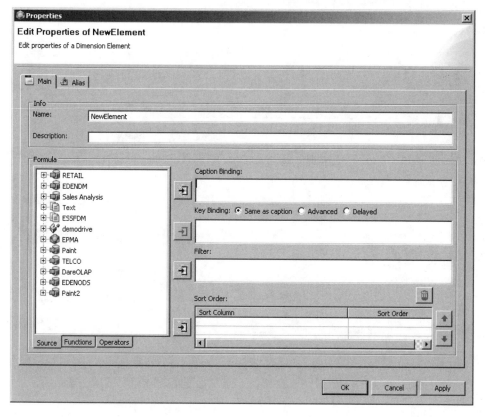

2. Specify a name for the new element. For this example, enter **Quarter**.

3. Select the Functions tab below the Formula list box.

4. Expand Date.

5. Select the QuarterAsString function and click the Add button beside the Caption Binding area.

6. Select the Source tab.

7. Expand TBC, then Sales.

8. In the Caption Binding area, select the string $$DateOperand$$. With the string selected, select Transdate from the Source tab, and then click the Add button beside the Caption Binding area. Transdate should overwrite the $$DateOperand$$ string.

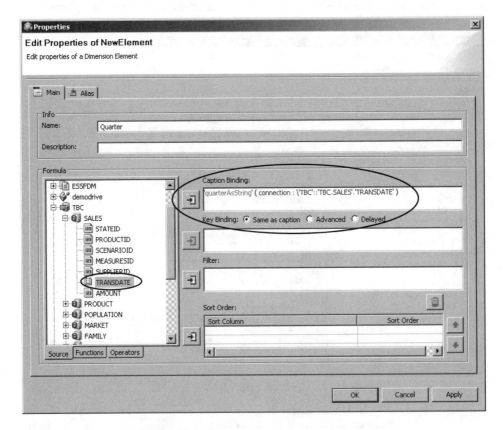

9. Click OK to add the element.

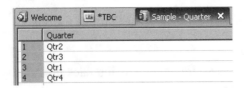

10. Repeat the process to create a new dimension named **Month**. Specify the MonthShortName function.

11. In the Hierarchies folder, create a hierarchy named **Year**. Make Quarter the top of the hierarchy, and nest Month underneath it.

Modeling the Essbase Database

In this part of the demonstration, we select the hierarchies (dimensions) to include in the Essbase database. The Essbase Studio console refers to this process as "creating a cube schema and model." Recall that *cube* is another name for a multidimensional database.

Let's take a step back for a moment. A cube schema is simply a representation of the actions you want Essbase Studio to take. This is different from a minischema, which describes how Essbase Studio should navigate the relational structure in order to retrieve numeric data across the set of tables. In the case of a cube schema, you are describing which dimensions you would like Essbase Studio to deploy to an Essbase database. The cube model is where you specify properties for deployment, such as the following:

■ Which dimensions are dense or sparse

■ The consolidation operator assigned to a member

■ Whether the resulting database should contain unique member names or allow for duplicate names

Depending on the nature of the data source, it is possible that all of the properties are being housed in the relational source. We have worked on a number of deployments where customers store all of the Essbase database information (metadata) in columns of the relational model. This might include consolidation operators, member formulas, member aliases, and user-defined attributes.

A centralized data warehouse or data mart makes it easier to manage changes to this information and to push them out to existing models. As the information changes in the data warehouse or mart, Essbase Studio automatically picks up those changes when it deploys the Essbase database. Once deployed, the implemented changes are available to the end users of the system. This way, you do not need to manage these changes on each deployed database individually.

The following procedures walk through the creation of the cube schema/model, as well as the assignment of various Essbase properties. Many of the Essbase properties for this model are stored in the relational database source, and the steps show you how to map these into your Essbase database.

Creating a Cube Schema and Model

Follow these steps to create the cube schema and model for this example:

1. In the Essbase Studio console's Source Navigator, select the Data Sources tab.

2. Expand TBC, and then the Sales table.

3. Drag AMOUNT from the Source Navigator to the Metadata Navigator, and drop it in the Dimension Elements folder.

4. In the Metadata Navigator, right-click the Cube Schemas folder and select New | Cube Schema.

5. Specify a name for the cube schema. For this example, enter **TBC1**.

6. Expand the Hierarchies folder and add the following hierarchies: Accounts, Year, Scenario, Product, and Market.

7. Expand the Dimension Elements folder and add Amount to the Measures area.

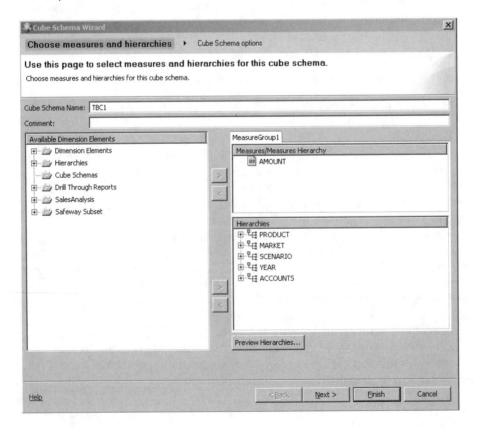

8. Click Preview Hierarchies. Review the dimension.

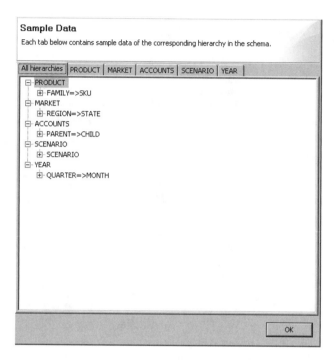

9. Click OK to close the preview, and then click Next.

10. On the Cube Schema Options page, select Create Essbase Model.

11. From the Accounts Dimension drop-down list, select Accounts.

12. Click Finish to create the cube schema.

The next task is to set all the Essbase properties in the Essbase model.

Setting Properties in the Essbase Model

To set properties for the model, follow these steps:

1. If the TBC1 model is not displayed, double-click TBC1 in the Metadata Navigator.

2. Right-click in the model and select Essbase Properties to display the properties of the model.

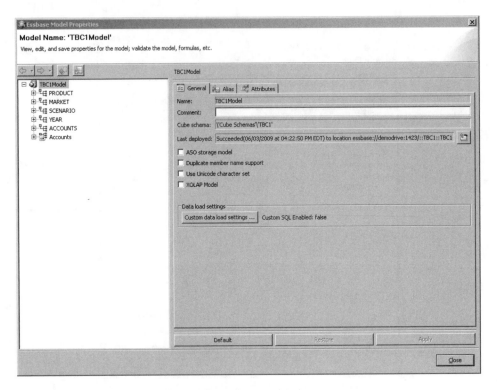

3. Expand Accounts and PARENT, and then select CHILD.

4. Select the Info tab and specify the settings as follows:

   ■ **Consolidation**   Select External source and then select CONSOLIDATION.

   ■ **Two Pass Calculation**   Select External source and then select TWOPASSCALC.

   ■ **Data Storage**   Select External source and then select Storage.

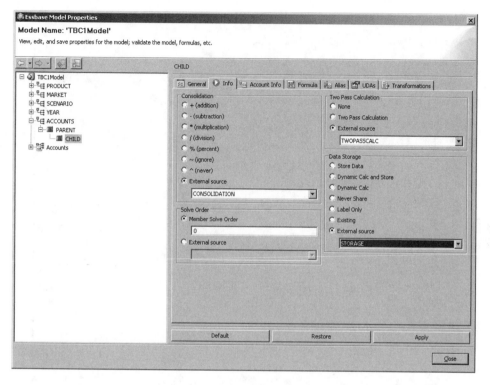

5. Select the Account Info tab and specify settings as follows:

- **Time Balance** Select External source and then select TIMEBALANCE.

- **Skip** Select External source and then select SKIP.

- **Variance Reporting** Select External source and then select VARIANCEREPORTING.

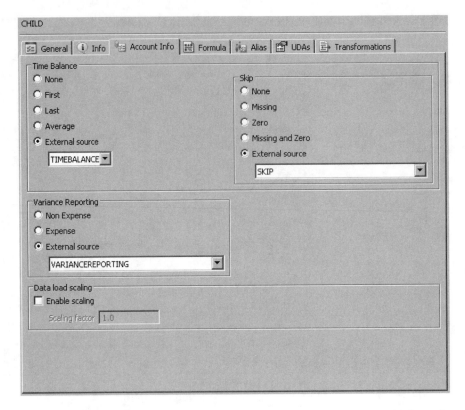

6. Select the Formula tab. Select External source and select Formula from the drop-down list.

7. Select the UDA tab. From the External source drop-down list, select UDA and click Add to List.

8. Click Apply to apply these member properties.

9. Select PARENT from the navigation tree. Repeat steps 4 through 8.

10. Expand the Product dimension and select OUNCES.

11. On the General tab, select Essbase Attribute for SKU.

12. Change the Attribute Type to Numeric.

13. Specify the remainder of the settings for this model as follows:

Hierarchy	Column	Tab	Property	Setting
Year	Year	Info	Dimension Type	Time
Year	Year	Info	Dimension Storage	Dense
Scenario	SCENARIO	Info	Consolidation	~
Product	PKGTYPE	General	Select Essbase Attribute for SKU	String (default)
Product	CAFFEINATED	General	Select Essbase Attribute for SKU	Boolean
Market	STATE (under REGION)	UDAs	External Source	UDAMKTSIZE
Market	STATE (under REGION)	UDAs	External Source	UDAMKTTYPE

14. Click Close. If you are prompted to validate the model, select Yes. Fix any issues identified. When the validation is complete, click Close.

NOTE

If you receive a message stating that the selection of External for data storage for the column Child can cause trouble, ignore this message. This message indicates that if not configured properly, the external settings can cause invalid configurations on cube deployment. The sample database source is free of data errors.

Deploying the Essbase Database

The actual deployment is the simplest of all steps. At this point, all you need to do is specify a destination for your database, select a few deployment options (if desired), and let the process run.

For the deployment target, you can specify an existing Essbase server that you previously defined in Essbase Studio, or you can define a new Essbase server directly from the Cube Deployment Wizard. For this demonstration, we will define the Essbase server during deployment to preserve a logical flow through the chapter. Alternatively, you can define a deployment target using the data source window when you map data sources. There is no advantage or disadvantage to defining the Essbase server at deployment or earlier in the process.

The deployment options allow you to specify how you want Essbase Studio to treat the build process. You can choose to deploy only the outline (metadata only), load data to an existing outline, or both. If you are updating an existing database, you can tell Essbase Studio to remove all members and rebuild, or tell it to build a dimension incrementally and update the numeric data accordingly. Many other deployment options are available. The intention of this demonstration is to provide a framework for the overall process. For specific information on the deployment options, see the *Oracle Essbase Studio User's Guide*.

Deploying the Database to an Essbase Server

Follow these steps to deploy the sample Essbase database:

1. With the TCB1 model open (if necessary, expand Cube Schemas in the Metadata Navigator and select the model), right-click TCB1Model and select Cube Deployment Wizard.

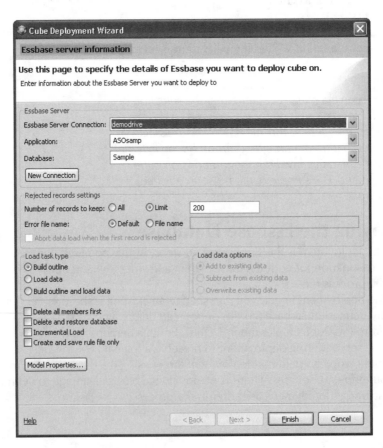

2. Click New Connection.

3. Define a new Essbase deployment target by completing the fields in the Essbase Login dialog box as follows, and then click Login.

Name	The name you want to display in the interface (for this example, specify **Demo)**
Description	An optional parameter allowing you to provide a description about the Essbase target (for this example, you can leave this field blank)
Server	Hostname or IP address of your Essbase server
Port	Port on which Essbase is listening (1423 is the default port; you should not change it unless you have been told specifically that the default Essbase port was not used)
User	User name that you specify when connecting to Essbase
Password	Password that you specify when connecting to Essbase

The following image is for illustrative purposes only; do not copy these values.

NOTE
The login information you supply in the Essbase Login dialog box needs to reflect your implementation of Essbase. If you do not know this information, contact the person responsible for the Essbase server in your organization.

4. Select the new connection from the Essbase Server Connection drop-down list. In this case, select **Demo**.

5. Specify names for the application and database. For this example, name both of them **TBC1**.

TIP
Although the Application and Database fields are drop-down lists, you can also type the name of a new application and database into the fields.

6. Under Load Task Type, select Build Outline and Load Data.

```
Cube Deployment Wizard                                             [X]

Essbase server information

Use this page to specify the details of Essbase you want to deploy cube on.
Enter information about the Essbase Server you want to deploy to

┌─ Essbase Server ──────────────────────────────────────────────────┐
│ Essbase Server Connection: │Demo                              │▼│ │
│                                                                    │
│ Application:               │TBC1                              │▼│ │
│                                                                    │
│ Database:                  │TBC1                              │▼│ │
│ │New Connection│                                                   │
└────────────────────────────────────────────────────────────────────┘
┌─ Rejected records settings ───────────────────────────────────────┐
│ Number of records to keep:  ⊙ All    ○ Limit    │200          │   │
│ Error file name:            ⊙ Default  ○ File name │           │   │
│ □ Abort data load when the first record is rejected                │
└────────────────────────────────────────────────────────────────────┘
┌─ Load task type ──────────┐  ┌─ Load data options ─────────────┐
│ ○ Build outline           │  │ ⊙ Add to existing data          │
│ ○ Load data               │  │ ○ Subtract from existing data   │
│ ⊙ Build outline and load data│ ○ Overwrite existing data       │
└───────────────────────────┘  └─────────────────────────────────┘
  □ Delete all members first
  □ Delete and restore database
  □ Incremental Load
  □ Create and save rule file only

  │Model Properties...│


Help                    │ < Back │ │ Next > │ │ Finish │ │ Cancel │
```

7. Click Finish. Essbase Studio initiates the deployment of the database.

Taking a Look at the Load Rules

As mentioned earlier in this chapter, Essbase Studio is a graphical load rule generator. You can use the Administration Services console to look at the TBC1 database we just deployed and see the load rules that were created by Essbase Studio. Figure 5-3 shows the Administration Services console with the rules files displayed in the left navigation panel. The TBC1 rules file is open in the Data Prep Editor.

In the Data Prep Editor, the upper half of the window shows the original data source. The lower half shows the load rule that was created based on the data source and the selections made while building the database. The rows represent records, and the columns are the dimensions. There is a single metric per record, which is located in the last column, entitled *Data*.

You can use these load rules to automate your processes, as discussed in the "Automating Processes" section later in this chapter. You can also create custom load rules, as explained in the "Creating Custom Load Rules" section later in this chapter.

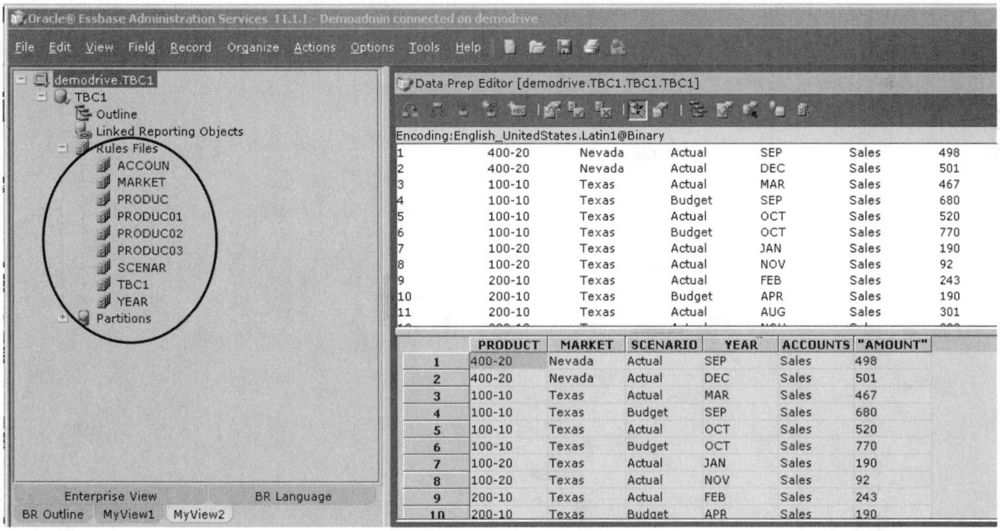

FIGURE 5-3. *Autogenerated rules files for the database*

Summary of the Database Building Process

At this point, we have successfully deployed an Essbase database from scratch. Before we move forward, let's review the steps that we have covered so far and look at how they map to our overall architecture.

Recall the first four steps:

1. Map the data source.

2. Model the data source.

3. Build dimensions (hierarchies).

4. Model the Essbase database

Figure 5-4 shows the components used in the process. We used the Essbase Studio console to complete all the steps. First, we mapped the data source, which connected the Essbase Studio server to the data source. We then modeled the data source so that load rules could be created, and we created the hierarchies that represent our dimensions. Finally, we modeled the Essbase database and pushed information about our dimensions and the Essbase database structure into the metadata repository.

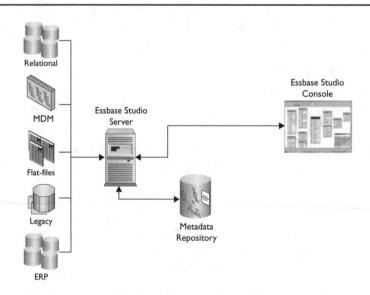

FIGURE 5-4. *Components used in the first four steps of the demonstration*

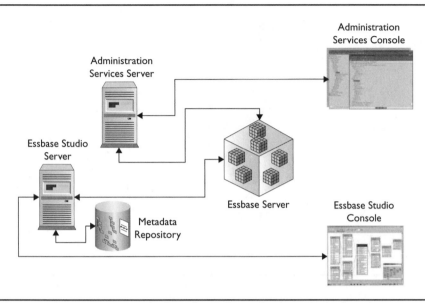

FIGURE 5-5. *Components used when the Essbase database is deployed*

In the fifth step, the Essbase server enters the picture. As shown in Figure 5-5, when the Essbase database is deployed to the Essbase server, a physical database is created on that server.

Figure 5-5 also includes the Administration Services server and console. After deployment, we used the Administration Services console to view a generated load rule.

NOTE
So far, we have worked completely in the user interfaces. This is not, however, how deployments operate after the prototype stage. Essentially, you would use the Essbase Studio console for modeling, but leverage the standard Essbase automation capabilities to deploy a production-level database. For more information, see the "Automating Processes" section later in this chapter.

The next steps are to calculate the Essbase database and then validate the data.

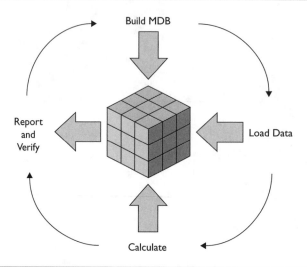

FIGURE 5-6. *A database needs to be calculated to be usable.*

Calculating the Essbase Database

You now have a database with data loaded. However, as illustrated in Figure 5-6, your database is generally not usable until you run a calculation process.

It is important to understand why calculation is required. To make this clear, let's take a look at the simple hierarchy shown in Figure 5-7. If you load the sales value 10 into all of the bottom level (leaf node) markets, then a generated report might look like the report in Figure 5-8.

If the values at East and Market are not dynamically calculated (derived at request time), then there is no total at East or Market. To get a value to appear at that level, you need to execute a calculation to tell Essbase to, at the very least, read the outline and do what the consolidation operators tell it to do. From Figure 5-7, you see that this is simple addition. The value for East is the sum of the values for the individual states—that is, 50. This total is then added to the totals for the other regions (not pictured) and rolled up to produce a Market total.

FIGURE 5-7. *A simple hierarchy*

	A	B	C
1		Sales	
2	New York	10	
3	Massachusetts	10	
4	Florida	10	
5	Connecticut	10	
6	New Hampshire	10	
7	East	–	
8	Market	–	
9			

FIGURE 5-8. *Report showing the output of the simple hierarchy and its data*

To accommodate simply moving data through the model, every database comes with a prebuilt calculation, called the *default calculation*, which reads the outline and does exactly what the consolidation operators say to do. Aggregate Storage databases calculate all upper level intersections dynamically at query time. As such, there is no need to run a calculation to see data at a given intersection. Performance is greatly improved by running at least the default aggregation set. Running the default aggregation set after a build is the recommended process. For block storage databases, you need to run the default calculation yourself, as follows:

1. In the Administration Services console, expand Essbase Servers, then your server, then Applications, then Sample.

2. Right-click the database node and select Execute Calculation.

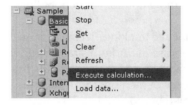

3. In the Execute Calculation dialog box, select Default calculation, and then click OK.

Sometimes you need to do something more complex than just aggregate the model. You might want to clear data in a certain portion of the database, and aggregate it in a different fashion. For example, you may need to recalculate a portion of the model when comparing exchange rates between actual and forecast scenarios. To handle situations like this, you can create member formulas and custom calculation scripts. Both of these topics are discussed in the "Creating Member Formulas and Calculation Scripts" section later in this chapter.

Note that when we built the dimensions for the database, we linked a formula that is defined in the metadata repository to the PARENT and CHILD members of the Product hierarchy. When the database is calculated, these formulas are also processed.

Validating the Essbase Database

The model is built, the data loaded, and a calculation is run. The next step is to validate the data and metadata in the database by running a series of reports on the Essbase database and comparing the results to the original data and reports. Be sure to share the results with your business users and investigate any analytic challenges. You should expect to need to tweak dimensions, members, hierarchies, attributes, and formulas based on their feedback. This will drive the greatest flexibility for future use.

You can create reports for Essbase in many ways, including with Oracle Hyperion Smart View, Oracle Essbase Spreadsheet Add-in, Oracle Business Intelligence Answers, Oracle Hyperion Financial Reporting, Oracle BI Publisher, plus a variety of third-party reporting tools. Most of these tools make use of the built-in Essbase reporting languages to query the Essbase database. If you want, you can use the built-in reporting languages directly to create your reports. For more information, see the "Using Essbase Query Languages for Reports" section later in this chapter.

Using Essbase Features

The preceding demonstration covered the basic workflow for building, deploying, calculating, and validating an Essbase database. In this section, we will address some optional features and more complex functionality available with Essbase.

We start by introducing two powerful features available with Essbase Studio: drill-through reports and lineage tracking. Then we move from Essbase Studio to Administration Services. We use the Administration Services console to take a closer look at the anatomy of a load rule and show you how to create custom load rules. We then return to the concept of member formulas, introducing the scripting languages and creating a member formula and a calculation script. We wrap up the section with a look at how to use the built-in reporting languages available with Essbase.

Many of the examples in this section use the Sample Basic database, which contains the same data as the TBC1 database used in this chapter's demonstration.

Creating Drill-Through Reports

Drill-through reports provide one way to implement an HOLAP architecture, where summary data is stored in the Essbase database, but detailed data remains in the relational source. The ability to create a drill-through report is a distinct advantage Essbase Studio has over the traditional load rule approach.

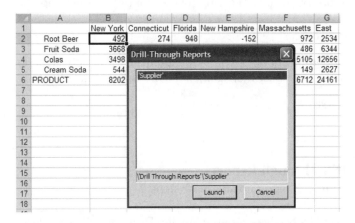

FIGURE 5-9. *Smart View finds a drill-through report for Supplier detail.*

Understanding How Drill-Through Works

Drill-through is the ability to navigate from your intersection in an Essbase reporting environment to data found in another source. Essbase Studio passes your current context to the other data source. For example, Figure 5-9 shows a typical spreadsheet report for the TBC1 database. When you drill into the cell at the intersection of New York and Root Beer, Oracle Hyperion Smart View checks for the existence of a drill-through report for this data cell and finds one for Supplier detail.

When the report is launched, the context of the data cell—that is, New York and Root Beer—is passed into a SQL statement. The resulting report, shown in Figure 5-10, lists only the suppliers of Root Beer to New York

	A	B	C	D	E	F	G	H
1	SUPPLIER ALIAS	ADDRESS	City	Country				
2	Cool Canadian	1250 Boul Rene Levesque	Montreal	Canada				
3	East Coast Bever:	900 Long Ridge Road	Stamford	United States				
4								
5								
6								
7								
8								
9								
10								
11								
12								
13								
14								
15								
16								
17								

Sheet1 / Sheet2 / Sheet3 / **Sheet4** / Sheet5

FIGURE 5-10. *The Supplier report lists the suppliers of Root Beer in New York.*

Essbase Studio supports the following sources for drill-through reports:

■ Relational sources

■ URL, standard (manual) or within the template for Oracle Hyperion Financial Data Quality Management (FDM) or for Oracle BI EE

■ Custom SQL

■ Java method

Creating a Drill-Through Report

To create a drill-through report, follow these steps:

1. In the Metadata Navigator, right-click the Drill Through Reports folder (under SalesAnalysis) and select New | Drill-through Report.

2. Specify a name for the report. For this example, enter **Supplier**.

3. In the Intersections area, click Add.

4. Expand SalesAnalysis and Hierarchies.

5. Select Product, and then click OK.

6. Change the intersection level to be only Family.

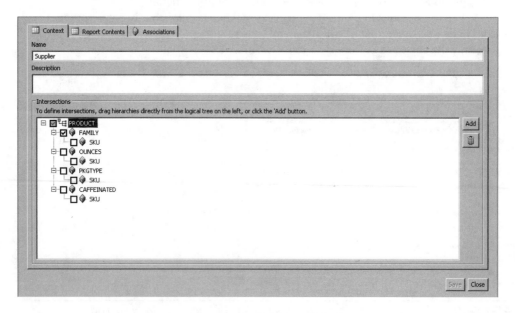

7. Select the Report Contents tab.

8. Add the following columns to the reports (you can drag and drop from either the Data Sources area or the Metadata Navigator): Supplier Alias, Address, City, State, and Zip.

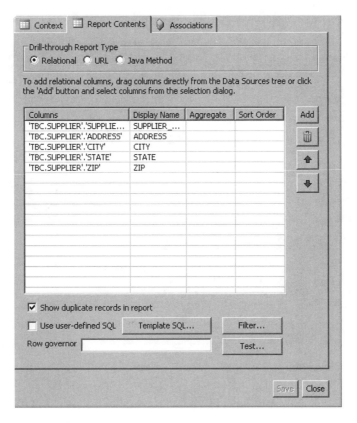

9. Select the Associations tab.

10. Select SalesAnalysisModel, and then click Save.

11. Select the Report Contents tab.

12. Deselect Show Duplicates in Report, and then click Test.

13. For Family, enter a value of **200**. Press ENTER and click Show Result. Ensure that the result looks similar to the following report.

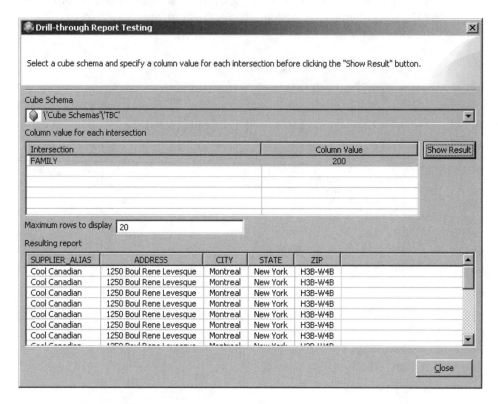

14. Click Close twice.

The report is now available; no further deployment steps are required.

Leveraging Lineage Tracking

The ability to track lineage on an Essbase database and the individual dimensions that make up that database is another advantage of using Essbase Studio. A constant issue with analytical systems is adapting to change. By the time, the data is cleansed and ultimately moved to an analytical database, the needs on the data change. For example, the economic conditions vary, competitive changes alter the business model, or new data sources are identified. In many cases, this results in changes to the analytical structure or the sources upon which it is built. You need to consider what impact a change in structure or source has on your analytical environment. Additionally, after the data models are deployed, you will want to be able to track data from the source to target and back.

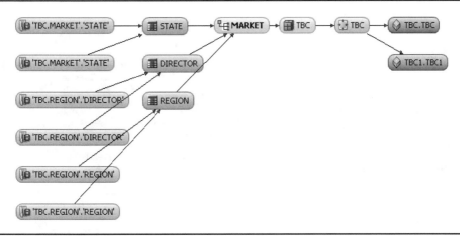

FIGURE 5-11. *Lineage chart for the Market hierarchy*

To help solve both of these problems, Essbase Studio provides lineage tracking. Through either the context menu or standard menu selection, you can request lineage diagrams for any metadata element (up to and including deployed models). Figure 5-11 shows a lineage chart for the Market hierarchy. As you can see, the chart displays information back to the original source columns or fields. It also shows the Essbase databases in which the Market dimension is used; in this case, it is used in two Essbase databases TBC and TBC1. Moreover, you also have the ability to review individual object properties from the lineage chart. For example, you can right-click the Market hierarchy object and see specific storage properties.

Creating Custom Load Rules

While Essbase Studio automatically generates rules, you may find yourself in a situation where you want to do a highly custom build or load process on a database. In this case, it may be necessary to use the Data Prep Editor in the Administration Services console to create a load rule directly. Figure 5-12 shows the Administration Services architecture with the Data Prep Editor noted.

A load rule is a mapping object that tells the Essbase server how to read a data source (flat file or relationally based). Load rules have two functions: dimension build and data load. A single rule can perform both functions if required. Let's look at both types, and then create a dimension build rule from scratch.

Dimension Build Rules

The goal of a dimension build rule is to add dimensionality to a database or to alter existing dimensionality. For example, you can use a build rule to update the corporate reporting structure in the database or to add additional SKUs to a product

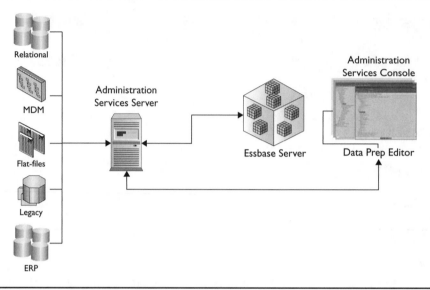

FIGURE 5-12. *Administration Services architecture*

dimension. You can have a build rule reorder or incrementally build portions of your database. In addition, a build rule can do something as simple as change an alias on a member.

Figure 5-13 shows a flat file, displayed in Notepad, which we will use as a data source on which to create a dimension build rule. The file, from left to right, presents a hierarchy. In Chapter 2, we introduced the concepts of generations and

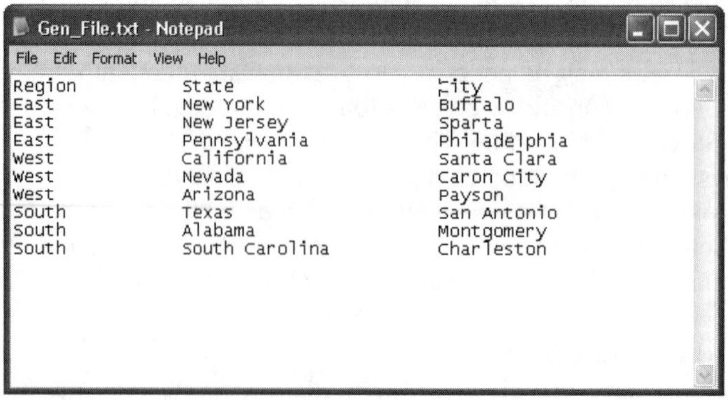

```
 Gen_File.txt - Notepad
File  Edit  Format  View  Help
Region      State           City
East        New York        Buffalo
East        New Jersey      Sparta
East        Pennsylvania    Philadelphia
West        California      Santa Clara
West        Nevada          Caron City
West        Arizona         Payson
South       Texas           San Antonio
South       Alabama         Montgomery
South       South Carolina  Charleston
```

FIGURE 5-13. *Creating a dimension build rule starts with a data source.*

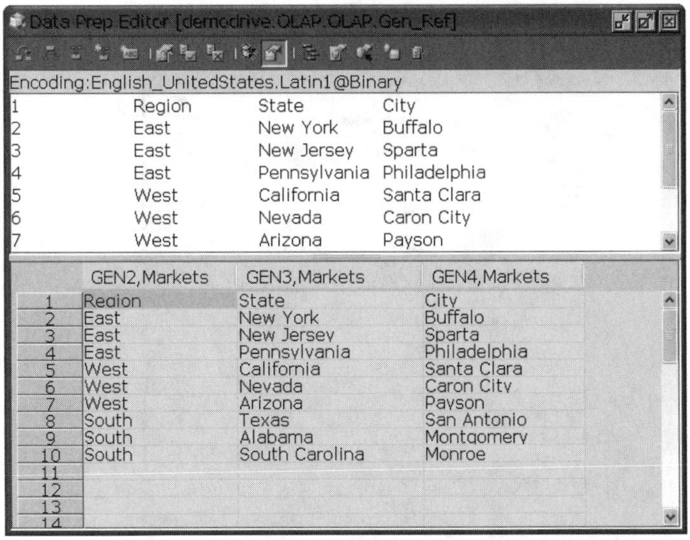

FIGURE 5-14. *A dimension build rule maps column headings to members in a hierarchy.*

levels in Essbase. The contents of this file represent generations in a geographic dimension (for example, Market or Regions).

The rule file (shown with a .RUL extension in the database directory) for this data source might look similar to the rule displayed in Figure 5-14.

The Data Prep Editor has two view areas. On the top is the source file in its original state. On the bottom, the load rule shows how Essbase would interpret the data source. For example, the first column should be placed at the second generation of the Markets dimension (GEN2,Markets). The other columns continue to subsequent generations in the hierarchy. In addition, the first line is ignored as a column header and is not built into the model. This is not explicitly shown, but is a simple setting in the rule.

The settings are exactly the same whether you are working with a flat file or querying the metadata directly from a relational source. Essentially, columns in a table are not treated any differently from columns in a file.

Figure 5-15 shows the resulting database outline after this rule is run. Essbase parses the data file and reads it as instructed by the load rule.

This is a very simple example. A dimension build rule can handle much more complex build cases. It can be used to add, ignore, reorder, concatenate, split, or truncate columns. You can also perform string replacements, record selection/rejection,

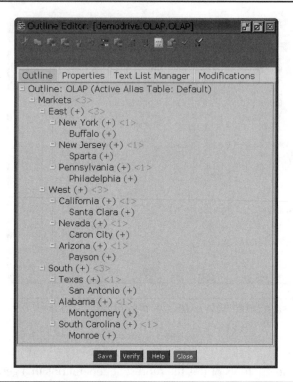

FIGURE 5-15.   *When run, the database outline is updated to include the hierarchies.*

and conversions where required. Furthermore, the rules file does not need to be structured from the top down using generations; you can easily create rules to handle building from the bottom up (levels) through recursive (parent-child) relationships.

Data Rules

You can have load rules that load numeric or textual data into the model. As is the case with dimension build rules, data rules are simply instructions to the Essbase server on how to process the file.

For example, the data source, shown in Figure 5-16, contains columns for each of five dimensions—Market, Product, Scenario, Time, and Measure—plus a Data column. All dimensions are represented for each record (row), and the single numeric fact is listed at the end of each record.

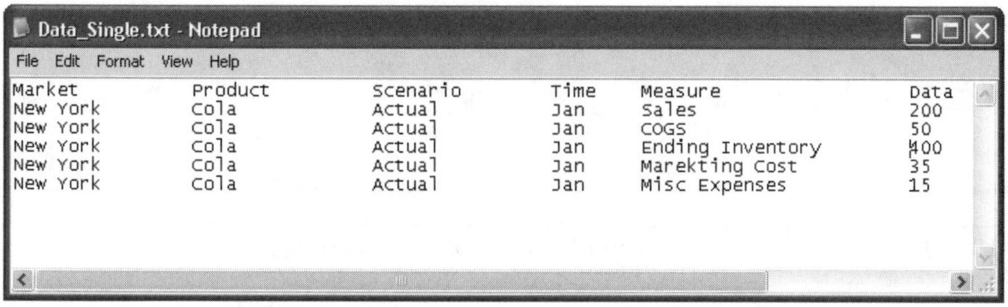

FIGURE 5-16. *Flat file with five column headers that map to dimensions*

Figure 5-17 shows a sample rules file for this source. The data-load rule simply tells Essbase which dimension to scan in order to find the matching members. For instance, Essbase will look for Jan in the dimension named Year. It is important to note that the last column is specified as the data value. After identifying the specific intersection denoted by the dimension members, Essbase places the value in the Data column into the database at that intersection.

Figure 5-18 illustrates a different data source example. In this case, the Measure members are presented as column headers. The data rule to interpret this data source presentation is shown in Figure 5-19. Notice that this rule handles the Measure dimension differently than in the first example. Each row includes multiple values of the Measures dimension for a single Market-Product-Scenario-Year intersection.

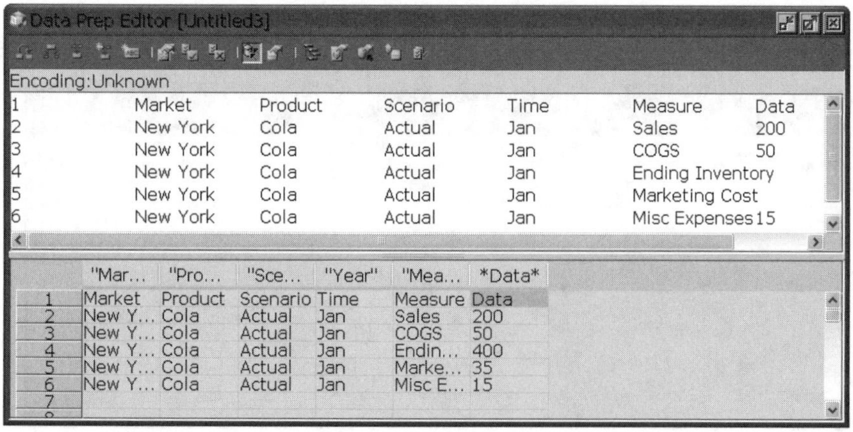

FIGURE 5-17. *Data rule for the preceding data source*

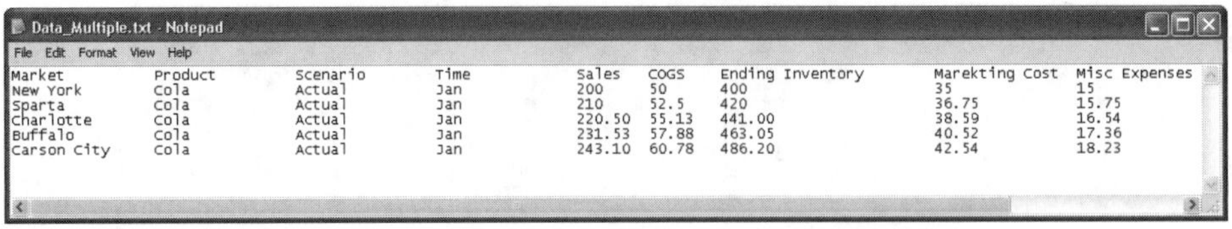

FIGURE 5-18. *Flat file with Measures members as column headings*

Creating a Load Rule Manually

In this section, we build a load rule that uses a flat file as its data source. The flat file accompanies the Sample Basic database example that ships with Essbase. This is the same sample application used in the *Oracle Essbase Database Administrator's Guide*. If you do not have this sample, you can download it from the Oracle Technology Network (OTN) web site.

This procedure provides a general guideline for working with load rules. While it focuses on creating a dimension build rule, the process for creating a data rule is similar. For more information, see the *Oracle Essbase Database Administrator's Guide*.

As was the case with the Essbase Studio example, this procedure is for illustrative purposes only. The specific process to create a custom rule varies based on many factors, including the data source and the type of structure you want to build in the Essbase database.

Finally, it is worth repeating that Essbase Studio eliminates the necessity (in most cases) to create load rules manually, as it generates the load rules based on the actions you take in the Essbase Studio console.

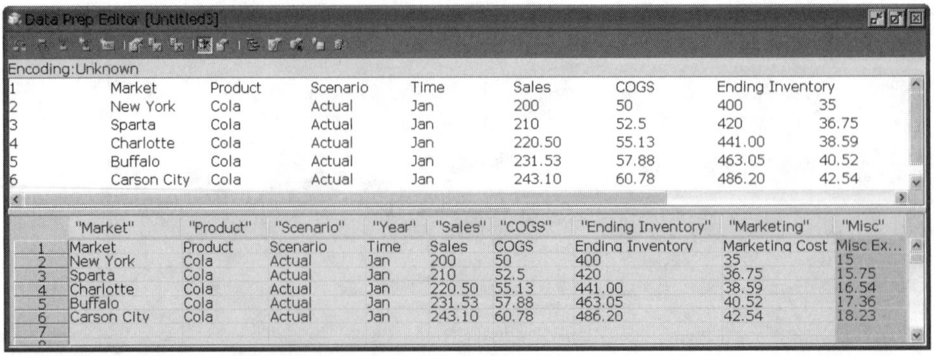

FIGURE 5-19. *Data rule for the second data source*

Selecting the Data Source for a Load Rule   Follow these steps to start Administration Services and select the data source for the load rule:

1. To start the Administration Services server, select Start | Programs | Oracle EPM System | Essbase | Administration Services | Start Administration Services (Embedded Java Container). If you have the Administration Services server installed as a service in your environment, you can start the service by issuing the specific operating system command or by using the specific operating system user interface. For example, in Windows, open the Services Management console and start the Hyperion Administration Services service.

2. To start the Administration Services console, select Start | Programs | Oracle EPM System | Essbase | Administration Services | Start Administration Services Console.

3. In the Metadata Navigator, expand Essbase Servers, then Applications, then Sample, then Basic.

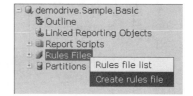

4. Under demodrive.Sample.Basic, right-click Rules File and select Create Rules File.

5. The Data Prep Editor appears in the work area of the Administration Services console. Select File | Open Data File. The Open dialog box displays a series of files stored directly on the Essbase Server.

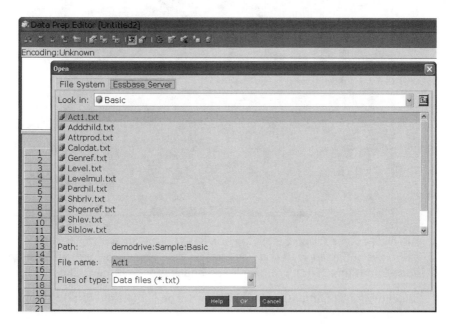

TIP
You can browse to a file located elsewhere by selecting the File System tab of the Open dialog box.

6. Select Genref.txt and click OK. Genref.txt is a metadata file. There are no numeric data values like those for sales or cost. We will use it to build an outline.

7. To specify that you are building the outline (not loading data), select View Dimension Build Fields from the toolbar or the View menu.

Specifying File-Based Settings for the Rule Now, you need to specify any file-based settings, such as file headers that you want to skip during the build process. Follow these steps:

1. Select Options | Data Source Properties. The Data Source Properties dialog box appears.

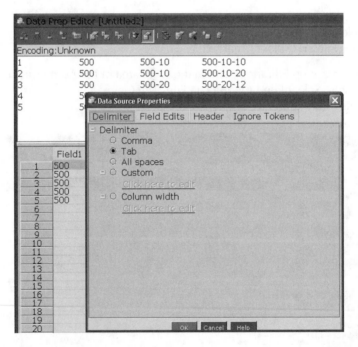

2. The Data Source Properties dialog box lets you specify things like file delimiters and headers, If you need to specify any settings for the data source, do so at this time. For this example, no changes are required. Click Cancel.

3. Select Options | Dimension Build Settings. The Dimension Build Settings dialog box appears.

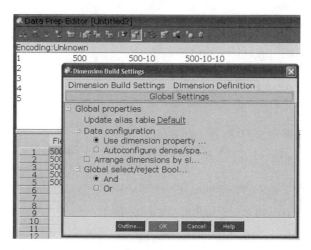

4. Select the Dimension Build Settings tab. We will add the members in the sample file to the Product dimension.

5. In the Dimension area, double-click Product.

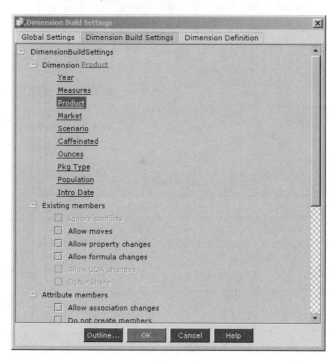

6. In the Build Method area, ensure that Use Generation References is selected, and then click OK.

This denotes that this file will build the dimension from the top to the bottom. In this case, the member 500 will be placed toward the top of the outline and subsequent members organized underneath.

Specifying Field Properties for the Rule   The next task is to specify field properties, as follows:

1. Select field1 in the Data Prep Editor.

2. Select Field | Properties.

3. In the Field Properties dialog box, select the Dimension Build Properties tab.

4. In the Dimension area, double-click Product.

5. In the Field area, double-click Generation.

6. In the Number area, enter **2**. This specifies that the member 500 will be placed directly below the Product dimension name as a product line.

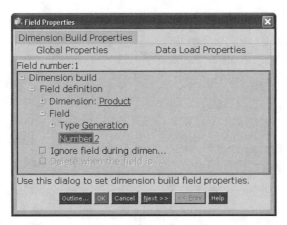

7. Click Next to move the focus to the next field of the source file.

8. Repeat the process using the following values for the fields:

Field Number	Dimension	Field Type	Field Number
2	Product	Generation	3
3	Product	Generation	4

9. When you are finished, click OK.

In the Data Prep Editor, the column headings represent the fields. The headings contain an abbreviation of the Field Type and Field Number (for example, GEN2), followed by the Dimension name (in this case, Product). The values in the table match the values for each of the fields in the original source file.

Data Prep Editor [Untitled2]			

Encoding: Unknown

1	500	500-10	500-10-10
2	500	500-10	500-10-20
3	500	500-20	500-20-12
4	500	500-20	500-20-15
5	500	500-20	500-20-20

	GEN2, Product	GEN3, Product	GEN4, Product
1	500	500-10	500-10-10
2	500	500-10	500-10-20
3	500	500-20	500-20-12
4	500	500-20	500-20-15
5	500	500-20	500-20-20
6			

NOTE
If the field labels are not showing, ensure that the Dimension Build Fields option is selected (via the toolbar button or the View menu).

Validating and Saving the Load Rule   Follow these steps to validate and save your new load rule:

1. Select Options I Validate. A message tells you whether the rule is valid. Click OK to close the message box.

2. If the rule was not valid, edit the rule and rerun the validation process.

3. To save the load rule, select File I Save. Specify a name for the new load rule.

4. Close the rule.

Executing the Load Rule   You can execute the load rule against the database in a couple ways. If you use the Update Outline option (as specified in the following steps), you can test the impact on the database before saving it (this option is available only on block storage databases).

1. Open the Sample Basic outline.

2. Select Outline I Update Outline.

3. Click Find Data File. Browse to and select the original data file, and then click OK.

4. Click Find Rules File. Browse to and select the rule you just created, and then click OK.

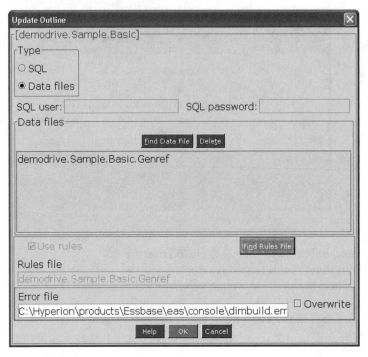

5. Click OK. The load rule should complete with a message stating that the file loaded with no errors. Click Close to dismiss this message.

6. Expand the Product dimension in the outline. The additional chain starting with the member 500 should be visible.

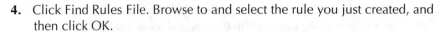

7. If you want to keep the updates, click Save, and then close the outline.

Note that while this rule simply added a chain to an existing dimension, a rule could have been built to create a new dimension in the model.

Load Rules and the SQL Interface

Up to this point, our discussion of custom load rules has concentrated on using flat files for the data source. Quite often, however, load rules are written to source a relational database. The Data Prep Editor provides an interface that lets you connect directly to a relational source. You can create dimensions and load data based on a SQL connection instead of relying on a flat file.

The steps for the creating a rules file from a SQL source are basically the same as those used when creating a standard load rule, after you select the SQL data source. Instead of selecting File | Open Data File, you select File | Open SQL. As shown in Figure 5-20, you then choose the appropriate database source (in this example, the TBC database) from the SQL Data Sources drop-down list.

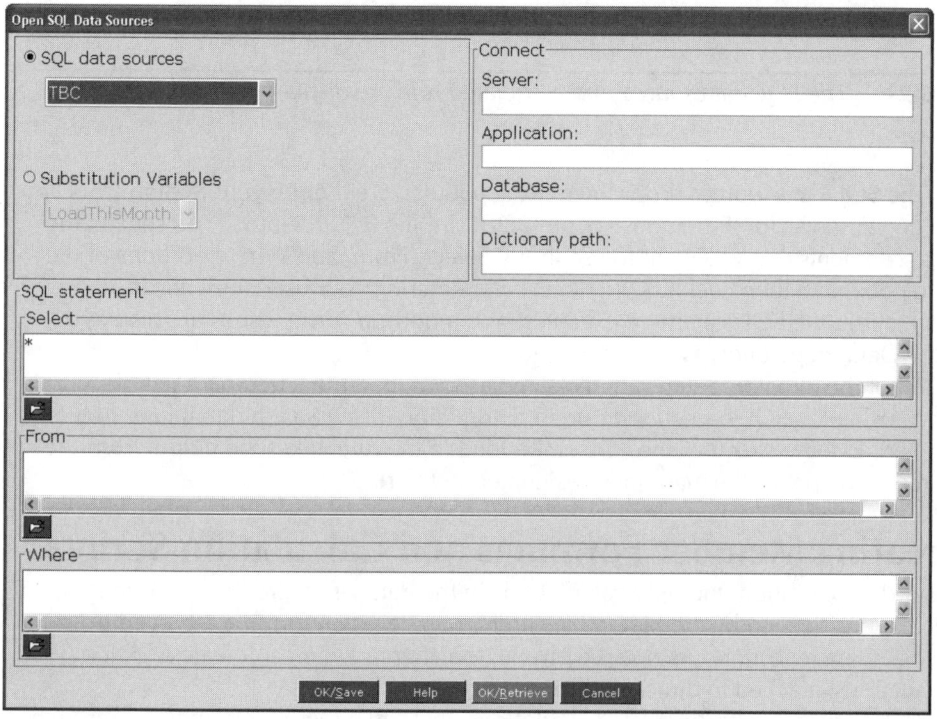

FIGURE 5-20.   *You map a relational source using the Open SQL Data Sources dialog box.*

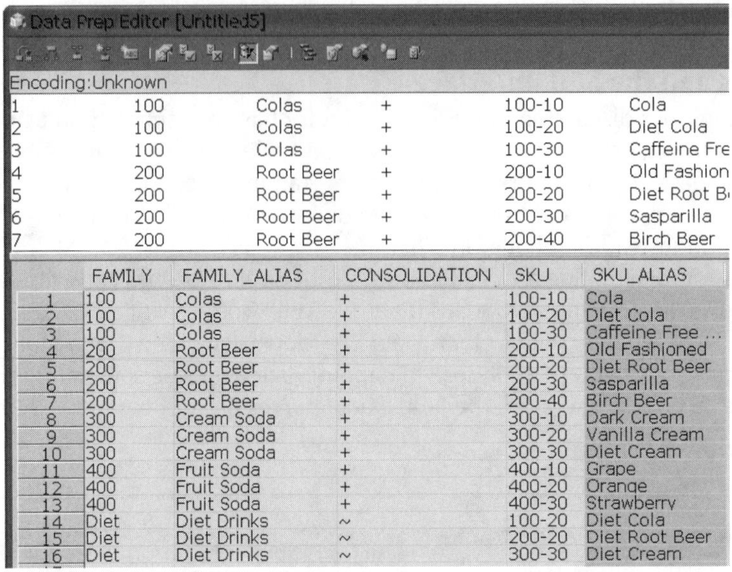

	FAMILY	FAMILY_ALIAS	CONSOLIDATION	SKU	SKU_ALIAS
1	100	Colas	+	100-10	Cola
2	100	Colas	+	100-20	Diet Cola
3	100	Colas	+	100-30	Caffeine Free ...
4	200	Root Beer	+	200-10	Old Fashioned
5	200	Root Beer	+	200-20	Diet Root Beer
6	200	Root Beer	+	200-30	Sasparilla
7	200	Root Beer	+	200-40	Birch Beer
8	300	Cream Soda	+	300-10	Dark Cream
9	300	Cream Soda	+	300-20	Vanilla Cream
10	300	Cream Soda	+	300-30	Diet Cream
11	400	Fruit Soda	+	400-10	Grape
12	400	Fruit Soda	+	400-20	Orange
13	400	Fruit Soda	+	400-30	Strawberry
14	Diet	Diet Drinks	~	100-20	Diet Cola
15	Diet	Diet Drinks	~	200-20	Diet Root Beer
16	Diet	Diet Drinks	~	300-30	Diet Cream

FIGURE 5-21. *The SQL data source and associated rule are displayed in the Data Prep Editor.*

The SQL data sources drop-down list is populated either by your System DSN list (on Windows) or through use of an ODBC.ini file (UNIX/Linux). You specify the SQL statements that you want to use in the Select, From, and Where portions of the dialog box, and then click OK/Retrieve. After entering your user authentication information, the SQL statement executes, and a portion of the results are displayed in the Data Prep Editor, as shown in Figure 5-21.

All of the remaining steps are the same as for a load file based on a flat file. When using the SQL-based load rule in automation (discussed in detail later in this chapter), Essbase executes the SQL embedded in the rule, takes the output from the source, and applies the mappings designated in the rule.

Creating Member Formulas and Calculation Scripts

In our demonstration, the only calculations in the database were the consolidation calculations defined by the hierarchies and an unidentified formula retrieved from the metadata repository. As noted earlier in the chapter, you can create additional calculations attached to dimension members.

There are two ways to create calculations: through a member formula or through a calculation script. Depending on the nature of what you are doing, you can often accomplish similar tasks with either approach. While there may be slight syntactical differences between commands in member formulas and those in calculation scripts, the general logic and process of creation is similar.

For example, what if 25% of the cost and revenue of Florida is assigned to the East region, while the remainder is assigned to the South. You can easily create a formula with a weighted total to reflect this situation. The formula for the East member might look like this:

```
@SUM ("New York", "Massachusetts", "Connecticut", "New Hampshire") +
    ("Florida"*.25);
```

You would need to create a similar formula for the South member to account for the other 75% of Florida's cost and revenue. In this example, all metrics in the database would be subject to the weighted aggregation. Furthermore, this assignment would apply to all scenarios (Actual, Budget, Forecast, and so forth).

You can expand this formula to include a series of logical tests. The test would validate the intersection and take appropriate actions. For example, you might be considering moving Florida's reporting hierarchy from East to South. You can calculate Actual numbers one way and put a check in to calculate a scenario for reorganization (ReOrg1) in a different way.

```
IF (@ISMBR("Actual"))
    "East"=@SUM ("New York": "New Hampshire");
ElseIf (@ISMBR("ReOrg1"))
    "East"=@SUM ("New York", "Massachusetts", "Connecticut",
"New Hampshire") +
    ("Florida"*.25);
ENDIF
```

Another common type of calculation (and one used in the following examples) is the creation of variances inside Essbase. For example, if you wanted to create a variance to compare quarter over quarter changes, the formula might look like this:

```
"Q1 vs Q2"=@VAR("Qtr1","Qtr2");
```

If you wanted a percentage difference, you could use the @VARPER function instead. (The @VAR and @VARPER functions reverse the variance reporting for items flagged as Expense within the Accounts dimension.)

In the preceding example, the formula would always do a variance between Qtr1 and Qtr2, only. For more flexibility, you could make the formula reusable. For instance, you could build a formula that takes the current quarter and does a variance comparison to the previous quarter. The process for designing reusable calculations is covered in Chapter 8.

Calc Scripting Language Versus MDX

Chapter 3 described the two database storage methodologies within Essbase: block storage (BSO) and aggregate storage (ASO). Depending on the storage method you choose for a specific database, the language you use to write a member formula is either the native Essbase Calc Scripting Language for block storage databases or the Multidimensional Expressions (MDX) language for aggregate storage databases. The following sections provide a general overview of the language specifications. For detailed information, see the *Oracle Essbase Technical Reference*.

Block Storage Databases and the Essbase Calc Scripting Language   Block storage database formulas use the Calc Scripting Language. This language is a series of functions and commands that lets you select and calculate members of your Essbase database. The Calc Scripting Language is divided into two categories: Commands and Functions.

Commands provide broad capabilities across a database (as opposed to deriving a value for or working with a specific member). For example, you can use the `DATACOPY` command to copy a slice of data from one portion of the database to another (such as copying last year's actual values to seed this year's budget).

Functions work on individual members, either by selecting a member for calculation or by deriving a value for a member. For example, the `@SUM` function adds the specified members together. Functions are divided into a series of subcategories. Here is an overview of some of the key areas:

- **Boolean**   These functions are used to perform logical tests on values. For example, they can be used to check if the active member matches a given string, as in `@ISMBR("Actual");`.

- **Relationship**   These functions retrieve a value from a member in the database based on its relationship to another member. For example, you could request the total sales value for the East market by specifying one of its children, using `@PARENTVAL ("New York", "Sales");`. This would return the total Sales value for East (the parent of New York).

- **Mathematical**   These functions perform arithmetic and mathematical operations on a member or set of members. For example, you can add a range of values, as in `@SUM("Jan":"Mar");`.

- **Member Set**   These functions specify a set of members on which to perform actions. For example, to get all of the months in Qtr1 to do an average, you can use `@CHILDREN("Qtr1");`.

There are also Statistical, Forecasting, Allocations, and a whole host of other categories from which you can choose functions. In total, there are hundreds of prebuilt functions in the Essbase engine.

You should be aware of a few Calc Scripting Language syntax rules:

■ Functions must end in a semicolon (;).

■ Any member name containing a space, number, or special character (*, &, $, and so forth) must be enclosed in double quotes.

■ Functions start with the @ symbol; commands do not.

For a complete list of functions, commands, and syntax requirements, see the *Oracle Essbase Technical Reference*, which is part of the Oracle Essbase documentation set.

Aggregate Storage Databases and MDX When creating formulas for an aggregate storage database, you use MDX. MDX is a standardized query and calculation language for multidimensional databases such as Essbase, Microsoft Analysis Services, and SAP BW. When the aggregate storage option was added to Essbase, MDX was chosen over the Calc Scripting Language in order to embrace the industry-standard query methodology.

Although formulas created in MDX can be used only for aggregate storage databases, MDX can be used to *query* any Essbase database—block or aggregate storage. This is because the syntax and functions described in this section are universal, regardless of whether they are used in formulas or queries. For more information, see the "Using Essbase Query Languages for Reports" section later in this chapter.

In general, MDX formulas are very similar to Calc Scripting Language formulas. For example, to perform the same summation we looked at previously, the formula would be `SUM([Jan]:[Mar])`. Aside from a few apparent syntactical differences, the logic and function are the same.

Unlike the Calc Scripting Language, MDX is not divided into functions and commands. MDX contains a series of functions to perform similar grouping and mathematical operations. MDX functions are organized by action:

■ **Member return** These functions return a member. For example, to see the parent of a Jan, you use the `Parent` function (returns the member Qtr1): `[Jan].parent` or `Parent([Jan])`.

■ **Set return** These functions return a set of members. For example, to see the children of Qtr1, you can use the `Children` function (returns Jan, Feb, and Mar): `[Qtr1].children` or `Children([Qtr1])`.

■ **Number return** These functions are mathematical, such as Average. For example, you can get the average sales for Qtr1 using the `Avg` function: `Avg([Qtr1].children, [Sales])`.

There are many additional functions in the MDX specification. For a complete list of functions, including examples, see the *Oracle Essbase Technical Reference* in the Oracle Essbase documentation set.

Some syntactical rules for MDX include the following:

■ Any member name containing a space, number, or special character (*, &, $, etc) must be enclosed in hard brackets [ ].

■ You can often call a function as a property of a given member by using a dot (.) notation. For example, [Qtr1].children is the same as Children([Qtr1].

Now let's take a look at how to create a member formula and a calculation script. The following examples are based on the Sample Basic database. Because this database is a block storage database, we use the Calc Scripting Language syntax.

Creating a Member Formula

The sample member formula calculates the variance between Quarter 1 and Quarter 2. Follow these steps to create this member formula:

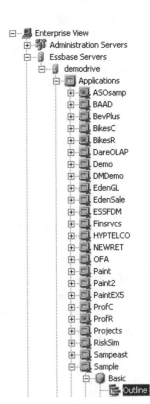

1. In the Administration Services console, expand Essbase Servers, then your server, then Applications, then Sample, then Basic.

2. Double-click the Outline node to open the Sample Basic outline.

3. Expand the Year dimension.

4. Right-click Qtr4 and select Add Sibling.

5. In the dialog box, type **Time Variances**. Press the ENTER key to accept the name, and then press the ESC key to leave member-entry mode.

6. Right-click Time Variances and select Add Children.

7. In the dialog box, type **Q1 vs Q2**. Press the ENTER key to accept the name, and then press the ESC key to leave member-entry mode.

8. Press and hold the CTRL key and select both Time Variances and Q1 vs Q2.

9. Click the ~ icon on the toolbar to ensure these do not consolidate on a calculation process.

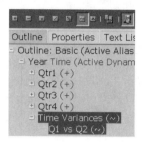

10. Right-click Q1 vs Q2 and select Edit Properties.

11. In the Member Properties dialog box, select the Formula tab. The Member Formula Editor is divided into three areas: outline viewer, function selector, and text editor.

12. In the text editor, type the formula: **@VAR("Qtr1", "Qtr2");**

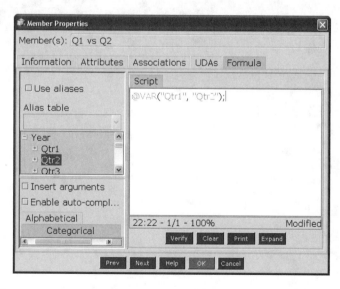

13. Click OK.

14. In the outline editor, click Save.

15. If you are prompted to restructure the model, ensure All Data is selected, and then click OK.

Creating a Calculation Script

The sample calculation script clears data on the Budget scenario, copies Actual into Budget, increments the copied values by 5%, focuses the process on the Budget scenario, and then aggregates the new values across the other dimensions. Follow these steps to create this calculation script:

1. In the Administration Services console, right-click the Sample Basic database and select Create | Calculation Script. You will see that the Calculation Script Editor (like the Member Formula Editor) is divided into three areas: outline viewer, function selector, and text editor.

2. In the function selector, select the Alphabetical tab.

3. Expand the tree and double-click FIX. This inserts the FIX command into the script. This command is used to focus the script on a specific subsection of the database.

4. In the text editor, type the remainder of the script to match the following image.

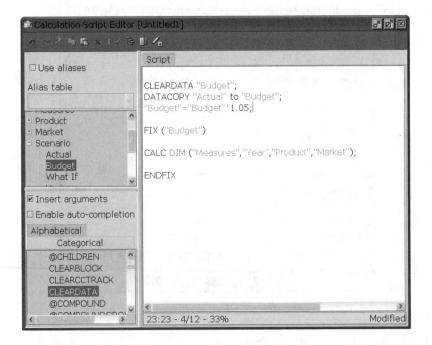

5. On the toolbar, click the Validate button (green checkmark).

6. After validating the script, select File I Save.

7. Name the script, and then click OK.

8. To execute the script, click the Execute button on the toolbar.

Using Essbase Query Languages for Reports

Essbase provides two built-in reporting options: MDX scripts and report scripts. Generally speaking, neither option is normally used in raw format for reporting. Both MDX and report scripts represent language specifications (similar to SQL) to query data and dimensionality from an Essbase database. Both are often used by front-end reporting tools to interface with an Essbase database. Oracle BI EE, for example, generates MDX queries when sourcing data from Essbase. From a batch processing and automation perspective, you might use either MDX or report scripts to export data from an Essbase database or to validate numbers. This section provides a brief overview of each scripting language.

Querying with MDX

Recall that MDX can be used to query either a block storage or an aggregate storage database. MDX is a standardized query calculation language for OLAP sources. It is similar to the relational database SQL language. An MDX query is divided into three key areas:

- **Select**   This specification denotes what information you want on the axes of your reports. What do you want on rows and columns?

- **Data source**   This specification identifies the Essbase database you are using for the query.

- **Where**   This optional specification filters the results. For example, you could request on data values for April.

Here is a simple MDX query to get all of the Profit subaccount details for the specified market regions in the first quarter:

```
SELECT Descendants([Profit]) ON ROWS, Children ([Market]) ON COLUMNS
FROM [Sample.Basic]
WHERE [Qtr1]
```

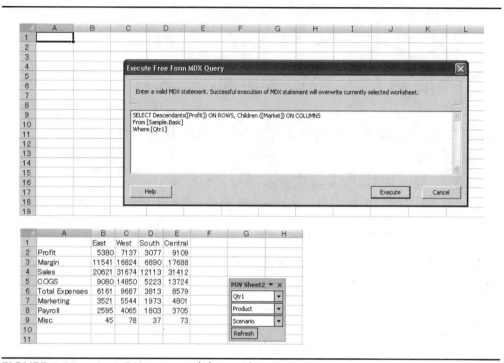

FIGURE 5-22. *An MDX query and the resulting report*

This request can be passed into Smart View via the Execute Free Form MDX Query dialog box. Figure 5-22 shows the formula within this dialog box, followed by the results of the query in Microsoft Excel.

The specific format of the output is determined by the front-end client. MDX does not contain specific formatting functions. Instead, MDX focuses on data and metadata queries.

The Administration Services console also includes an MDX editor and viewer. Follow these steps to create a sample MDX query using the Administrative Services console:

1. In the Administration Services console, select File | Editors | MDX Script Editor.

2. In the text editor, type the following query:

```
SELECT [Year].Children ON ROWS,
[Profit].Children ON COLUMNS
FROM [Sample].[Basic]
WHERE [Actual]
```

3. From the menu bar, select MDX | Execute Script.

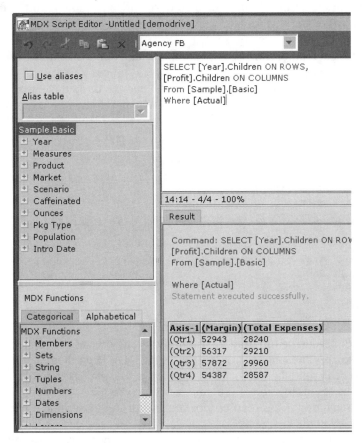

Querying with Report Scripts

Report Script is a legacy Essbase script-based reporting interface. Like MDX, you can use report scripts on either aggregate storage or block storage databases.

The report script language contains functions and is divided into a series of categories:

- **Data layout**   Positioning of a dimension on a report

- **Data range**   Ordering, top, and bottom functions

- **Formatting**   Commands dedicated to specifying overall report formats (such as column width)

The complete report scripts specification is detailed in the *Oracle Essbase Technical Reference*.

A series of report scripts is included with the Sample Basic database. The following is an example of one of these scripts, which retrieves the top ten products for specified markets:

```
<Sym
//Suppress shared members from displaying
<Supshare
     <Column (Scenario, Year)
     Actual Budget
     Jan Dec
<Row (Market, Product)
<Desc Market
//Use bottom level of products
<DimBottom Product
<Top (10, @DataColumn(3))
!
```

Figure 5-23 shows the output of the script.

Report scripts can be run from the Administration Services console or via the Essbase command-line languages (MaxL and ESSCMD). Regardless of the execution medium, you can send the output of a report script to a file or the screen, or you can stream the results to another program. For example, Financial Reporting (an Oracle reporting tool) issues report script commands to Essbase and displays the data in its user interface.

To create a report script using the Administrative Services console, follow these steps:

1. This sample report script, when executed, shows the actual and budget values for January and December (as columns) for all market and product

```
|
                                              Measures

                                 Actual               Budget
                            Jan      Dec         Jan       Dec
                         ======== ========    ======== ========

New York       100-10       273      271         260       250
               200-40       175      312         200       320
               400-10       101       89         120        90
               400-20        94      133         110       150
               300-10       111      309         100       210
               400-30        54       52          70        60
               300-20      (113)    (189)        (70)     (150)
               200-10      (172)    (224)       (170)     (210)
Massachusetts  100-10       367      390         360       360
               200-40       100       87         110        80
               400-10        29       29          40        40
               400-30        29       25          40        30
               300-10        17        7          30        10
               200-10       (23)     (20)        (10)      (10)
Florida        100-10        68       73          70        80
               100-20        67      122          70       110
               200-20        50       58          60        70
               300-20        39       50          40        30
               400-10        28       26          40        30
               400-30        28       30          40        40
               200-10         9       21          30        30
               300-30        34       12          30        20
               300-10        13       23          20        20
```

FIGURE 5-23.   *Report output created by the sample report script*

combinations (on rows). In the Administration Services console, right-click the Sample Basic database node and select Create | Report Script.

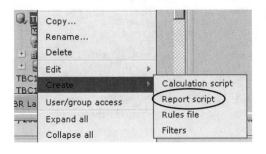

2. In the Report Script text editor, type the following query:

```
<Sym
<Column (Scenario, Year)
Actual Budget
Jan Dec
<Row (Market, Product)
<Ichild Market
<Ichild Product
!
```

3. From the menu bar, select File | Save.

4. In the Save dialog box, name the script, and then click Save.

5. Select Options | Execute Script.

6. When prompted, select Console for output, and then click OK.

Report Viewer [demodrive.Sample.Basic.Sample]

Agency FB

```
                           Measures

                    Actual        Budget
                   Jan   Dec      Jan   Dec
                  ======== ======== ======== ========

East      100      924   1,026    960    990
          200      158    233     280    340
          300      184    277     240    210
          400      466    501     600    580
          Diet     181    213     200    240
          Product 1,732  2,037   2,080  2,120
West      100      378    223     830    530
          200      752    820     850    860
          300      755    971     830    950
          400      454    434     470    370
          Diet     663    629     850    730
          Product 2,339  2,448   2,980  2,710
South     100      329    432     540    640
          200      480    496     520    390
          300      188    213     270    240
          400     #Missing #Missing #Missing #Missing
          Diet     355    404     490    430
          Product  997   1,141   1,330  1,270
Central   100      724    792     900    890
          200      751    753    1,060  1,220
          300      790    824     930    810
          400      691    785     660    650
          Diet    1,080  1,064   1,340  1,300
```

Automating Processes

Up to this point in this chapter, we have done almost everything in the various user interfaces. We modeled the database in the Essbase Studio console. We used the Administration Services console to view and create load rules, to create a drill-through report, and to create member formulas. We even generated a report (via MDX) using Smart View.

From a practical deployment perspective, however, most databases processes are automated. After you create the initial database using Essbase Studio (or custom load rules in the Data Prep Editor), you create automation scripts to use these objects in a larger batch process. This section focuses on the command-line capabilities inherent in Essbase.

The two command-line languages available are ESSCMD and MaxL. ESSCMD is a supported and actively used scripting language for Essbase automations. However, the majority of recent development efforts from both a user and an Oracle product direction perspective—use MaxL. This section provides an overview of using ESSCMD and MaxL. For a complete listing of all MaxL and ESSCMD capabilities, see the *Oracle Essbase Technical Reference*.

Using ESSCMD

ESSCMD is a legacy scripting language that lets you create, use, and modify database objects. It was the first command-line language provided for Essbase. ESSCMD is primarily numeric-based in its command syntax. For example, to execute a load rule using ESSCMD, the syntax is as follows:

```
BUILDDIM 2 "GenRef" 2 "GenRef" 4 "GenRefError";
```

Decoding the syntax, this command does the following:

- `BUILDDIM` executes a dimension build rule.

- `2 "GenRef"` leverages a server-based load rule named GenRef.

- `2 "GenRef"` leverages a server-based data file named GenRef.

- `4` tells Essbase that the source is a text file.

- `"GenRefError"` writes any errors out to an error file named GenRefError.

Using MaxL

MaxL is the newer of the two command-line languages for Essbase. It provides commands for building, calculating, and managing Essbase processes. Unlike ESSCMD, MaxL's command structure is closer to common language. In many respects, it is similar to the Oracle SQL*Plus command-line language.

To perform the preceding data load example using MaxL, the command is as follows:

```
import database sample.basic dimensions from server text data_file
'GenRef.txt'
using server rules_file 'GenRef.rul' on error append to
'GenRefError.txt';
```

As you can see, MaxL syntax is easier to interpret than the ESSCMD commands. The following are some key syntactical requirements of MaxL:

- MaxL statements end in a semicolon (;).

- Paths with spaces and special characters require single quotes (').

- To insert comments into a script, open the comment block with /* and close it with */. Anything within these markers is ignored when the script is executed.

With MaxL, you can automate other tasks beyond building a database, such as the following:

- Logging out users and disabling connections during batch processes (if desired)

- Exporting data and objects for backup

- Encrypting user names and passwords

- Creating calculation and report scripts

- Setting database caches

In short, the MaxL command-line language provides a full range of capabilities for managing all database processes.

A Sample MaxL Script

You can automate all the processes modeled in this chapter in a single MaxL script, as presented in this section. This script assumes that the application name is Sample, the database name is Basic, and the calculation script created earlier is named BudInc. It also assumes the load rules generated by the Essbase Studio process are as follows:

- ACCOUN builds the Account dimension.

- MARKET builds the Market dimension.

- **PRODUC** builds the Product dimension.

- **SCENAR** builds the Scenario dimension.

- **YEAR** builds the Year dimension.

- **BASIC** loads numeric data into the model.

The following script contains commented sections that explain the purpose of each command or block of commands.

```
/* Create a log file of the process and log into the Essbase sever.*/
spool on to 'c:/MaxL_Logs/output.txt';
login 'admin' 'password';

/* Build the Essbase database using the rules created by Essbase
Studio*/
import database sample.basic dimensions
connect as 'admin' identified by 'password' using server rules_file
'ACCOUN',
connect as 'admin' identified by 'password' using server rules_file
'MARKET',
connect as 'admin' identified by 'password' using server rules_file
'PRODUC',
connect as 'admin' identified by 'password' using server rules_file
'SCENAR',
connect as 'admin' identified by 'password' using server rules_file
'YEAR'
on error append to 'C:/MaxL_Error/dimbuild.txt';

/* Load data into the Essbase database using the rule created by
Essbase Studio*/
import database sample.basic data
connect as 'admin' identified by 'password' using server rules_file
'BASIC'
on error append to 'C:/MaxL_Error/data.txt';

/* Execute the BudInc calculation script */
Execute calculation sample.basic.budinc;

/* Execute the Top report script*/
export database sample.basic using server report_file 'top.rep' to
data_file
'c:/MaxL_Reps/top.txt';

/* Close log file and exit*/
spool off;
exit;
```

```
C:\HYPERION\ESSBASE\bin\essmsh.exe                                    _ □ X

MAXL> login demoadmin Demov52 on 192.168.109.138;

 OK/INFO - 1051034 - Logging in user [demoadmin].
 OK/INFO - 1051035 - Last login on Wednesday, March 18, 2009 10:04:17 PM.
 OK/INFO - 1241001 - Logged in to Essbase.

MAXL> execute calculation default on sample.basic;

 OK/INFO - 1012714 - Regular member [Q1 vs Q2] depends on dynamic-calc member [Q
tr1]..
 OK/INFO - 1012714 - Regular member [Q1 vs Q2] depends on dynamic-calc member [Q
tr2]..
 OK/INFO - 1012714 - Regular member [Market] depends on dynamic-calc member [Wes
t]..
 OK/INFO - 1012684 - Multiple bitmap mode calculator cache memory usage has a li
mit of [50000] bitmaps..
 OK/INFO - 1012669 - Calculating [ Measures<All members> Year<All members> Scena
rio<All members> Product<All members> Market<All members>].
 OK/INFO - 1012677 - Calculating in serial.
 OK/INFO - 1012550 - Total Calc Elapsed Time : [0.047] seconds.
 OK/INFO - 1013274 - Calculation executed.

MAXL> _
```

FIGURE 5-24. *An Essbase MaxL Shell window*

Executing a MaxL Script

MaxL is a command-line shell similar to a standard Windows command line. The Essbase MaxL Shell (ESSMSH), shown in Figure 5-24, inherently knows how to execute the MaxL commands.

Once you have created a script file, you execute the script in a batch process by invoking the MaxL shell and passing the name of the script object. This can be done, for example, with a Windows BAT file. For instance, if you named the previous script sample.mxl, the batch file to execute this script might contain a single command:

```
ESSMSH sample.mxl
```

In this case, the batch file starts ESSMSH and passes the sample.mxl file to the shell. The MaxL shell reads the commands in the file and executes them as specified.

Note also that parameters can be passed to the script, so you could pass the user name and password when calling the script. In addition, you can encrypt the script, so that the password is not visible. Furthermore, you can incorporate MaxL commands into the Perl language for greater integration into other business processes.

Creating a Script in the MaxL Script Editor

This script creates an application and database named test, and then shuts down the running application.

Follow these steps to create a script using the Administration Services console:
In the Administration Services console, select File | Editors | MaxL Script Editor.

1. In the MaxL Script Editor window, type the following script:

    ```
    create application 'test';
    create database 'test'.'test';
    alter system unload application 'test';
    ```

2. From the menu bar, select MDX | Execute.

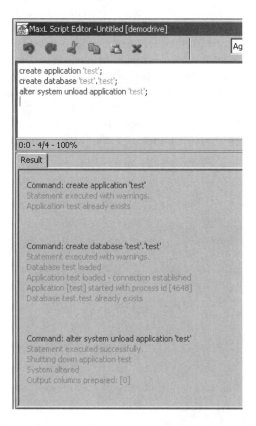

After you have the script created, you can save this as a text file and use a batch
file to execute the script (as shown in previous section). While you could have
created the script in any text editor, the MaxL editor provides valuable syntax-
checking capabilities, as well as an autocomplete option.

Conclusion

There is not a single method or philosophy for designing and building an Essbase database. After so many years of doing something, you often take for granted how difficult or easy it is to do. A number of years ago, I was working with a friend on an Essbase design project. He remarked on how easy it is to build an Essbase database. From his perspective, it is no more difficult than counting to three. While I never thought building an Essbase database was difficult, I never really would have thought it as simple as 1-2-3. Rather, like most things in the world, it is somewhere in between. The steps outlined in this chapter provide a method for building an Essbase database. For sake of simplicity, the chapter did not include ETL tools such as Oracle Data Integrator or Informatica. You could just as easily build a database leveraging adapters in numerous ETL tools. The specific methodology you use to build an Essbase database will vary depending on the specifics of your data source(s), your analytical needs, and your comfort level with the product.

In this chapter and the preceding chapter, we showed you how to build OLAP applications for ad hoc analysis. In the next chapter, we discuss ways to share OLAP results with business users throughout your organization using web-based and desktop-based reports.

CHAPTER
6

Reporting from an OLAP Application

ven the most sophisticated technical implementation of an OLAP solution can fail if put into production without thought to the reporting needs of the users. Without user input, the system will not meet user expectations.

Frequently, we hear how the user community simply wants one reporting tool—an idea that speaks to simplicity, but is unfortunately flawed. The reality is there is not a single "silver bullet" reporting tool, because there is no single type of user. Typically, several use cases are needed to drive the application design. For example, an executive "big-button" user needs technology to be simple and guide him, while a technical analyst wants technology to get out of the way and let her quickly perform ad hoc analyses. The OLAP application developer must discover the needs of all interested users, and make sure they have options available that meet their requirements.

Oracle offers an approach that fits in with this reality. When looking at the different reporting tools an organization may need, the solution may indeed be a suite of tools to suit different users. Oracle Business Intelligence Suite Enterprise Edition Plus (OBIEE Plus) delivers reporting tools to support a wide range of end-user reporting needs.

Underlying the OBIEE Plus philosophy is delivery of tools that can be used for different purposes, yet should be integrated, so they are easy to maintain, regardless of data source. OBIEE Plus is the strategic platform for BI reporting from Oracle, and the examples in this chapter come mainly from that set of tools.

In addition, OBIEE Plus allows access to many different data sources, including both Oracle OLAP and Oracle Essbase, as well as relational sources. Companies can use OBIEE Plus to report from a single source, as well as to combine data from many different data sources by means of a federated query engine supported by a single semantic model, interface, dashboard, or report. OBIEE Plus will serve as the central reporting interface for Oracle for years to come. So, invest time to learn its tool set and many capabilities.

In this chapter, we cover many of the considerations necessary to support reporting from an OLAP application. We start by focusing on user discovery, followed by an introduction to the types of reports that are available. After you have a sense of what is possible, we bring the possible into the realm of what is doable with a discussion of deployment options and architectural considerations for your organization. Finally, we spend some time discussing the types of functionality you should look for in web-based and desktop-based reporting tools.

User Discovery

One consistent, successful strategy for OLAP applications is the formation of a user committee. This committee—whether formal or informal—helps to secure buy-in from relevant people throughout all phases of the project. A user committee generally starts with the people who championed the purchase of an OLAP system, and expands to include anyone with a vested interested in OLAP results. A well-rounded, representative user committee—that is, one with members from all areas of the organization that may use the OLAP application and the OLAP reports—is ideally suited to take on the task of user discovery.

Identifying the Consumers of OLAP Reports

Early in the process, use the committee to identify the potential content consumers, or end users, of OLAP reports in your organization. Typical consumers are executives, managers, and analysts. Do you have additional consumers in your organization? Identify the departments to which your consumers belong. Where, geographically speaking, are your consumers located?

For example, Company XYZ envisions a roll out to 1,000 users around the world. The company's purchase of software follows the standard breakdown of users: about 80 percent are strict report consumers, 15 percent need more interaction and analysis, and 5 percent are power or administrative users. The majority of these users are in the United States, but given the global nature of the company, it is probably a 60/40 split. The users require 24-hour support. As this software is implemented, the user breakdown and global nature of the company must be taken into consideration.

Gathering Information About Your Users

The next step is to find out how your users prefer to consume their information. You might use a questionnaire or conduct interviews with interested parties. You do not need to collect exact numbers; rather, just get a feel for the needs of your different users. Your questions should suit your environment, but as a starting point, you may need to ask a few key questions. A good guide for determining the type of questions to ask is *Oracle's Comprehensive Guide to Realizing Enterprise Performance Management Version 2.2*. Here is a sample of questions that you may want to ask your users, paraphrased from that white paper:

- Do you expect to consume static reports with no interaction?

- Do you need reports that you can customize through interacting with the report? In what ways would you want to modify the report?

- Do you want a big-button approach to reports, such as dashboards that contain summary reports from multiple sources?

- Do you prefer to build reports from scratch, rather than using prebuilt reports?

- How do you expect to access reports? From the desktop, Web, or both?

From your users' responses, you can begin to determine how many people in the organization will require which kinds of reports. Some need just one type of report, while others need three or four to provide context while analyzing data.

Discussing the Reporting Needs of Your Users

After you have formed a picture of what your users expect, you can begin to piece together the style of reports they may want to consume. Here are some questions that the user committee can use to discern which reports may be needed (also from the white paper):

- Are predefined dashboards part of the user vision?

- Is there a need for delivery via a corporate standard portal?

- Is there a "start from scratch" set of users who require ad hoc analysis and reporting? These users might require drill-down, pivot, and "slice-and-dice" capabilities.

- Do users need to integrate multiple data sources into one report? What about into one dashboard?

- Do some users need standard drag-and-drop controls along with a right-click context menu for ease of use?

- Is there a need for deployment through Microsoft Office?

- Do you need to provide the ability to drill through from the analytic measures to the underlying transactional detail?

- Is there a need for offline analysis?

- What about scheduling and batch bursting of reports?

NOTE
Batch bursting *allows for secure delivery of hundreds or thousands of individual reports using one template. It can be run for the portion of data allowed to a particular user, instead of needing to build multiple reports.*

Suppose that Company XYZ ended up purchasing 1,000 OLAP licenses to support enterprise performance management (EPM) and BI applications. Two different departments were involved in the purchase: the finance department needed 700 licenses, and the operations department claimed 300. Now that the user committee has done its work, the project team must work with each department and get more details about their users and reporting needs.

In the interview with the finance department representatives, they list several current reporting projects and the need to improve them. Executives have a 50-page book of reports created mainly in Microsoft Excel that takes a team of analysts two weeks each month to create. Around 200 executive users want to consume the reports in this book. Currently, they receive the book via interoffice mail, and keep copies of past and present books on their local computer hard drives. The executives would prefer to view the reports online in static dashboards and have links to PDF versions of past books stored in a central archive to support future audits.

The team that creates the monthly book still wants interaction with the Microsoft Office suite of tools, but with much more flexibility and speed. They want the ability to link data points from Excel to Word to PowerPoint. Instead of spending weeks to create the reports, they want a set of reports that they can simply refresh with the new monthly data. They also want any changes in hierarchy structure to flow through to the reports automatically, removing the need for manual updates.

Each of these executives has a team of around 500 managers and analysts who truly need both ad hoc reporting and the ability to start from scratch against that monthly data. They want to consume a group of dashboards as a starting point—to see the same information as the executives—but they also want to be able to modify the report sections and work free-form to do additional analysis. These users also want to do forecasting based on the seasonal monthly trends. They decide that an Excel add-in would suit their requirements, allowing them to drill down to detail data and pivot data, and write back to a database. The higher-level visual analysis features are appealing to a group of about 50 users that do statistical trending.

The operations department has a brand-new sales reporting project to meet the requests from its field sales team. All 300 users will be mobile, and they need to be notified when the sales reports for the previous day are ready. They want to receive an e-mail message that has a link to the online system, but also an attached static sales report for just their customers. The static report keeps them informed of the sales activity, and the ability to link to the online system gives them the flexibility to do some ad hoc reporting via the Web. They also need offline analysis capabilities, so they can work in an airplane or a location without Internet access.

To summarize, Company XYZ needs to deliver a unified reporting system to meet the requirements of both departments, starting with a single sign-on to corporate dashboards that everyone uses to see total company results. These dashboards provide links to additional reports and tools that make sense for the users' daily jobs. The reports need to be available via the desktop and the Web.

Clearly, a project team needs to be ready with reporting options and tools already in mind for the different styles of reports each user community mentioned. In the next section, we review the types of reports that are generally available in a reporting tool. After that, we look at possible deployment options.

Types of Reports

As discussed in the previous section, many users will want different interfaces for different requirements. You cannot meet the needs of power users who want ad hoc analysis by giving them only dashboards. Similarly, you cannot meet the needs of big-button executive users if you provide only a reporting tool to start reports from scratch. The best approach is to deliver a reporting system that leverages a common back end but provides different delivery mechanisms based on requirements.

To help you select appropriate reports for your various users, this section presents some of the typical report types. The screen captures in this section reflect output from a variety of software reporting tools. These are just a few examples; additional styles of reports may be needed by an organization.

Basic Report

The simplest of report types, a basic report has a single source of data presented in a grid format made up of rows and columns. Figure 6-1 shows a basic report for product family, time scenarios, and sales data. A basic report can be used as a component of a dashboard report.

FIGURE 6-1. A basic report

Compound Report

A compound report adds a visual analysis component to the grid of data. The visualization contains the same data as in the grid. For example, Figure 6-2 contains the same grid as Figure 6-1, as well as a bar chart summarizing the sales data for all scenarios by product. A compound report can be used as a component in a larger dashboard.

Dashboard Report

A dashboard report is a compilation of reports containing summary-level data. Its purpose is to provide a complete picture of a certain group of metrics. Many times, this can include the use of basic or compound reports brought together across similar metrics. In his book *Information Dashboard Design*, Stephen Few defined a dashboard as "a visual display of the most information needed to achieve one or more objectives which fits entirely on a single computer screen so it can be monitored at a glance."

A dashboard usually has some common information across all of the elements, such as revenue, viewed from different perspectives. Dashboards have controls on

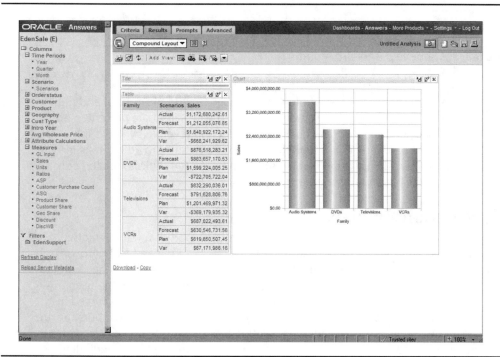

FIGURE 6-2. *A compound report*

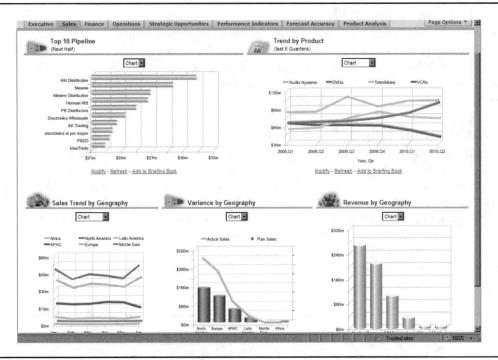

FIGURE 6-3. *A sample dashboard report*

either individual sections or the whole report, depending on the control and the requirement. Figure 6-3 shows a sample dashboard with sales data presented from a variety of perspectives, such as trends by product and revenue by geography.

Often, dashboards serve as a launch pad to more detail, providing links to additional reports or information. For example, in Figure 6-4, links to related content are located to the left and right of the graphs.

Production Reports

A production report (also called a static management report) is a noninteractive report that is pixel-perfect. Strict requirements dictate the look and feel of rows, columns, headers, and images. This style of report is typically created ahead of time as a "snapshot" in time from a database, and the report does not give the user any interactive capabilities. What you see in this report online is what is expected in PDF and printed versions of the report. Scheduling of reports and batch bursting are typical requirements associated with production reports.

Figure 6-5 shows a production report with a strict landscape layout, including spacing requirements, underlining on certain rows, a logo, and a context-sensitive

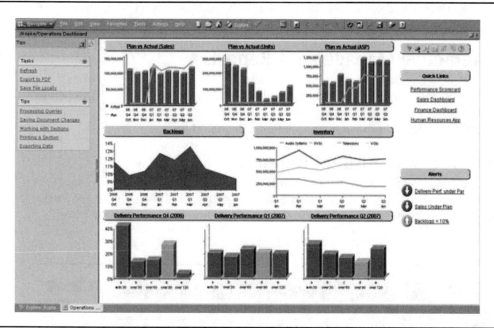

FIGURE 6-4. *A dashboard report with links to related content*

Eden Corporation
Total Geography - Income Statement Trend
2009
Report Run Date: 25-Feb-09 3:03:17 PM by demoadmin

	January Actual	February Actual	March Actual	April Actual	May Actual	June Actual
Net Revenue	158,492,773	268,343,301	344,897,592	421,770,757	559,856,251	693,196,333
Cost of Sales	105,875,345	175,361,994	220,506,345	264,598,873	348,256,845	441,527,943
IC Revenue and Costs Difference	-	-	-	-	-	-
Gross Profit	50,617,428	90,981,307	124,391,247	157,171,884	211,399,406	251,668,390
Oper Exp before Alloc	43,957,926	70,942,289	83,457,950	98,567,062	133,147,044	172,057,510
Allocations	-	-	-	-	-	-
Operating Expenses	43,957,926	70,942,289	83,457,950	98,567,062	133,147,044	172,057,510
Pretax Income From Operations	6,659,502	20,019,018	40,933,297	58,604,822	78,252,362	79,610,880
Other Exp (Inc)	3,796,332	6,159,172	7,139,001	8,534,918	11,050,824	14,745,439
Total Pretax Income	2,863,170	13,859,846	33,494,297	50,069,903	67,201,538	64,865,441
Provision for Income Tax	5,402,002	8,695,580	10,303,815	12,097,297	16,673,613	21,223,282
Minority Interest Income	-	-	-	-	-	-
Earnings from Investments in Subs	263,489	459,301	534,487	635,914	834,094	1,103,387
Extraordinary Income	-	-	-	-	-	-
Net Income	$ (2,288,343)	$ 5,623,567	$ 23,724,949	$ 38,609,520	$ 51,361,819	$ 44,745,565

	July Actual	August Actual	September Actual	October Actual	November Actual	December Actual	[Year] Actual
Net Revenue	828,513,821	941,273,058	1,094,402,714	1,288,880,583	1,454,030,211	1,636,614,168	1,636,614,168
Cost of Sales	531,723,620	602,116,483	702,056,834	807,086,857	925,917,019	1,040,810,724	1,040,810,724
IC Revenue and Costs Difference	-	-	-	-	-	-	-
Gross Profit	296,790,201	339,156,595	392,345,880	459,593,705	528,113,193	595,803,444	595,803,444
Oper Exp before Alloc	208,942,987	236,753,694	282,669,663	366,507,994	452,899,978	533,278,478	533,278,478
Allocations	-	-	-	-	-	-	-
Operating Expenses	208,942,987	236,753,694	282,669,663	366,507,994	452,899,978	533,278,478	533,278,478
Pretax Income From Operations	87,847,234	102,402,901	109,676,217	93,085,712	75,213,216	62,524,966	62,524,966
Other Exp (Inc)	18,035,437	20,414,933	24,614,528	32,488,834	40,050,789	47,127,747	47,127,747
Total Pretax Income	69,811,797	81,987,968	85,061,689	60,596,878	35,162,428	15,397,218	15,397,218
Provision for Income Tax	25,663,510	29,118,678	34,596,558	44,458,984	55,005,583	64,789,250	64,789,250
Minority Interest Income	-	-	-	-	-	-	-
Earnings from Investments in Subs	1,347,012	1,525,150	1,834,134	2,409,629	2,972,329	3,496,134	3,496,134
Extraordinary Income	-	-	-	-	-	-	-
Net Income	$ 45,475,298	$ 54,396,441	$ 52,299,265	$ 18,547,524	$ (16,870,805)	$ (45,893,898)	$ (45,893,898)

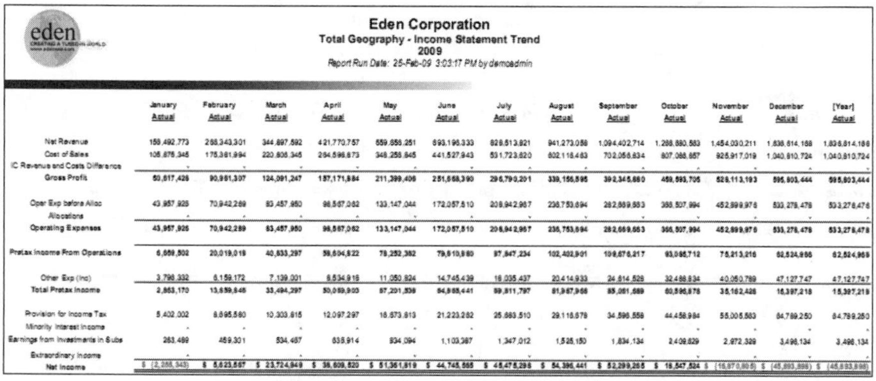

FIGURE 6-5. *A production (static management) report*

header. The title updates automatically based on the point of view (POV) for the user, but no changes can be made.

Interactive Management Reports

An interactive management report is very similar to a production report in its formatting, but retains the ability to be modified slightly by an end user. The report in Figure 6-6 allows a user to do some minor query changes and update the dimensional selections using the POV bar across the top of the report page.

Ad Hoc Spreadsheet Reports

Ad hoc reporting for OLAP is often done in Microsoft Excel. From the familiar Excel interface, analysts can connect to an Essbase database or Oracle OLAP analytic workspace, retrieve data, format the data, navigate the data, change the POV,

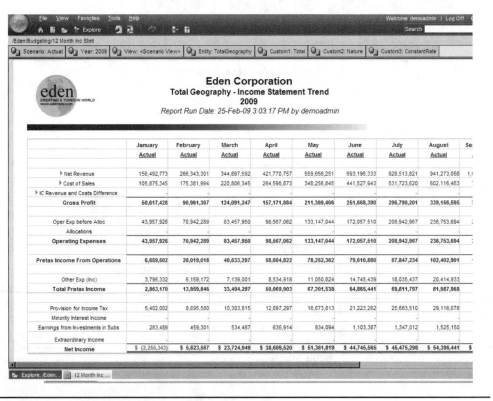

FIGURE 6-6. *An interactive management report*

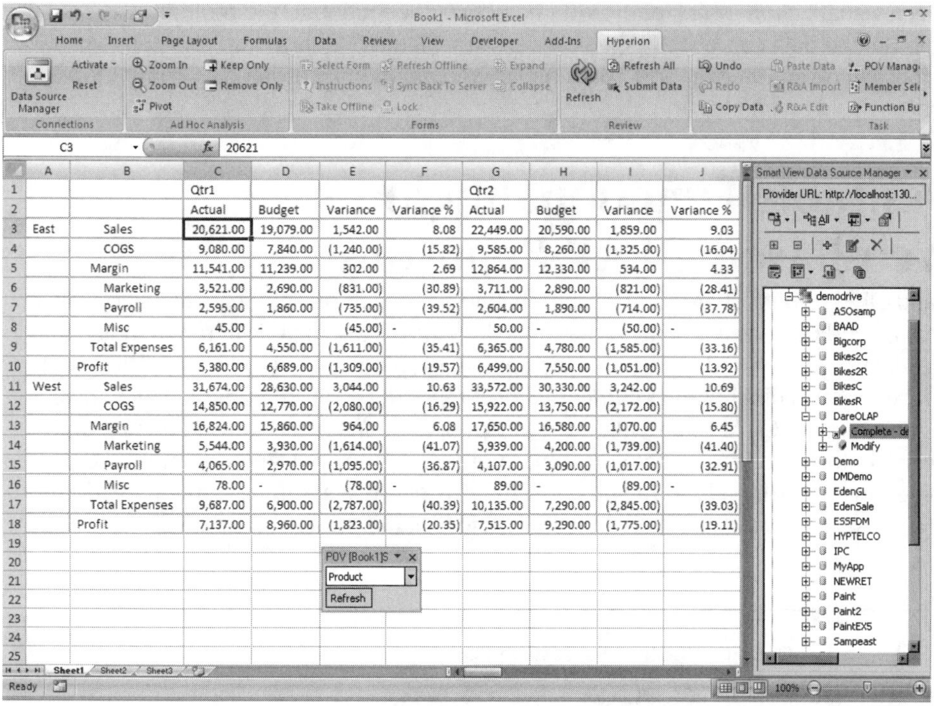

FIGURE 6-7.   *An ad hoc spreadsheet report*

calculate the data, refresh the data, and (with the appropriate permissions) write back to the database. Ad hoc spreadsheet reports are attractive to power users who like to build reports from scratch and to users who want the ability to experiment with the numbers to create what-if scenarios. Both basic users and advanced analysts use these types of reports on a daily basis.

Figure 6-7 contains an ad hoc spreadsheet report created using the Spreadsheet Add-in. While the user interface is specific to Essbase, the example applies equally well to Oracle OLAP. The report shows a Measures dimension in the rows and a Time dimension in the columns. The indentations in the row text for the Measure members represent the dimension hierarchy. In this example, actions related to the Essbase database are available from the main menu via a Hyperion menu.

Custom Microsoft Office Reports

Custom Microsoft Office reports include live data in an otherwise static document or slide. Report creators can copy a data point from Excel and paste it anywhere in a Word document or PowerPoint slide. They can then specify how that data is displayed using a visualization tool. Finally, with an active connection to the multidimensional database, the data can be refreshed on demand. Figure 6-8 shows an example of a custom Microsoft Office report containing two data points presented as compound reports (a grid and a chart).

Desirable Functionality in Web-Based OLAP Reporting

BI and OLAP reports share some commonalities. For example, at the presentation layer (what an end user sees), a static BI report is the same as a static OLAP report; regardless of its data source or underlying analytic engine, each must meet the user requirement that the report is pixel-perfect. Similarly, most reporting tools, regardless of whether they are for BI or OLAP, start with the concept of data organized in rows and columns. You select the criteria for what you want to display in the rows and columns, and the tool returns a report. Where BI and OLAP reports part ways is in how much freedom the end user has to interact with the data and format the presentation.

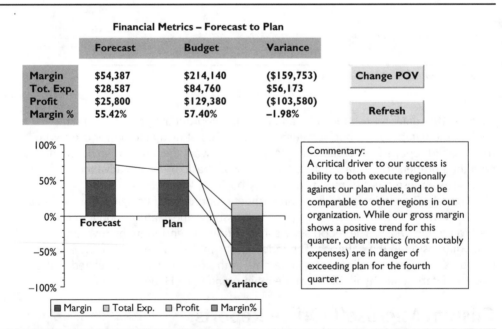

FIGURE 6-8. *A custom Microsoft Office document with dynamic content*

		East	West	South	Central
Forecast	**Profit Contribution %**	21.250000	28.180000	13.100000	35.720000
	Revenue Contribution %	22.350000	31.560000	13.410000	32.690000
	Cost Contribution %	21.750000	34.600000	13.700000	29.950000
Budget	**Profit Contribution %**	21.250000	28.360000	13.520000	36.870000
	Revenue Contribution %	21.120000	30.910000	13.520000	34.450000
	Cost Contribution %	20.910000	35.100000	13.510000	30.470000
Variance	**Profit Contribution %**	1.760000	–0.180000	–0.420000	–1.150000
	Revenue Contribution %	1.230000	0.650000	–0.110000	–1.760000
	Cost Contribution %	0.840000	–0.500000	0.190000	–0.520000

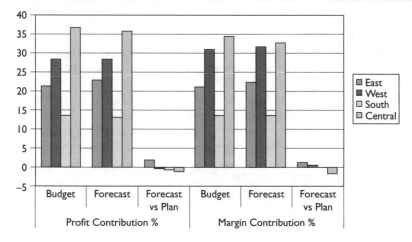

Forecasted Overhead per Region

The current forecasted corporate overhead allocation for the Eastern region stands at -

...

FIGURE 6-8. *A custom Microsoft Office document with dynamic content* (continued)

In discussing desirable functionality with web-based tools, consideration must be given to performance over a network, amount of images, caching, and comparisons between what users get on the desktop. As is commonly known, desktop tools typically deliver a richer and more interactive user experience for nearly all software.

In this section, we review some of the most desirable functionality in an OLAP reporting tool. We start with member selection and data aggregation, which is common to most BI and OLAP reporting tools. Then we move to OLAP-specific functionality, discussing pivoting and POV. Lastly, we explore how OLAP enables analysts to dig down into dimensions and create reports with data sets that are meaningful to the OLAP report consumer. Note that the screen captures in this section reflect a variety of software reporting tools, yet the basic capabilities are very similar. In many cases, business users need to view the data summarized, or in aggregate, to start to understand the underlying business issues.

Creating the Skeleton of a Report

All OLAP reports start with the selection of dimensions for the rows and columns. You might make this selection from a conventional selection tool similar to those used by BI tools or from an OLAP pivot table. In addition to rows and columns, OLAP reports often use filtering or POV options to focus the data to display. Let's begin with a look at conventional member selection.

Conventional Member Selection

Any basic BI reporting tool allows for the selection of members, fields, or columns, regardless of the data source with which you are working. The initial selection becomes the starting point for a query. In an OLAP reporting tool, the selection of members starts with the dimensions. For example, in Figure 6-9, an analyst has selected members from the Product, Scenario, and Measures dimensions as the initial query.

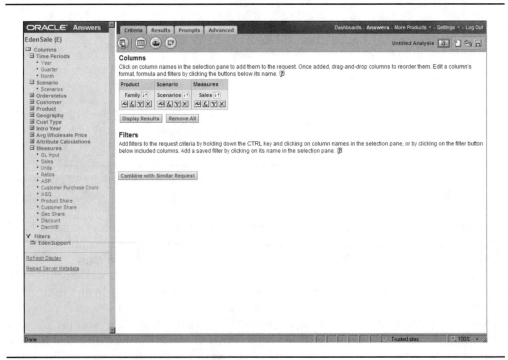

FIGURE 6-9. *Standard selection of dimensions*

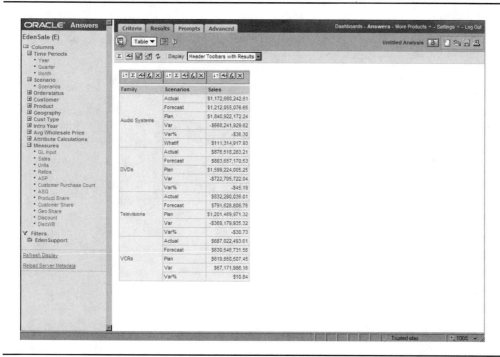

FIGURE 6-10.   *Results from the OLAP query*

When the analyst processes the query, the resulting report displays the data for each of the selected dimension members. Figure 6-10 shows the results of a query displayed in a simple column format.

The next step may be to change the representation of the aggregated data, creating a grid, a graph, or a chart. Figure 6-11 shows a compound report containing a grid and a bar chart side by side. This type of compound report is one we see used very often, sometimes side by side, sometimes top to bottom, and sometimes with a toggle or drop-down window listing choices to let the consumers of the report choose the orientation that suits their needs.

Member Selection Using a Pivot Table

Where OLAP shines is when users are looking to go beyond static and traditional styles of reporting. You can truly empower end users to analyze data with interactive, free-form, speed-of-thought query responses. In effect, the end users can change what data is aggregated and displayed on the fly. Starting from a pivot table is a great way to do this. Members left in the filter area can then be used to make specific choices in other dimensions or separate POVs.

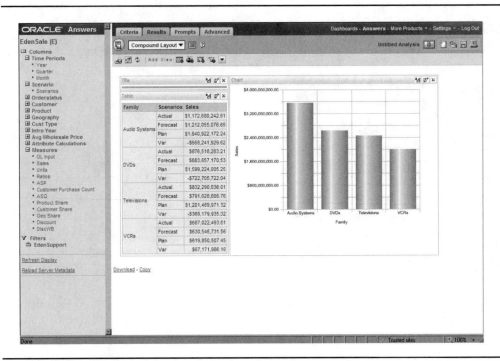

FIGURE 6-11. *Results of the query displayed as a compound report*

One main difference between a typical BI reporting tool and an OLAP reporting tool is that an OLAP report is more appropriately designed using a pivot table to create cross-dimensional displays. While a pivot table can also be used by relational tools, it is the best practice way to look at multiple dimensions at the same time. For example, rather than just a cross-tab comparison of sales greater than 1,000, you can generate a report that shows product sales greater than 1,000 sorted by region, month, scenario, and customer category. It is this in-depth, multidimensional analysis that OLAP so easily conveys.

In a pivot table, you assign dimension members to both columns and rows, and you select at least one data element—a measure, account, or fact (like sales or units). The results are displayed in a grid format. This cross-dimensional view of data can allow for detailed analysis by adding more dimensions to both rows and/or columns.

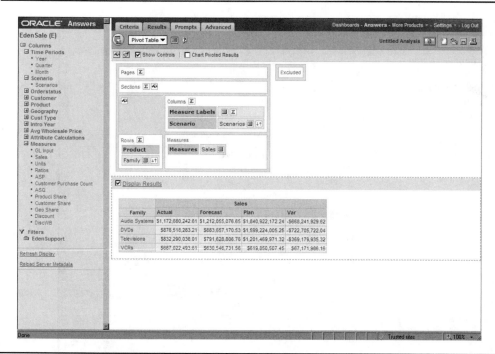

FIGURE 6-12. *A pivot design layout*

Figure 6-12 shows an example of a pivot table with the Product dimension assigned to rows and Scenario assigned to columns. In Figure 6-13, another example of a pivot table implementation shows the Scenario dimension assigned to rows and the Time Periods dimension assigned to columns.

Reports can be designed with multiple dimensions nested within each other in both rows and columns, so you get a full picture of the results by perspective.

Filters and Points of View

A report needs additional perspective for the data displayed, which is provided by filters. You can filter on the dimensions that are not in the rows or columns, such as sales amount or units. Items that are filters can be thought of as a POV for the report, and can be used to filter a single selection in the report. Filters can be driven from drop-down windows, parameter selections before running a report, or free-form

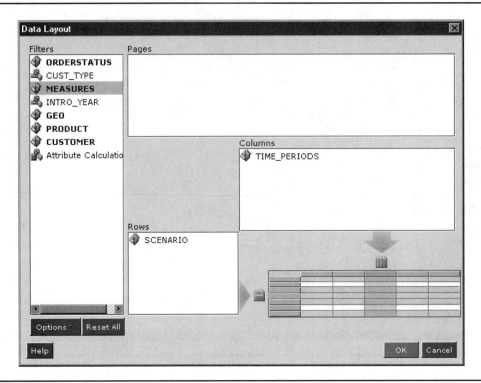

FIGURE 6-13. *Another pivot design layout*

selection by end users. It is a best practice to design reports that allow users to change their POV and alter the report to display only what they need to see.

Adding Functionality to a Report

Selecting dimension members for rows and columns and adding filters creates the skeleton of an OLAP report. Now you can add some muscle by selecting details to include in the report. This section covers dimension browsing, time-specific member selection, formatting, and some advanced options.

Dimension Browsing

To make more complex selections from a dimension, you need a tool that enables you to browse and select the members of a dimension. Figure 6-14 shows an OLAP dimension browser. Using the dimension browser, you can go into each dimension and browse the members until you find the ones you want to select, not just by picking members from a list, but also using functions like Parent, Children, Descendants,

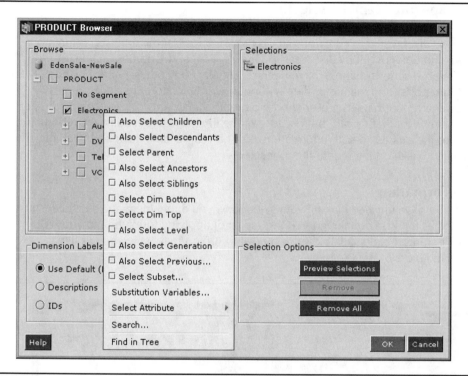

FIGURE 6-14. *A dimension browser*

Siblings, Dimension Bottom, and so forth. This is where the real OLAP advantage starts to show. You cannot easily do this level of specific complexity in a relational model.

OLAP allows you to select individual members from any level or combination of levels, or you can select a member and then include other members based on their relationship to a member. A powerful attribute of reporting tools that are designed to work with OLAP is that they help the end user with these concepts and guide the end user with the analysis, making it much easier to accomplish.

For example, with the dimension browser shown in Figure 6-14, you can right-click a member—in this case, Electronics—and display a context menu that contains the select-based-on-relationship options. Because Electronics has children of four different product types, the design that allows for the easiest report maintenance of this dimension would be to choose either Also Select Children or Also Select Descendants. If you choose Also Select Descendants, the report can query the cube for all members that appear beneath Electronics, regardless of ragged and changing hierarchies. This means that if anything ever changes in the product structure below Electronics, the report will still display it correctly.

Time-Specific Member Selection

Figure 6-15 shows another dimension selection window, this time with the functions displayed in a Functions tab. Let's take a look at the time-series functions shown at the bottom of the list: Year-to-Date (Y-T-D) and Quarter-to-Date (Q-T-D).

The time-series functions have been set up on the database, and they can be used in reports for dynamic update without needing to store these data points. Consider a report that lets a user choose a month via a prompt. The generated report has columns for that month, but because of the time-series functions, the report also includes the quarter-to-date information and the year-to-date data, both dynamically generated based on the month the user selects.

Grid Formatting

Once you have finished making your selections, you apply them and see the results returned as a grid. You then go into the aspect of applying formatting to your grid (spacing, fonts, headers, data display, and so on). You may have choices like those shown in Figure 6-16.

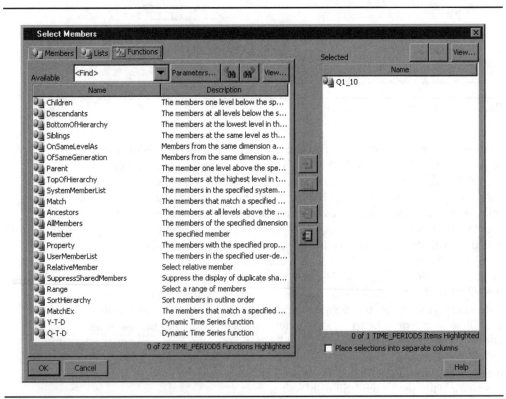

FIGURE 6-15. *Time-specific functions*

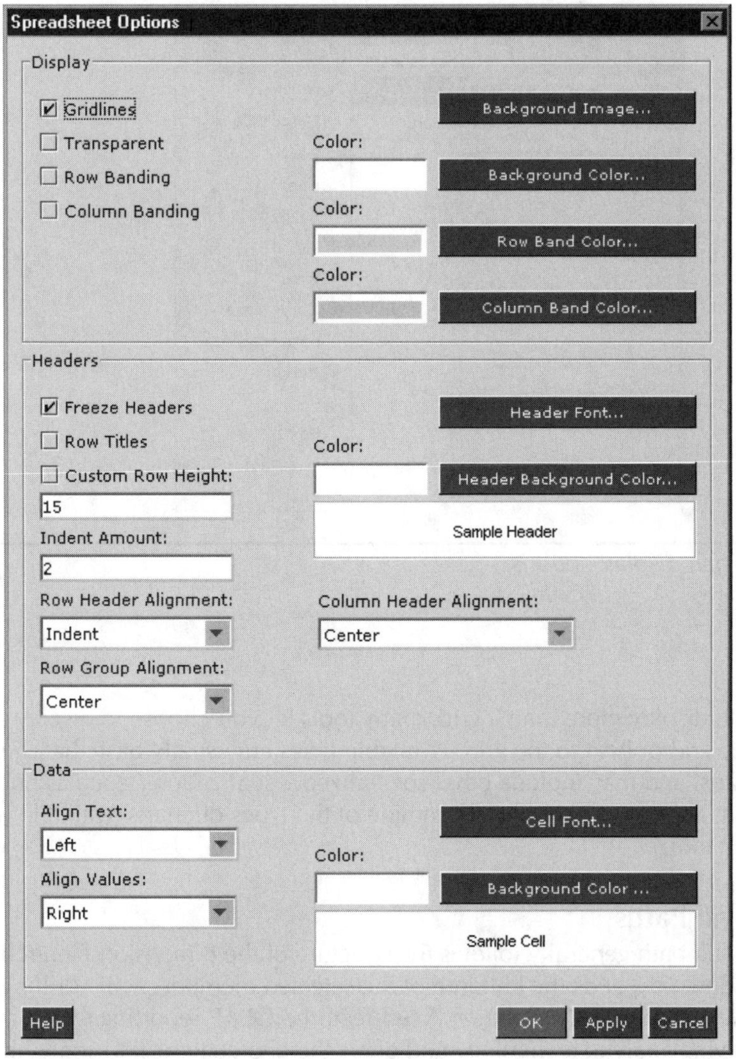

FIGURE 6-16. *Grid display options for formatting*

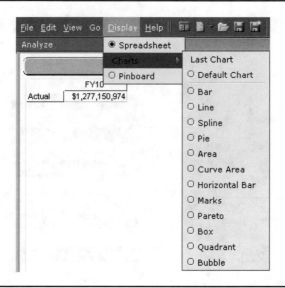

FIGURE 6-17. *Chart display options*

Charts

If you need to display more than a grid, many tools let you choose to display a chart instead of the grid or next to the grid. Available types are usually basic bar, line, pie, and area charts, and may include other specialized visualizations, such as bubble and quadrant. Figure 6-17 shows an example of the types of charts available with one reporting tool.

Custom Drill Paths

The default drill path generally follows the structure of the dimension hierarchy, so that drilling down expands the children of the selected member, while drilling up hides the selected member's children. A full-featured OLAP reporting tool is aware of the underlying analytic technology and offers the choice to drill to something other than children, such as all descendants, siblings, or levels. This flexibility in reporting and analysis is why OLAP is popular.

Advanced Analysis Options

Web-reporting tools offer a wide variety of analysis options. In addition to standard slice-and-dice analysis (retaining and removing dimensional slices; see the "Powerful

Ad Hoc Analysis Features" section later in this chapter), web-reporting tools may offer the following types of advanced analysis:

- "Traffic lighting" of cells to visually highlight important thresholds in the data

- Sorting

- Retrieval options (such as top five or bottom ten products)

- Thresholds to restrict data (such as show only members with data over a certain value)

- End-user calculations (such as when the calculation is not available from the database)

- Show or hide members based on criteria

- Advanced formatting options

As you can see, end users are given wide flexibility to do analysis, and are enabled to do it themselves, instead of being reliant on static reports.

Suppress Missing Data Values

A very useful feature for OLAP reporting is the ability to suppress missing data values. Because of the inherent sparsity of OLAP cubes, many combinations of members have no data value. The result can be reports with too many null values. A suppress missing values feature provides an easy way to avoid taking up large amounts of screen real estate with null or empty cells returned from a symmetric result set. Such a feature may allow you to suppress missing rows, missing columns, or even zero rows (when the data stored is actually the numeral 0). This level of suppression selection again helps OLAP reporting be more flexible and stand out compared with relational reporting tools.

Display of Dimension Members

The last report item that is frequently requested in OLAP reporting is changing how a user can display the rows. This feature allows the end user to decide where the parent of a member is displayed—perhaps at the top or at the bottom of the list of members. For example, financial statements such as net income reports are typically made from dimensions that roll up, so the parent is best displayed below its children.

Desirable Functionality in Desktop-Based Reporting

Earlier in this chapter, we mentioned that desktop-based reporting is most often done from within Microsoft Excel. This means that you can take advantage of many of the features that come standard with Excel, including formatting, sorting, and other spreadsheet-related functionality. When selecting a desktop-based reporting tool—whether it is from Oracle, a third-party, or created in-house—you should make sure that you are getting the OLAP functionality you need to produce the types of reports you want.

Desirable functionality for desktop-based reporting includes:

- Integrated database connection for data retrieval, calculation, refresh, and write-back

- Powerful ad hoc analysis features, such as the ability to drill down on dimension hierarchies, pivot rows and columns, change the POV, and keep or remove subsets of data

- Easy report-creation tools, such as member selection, saved queries, and free-form reports

- Visualization tool to create charts and graphs based on the data in the spreadsheet

In the following sections, we review each group of features in more detail. We use two tools in our examples: Smart View and Discoverer Plus OLAP. Discoverer Plus OLAP is the OLAP component of Oracle Business Intelligence Discoverer Plus, which is described later in this chapter.

Integrated Database Connection

To perform an effective OLAP analysis, you need a connection to live multidimensional data. Therefore, your desktop-based reporting tool should provide an integrated way of connecting to databases. Desirable features include the ability to retrieve, calculate, and refresh data, as well as write back to the database (with the appropriate permission). For example, Smart View offers an integrated way to connect to Essbase databases and enables all of these data-related features. The features for running calculation scripts on the database and writing back to the database are restricted to users with the appropriate security permissions.

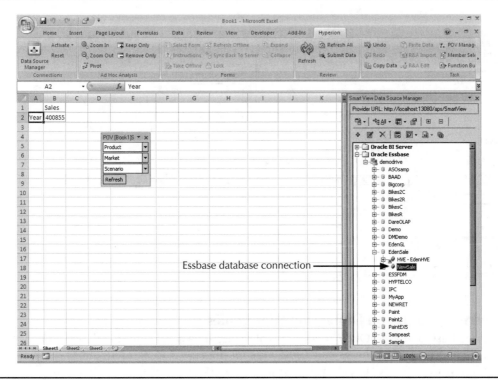

FIGURE 6-18. *Smart View integrated database connection*

Figure 6-18 shows the Data Source Manager, which allows connection not just to Essbase, but also to Oracle BI Server content. Here, we will focus on Essbase as the data source.

Powerful Ad Hoc Analysis Features

In addition to standard spreadsheet features such as formatting and sorting, a competent ad hoc analysis tool should provide the following OLAP-related capabilities:

- Zooming in/out on dimension hierarchies

- Setting the POV

- Pivoting dimensions

- Retaining and removing dimensional slices

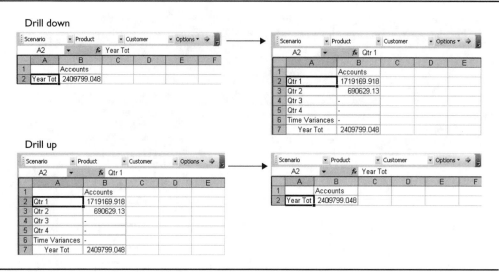

FIGURE 6-19. *Navigation of hierarchies*

Zooming In/Out on Dimension Hierarchies

A good desktop-based OLAP reporting tool makes it easy to explore a dimension hierarchy from within the spreadsheet. Look for the ability to zoom in/out (drill down/up) on a data cell. When you zoom in on a dimension member, you should see (by default) data for the children of the selected member. For example, if you zoom in on a Year dimension, data for the quarters is displayed in the spreadsheet. Drilling down on a quarter then reveals the months in the quarter. You should be able to reverse this process by zooming out.

More advanced tools will provide a way to modify what happens when you zoom in and out. For example, you may be able to show all descendants, instead of just the children, or to explore the siblings. In a hybrid architecture, you may want the ability to drill down to dimensional data stored in a relational source.

Figure 6-19 shows what happens when you zoom in on Year Tot and then zoom out using Smart View. Smart View makes zooming in/out as simple as double-clicking a cell. It supports changing the zoom actions, as well as drilling down to data in a relational source (requires Essbase Studio).

Changing the POV

As previously mentioned, a POV enables you to see a subset of data. A POV feature makes it easy to filter out extraneous data and focus in on what is important to you. The desktop-based reporting tool that you choose should offer a convenient and intuitive way to set and change the POV.

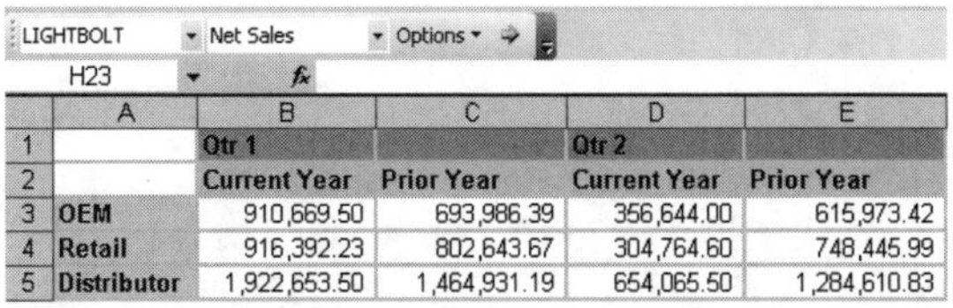

	LIGHTBOLT ▾	Net Sales ▾	Options ▾ ⇒	
	H23 ▾	*fx*		

	A	B	C	D	E
1		Qtr 1		Qtr 2	
2		Current Year	Prior Year	Current Year	Prior Year
3	OEM	910,669.50	693,986.39	356,644.00	615,973.42
4	Retail	916,392.23	802,643.67	304,764.60	748,445.99
5	Distributor	1,922,653.50	1,464,931.19	654,065.50	1,284,610.83

FIGURE 6-20. *Smart View POV toolbar*

Figure 6-20 shows the Smart View POV toolbar. The selections made in the POV toolbar control what data is displayed in the spreadsheet. In this example, the POV is set to show the net sales for the Lightbolt product only. You can select a new POV by using the drop-down lists on the POV toolbar.

Pivoting Dimensions

When following a path of investigation, it can be very useful to change the orientation and order of dimension data in the spreadsheet. Desirable pivoting features include the ability to perform the following actions:

- Pivot a dimension from a row to a column

- Pivot a dimension from a column to a row

- Pivot a dimension from the spreadsheet to the POV

- Pivot a dimension from the POV to a row or column

- Change the order of dimensions in the rows

- Change the order of dimensions in the columns

Figure 6-21 shows a sample spreadsheet and the results of several pivot actions related to the Current Year and Prior Year dimensions. On the bottom left, the selected dimensions are moved from the second column to the first column. On the upper right, the selected dimensions are pivoted from rows to columns. The bottom right shows what happens when the row order is then changed.

Slicing and Dicing

For effective OLAP analysis, you need to be able to remove dimensional slices (data subsets) without deleting individual cells. A dimensional slice is made up of one or

Product ▾ | **Accounts** ▾ | **Options** ▾ ➪
B2 ▾ ƒx Current Year

	A	B	C	D
1			OEM	Retail
2	Qtr 1	Current Year	414303.25	471800.8175
3		Prior Year	370420.0044	473494.6201
4	Qtr 2	Current Year	173221.15	174343.03
5		Prior Year	368003.4063	465615.9328
6	Qtr 3	Current Year	-	-
7		Prior Year	349006.774	469705.1217
8	Qtr 4	Current Year	-	-
9		Prior Year	351801.0503	408167.8464
10	Time Variances	Current Year	-	-
11		Prior Year	-	-
12	Year Tot	Current Year	587524.4	646143.8475
13		Prior Year	1439231.235	1816983.521

Product ▾ | **Accounts** ▾ | **Options** ▾ ➪
B1 ▾ ƒx Current Year

	A	B	C	D	E
1		Current Year		Prior Year	
2		OEM	Retail	OEM	Retail
3	Qtr 1	414303.25	471800.8175	370420.0044	473494.6201
4	Qtr 2	173221.15	174343.03	368003.4063	465615.9328
5	Qtr 3	-	-	349006.774	469705.1217
6	Qtr 4	-	-	351801.0503	408167.8464
7	Time Variances	-	-	-	-
8	Year Tot	587524.4	646143.8475	1439231.235	1816983.521

Product ▾ | **Accounts** ▾ | **Options** ▾ ➪
A2 ▾ ƒx Current Year

	A	B	C	D
1			OEM	Retail
2	Current Year	Qtr 1	414303.25	471800.8175
3		Qtr 2	173221.15	174343.03
4		Qtr 3	-	-
5		Qtr 4	-	-
6		Time Variances	-	-
7		Year Tot	587524.4	646143.8475
8	Prior Year	Qtr 1	370420.0044	473494.6201
9		Qtr 2	368003.4063	465615.9328
10		Qtr 3	349006.774	469705.1217
11		Qtr 4	351801.0503	408167.8464
12		Time Variances	-	-
13		Year Tot	1439231.235	1816983.521

Product ▾ | **Accounts** ▾ | **Options** ▾ ➪
B2 ▾ ƒx Current Year

	A	B	C	D	E
1		OEM		Retail	
2		Current Year	Prior Year	Current Year	Prior Year
3	Qtr 1	414303.25	370420.0044	471800.8175	473494.6201
4	Qtr 2	173221.15	368003.4063	174343.03	465615.9328
5	Qtr 3	-	349006.774	-	469705.1217
6	Qtr 4	-	351801.0503	-	408167.8464
7	Time Variances	-	-	-	-
8	Year Tot	587524.4	1439231.235	646143.8475	1816983.521

FIGURE 6-21. *Pivot examples*

more dimensions and/or dimension members. When a dimensional slice is selected, you should be able to choose whether to remove the slice from the data displayed or to display only the slice.

For example, Figure 6-22 shows the results of the Essbase Keep Only and Remove Only actions on a sample spreadsheet. In Smart View, you specify the dimensional slice by selecting the desired rows and columns in the spreadsheet. In this case, the dimensional slice is made up of Qtr 1 and Qtr 2 (rows) and Performance and Value (columns). The image on the left shows the result of keeping only the slice; that is, the selected rows and columns are retained and everything else is removed from the spreadsheet. The image on the right shows what happens if the same slice is removed.

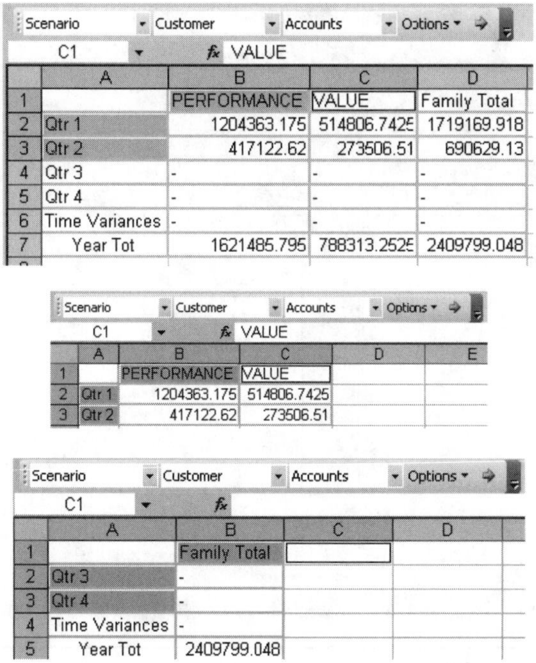

FIGURE 6-22. *Examples of Keep Only and Remove Only in Smart View*

Easy Report-Creation Tools

Ad hoc analysis takes time because you are exploring the dimension members and data as you build the report. A desktop-based tool that provides shortcuts for report creation and reuse can be invaluable. Desirable report-creation features may include the following:

- Member selection
- Query creation
- Free-form reports

Member-Selection Tool

When you are dealing with millions of members organized within dimensions, finding the members that you want in a report using only ad hoc features can be

FIGURE 6-23. *Member selection*

a daunting task. A good member-selection tool can make the process faster and easier. At minimum, you need to be able to browse members by dimension and select multiple members at the same time. You may also want the ability to filter results, search for members, and specify conditions and criteria for member inclusion. The end result of your selection is a query that you can use to retrieve data from the database.

Figure 6-23 shows the Member Selection dialog box in Smart View, which offers all of the desired abilities.

Query Creation

After spending the time to create the query for a report, it would be useful to be able to save it and share it with others, without needing to save the data contained in the actual report. The saved query can be used to generate the report as exactly as designed, or the query can function as a quick starting point for creating new report queries.

With Smart View, you can create queries and save them to the server, allowing the query to be reused and shared with others. Figure 6-24 shows a simple report query with Market and Time dimensions assigned to rows and members of the Measures (or Accounts or Facts) dimension in columns. Note that you can also select a POV and attributes from the query window.

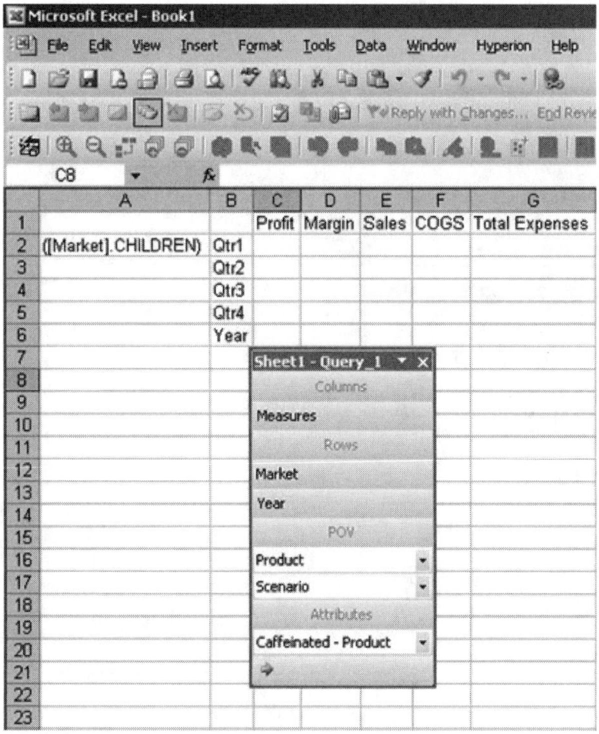

FIGURE 6-24.   *A report with a query designer*

Some tools offer advanced query construction, where you can select conditions as well as members. For example, Figure 6-25 shows a query-creation tool from Discoverer Plus OLAP with an option to select the top ten items based on a variety of criteria.

Free-Form Reporting

Free-form reporting lets you converse with data in the connected database. The concept is straightforward. You enter the dimension or member names in the data cells of the spreadsheet, laying out the elements in the orientation you would like used for the report. A report is automatically generated from that information.

Free-form reporting is unique to Smart View. Figure 6-26 shows two ways to create a free-form report: specifying all dimensions/members or specifying some dimensions/members. If only some dimensions/members are included, Essbase completes the query and returns all other dimensions as top-level entries.

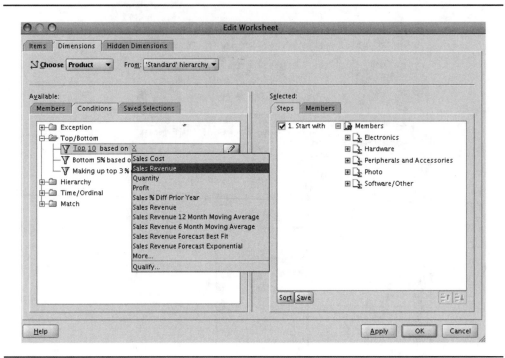

FIGURE 6-25. *Query creation*

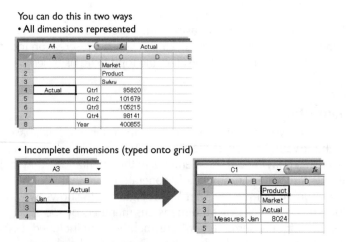

FIGURE 6-26. *Free-form reporting techniques*

Visualization

The notion of visualization has been around for years. Visualization provides a means by which you can gain insight into your data. For some, visualization can be a report that appears in their e-mail inbox or on a web page. For others, it could be a grid of numbers with a chart in Excel. The key is to provide the correct, most efficient approach to allow users to view what there is to see.

Grids (such as tables and spreadsheets) are a simple and very powerful form of visualization, but when it comes to presenting multidimensional OLAP results, they tend to take up a lot of real estate—so much real estate that you may need to scroll through subsets at a time. Because scrolling can be very time-consuming and tedious, important information may be overlooked, if ever even seen. Other kinds of visualization can enhance users' ability to interpret large sets of OLAP results. For example, the scatter plot is ideal for revealing patterns and anomalies in large data sets.

Here, we will go into some detail on visualization—starting with the limitations of traditional grids for OLAP querying and reporting, and then showing some effective visualization means you might consider for visualizing OLAP results.

Limitations of the Grid Format for OLAP Reporting

Not so long ago, people would run a report per a set of parameters and sift through the details. In some instances, data would be transferred to a spreadsheet for some additional analysis. Once in a spreadsheet, consumers could apply graphs to spot trends or color-coding to find outliers. With smaller amounts of data, these tasks were important, but basic.

OLAP analysis can produce very large sets of data. Analysts often miss important information, because the sheer amount of data can be overwhelming. Thus, decision-making suffers. Spreadsheets exacerbate this issue. Though spreadsheets are very user-friendly, the ability to store millions of cells by row and column inhibits the ability to see the entire data set at once.

It is far easier to spot trends, patterns, anomalies, and so on when you can examine the data in its entirety in a single view. If the data set is so large that you find yourself scrolling up and down and side to side, your analysis will suffer. It is virtually impossible to remember all of the data as you scroll. Enter the scatter plot.

From Grid to Scatter Plot

To meet the challenge posed by larger data sets, software vendors have begun creating new ways to query data that promote better visualization. In this section, we compare OLAP results in a grid format with the same data in a scatter plot. The demonstration starts with a small data set made up of sales and marketing data for a year. After you see how that data set maps to a scatter plot, we add the Market and Product dimensions to increase the size of the data set. Important information, hidden in the detail of a grid, becomes readily apparent in the scatter plot.

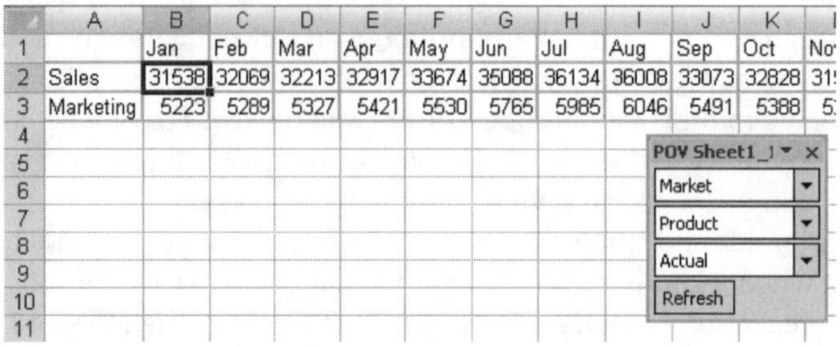

	A	B	C	D	E	F	G	H	I	J	K	
1		Jan	Feb	Mar	Apr	May	Jun	Jul	Aug	Sep	Oct	No
2	Sales	31538	32069	32213	32917	33674	35088	36134	36008	33073	32828	31
3	Marketing	5223	5289	5327	5421	5530	5765	5985	6046	5491	5388	5

POV Sheet1_J ▾ ✕

Market ▾
Product ▾
Actual ▾
Refresh

FIGURE 6-27. *Sales and marketing values by month in a grid*

Let's get started. Figure 6-27 shows OLAP results in a simple grid. In this case, Smart View was used to query an Essbase database and populate an Excel spreadsheet. Grids show values explicitly. For example, cell B2 reflects the value associated with Jan Sales: $31,538. Figure 6-28 presents the same data in a scatter plot.

So, what is the difference? Well, instead of the 24 numbers shown in the grid, we see 12 data points in the scatter plot. The scatter plot still reflects all 24 values,

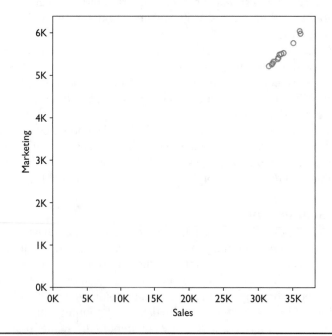

FIGURE 6-28. *Sales and marketing by month in a scatter plot*

except that the data is plotted by sales and marketing. This is a subtle but extremely powerful difference. In addition, instead of showing the numeric value in each cell, a plot point represents the value as an intersection with each axis. One drawback is that, initially, it may be difficult to discern which data point is which. We will demonstrate techniques to address this issue in the next section. But first, let's review how the scatter plot works. Then we will look at larger examples using the same size scatter plot object.

Creating plots in a scatter plot is a matter of simple geometry. In our example, each data point reflects a given month. So, to find the data point for sales and marketing for January, locate 31,538 on the x-axis (Sales) and draw a line upward, parallel to the y-axis. Locate 5,223 on the y-axis (Marketing) and draw a line to the right, parallel to the x-axis. As shown in Figure 6-29, the data point is found at the intersection of the two lines. The lines are sometimes referred to as *drop lines.*

Now that you have the basics, let's expand the data set to include market data. Figure 6-30 shows that as the domain size increases, the grid takes up more space. For each market, we need two rows by 12 columns to present 24 values. With 20 markets, we need 40 rows by 12 columns to present 480 values. In a scatter plot, the 20 additional markets are presented as 240 marks in the same space used before we introduced the additional markets, as shown in Figure 6-31.

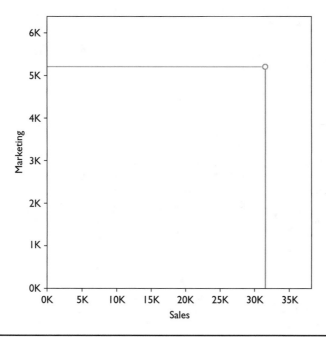

FIGURE 6-29.   *Sales and marketing by January*

	A	B	C	D	E	F	G	H	I
1			Jan	Feb	Mar	Apr	May	Jun	Jul
2	Florida	Sales	1321	1383	1428	1498	1562	1705	1837
3		Marketing	223	237	246	254	262	292	316
4	New York	Sales	2479	2625	2601	2835			
5		Marketing	474	494	504	515			
6	Massachusetts	Sales	1251	1206	1203	1210			
7		Marketing	165	156	150	147			
8	Connecticut	Sales	1197	1157	1118	1083			
9		Marketing	206	194	188	184			
10	New Hampshire	Sales	532	549	571	587	610	680	727
11		Marketing	93	94	97	100	102	116	128
12	California	Sales	3602	3699	3755	3814	4031	4319	4493
13		Marketing	585	612	625	649	678	737	786
14	Oregon	Sales	1741	1667	1650	1661	1617	1615	1624
15		Marketing	270	255	250	251	247	241	238
16	Washington	Sales	1605	1629	1601	1552	1574	1568	1576

POV Sheet1 ▾ ×
Product ▾
Actual ▾
Refresh

FIGURE 6-30. *Sales and marketing by month by market in a grid*

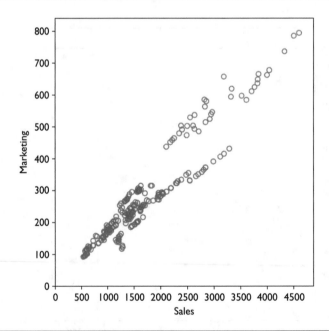

FIGURE 6-31. *Sales and marketing by month by market in a scatter plot*

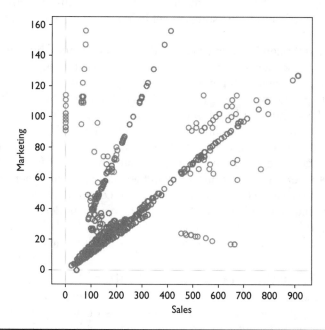

FIGURE 6-32.   *Sales and marketing by month by market by product in a scatter plot*

When we add the Product dimension with its 12 members to the mix, the spreadsheet gets even larger and more unwieldy, while the scatter plot simply adds more data points. Figure 6-32 shows the scatter plot. (The spreadsheet version is too large to show.)

It may be useful to look at the progression of the scatter plots we have discussed. Figure 6-33 demonstrates the increased data points plotted as we add 20 markets,

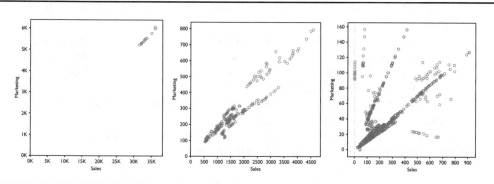

FIGURE 6-33.   *From 12 values to more than 2,700 values*

followed by 12 products. Throughout, the footprint used remains the same. In contrast, the number of rows in the spreadsheet increases tremendously as we add markets and products.

More interesting though is the information that can be gleaned by a quick glance. The rightmost scatter plot in Figure 6-33 has some stunning information. What appeared to be a consistent pattern has been broken, yielding very interesting data in both the upper-left and lower-right portions of the result. We refer to these anomalies as *outliers*, and their location in the scatter plot is critical. In this case, some of the outliers are good news and some are potentially bad news.

Considering that our analysis compares sales to marketing, the outliers found at the lower right are good news. These data points represent our ability to sell with little to no marketing expense. In contrast, the outliers found at the upper left warrant further investigation, because the opposite is true—the company is spending money on marketing with little return in sales. These outliers may be understandable; for example, a new product entering the market could have this kind of profile. If the product has been around for some time, however, this result is cause for attention.

Improving the Presentation of Data in a Scatter Plot

One challenge presented by the scatter plot is visibility. For example, it is hard to tell which market-by-product-by-time combination is associated with a given data point. To solve this problem, we can associate dimensional information with any combination of color, shape, size, and/or text. Color, shape, and size generally provide the most value. Text is nice to use with smaller sets of data. A legend is also important to aid comprehension. Another useful technique is to make the values along the axes suit the range of values contained in the chart. Let's take a look at a few examples.

Figure 6-34 presents a side-by-side view of our very first scatter plot—the one showing sales and marketing by month—with text labels added to each data point. The left chart reveals that, because the data points are clustered so close together, much of the text cannot be displayed. The solution, as shown in the right chart, is to use more appropriate axes values in order to provide the space necessary to display the text labels.

As you might guess, the challenge with text for larger data sets is that text uses a good deal of space. In essence, for larger data sets, the problem is the same one that led to using a scatter plot in the first place: lack of real estate. So, let's look at some other techniques for improving comprehension using larger data sets.

In the next example, we turn our attention away from months and focus on market. Figure 6-35 contains the scatter plot originally shown in Figure 6-32 (sales and marketing by month by market by product) with color assigned to the Market dimension. A legend maps a color to each of the markets.

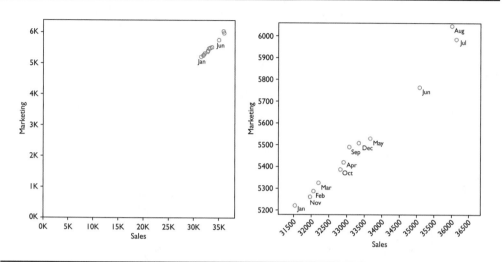

FIGURE 6-34.   *Text labels are used to identify months.*

NOTE
As this book is printed in black and white, the colors in the following images are rendered in shades of gray. In the real world, you would be viewing the scatter plot—and the colors—online.

We can quickly determine a pattern in the data after color is applied. The cluster of good outliers (lower right) is from Massachusetts, while the two clusters of poor outliers are from Nevada (leftmost) and New York State, respectively. We have figured out that our problems are isolated to particular markets. This is very helpful information that would be a challenge to discover using a spreadsheet.

Now, by applying shape to product data in Figure 6-36, we can see other patterns emerge. Particular products are associated with the good and poor outliers. Referring to the legend, which contains a subset of information, we discover that Cola is the product that is selling very well in Massachusetts (good outlier). The poor performing product is Old Fashioned in New York State. With the information gleaned from increased visibility, we can contact the product managers for those markets and determine a course of action.

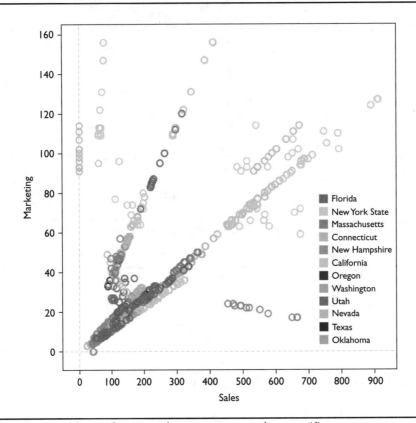

FIGURE 6-35. *Adding color to markets causes a market-specific pattern to emerge.*

Up to this point, we have used two measures, Sales and Marketing, on the x and y axes. Each data point represents the intersection of the values associated with these measures in terms of months, market, and products. We then highlighted markets with color and products with shapes. Now we are going to layer on yet another dimension member: ending inventory. We will use size to represent the value of the ending inventory—the larger the plot point, the greater number of units in inventory. Figure 6-37 confirms that in the poorest performing area (upper left), the data points are indeed larger than those found in the best performing area (lower right).

From Figure 6-37, we can conclude that we may be able to apply production capacity from the products at the upper left to the more profitable products at the lower right. After all, we are producing more product than we can possibly sell. In addition, if this excess inventory could be sold in the markets found at the lower right,

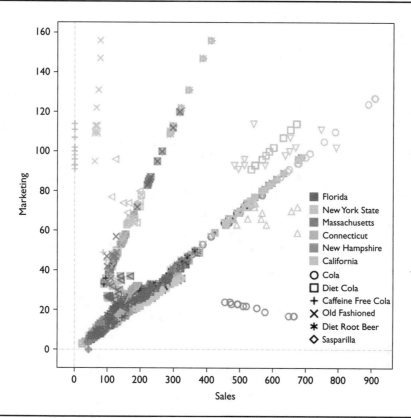

FIGURE 6-36.   *Adding shape to products reveals a product-specific pattern.*

a simple distribution change would help. In either case, having the information quickly provides us with the power to make a better decision.

The preceding examples demonstrated some basic functionality shared by many different visualization tools. We showed how properties such as shape, color, size, and text could be used to identify the data points and reveal patterns within the data. Most of what we demonstrated had to do with outliers. These values are simply anomalies that appear outside a typical pattern. Visualizations such as the scatter plot are great for this type of analysis.

Other Types of Visualizations

In general, visualizations should provide the most appropriate method for presenting the data, given the analytic need. Our intent was to present an alternative approach

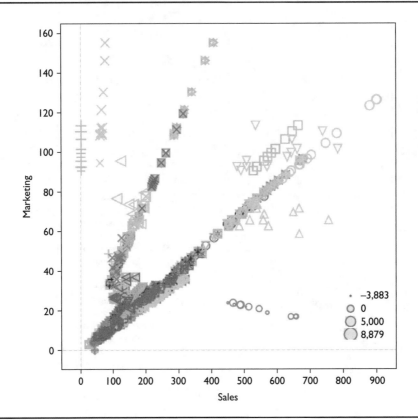

FIGURE 6-37. *Size represents the value of ending inventory.*

to the grid- and chart-based methods. If you are simply after a report comparing this year to last, a grid or bar chart may fit the need. However, when heavy data volumes or no clear-cut output is needed—meaning the exercise is more analytic than static—other visualizations are a better fit. Both Oracle OLAP and Oracle Essbase can leverage Excel to perform similar tasks, allowing users to get more depth of analytics and insight, not just rows of data.

Many other types of visualizations are possible, including the following:

■ Bar charts are a great way to compare data across categories or to break data down into stacked bars.

■ Text tables (also called cross-tabs or pivot tables) provide an easy way to display the numbers associated with categorical data.

- Line charts connect individual data points in a data view. They provide a simple way to visualize a sequence of values, and they are especially useful when you want to see trends over time.

- Heat maps are a great way to compare categorical data using color. They are typically constructed as a table using colored squares to represent the data and a continuous range of colors. Heat maps allow you to see variations in the data via variations in color.

- Gantt charts are typically used when you want to display the duration of one or more categories of interest against the progression of time.

This section has covered the wide variety of functionality that you may want in a desktop-based OLAP reporting tool. Whichever tools you choose, ensure that you are getting the features you need to produce the types of ad hoc reports and custom reports that your users want.

Understanding Deployment Options

So far, we have discussed a general approach for determining what may be needed in a reporting solution. However, types of users and styles of reports are not the only factors that need to be taken into consideration. The project team needs to know which deployment options are feasible within the existing IT infrastructure. Sometimes, the ideal reporting solution is simply not possible based on security requirements or previous investments in technology. The team needs to manage expectations and be wary of letting pie-in-the-sky notions become requirements.

The project team works with the user committee to provide the best possible solution for their environment—one that adheres to enterprise standards while also providing the required functionality both for web-based and desktop-based reporting.

Fitting in with Enterprise Standards

Organizations may have strict policies about what can be delivered to end users. To follow best practices, many different interfaces need to be used to meet the requirements of different user types, but all of them need to comply with corporate standards for technology, security, and single sign-on end-user restrictions. Many companies do not allow employees administrator-level control over their desktop or laptop, may have data restrictions to different databases, and may assign different access to different reports.

Most likely, the project team members who selected the software are already aware of the possible options for deployment. If not, they can poll the user committee or user community for requirements based on what they know will fit in with their standards.

Web-Based Deployment Options

The majority of examples shown so far in this chapter have been from web-based reporting tools, so let's first look at the different ways you can deliver reports over the Web:

- **Interactive reporting** A good way to look at web-based interactive reporting is that it provides all the functionality for doing detailed analysis—functionality that is as close as possible to that available in a desktop application—yet delivered securely through the Web for ease of maintenance. There is always a need to deliver ad hoc analytics and what-if capabilities through the Web, and this style of reporting comes closest to satisfying the needs of users who are used to desktop analytic tools. Examples of deployment options include Hyperion Web Analysis, Oracle Business Intelligence Answers, and custom web portals.

- **Dashboard reporting** Web-delivered dashboards have been a buzz topic for many years now, because they provide a great overview into a particular subject area on one or just a few screens. Ideally, a dashboard is a starting point, containing high-level information, which can then be drilled into for additional detail, investigation of a certain problem, and links to additional areas that may be of interest. Examples of deployment options include Oracle Business Intelligence Interactive Dashboards and Hyperion Interactive Reporting.

- **Production reporting** Also known as pixel-perfect reporting, production reporting delivers a report that must look a certain way to meet requirements, but has little or no interactivity. Statements, checks, formatted management reports like income statements, balance sheets, and cash flow reports fall into this category. Examples of deployment options include Oracle Business Intelligence Publisher, Hyperion Financial Reporting, and Hyperion SQR Production Reporting.

Desktop-Based Deployment Options

Desktop-based reporting is generally delivered via Microsoft Office products—in particular, Excel. However, some third-party tools exist that offer other spreadsheet-based interfaces with built-in Essbase or Oracle OLAP features.

Ad Hoc Spreadsheet Reporting

As previously mentioned, ad hoc spreadsheet reports are most often created in Excel by power users. OLAP features are integrated into the Excel interface. Analysts can connect to and retrieve data from either an Essbase database or an Oracle OLAP analytic workspace. They can also set the POV, navigate the data, calculate the data, and format the report—all from within the spreadsheet. With the appropriate permissions, they can even write back to the database. End users can modify the report to create what-if scenarios.

Essbase Tools for Ad Hoc Reporting   You can add Essbase features to Excel using either the classic Spreadsheet Add-in or the next-generation Smart View, which both come standard with Essbase. Smart View has the added advantages of being able to connect to and retrieve content from other EPM applications, such as Planning and Financial Management, as well as offering the ability to create custom Microsoft Office reports (as described shortly).

Some third-party tools, such as Dodeca from Applied OLAP, offer an Excel-compatible spreadsheet interface and integrated Essbase features. Dodeca is described in more detail later in this chapter.

Oracle OLAP Tools for Ad Hoc Reporting   For Oracle OLAP, several desktop options are available for displaying and reporting data. These tools include those provided by Oracle and some third-party tools that support Oracle OLAP 11g features.

We have already discussed OBIEE Plus and its support for Essbase and Oracle OLAP, but there is also Oracle Business Intelligence Standard Edition, which is based on the Oracle Business Intelligence Discoverer tool set.

BI Discoverer has two components that can be used with OLAP data.

- **Oracle Business Intelligence Discoverer Plus**   BI Discoverer Plus is a Java-based tool delivered via a browser. It provides a rich report development and viewing environment. Because BI Discoverer Plus is a Java application, it can run on any operating system capable of running the Java environment, including Windows, Linux, and Mac OS X. BI Discoverer Plus has been available for quite some time for relational data. Several years ago, an OLAP component was released, called Discoverer Plus OLAP. Discoverer Plus OLAP directly accesses the data in Oracle OLAP cubes. Unlike earlier versions of BI Discoverer Plus, there is no need to use an administrator tool to create the metadata; in this case, an end user layer (EUL) can directly access the OLAP data stored in an Oracle database.

- **Oracle Business Intelligence Discoverer Viewer**   BI Discoverer Viewer is a web-based, thin client viewer that allows for viewing of reports and workbooks created with BI Discoverer Plus.

To view OLAP data in Discoverer Plus OLAP, start Discoverer Plus OLAP and select the data you want to view using the Workbook Wizard. Figure 6-38 shows a sample report. The feature-rich multidimensional query builder contained in this tool allows users to build very powerful presentations and briefing books.

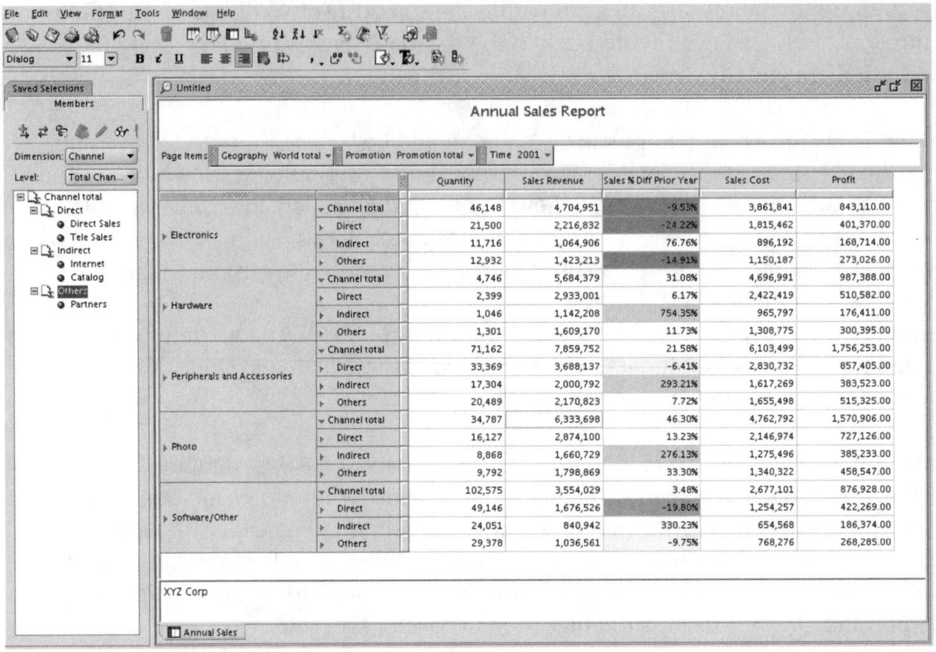

FIGURE 6-38. *Discoverer Plus OLAP report*

After you have selected all the data and filtered the dimensions, you will see your new Discoverer Plus OLAP workbook. You can now create reports. You have the option of viewing the reports in BI Discoverer Plus or allowing authorized web users to view the reports as well using BI Discoverer Viewer, as shown in Figure 6-39.

You can also use the BI Spreadsheet Add-in to display OLAP data in Excel. The BI Spreadsheet Add-in can be downloaded from the Oracle Technology Network (OTN) site or installed as part of the Oracle Business Intelligence Standard Edition Client bundle.

The BI Spreadsheet Add-in adds the following enhancements to Excel:

■ Common business rules and definitions on the OLAP catalog

■ Leverage of the scalability of Oracle OLAP

■ Access to the advanced calculations and power of the OLAP engine

■ Storage of data in a central repository—one version of the data!

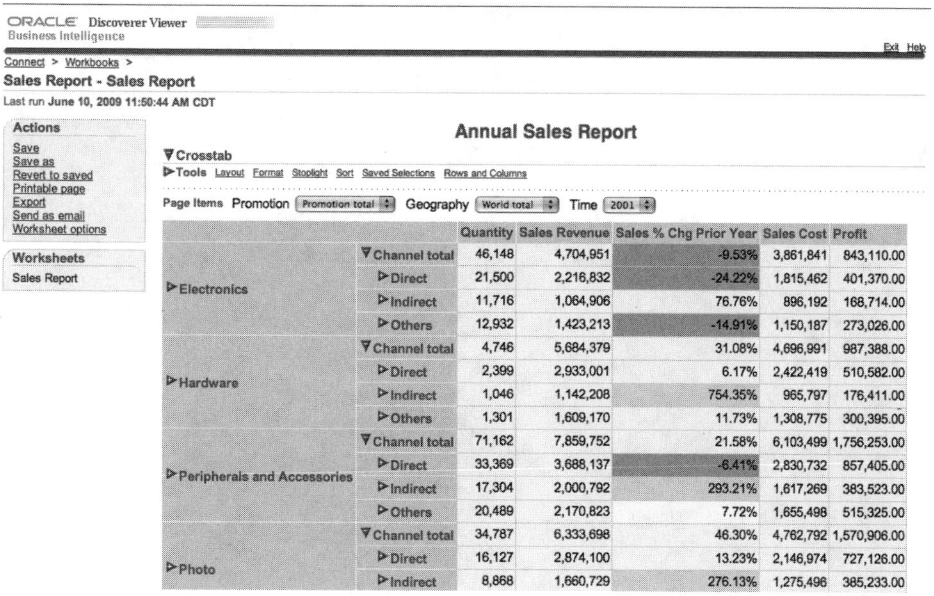

			Quantity	Sales Revenue	Sales % Chg Prior Year	Sales Cost	Profit
Electronics	▼ Channel total		46,148	4,704,951	-9.53%	3,861,841	843,110.00
	▷ Direct		21,500	2,216,832	-24.22%	1,815,462	401,370.00
	▷ Indirect		11,716	1,064,906	76.76%	896,192	168,714.00
	▷ Others		12,932	1,423,213	-14.91%	1,150,187	273,026.00
Hardware	▼ Channel total		4,746	5,684,379	31.08%	4,696,991	987,388.00
	▷ Direct		2,399	2,933,001	6.17%	2,422,419	510,582.00
	▷ Indirect		1,046	1,142,208	754.35%	965,797	176,411.00
	▷ Others		1,301	1,609,170	11.73%	1,308,775	300,395.00
Peripherals and Accessories	▼ Channel total		71,162	7,859,752	21.58%	6,103,499	1,756,253.00
	▷ Direct		33,369	3,688,137	-6.41%	2,830,732	857,405.00
	▷ Indirect		17,304	2,000,792	293.21%	1,617,269	383,523.00
	▷ Others		20,489	2,170,823	7.72%	1,655,498	515,325.00
Photo	▼ Channel total		34,787	6,333,698	46.30%	4,762,792	1,570,906.00
	▷ Direct		16,127	2,874,100	13.23%	2,146,974	727,126.00
	▷ Indirect		8,868	1,660,729	276.13%	1,275,496	385,233.00

FIGURE 6-39. *BI Discoverer Viewer in a browser*

After the BI Spreadsheet Add-in is installed, you start up Excel, navigate to the OracleBI menu item, and create a new query. After creating a connection to the database schema that has access to the OLAP cubes, the Query wizard is displayed. The wizard uses the same set of dialog boxes used to create a query in Discoverer Plus OLAP. Figure 6-40 shows an example of an Excel spreadsheet with the same data we showed in Discoverer Plus OLAP.

The BI Spreadsheet Add-in cannot use the same presentations that were created in Discoverer Plus OLAP, but they can share calculated measures and calculated members. One excellent offering of the BI Spreadsheet Add-in is a write-back feature that allows authorized users to write data directly back to the OLAP cubes. While this is only single user, the BI Spreadsheet Add-in does a good job of managing contention and opens the data in read-write mode only when data is actually being written.

As of this writing, the BI Spreadsheet Add-in supports only Oracle OLAP 10*g*. A couple third-party products support Oracle OLAP 11*g* in Excel, as discussed in the "Third-Party Reporting Tools for Oracle OLAP" section later in the chapter.

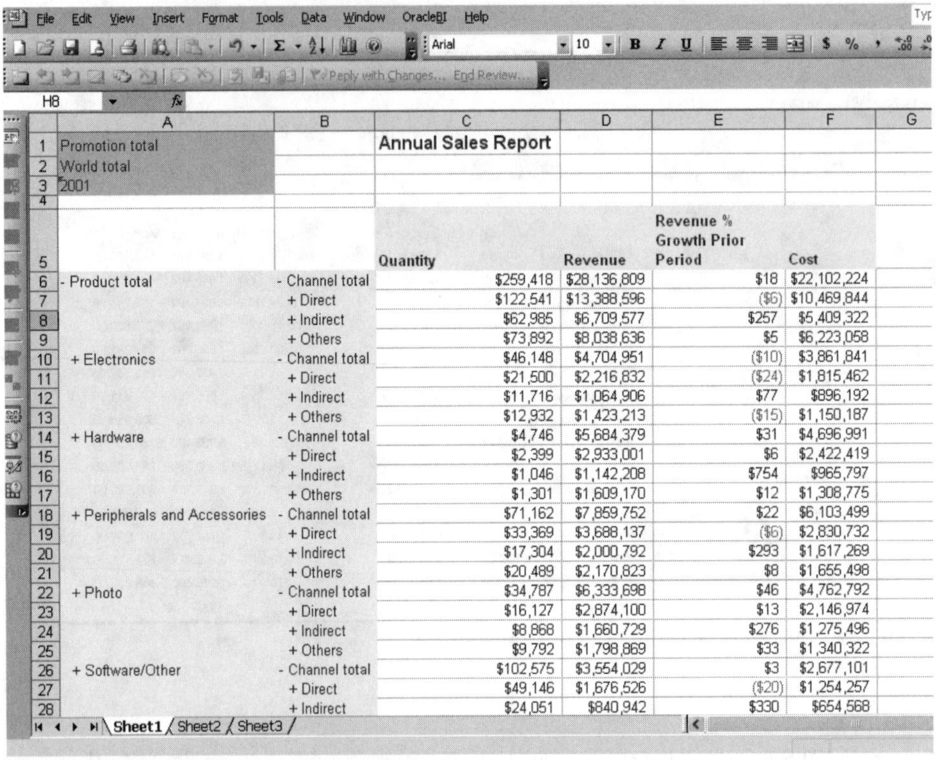

	A	B	C	D	E	F
1	Promotion total		Annual Sales Report			
2	World total					
3	2001					
4						
5			Quantity	Revenue	Revenue % Growth Prior Period	Cost
6	- Product total	- Channel total	$259,418	$28,136,809	$18	$22,102,224
7		+ Direct	$122,541	$13,388,596	($6)	$10,469,844
8		+ Indirect	$62,985	$6,709,577	$257	$5,409,322
9		+ Others	$73,892	$8,038,636	$5	$6,223,058
10	+ Electronics	- Channel total	$46,148	$4,704,951	($10)	$3,861,841
11		+ Direct	$21,500	$2,216,832	($24)	$1,815,462
12		+ Indirect	$11,716	$1,064,906	$77	$896,192
13		+ Others	$12,932	$1,423,213	($15)	$1,150,187
14	+ Hardware	- Channel total	$4,746	$5,684,379	$31	$4,696,991
15		+ Direct	$2,399	$2,933,001	$6	$2,422,419
16		+ Indirect	$1,046	$1,142,208	$754	$965,797
17		+ Others	$1,301	$1,609,170	$12	$1,308,775
18	+ Peripherals and Accessories	- Channel total	$71,162	$7,859,752	$22	$6,103,499
19		+ Direct	$33,369	$3,688,137	($6)	$2,830,732
20		+ Indirect	$17,304	$2,000,792	$293	$1,617,269
21		+ Others	$20,489	$2,170,823	$8	$1,655,498
22	+ Photo	- Channel total	$34,787	$6,333,698	$46	$4,762,792
23		+ Direct	$16,127	$2,874,100	$13	$2,146,974
24		+ Indirect	$8,868	$1,660,729	$276	$1,275,496
25		+ Others	$9,792	$1,798,869	$33	$1,340,322
26	+ Software/Other	- Channel total	$102,575	$3,554,029	$3	$2,677,101
27		+ Direct	$49,146	$1,676,526	($20)	$1,254,257
28		+ Indirect	$24,051	$840,942	$330	$654,568

FIGURE 6-40. *Excel spreadsheet with the Oracle BI menu*

Custom Reporting with Microsoft Office

Recall that custom Microsoft Office reports enable analysts to create documents and slides with live data points. Analysts can create the report once and reuse it month after month, simply by updating the content of the data points. The data points can be presented in the default grid format and in a variety of other visualizations, such as a scatter plot, bar chart, heat map, and so forth.

OBIEE includes the Oracle Business Intelligence Add-in for Microsoft Office which allows data from the BI Server to be used in Office products such as Excel and PowerPoint. Because Oracle OLAP and Oracle Essbase data can be used with OBIEE Plus and the BI Server, this same data can be used in the Oracle Business Intelligence Add-in as well. Oracle also offers the ability to create custom Microsoft Office reports out of the box with Smart View and its integrated visualization tool, Visual Explorer. Smart View offers the ability to view Essbase data directly or use data from the BI Server, which includes Oracle OLAP data.

Third-Party Reporting Applications

All the reporting tools that have been used as examples in this chapter are Oracle products. There are also some high-quality third-party reporting tools available for both Oracle OLAP and Oracle Essbase.

Third-Party Reporting Tools for Oracle OLAP

Over the years, several products have been able to access the data in Oracle OLAP workspaces. Recently, with all the BI software company consolidations and mergers, the landscape has changed. Several of the smaller independent companies that produced some very good tools are no longer with us, but others have emerged to take their place. The three products we address here are the Simba MDX Provider, ClearView, and Escendo Analyzer. The Simba MDX Provider and ClearView both work with Microsoft Excel, but provide different levels of integration and features. Escendo Analyzer is a stand-alone application that works directly with the Oracle OLAP data.

Simba MDX Provider

Simba Technologies has been a leader in relational and multidimensional connectivity tools and drivers for more than 18 years. The company has been providing multidimensional drivers for front-end tools for Microsoft and Hyperion since 2002. In the summer of 2009, Simba came out with another first: a native Microsoft Excel 2007 connector for Oracle OLAP 11*g*. This product uses Simba's MDX query language technology to access Oracle OLAP. Just about all other multidimensional databases have MDX providers; up until now, Oracle OLAP has been an exception. This will help level the playing field.

The primary purpose of the MDX Provider is to provide the same level of functionality within Excel as Microsoft Analysis Services. As far as Excel is concerned, the Oracle OLAP data looks just like Microsoft Analysis Services data. End users familiar with using the Excel PivotTable feature will view the Oracle OLAP data the same way they would see the Microsoft Analysis Services data. This is not an Excel add-in or bolt-on like other solutions; it works natively with Excel.

The Simba MDX Provider works seamlessly to parse and process multidimensional queries from Excel and integrate with Oracle OLAP 11*g* via SQL/ODBC. It translates Excel's MDX queries to SQL to retrieve Oracle OLAP cube information. The result is a fast and secure means to use popular, multidimensional tools like Excel to access your Oracle OLAP data directly.

The Excel 2007 PivotTable can now be used with Oracle OLAP to take advantage of all the BI analysis and presentation features that Microsoft provides. Connection to the database is simple. It is set up in the same way as any other MDX multidimensional data store, as you can see in Figure 6-41.

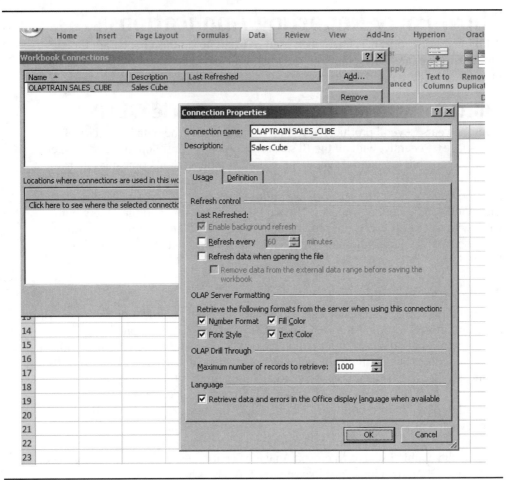

FIGURE 6-41. *Connection to Oracle OLAP data via the Simba MDX Provider*

As you can see from Figure 6-42, the OLAP data is presented in the native Excel interface supported by Microsoft. No additional menus or user interfaces are necessary.

NOTE
The native Excel PivotTable functionality does not allow for data write-back. As a result, the Simba MDX Provider does not currently support writing data back to the database.

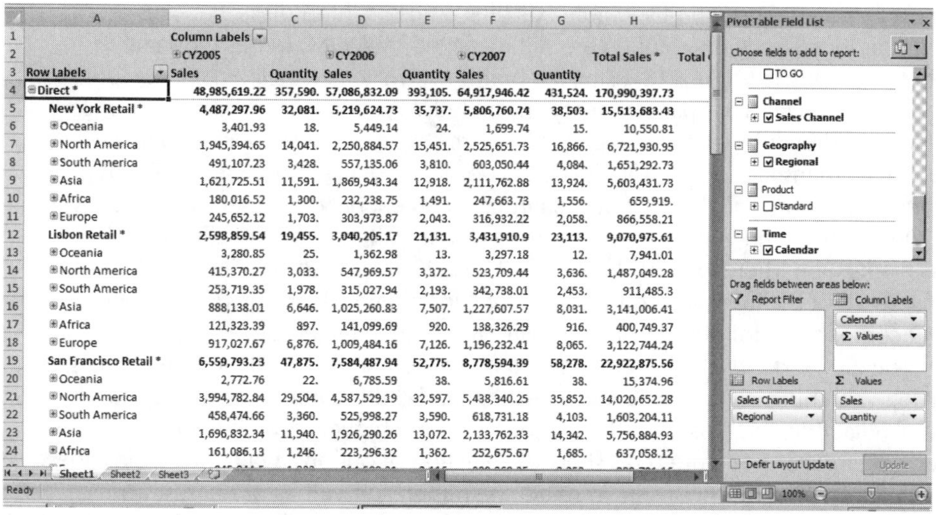

FIGURE 6-42. *Simba MDX Provider accessing OLAP data in Excel*

The Simba MDX Provider requires Oracle OLAP 11*g* (support for version 10*g* is currently not planned). This is the first release of the product, and Simba plans for this to eventually become a full MDX provider, compatible with other MDX data consumers. As you can see, this product provides a different layer of compatibility than other tools. While it may be limited by not supporting write-back, it also has the brightest future. If Simba is able to enhance the provider to support integration into other tools that currently support only Microsoft Analysis Services or other MDX multidimensional databases, this will expose Oracle OLAP to a much broader reporting tool base.

ClearView

ClearView 2.0, by Collaborative Concepts Consulting, Inc., allows Microsoft Excel users a great way to access data in Oracle OLAP cubes. ClearView is a rich Excel add-in that enables users to view data with a powerful query builder tool for ad hoc reporting, boardroom-ready reporting analysis, and what-if analysis. ClearView supports full write-back to Oracle OLAP cubes and can be used for a complete analysis solution.

ClearView 1.0 was originally developed for Oracle Financial Analyzer users. ClearView 2.0 extends support to Oracle OLAP cubes and adds a great number of features. ClearView is developed as an Excel add-in, using the Excel worksheet as a presentation vehicle. This solution is designed for a collaborative, multiuser environment.

It supports a workbook management catalog system, storing all workbooks in the Oracle Database, instead of separate .xls files on users' hard disks.

Cubes in a ClearView solution are still managed by AWM. It uses the same metadata as Oracle OLAP 11*g*, using the built-in views to access the data. For Oracle OLAP 10*g* analytic workspaces, ClearView includes routines that produce 11*g*-style metadata and built-in relational views. There are stored procedures and relational tables that are installed in the Oracle Database as part of ClearView setup. This type of architecture allows collaboration and sharing of content between users in a secure way.

On the front end, ClearView is a single DLL installed as an Excel COM add-in. This works with Microsoft Excel versions 2002, 2003, and 2007. The Excel add-in provides all of the interface components for ClearView. ClearView uses Oracle ADO components for communication with the Oracle Database.

ClearView extends the Excel menus to include standard OLAP actions such as ranking, matching, sorting, rotating, selecting, and drilling down, as well as more advanced actions such as spreading amounts from a higher level to lower levels (for allocating forecasts). Figure 6-43 shows a selection of options available in ClearView.

ClearView also allows users to select the dimension values of interest from within Excel using the Easy Select feature (autocomplete), without needing to pop up another data selection window. The newly inserted row or column inherits all the formatting from the previous row or column. The Easy Select feature, shown in Figure 6-44, can be used to append or insert records to a range of data without affecting other formats on the worksheet.

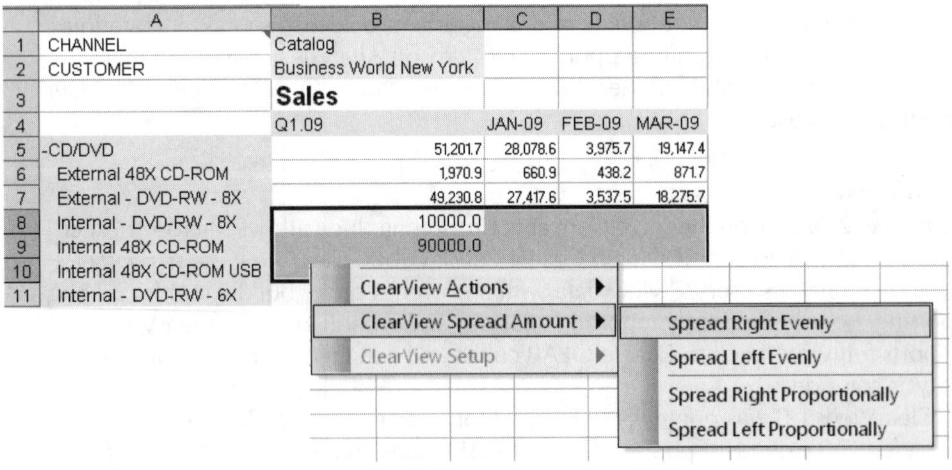

FIGURE 6-43. *ClearView Spread Amount feature*

	A	B	C	D	E
1	CHANNEL	Total Channel			
2	CUSTOMER	Total Customer			
3		Sales			
4		JAN-07	FEB-07	MAR-07	APR-07
5	OS DOC ENG - OS Doc Eng	80439.30	77232.45	87372.95	84678.34
6	OS DOC FRE - OS Doc Fre	10789.12	16074.52	13332.96	13699.80
7	doc				
8	DOC - Doc				
9	OS DOC ENG - OS Doc Eng				
10	OS DOC FRE - OS Doc Fre				
11	OS DOC GER - OS Doc Ger				
12	OS DOC ITA - OS Doc Ita				
13	OS DOC KAN - OS Doc Kan				
14	OS DOC SPA - OS Doc Spa				

FIGURE 6-44. *Inserting additional rows by using the Easy Select feature*

ClearView allows users to create a highly formatted deck of reports that can be periodically refreshed to reflect the latest data. These reports use qualified data reference (QDR) format, which allows users to create customized asymmetric reports with ease. Excel formulas and Excel charts, along with other native Excel features, can be used within the same report, as shown in Figure 6-45.

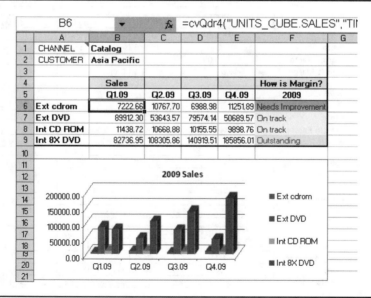

FIGURE 6-45. *Sample boardroom-ready report*

Users can enter data directly into Excel to be written back to Oracle OLAP cubes. When this occurs, this data is submitted to a task processor. This allows administrators to have fine control over what is actually written back and to trigger calculation rules that can calculate other data based on what was written back. ClearView's Aggregate function allows users to do a what-if analysis before committing the data to the database. This means that users can type in data, submit data in a read-only instance of the analytic workspace, compute the totals in the database, and redisplay the results in the worksheet. Based on the analysis of the aggregated results, the data can then be permanently submitted, as shown in Figure 6-46.

ClearView's write-back functionality supports all the AWM data types (text, date, and numeric). Security defined at the cube cell level within AWM is enforced for write-back. The task processor supports multiple queues, which can be configured for different cubes, facilitating multiuser write-back. An intelligent processor optimizes the queue processes to minimize the number of aggregations. It also supports Sarbanes-Oxley compliance with change tracking for reports and all data adjustments.

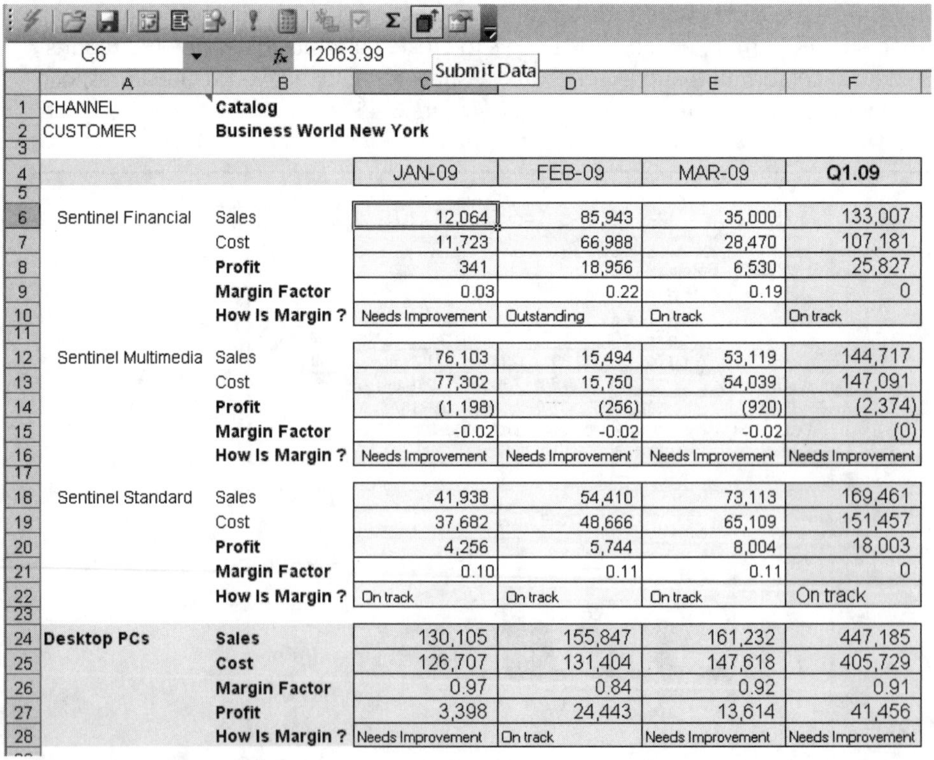

	A	B	C	D	E	F
1	CHANNEL	Catalog				
2	CUSTOMER	Business World New York				
3						
4			JAN-09	FEB-09	MAR-09	Q1.09
5						
6	Sentinel Financial	Sales	12,064	85,943	35,000	133,007
7		Cost	11,723	66,988	28,470	107,181
8		Profit	341	18,956	6,530	25,827
9		Margin Factor	0.03	0.22	0.19	0
10		How Is Margin ?	Needs Improvement	Outstanding	On track	On track
11						
12	Sentinel Multimedia	Sales	76,103	15,494	53,119	144,717
13		Cost	77,302	15,750	54,039	147,091
14		Profit	(1,198)	(256)	(920)	(2,374)
15		Margin Factor	-0.02	-0.02	-0.02	(0)
16		How Is Margin ?	Needs Improvement	Needs Improvement	Needs Improvement	Needs Improvement
17						
18	Sentinel Standard	Sales	41,938	54,410	73,113	169,461
19		Cost	37,682	48,666	65,109	151,457
20		Profit	4,256	5,744	8,004	18,003
21		Margin Factor	0.10	0.11	0.11	0
22		How Is Margin ?	On track	On track	On track	On track
23						
24	Desktop PCs	Sales	130,105	155,847	161,232	447,185
25		Cost	126,707	131,404	147,618	405,729
26		Margin Factor	0.97	0.84	0.92	0.91
27		Profit	3,398	24,443	13,614	41,456
28		How Is Margin ?	Needs Improvement	On track	Needs Improvement	Needs Improvement

FIGURE 6-46. *ClearView submits data tasks to a task processor for processing.*

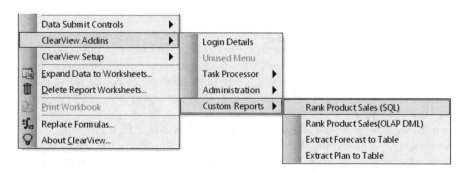

FIGURE 6-47.   *ClearView add-ins provide ways to extend OLAP functionality.*

As shown in Figure 6-47, ClearView can be configured to support custom add-ins to extend the OLAP functionality. For example, a custom add-in could be output coming from a relational query, OLAP DML program, or stored procedure.

While ClearView allows you to place Oracle OLAP data in any cell, by using formulas that access data at the cell level, it also fetches all cells of the same measure in bulk, providing excellent performance even on large data refreshes. Sparse data is handled in the back end to minimize communications between the front end and back end.

We have covered only a sampling of the capabilities of ClearView. Any company that is looking for a complete OLAP analysis solution using Oracle OLAP data with an Excel front end should investigate ClearView. ClearView's advanced write-back functionality makes it an ideal choice for clients who need a low-cost planning and forecasting application solution on top of Oracle OLAP. The task processor provides for orderly submission of data and tracking of multiple changes. The workbook management catalog system gives users the ability to store workbooks directly in the Oracle Database, mitigating one of the major problems with spreadsheet access to OLAP data—the proliferation of data.

Escendo Analytics

Escendo provides an application development environment for developing, deploying, and analyzing Oracle OLAP cubes. Escendo is built by long-time Express and Oracle OLAP consultants for migrating Express applications and developing new analytic applications on top of Oracle OLAP. Rather than using AWM, they wrote their own Escendo Architect tool for building cubes.

Escendo Analytics consists of two related products. Escendo Architect replaces AWM for cube development and deployment. Escendo Analyzer provides a web-enabled front end for reporting and analyzing Oracle OLAP cubes.

Escendo cubes are built with Escendo Architect, a Java application used by Oracle OLAP administrators. Components live on the server as well as on the client side. Escendo works with Oracle OLAP 10g as well as Oracle OLAP 11g, but uses its own metadata to include features such as version control on OLAP objects, customized SQL for loading data into cubes, a deployment manager, security administration, and migration from Oracle Express. As a result, some of the features available with Oracle OLAP 11g, such as cube-organized materialized views and query rewrite, are not yet available for cubes built with Escendo.

Escendo Analyzer is a Flash-based front end built on a Java EE framework. Deployments have a hierarchical structure, giving users the ability to control who gets to see what data or approve changes, carrying forward some of the features available with Oracle Financial Analyzer.

Escendo Analytics, shown in Figure 6-48, includes standard OLAP actions such as rotating, selecting, and drilling down. It also adds a Business Perspectives feature,

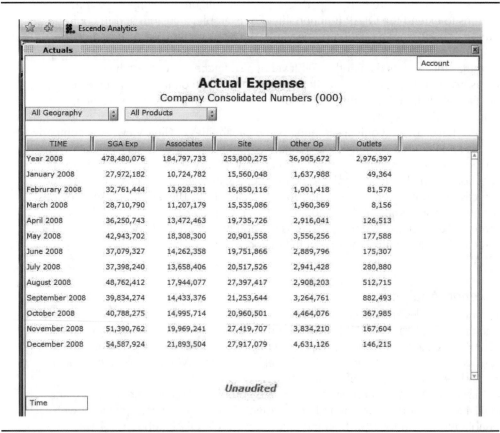

TIME	SGA Exp	Associates	Site	Other Op	Outlets
Year 2008	478,480,076	184,797,733	253,800,275	36,905,672	2,976,397
January 2008	27,972,182	10,724,782	15,560,048	1,637,988	49,364
Februrary 2008	32,761,444	13,928,331	16,850,116	1,901,418	81,578
March 2008	28,710,790	11,207,179	15,535,086	1,960,369	8,156
April 2008	36,250,743	13,472,463	19,735,726	2,916,041	126,513
May 2008	42,943,702	18,308,300	20,901,558	3,556,256	177,588
June 2008	37,079,327	14,262,358	19,751,866	2,889,796	175,307
July 2008	37,398,240	13,658,406	20,517,526	2,941,428	280,880
August 2008	48,762,412	17,944,077	27,397,417	2,908,203	512,715
September 2008	39,834,274	14,433,376	21,253,644	3,264,761	882,493
October 2008	40,788,275	14,995,714	20,960,501	4,464,076	367,985
November 2008	51,390,762	19,969,241	27,419,707	3,834,210	167,604
December 2008	54,587,924	21,893,504	27,917,079	4,631,126	146,215

FIGURE 6-48. *Escendo Analytics*

which helps to define which users get to see what data in what format. Users can write back data to the cubes.

Escendo allows companies to develop OLAP applications using Oracle OLAP. With Oracle OLAP moving more toward the IT organization, Escendo extends its use back to the user community for classic OLAP applications, developed and managed by line-of-business users.

Escendo should be considered by organizations that are attracted to many of the features of Essbase (but not necessarily the Excel interface), but want to store their data in an Oracle Database in Oracle OLAP cubes. Users can write back data to cubes using Escendo.

Third-Party Reporting Tools for Essbase

Nearly all of the reporting tools that have been used as examples in this chapter are Oracle products, from the OBIEE Plus tool set. Given the openness of Essbase and its use of standard MDX for querying, over the years, many companies have introduced great interfaces for Essbase. The software industry has gone through some major changes in the last few years, however, and many independent reporting tool companies were acquired by larger companies. Reporting tools for Essbase that were previously offered by smaller companies such as Temtec and Alphablox are now tools positioned inside larger companies. Their offerings may or may not retain their former level of support for Essbase.

Applied OLAP is one independent company that has developed its product, Dodeca, to meet needs that might not be available out of the box with Oracle's own reporting tools. We know of several Essbase clients using Dodeca very successfully today. This section includes a case study that highlights when the purchase of a third-party tool may be useful.

Dodeca

Dodeca is a web-deployed solution that easily integrates with Microsoft Office. It addresses the typical range of reporting needs, while also bringing together information from disparate data sources, including OLAP and relational database systems, within a single integrated user interface. Quick and easy customization is one of Dodeca's strengths.

Based on a web services and a metadata-centric architecture, Dodeca is designed to create tailored, customized applications that are targeted for analysts, decision makers, and business users at all levels. It was architected for speed of deployment and ease of use, while centralizing and managing business rules and files.

The two main features of the Dodeca architecture are the modular design and a patent-pending metadata management engine. The modular design provides the flexibility necessary for customers to control an interface that fits their exact needs, while the metadata engine enables rapid, global deployment flexibility and support for best-practice application life-cycle management.

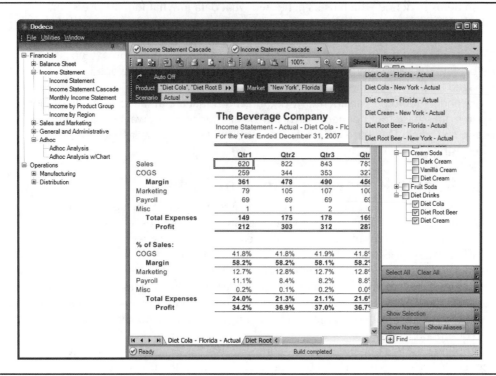

FIGURE 6-49. *The standard Dodeca user interface*

Typically, companies have a number of disparate data sources that contain related information, both relational and OLAP. Dodeca provides an interface that can bring those multiple sources together into a single custom application. Essbase analytics and underlying data sources, such as general ledger and other transaction systems, become part of a single experience. Figure 6-49 shows a standard Dodeca window, with user controls on the left, content in the center, and dimensional navigation on the right.

All of the features and functionality in Dodeca are provided by the underlying modular architecture. There are a large number of features that are available out of the box, including the following:

■ Dodeca provides essentially the same functionality found in the classic Essbase Spreadsheet Add-in, but also has some unique features. Specific operations can be made available within a given context, thus providing a more structured and guided user experience. For example, the zoom in and out operations can be enabled or disabled on a dimension-by-dimension basis for a specific report.

■ Dodeca includes its own Excel-compatible spreadsheet interface that can read and write Excel files that contain one or more sheets, calculate Excel formulas, render Excel formatting and charts, and enforce Excel element protection. It supports familiar editing operations, such as copy and paste special.

■ Intelligent navigation makes it easy for users to remain in context as they navigate between different views or reports. This capability allows users to remain within a continuous thought process without the distraction of logging in to multiple systems or reselecting the parameters in the supporting systems. For example, an existing Dodeca customer has both Essbase and PeopleSoft GL, and uses the right-click functionality of intelligent navigation to drill across from Essbase to the details from PeopleSoft.

■ Analytic commentary allows users to communicate variance explanations or other textual information related to an analysis in a systematic way. The commentary functionality delivered with Dodeca provides for threaded conversations and allows users to attach relevant documents to data points or partial data points within a view or report.

■ Dodeca automatically logs all changes to the Essbase database, including the user information, a timestamp, the old values, and new values.

■ All aspects of the Dodeca user environment are controlled centrally by administrators who manage the metadata that drives the application using a form-driven administration environment. Administrators control all aspects of both content generation and behavior—including the spreadsheet templates, available database connections, toolbars, and all user interface elements—to ensure that end users can easily and quickly get the correct information with minimal effort.

These are only a small sampling of the out-of-the-box features of Dodeca. For those customers who have other needs, Dodeca's object-oriented modular architecture is open, documented, and supported. Customers can create their own modules to satisfy their most demanding user requirements. Now we will look at a case study showing how Dodeca can be used.

Dodeca Case Study

Dodeca is often used when a company has a number of data sources, including a large number of Essbase databases, and wants to enable users to more easily explore and find the information they need.

A large international bank had hundreds of users using an Essbase flash reporting system to view daily results. Although popular with users, the flash reporting database lacked the level of detail necessary to get a complete understanding of the data. In order to access the detailed analytic data, a user had to connect to a different Essbase database that contained significantly more details for two of the dimensions. Next, to further investigate the underlying details stored in an external general ledger system, the user had to log in to the system and create one or more queries. Finally, to review a source document, such as an invoice, a request had to be submitted to the accounts payable department, who provided a copy within five working days.

Due to the cumbersome and time-consuming effort required to complete the analysis process, user productivity suffered. Further investigation was frequently skipped altogether, as the cost to dig into supporting details was often greater than the benefit gained.

The bank managers chose Dodeca for its Essbase functionality and Excel compatibility. They also looked to Dodeca's intelligent navigation feature to make it easier for users to complete more thorough analyses. As noted earlier, intelligent navigation enables users to move interactively between reporting systems in order to explore a particular point of interest, while staying within the same application. The context is automatically retained as a user navigates through and across the various systems.

The value of the intelligent navigation feature is demonstrated in this example during a training session with a corporate controller. He learned how to explore summary information from Essbase, and then, with a single mouse click, navigate to a more detailed analytic view. A report was created that allowed for drill through to details, like the one shown in Figure 6-50.

The controller was automatically connected to an Essbase database containing more detail in the account and entity dimensions. The view presented at the detailed level maintained the entity, month, scenario, and other dimensions of the selected data point as the starting point for the new report. At this point, he was able

Gold Standard Bank
Contribution, RPT_Calc
P&L By Entity (Var)

	2008 Actuals May	2008 Actuals Jun	Outlook (Jun) Jun	Variance B(W) Outlook
L92600 - PROTECTION	(158.57)	(184.93)	(169.99)	(14.94)
L92645 - INSURANCE	(30,108.34)	(38,597.00)	(36,116.12)	(2,480.87)
L92685 - DONATIONS	(765.37)	(553.50)	(943.32)	389.82
L92705 - LOSS ON EXTINGUISHMENT OF DEBT	60.40	354.27	200.00	154.27
L94899 - DIRECT NON-INTEREST EXPENSE	(492,453.57)	(504,824.01)	(525,683.04)	20,859.03

Line Detail Report
Source Detail Report
Cascade View   Ctrl+Shift+C

FIGURE 6-50. *Case study first report with right-click drill-through capability*

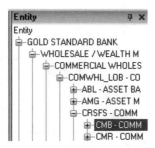

FIGURE 6-51.   *Drill-through details to CMB*

to navigate through certain dimensions to explore the detailed data further. For example, he could have selected to explore the CMB - Commercial Bank entity rollup instead of viewing data for the entire bank, as shown in Figure 6-51.

Once the controller found a number that required more detailed exploration, a simple right-click moved the analysis into the company's general ledger system.

When the controller selected the GLTXN link on the context menu, the context for the selected data point was automatically passed to the general ledger and produced a report showing the details. The controller selected a value that was the summary of more than 2,000 entities and over 100 accounts from the context menu shown in Figure 6-52.

The resulting general ledger report returned posting-level entities and accounts, and prepared a report for all postings that composed the number. Figure 6-53 shows an example of the GL Details Report.

The controller reviewed the details and found an accounts payable posting that was relevant from this detail, as shown in Figure 6-54. Once again, intelligent navigation allowed the controller to easily review the invoice image, where he discovered that one of his managers had a signature authority limit significantly higher than he believed appropriate. The continuous analytic thought process enabled by Dodeca gave the controller an insight into his business that led directly to action and to increased oversight within his department.

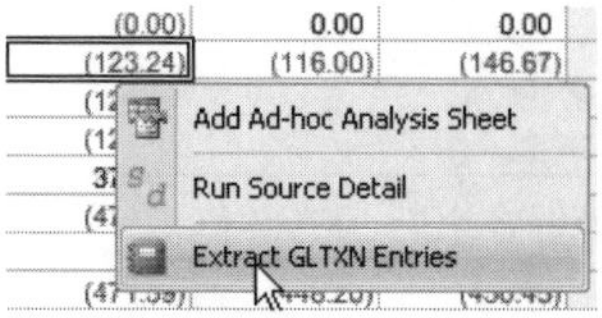

FIGURE 6-52.   *GLTXN drill-through selection*

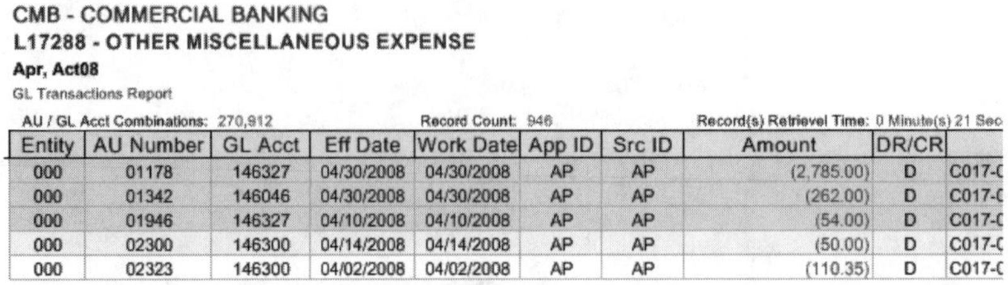

CMB - COMMERCIAL BANKING
L17288 - OTHER MISCELLANEOUS EXPENSE
Apr, Act08
GL Transactions Report

AU / GL Acct Combinations: 270,912 Record Count: 946 Record(s) Retrievel Time: 0 Minute(s) 21 Sec

Entity	AU Number	GL Acct	Eff Date	Work Date	App ID	Src ID	Amount	DR/CR	
000	01178	146327	04/30/2008	04/30/2008	AP	AP	(2,785.00)	D	C017-(
000	01342	146046	04/30/2008	04/30/2008	AP	AP	(262.00)	D	C017-(
000	01946	146327	04/10/2008	04/10/2008	AP	AP	(54.00)	D	C017-(
000	02300	146300	04/14/2008	04/14/2008	AP	AP	(50.00)	D	C017-(
000	02323	146300	04/02/2008	04/02/2008	AP	AP	(110.35)	D	C017-(

FIGURE 6-53. *Miscellaneous expense GL report*

t	DR/CR	Description
,785.00)	D	C017-0120247-CENTRAL AUT-001
(262.00)	D	C01
(54.00)	D	...9251-CENTRAL ...-063

Retrieve Invoice

BILL TO
Gold Standard Bank
555 Building Street
Silver City, CA 90124

SHIP TO
Gold Standard Bank
555 Building Street
Silver City, CA 90124

P.O. NUMBER	TERMS
	Net 30

QUANTITY	ITEM CODE	DESCRIPTION	PRICE EACH	AMOUNT
1	123456	Project Alpha 86419 Phase One	612,458.00	612,458.00

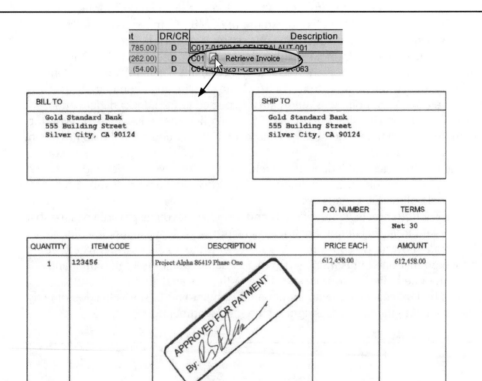

FIGURE 6-54. *Accounts payable posting and invoice*

Conclusion

This chapter touched on many areas that need to be taken into consideration for OLAP reporting. We showed that customers leverage many common elements—not just functionality and ease of use, but also terminology and common tools to deploy sophisticated OLAP reporting. You saw examples from many of the components in OBIEE Plus, as well as some additional reporting options from third-party companies. Oracle's strategy is to continue to offer functionality in a platform that works with both Oracle OLAP and Oracle Essbase, and extends current capabilities in both the web offerings and Smart View. This will make it easy for a large user base to extend their OLAP projects and leverage these common tools that work with both OLAP offerings.

We discussed determining the types of users and reports, the functionality they desire, and the many deployment options a project team can choose to use. In the next chapter, we look at front-end products that can leverage OLAP data and how they are commonly used in organizations.

References

Few, Stephen. *Information Dashboard Design: The Effective Visual Communication of Data*. O'Reilly Media, 2006.

Hatch, Toby and Raef Lawson. *Oracle's Comprehensive Guide to Realizing EPM Version 2.2*. White Paper. Oracle Corporation, October 2007.

Nader, Michael and Dave Collins. *Dare to OLAP*. Oracle Corporation, 2008.

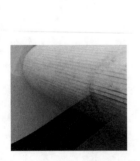

CHAPTER
7

Leveraging OLAP in
Your Organization

he reporting and spreadsheet tools discussed in Chapter 6 are powerful ways to interact with OLAP data and share results, but they are not the only ways. Many packaged applications can use Essbase or Oracle OLAP as a source of data and/or as a calculation engine. For example, you can find applications for planning, forecasting, and cost management. These packaged applications interact with Essbase or Oracle OLAP via Java APIs. The APIs are public, which means that anyone can develop a custom application to work with one of Oracle's OLAP engines.

In this chapter, we present some Oracle products that can be used with Essbase and Oracle OLAP. For Essbase, we showcase two enterprise performance management (EPM) products—Oracle Hyperion Planning and Oracle Hyperion Profitability and Cost Management—as well as Oracle Crystal Ball and Oracle Smart Space. For Oracle OLAP, we cover Oracle Application Express. We conclude with an introduction to the Java APIs for those who may be interested in developing a custom front-end application.

Performance Management Applications Leveraging Essbase

As described earlier in this book, you can create planning, budgeting, forecasting, and profitability and cost management systems using Essbase features embedded within custom Microsoft Excel or web applications. Custom applications come with challenges, including template creation (often by budget administrators), ease of use, end-user support, documentation, custom programming, a path for upgrades, and ongoing maintenance. For example, on one job, we had a situation where one employee created and owned the Excel-based planning models. The system was not documented, and it contained a lot of Visual Basic code leveraging the Essbase APIs. No one else in the organization had the knowledge necessary to maintain the application, and because the application was created by the finance department, it was not supported by the IT organization. Therefore, while this custom application did the job in the short term, the risks to the organization were high over the longer term.

Start-from-scratch solutions are obviously not for everyone. Fortunately, other options are available. As a result of the high demand for packaged applications, Oracle assembled the Oracle Enterprise Performance Management System. Two applications within that Oracle system leverage Essbase as their database and calculation engine: Planning and Profitability and Cost Management. Planning focuses on planning, budgeting, and forecasting. Profitability and Cost Management helps you to determine profitability and manage costs. With these Essbase-based applications, you gain all the advantages of a packaged application, without sacrificing the speed and power of an OLAP system.

In this section, we review the features and functionality of the Planning application and the Profitability and Cost Management application. We then look at the administration component called Oracle Hyperion Enterprise Performance Management Architect, which an administrator can use to create, manage, and deploy Planning and Profitability and Cost Management applications, as well as Essbase cubes. We end with a brief look at the architecture for all three applications.

Oracle Hyperion Planning

Planning is a centralized, OLAP-based application for planning, budgeting, and forecasting. Essbase is the underlying calculation engine and data repository.

Planning offers data-entry forms, custom context menus for ease of navigation, a graphical interface for creating rules and calculations, and built-in workflows. The workflow component helps drive collaboration throughout the planning, budgeting, and forecasting processes. For example, in the budget process, budget owners can submit their budgets for approval with commentary, and approvers can respond in a variety of ways, including sending comments back to the owner.

To satisfy the diverse needs of user communities within an organization, Planning provides a web-based interface and an Excel-based interface. A centralized server provides a single point of administration for both interfaces. For example, an administrator can create one data-entry template that is available from either a web browser or Excel.

Planning includes the following features:

- **Support for top-down and bottom-up planning**   Senior management can set high-level targets at upper levels and allocate the targets down to lower levels (top-down). Planners can also start building budgets from the lowest level (bottom-up) and have comparisons to the targets.

- **Multiple versions for iterative planning cycles**   Planners can set up multiple versions of the plan to create what-if scenarios. They can also capture plan iterations and create comparisons between the iterations.

- **Support for driver-based plans**   Planners can set up assumptions for drivers that may affect their financial plan, such as market share, inflation factors, interest rates, midpoint salaries, and FICA limits.

- **Graphical Calculation Manager**   Planners can create easy and complex business rules and allocations without having to write script.

- **Web-based and Excel-based data-entry forms and annotations**   Planners can create data forms to collect key plan information. A single data form definition is valid for both interfaces.

- **Process management of the planning cycle**   Planners have a hierarchical or matrix review and sign-off with collaboration.

- **Integration with other systems** Planning ships with Oracle Data Integrator Enterprise Edition (ODI). ODI can be used to load metadata (such as charts of accounts, departments, and products) and related data from a relational data source.

- **Currency conversion for multicurrency applications** Currency conversion is built into Planning.

- **Workforce Planning module** This module provides predefined and supported content for the planning, budgeting, and forecasting of headcount and salary expenses.

- **Capital Expense Planning module** This module provides predefined and supported content for the planning, budgeting, and forecasting of capital expenditures and related profit and loss, balance sheet, and cash flow statements.

- **Common administration** Planning ships with Performance Management Architect, which is a common tool for managing shared hierarchies and creating applications for Planning and Profitability and Cost Management.

In a packaged solution, administrators expect the supporting components of the system to adapt to changes made to the system. For example, if an administrator adds a new cost center to an application, then the business rules, data-entry forms, custom navigation menus, process management, and related reports should automatically become aware that the new cost center exists. The administrator should not need to make any manual changes. Planning makes use of Essbase features to meet the demand for adaptive software. For example, when designing a business rule or data-entry form, the user will use family-related functions like IDescendants (Total Company). With family-related functions, the business rule and data form can adapt automatically to the addition of a new cost center. The following sections describe the adaptive components of Planning: Calculation Manager, data-entry forms, custom menus, process management, and task lists.

Calculation Manager

Business rules and the related calculations are the backbone of a planning application. Oracle developed a common interface, called Calculation Manager, where users can design, validate, and administer business rules in a graphical environment. Calculation Manager leverages the power of the Essbase calculation engine without the need to write Essbase calculation scripts. For example, you can graphically create a rule to aggregate the IT departmental expenses and allocate the total to all other cost centers (excluding the IT department) based on the number of PCs they have in place.

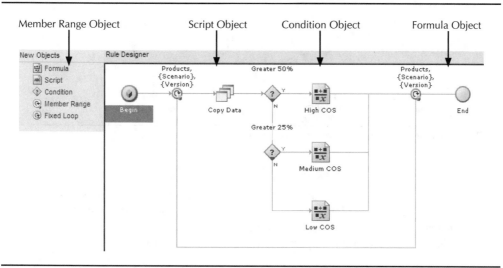

FIGURE 7-1. *Business rule flowchart*

Calculation Manager has four main components: business rules, templates, variables and run-time prompts, and rule sets.

Business Rules   A business rule consists of components that are dragged and dropped into a rule flowchart. Figure 7-1 shows a sample flowchart and points out the components of a business rule.

As summarized in the New Objects area of Figure 7-1, a rule has five possible components:

- **Formula**   This is the primary component of a business rule. Formulas contain calculation statements that assign values to accounts. For example, operating cost of sales (COS) can be assigned the value of 50 percent of operating revenue (Operating COS = Operating Revenue / 2). You can embed Essbase functions within formulas. Figure 7-2 shows two sample formulas within the Formula component.

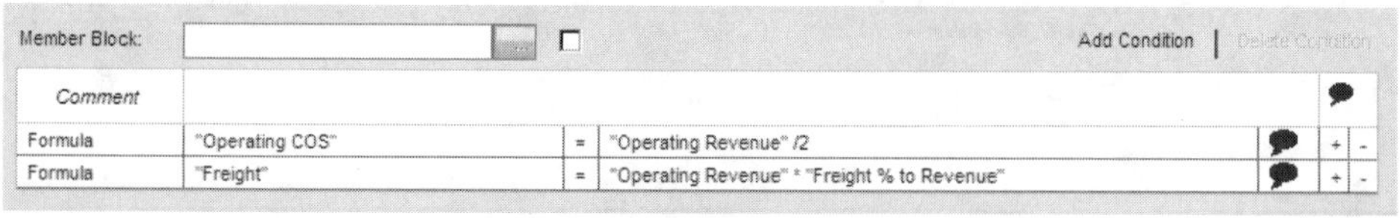

Member Block:						Add Condition	Delete Condition
Comment							💬
Formula	"Operating COS"	=	"Operating Revenue" /2			💬	+ -
Formula	"Freight"	=	"Operating Revenue" * "Freight % to Revenue"			💬	+ -

FIGURE 7-2. *Formula component of a business rule*

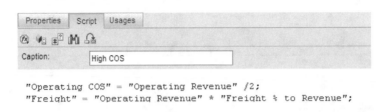

```
"Operating COS" = "Operating Revenue" /2;
"Freight" = "Operating Revenue" * "Freight % to Revenue";
```

FIGURE 7-3. *Script component of a business rule*

- **Script** With the Script component, those who are familiar with Essbase Script can add calculation statements to their rules using Essbase syntax instead of formulas. You can embed Essbase functions within scripts. Figure 7-3 shows the calculations from Figure 7-2 recast in Essbase Script.

- **Condition** You insert other rule components within the scope of the Condition component. A condition is an if-then statement. When the if part of the statement is true, Calculation Manager executes the statements within the Condition component. When it is false, the statements of the Condition component are skipped. You can specify conditions based on metadata or on the data itself. You can use Condition components to test which calculation should be executed. For example, the condition shown in Figure 7-4 states that if gross margin percent (Gross Profit / Net Revenue) is greater than 25 percent, execute the rule for medium COS.

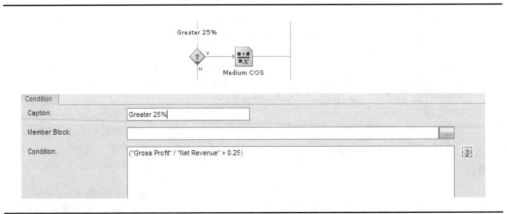

FIGURE 7-4. *Condition component of a business rule*

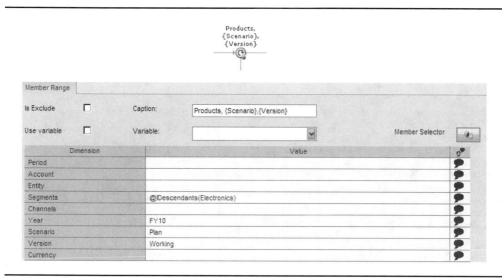

FIGURE 7-5. *Member Range component of a business rule*

- ■ **Member Range** This component creates a focus on a member or members where you would like the calculation to execute. For example, the range in Figure 7-5 specifies that this portion of the calculation will execute for all products under the Electronic category for the year FY10 for the Plan scenario and the Working version.

- ■ **Fixed Loop** This component indicates that a block of code is to repeat for a specified number of iterations. For example, you could specify that a loop execute the components within its scope ten times.

Templates The rule designer provides predefined business rules called *templates*. Templates can be used for clearing a portion of the database, copying a portion of the database, creating allocations, and aggregating a portion of the database. A Units/Rate/Amount template solves for any of the three variables, as long as two of the three variables are defined. Figure 7-6 shows a template specifying a revenue calculation based on units and price. Using this template, if a planner enters values for units and price, the template solves for operating revenue. If another planner enters values for price and operating revenue, the template will solve for the number of units.

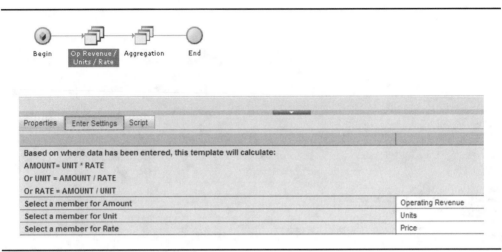

FIGURE 7-6. *Template rule designer*

Variables and Run-Time Prompts   Variables are user-defined values that are set at the global, application, rule, or Essbase level. For example, you can create a variable called CURRYEAR and set it to 2009. Rules containing this variable will use the year 2009 in all calculations. In subsequent years, you can reset CURRYEAR to the new current year, and all rules that contain the variable automatically use the new value. Using variables eliminates the need to update each rule manually when the value of a global variable changes.

Run-time prompts (RTPs) can be used to ask the user to enter required information during the execution of a calculation. For example, if you had a business rule to increase an account by a given percentage, the RTP would ask the user to enter the percentage value.

An advanced feature of RTPs uses members that are on the data-entry form. The form enters the tokens into the business rule, and executes when the form is saved without prompting the user. For example, consider a data-entry form where the point of view reflects these settings: Scenario=Plan, Year=2009, Version=Working, and Entity=Dallas. If the end user changes the point of view to show Houston instead of Dallas and saves the change, the rule is updated to specify Houston.

Rule Sets   Rule sets contain two or more rules that are calculated simultaneously or sequentially. For example, if you are allocating the IT department's expenses to all other cost centers, you first want to aggregate the expenses, and then run a series of allocations. You can create a rule set to automate the calculation and allocations.

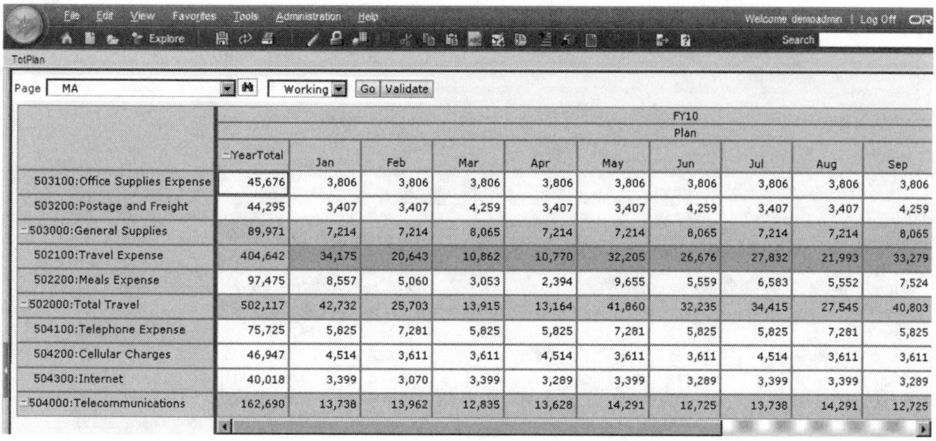

FIGURE 7-7.   *Data-entry form in a web browser*

Data-Entry Forms

Data-entry forms are spreadsheet-like grids with rows and columns for entering and modeling data. Figure 7-7 shows a sample Planning data-entry form displayed in a web browser.

Figure 7-8 shows the same data-entry form displayed in Microsoft Excel. In Excel, a companion line graph aids understanding of the relative differences among expenses.

Creating Forms   You design data-entry forms in a wizard by selecting the columns, rows, and page headers. Data-entry forms are designed using family-related functions (like IDescendants) and variables (like CURRYEAR) to minimize the number of forms required, and for monthly and annual maintenance during the monthly forecasting and annual planning processes. For example, if you set the variable CURRYEAR to FY10 for this year, all annual planning data-entry forms for the current annual operating plan will reference the year FY10. Next year, you can set the CURRYEAR variable to FY11, and these same forms will now reference FY11 as the current planning year. This use of variables and functions minimizes the amount of maintenance required for the system. Figure 7-9 shows an example of the column and row options for a data-entry form.

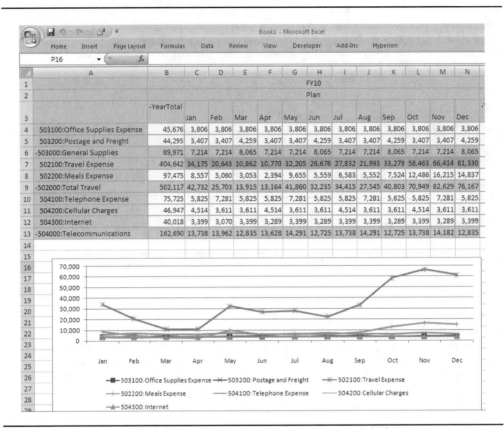

FIGURE 7-8. *Data-entry form in Microsoft Excel with line graph below*

Using Forms Planning includes various out-of-the-box data-entry features for entering and modeling data. End users can do the following with the data in a form:

- **Enter data** You can enter data directly into cells on a data-entry form. There are visual clues when data changes. When a cell has changed, the data-entry form marks the cell by changing the background of the cell to a darker yellow. After the data is committed to the application, the cell reverts to the original color. Figure 7-10 shows two data cells with changed values.

- **Spread data changes** You can spread data from summary to base time periods automatically. For example, in Figure 7-11 a planner changes the year total of Office Supplies from 45,000 to 50,000. The difference is spread down to the month proportionately based on the values that were previously there.

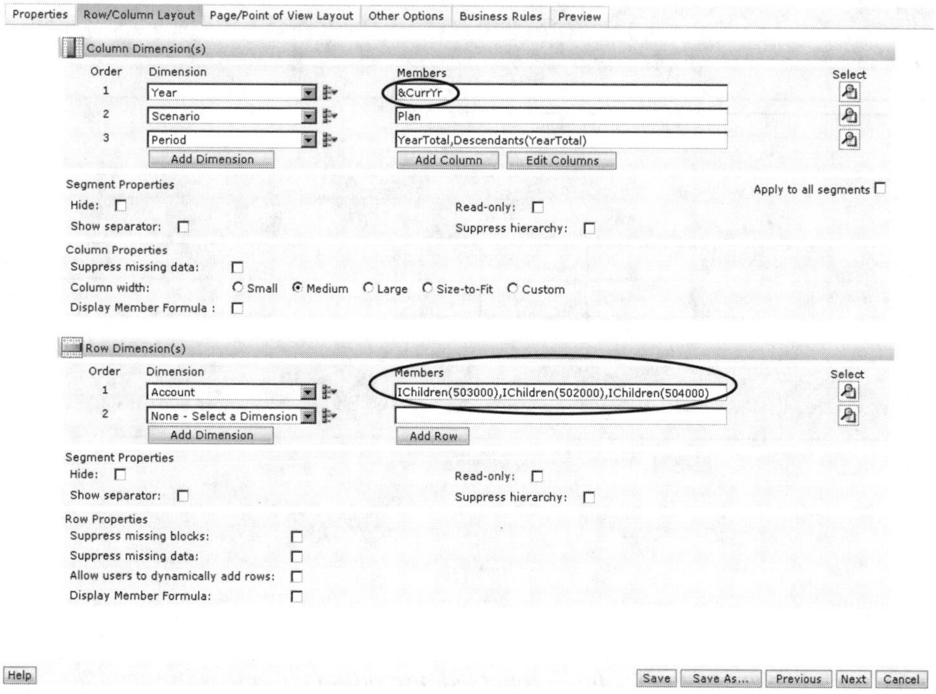

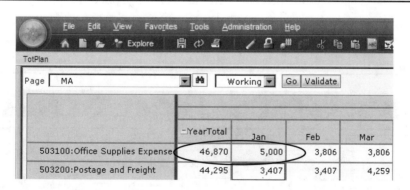

FIGURE 7-9.   *Data-entry form wizard*

FIGURE 7-10.   *Data cells with changed values are indicated with a yellow fill.*

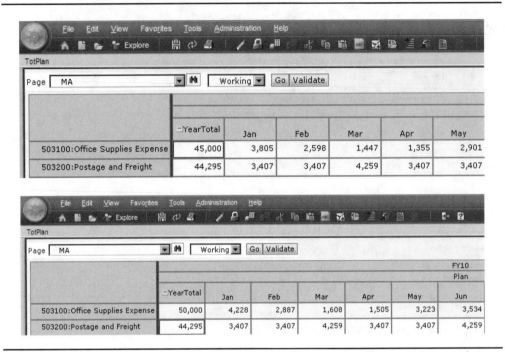

FIGURE 7-11. *A change to a total value is reflected proportionally across its members.*

- **Increase and decrease values for members** You can use the Adjust Data tool to increase or decrease data by a value or percentage. In Figure 7-12, a planner specifies a 5 percent decrease to Office Supplies Expenses.

- **Increase and decrease values for dimensions** You also have the ability to adjust data for dimensions. A planner can adjust the data by various spread

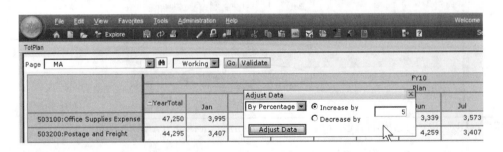

FIGURE 7-12. *Data for a member can be adjusted by user-defined values.*

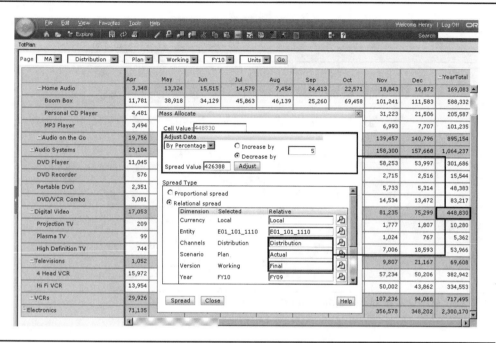

FIGURE 7-13. *Data for a dimension can be adjusted and spread according to user-defined values.*

methods, such as proportional spreads based on prior year actual values. In Figure 7-13, a planner decreases overall sales units by 5 percent for the DVD product line. She specifies a relational spread for the FY10 Working Plan based on the proportional values found in the Final version of the Actual scenario for FY09.

- **Execute predefined calculations** You can execute business rules to perform predefined calculations on data. For example, planners can enter key revenue drivers, and when the data is saved, execute a business rule to derive revenue and cost of sales based on the driver inputs. Figure 7-14 shows the drivers (Units through Sales Allowance %) followed by the business rule calculated accounts (Operating Revenue to Gross Profit).

- **Add comments and dates** You can add text comments directly into a data form. For example, a planner may need to enter a description or justification for the addition of a capital expenditure. You can also add dates directly into a data form, such as when a capital item was acquired for the purposes of depreciation. In Figure 7-15, a planner has added comments about

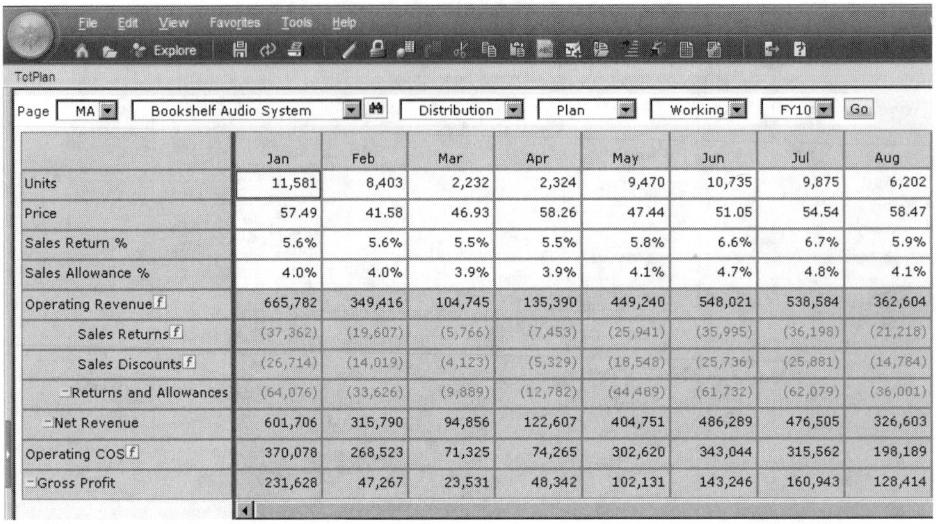

	Jan	Feb	Mar	Apr	May	Jun	Jul	Aug
Units	11,581	8,403	2,232	2,324	9,470	10,735	9,875	6,202
Price	57.49	41.58	46.93	58.26	47.44	51.05	54.54	58.47
Sales Return %	5.6%	5.6%	5.5%	5.5%	5.8%	6.6%	6.7%	5.9%
Sales Allowance %	4.0%	4.0%	3.9%	3.9%	4.1%	4.7%	4.8%	4.1%
Operating Revenue	665,782	349,416	104,745	135,390	449,240	548,021	538,584	362,604
Sales Returns	(37,362)	(19,607)	(5,766)	(7,453)	(25,941)	(35,995)	(36,198)	(21,218)
Sales Discounts	(26,714)	(14,019)	(4,123)	(5,329)	(18,548)	(25,736)	(25,881)	(14,784)
Returns and Allowances	(64,076)	(33,626)	(9,889)	(12,782)	(44,489)	(61,732)	(62,079)	(36,001)
Net Revenue	601,706	315,790	94,856	122,607	404,751	486,289	476,505	326,603
Operating COS	370,078	268,523	71,325	74,265	302,620	343,044	315,562	198,189
Gross Profit	231,628	47,267	23,531	48,342	102,131	143,246	160,943	128,414

FIGURE 7-14. *Drivers and calculated accounts in a business form*

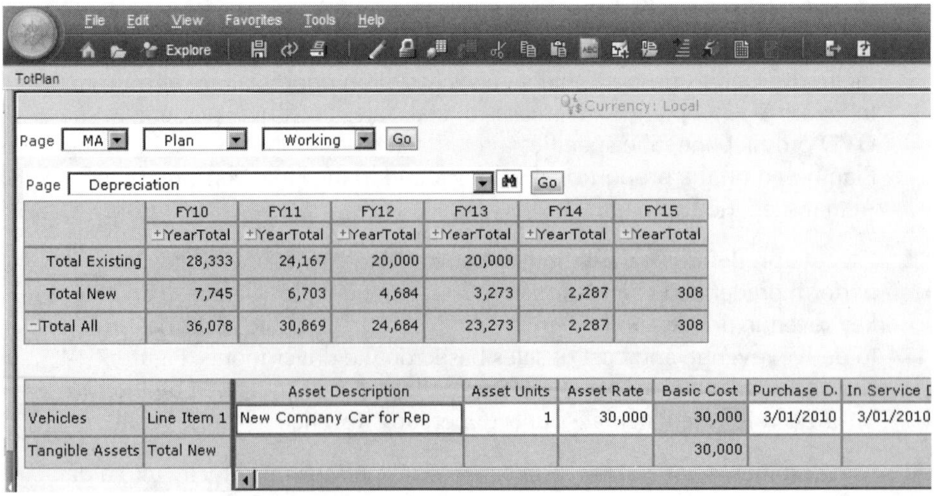

	FY10	FY11	FY12	FY13	FY14	FY15
	YearTotal	YearTotal	YearTotal	YearTotal	YearTotal	YearTotal
Total Existing	28,333	24,167	20,000	20,000		
Total New	7,745	6,703	4,684	3,273	2,287	308
Total All	36,078	30,869	24,684	23,273	2,287	308

		Asset Description	Asset Units	Asset Rate	Basic Cost	Purchase D	In Service D
Vehicles	Line Item 1	New Company Car for Rep	1	30,000	30,000	3/01/2010	3/01/2010
Tangible Assets	Total New				30,000		

FIGURE 7-15. *Comments and important dates can be added to data.*

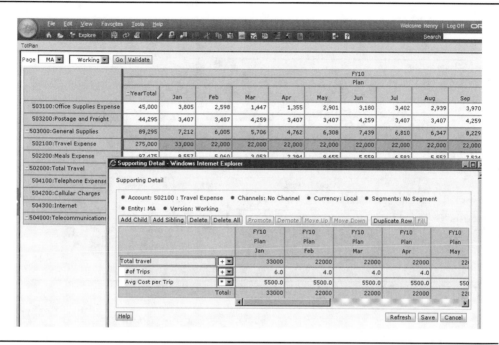

FIGURE 7-16.   *Planners can add detail to line items.*

a company car, its purchase date, and the date that it went into service. He likely has (or will create) a business rule to depreciate the value of the car automatically based on the In Service date.

- **Add detail to line items**   You have the ability to add line-item detail for base accounts. For example, your application may have an account for Travel Expense, but the planner wants to enter each trip. By using the line-item detail feature, the planner can build up the detail to derive the total Travel amount. In Figure 7-16, a planner has decided to record the number of trips and the average cost per trip.

- **Attach documents**   You can attach documents directly into a data form. For example, a planner may want to attach a copy of the funding document in PDF format for justification of the new capital expenditure, as shown in Figure 7-17.

You can make data-entry forms more dynamic by adding context menus, as discussed in the next section.

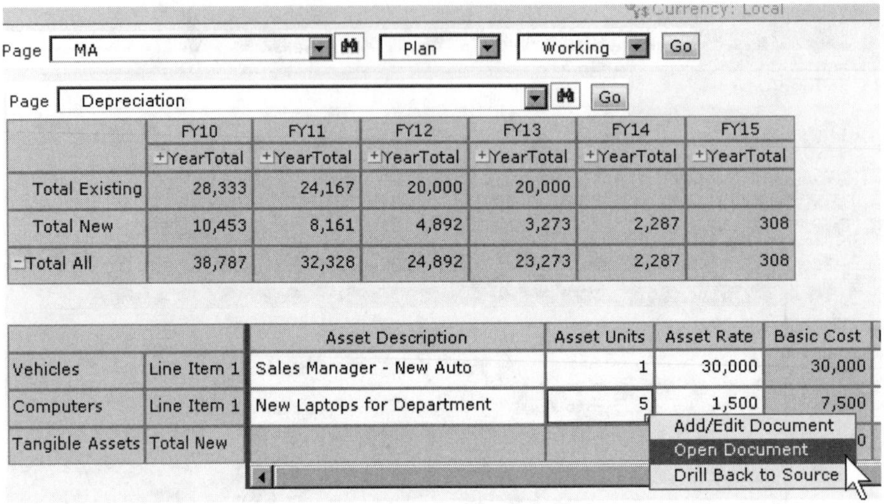

FIGURE 7-17. *Attach a document in a data form when detail is required.*

Custom Menus

While in a data-entry form, you can right-click a row or column to display a context menu with related actions. For example, after entering data, you may want to use the context menu to move to the Manage Process page, where you can approve a predefined scenario and version for use. Administrators are responsible for creating context menus and associating them with data-entry forms.

Here is a list of the types of tasks you may want added to the context menus:

■ Launch another application, URL, or business rule, with or without runtime prompts

■ Move to another data form

■ Move directly to the Manage Process page, with a predefined scenario and version

For example, in Figure 7-18, a right-click on the TBH1 row displays a context menu with related hiring actions, such as the option to add or remove a to-be-hired employee.

The context of the right-click is relayed to the next action. Any content that exists in the Page drop-down list (for example, the selected cost center) is passed to the next action, and the end user does not need to reenter that information. Figure 7-19 shows a sample form with inherited content.

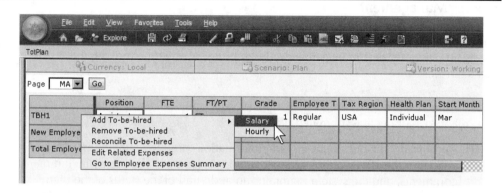

FIGURE 7-18. *Administrators create context menus and associate them with forms.*

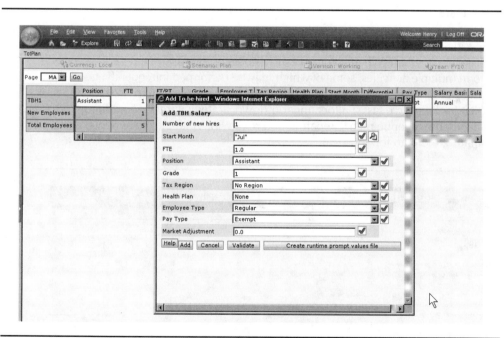

FIGURE 7-19. *Content is inherited from the page where the context menu action was initiated.*

Process Management

Process management enables you track the progress of your budget, view status information, identify ownership, and change the budget status at any level within the organization. Process management reduces budget cycle time through these key characteristics:

- **Approval process**   Preparers submit plans for approval and reviewers approve or decline submitted plans.

- **Audit trail**   Includes built-in audit information through annotations and process status. For example, preparers and reviews collaborate by including comments, and the system maintains an audit trail of the status of the plan.

- **E-mail notification**   E-mail notifications are sent when a status changes. For example, when a plan preparer submits a budget for approval, the reviewer receives an e-mail message stating that the plan is ready for review.

Task Lists

Task lists are a method of guiding users though the planning process. They provide a list of specific activities to complete within and outside the Oracle Enterprise Performance Management System. When an organization's plan or forecast requires end users to perform multiple activities, some of which may be performed infrequently, task lists provide guidance in completing these activities. For example, Figure 7-20 shows a task list that includes five tasks: allocating top-down strategic targets, compiling and reviewing the revenue plan, preparing and reviewing financial statements, and submitting the plan for approval.

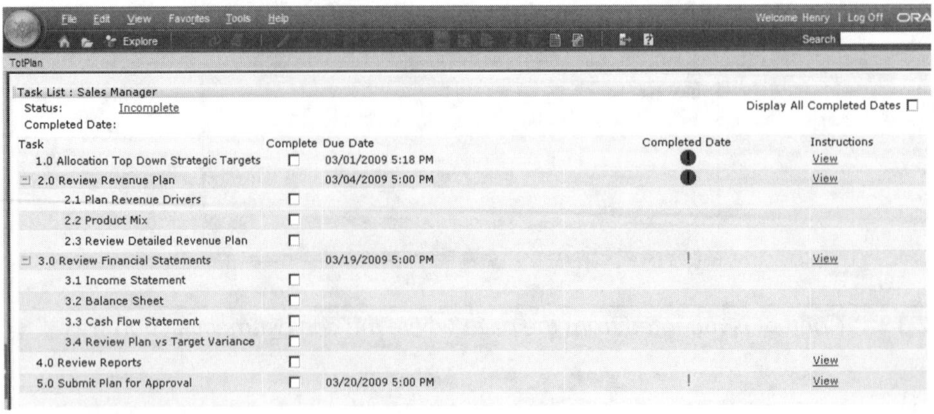

FIGURE 7-20.   *Sample task list*

Oracle Hyperion Profitability and Cost Management

Profitability and Cost Management is a packaged application that manages the cost and revenue allocations required to compute profitability for a business segment, such as a product, service, customer, region, or branch. The application provides a process that allows a business user to define allocation rules in business terms. The application translates these rules into underlying calculation scripts. By having a packaged application to create allocation definitions in business terms, business users are able to quickly create, deploy and maintain profitability and cost management solutions.

Before Profitability and Cost Management, it was common for business users to create complex Excel modules that linked a bunch of spreadsheets, and were difficult for other business users to decipher. Business users with access to Essbase would extend these Excel models by using the calculation functions within Essbase, but this usually required the assistance of an Essbase administrator to help write the complex calculations scripts required. While the combined Essbase/Excel solution was an improvement over Excel on its own, it did not provide business users with the flexibility to easily revise the allocation definitions to reflect changes in the business operations. Neither custom solution provided a user-friendly interface to define the profitability module or traceability of what was allocated and how it was allocated. Having a packaged solution for these tasks offers many benefits.

Building a Profitability and Cost Management Model

Profitability and Cost Management applications are referred to as *models*. A model represents part or all of an organization, and starts with costs and revenue values, often in a form similar to the organization's chart of accounts. These initial financial values are transformed through one or more allocations to assign reasonable and defensible cost values to ultimate cost (or profitability) objects—products, services, customers, and so on.

Building a Profitability and Cost Management model follows these steps:

- **Define stages** Define the number of cost or revenue transformations within an allocation process.

- **Create drivers** Define the methods used to calculate how source values are allocated to their destinations within a stage.

- **Select drivers** Choose which driver methods will be used by which source costs or revenues.

- **Make assignments** Map source cost and revenues to destinations.

■ **Collect data**   Use any number of existing utilities to load cost, revenue and driver data into the application's database (Essbase) or manually enter data through the Profitability and Cost Management data-entry forms.

The following sections detail each of these steps.

Defining Stages   Stages represent the network of allocations within your organization. They enable you to create allocations that require multiple steps by defining a calculation sequence. The allocation result calculated and stored in a prior stage becomes the source value to be allocated in the following stages. You can define up to nine stages in your model. For example, total labor costs for the department collected in stage 1 are allocated to the activities performed by each department in stage 2. The total for each activity, in turn, can act as a source value to be allocated in a subsequent stage. Stages can be skipped when certain costs do need to reflect that stage's specific transformation. For example, raw material costs collected in stage 1 can be allocated directly to the products in stage 3. Figure 7-21 shows five stages.

The overall process for transforming costs from stage to stage is that source costs from one stage will be assigned to destination costs in subsequent stages, using a mathematical method (a driver). The resulting model is a series of "source to destination using a driver" relationships. After the stages are defined, the business user will define the required drivers, identify which sources will use which drivers, and define the source-to-destination assignments.

Defining and Selecting Drivers   Drivers provide formulas for allocating the source intersections values to the destination intersections. For example, the wages for the manufacturing department could be split among the different activities based on the number of hours consumed by each activity. Profitability and Cost Management

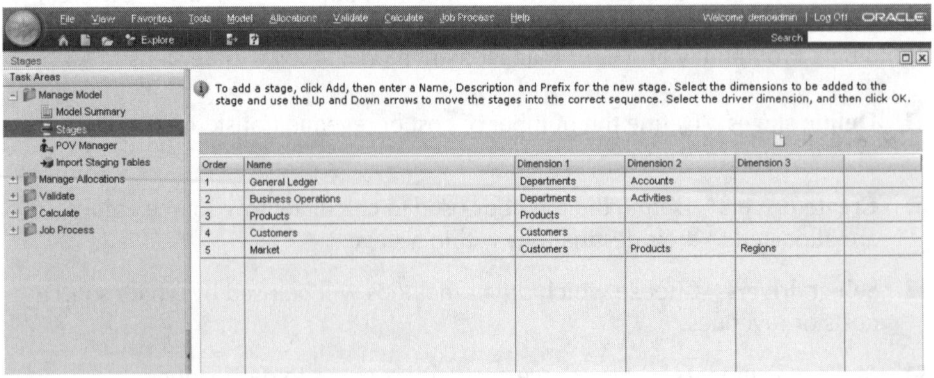

FIGURE 7-21.   *Defining stages*

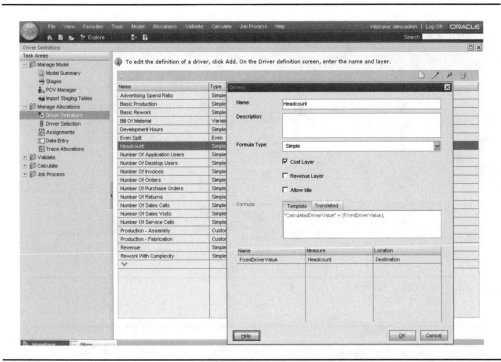

FIGURE 7-22. *Defining drivers*

enables you to create an unlimited number of drivers. When you create a driver, you can select from predefined formulas, such as even split, or you can create custom formulas. In Figure 7-22, drivers have been created for even split, headcount, number of application users, and so on.

After drivers have been defined, the business users assign the drivers to applicable source members for each stage. For example, in Figure 7-23, the activity of invoicing by the finance department is to be assigned based on the number of invoices created.

Making Assignments Assignments represent the links between data in stages. For each intersection of dimension members within a stage that contains source data, you assign downstream destinations. The destinations can be within the same stage as the source intersections. This assignment is called an *intrastage* assignment. Intrastage assignments can be reciprocal. For example, the HR department could have the IT department as an assignment, and the IT department could have HR as an assignment. Dimension intersections in later stages cannot have assignments in earlier stages. Figure 7-24 shows an assignment example that shows that corporate rent will be distributed to 45 department-activities based on a square footage driver.

After all assignments are made, it is time to collect data.

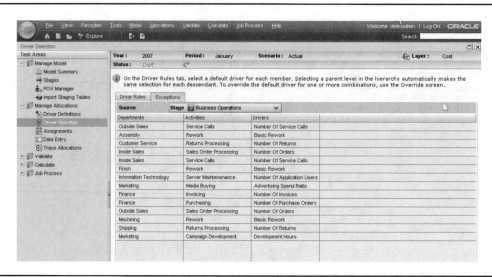

FIGURE 7-23. *Selecting drivers*

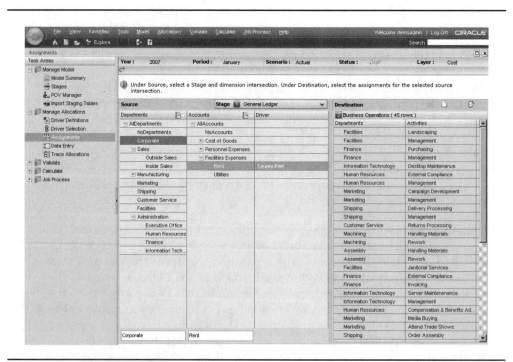

FIGURE 7-24. *Making assignments*

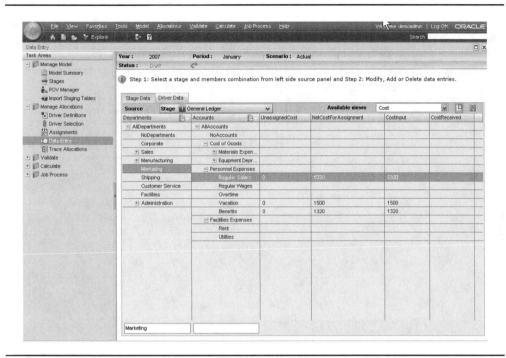

FIGURE 7-25. *Manually collecting data*

Collecting Data   You can import cost, revenue, and driver data into the underlying Essbase database by using Essbase load rules, Smart View, or ODI. After loading data into your model, you use the Data Entry window to verify the data, as shown in Figure 7-25. You can edit data or add missing data in this window, if necessary. The Data Entry window has separate tabs for Stage Data and Driver Data. On the Stage Data tab, you can view cost, revenue, or driver data for a selected stage and selected measures. You can save your measure selections as a view that you can reuse.

After all data has been collected, you can validate the model.

Validating Model

The model is verified against model validation rules to ensure the structure is sound before adding data. The structure validation checks to help ensure these criteria are correct:

■   You assigned a driver to each dimension intersection that is assigned destination members.

■   You assigned destination members to all dimension intersections to which a driver is assigned.

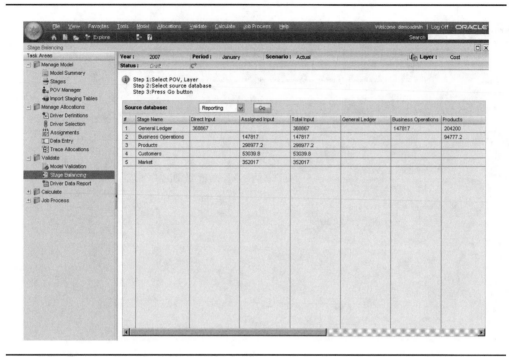

FIGURE 7-26. *Validating the model*

- Intrastage assignments are correct.

- Reciprocal assignments are correctly defined.

After the model is calculated, you can use built-in features to help validate the correctness of these calculations. Figure 7-26 shows the Stage Balancing report, which illustrates the high-level flow of costs across the stages. It will provide the user with a quick recap of the flow of costs and highlight where the allocations may need further work.

Tracing Allocations

A trace allocation report, such as the one shown in Figure 7-27, provides a graphical representation that enables you to trace allocations throughout the model. For a selected member intersection in a stage, the report lets you move backward or forward through the model. You can move backward from the intersection to view the source members that contributed to the value for the intersection and the amount that each contributed. You can move forward to view the destination members to which the value for the intersection was allocated and how much was allocated to each member.

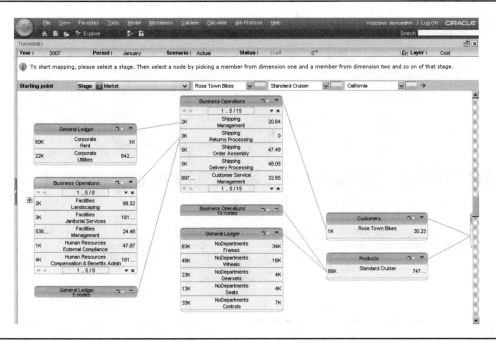

FIGURE 7-27.   *Tracing an allocation*

Oracle Hyperion Enterprise Performance Management Architect

Performance Management Architect offers a centralized interface where administrators can manage, create, and deploy Oracle Hyperion applications. Eligible products include applications for the Fusion Editions of Planning, Profitability and Cost Management, as well as Oracle Hyperion Financial Management and custom Essbase cubes.

Performance Management Architect enables administrators to perform the following tasks:

- Visually link and manage applications.

- Use dimensions and attributes across multiple applications. (For example, you can create one account dimension and use it in multiple applications.) Performance Management Architect leverages existing applications and dimensionality to spin off other applications with previously constructed dimensions.

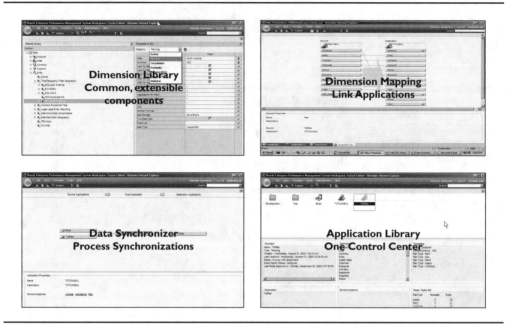

FIGURE 7-28. *Interfaces for the components of Performance Management Architect*

- Graphically manage data flows.

- Perform impact analysis—graphically view and model relationships across applications.

- Handle and evaluate the impact of exceptions and changes to all models.

- Eliminate manual dimensional and data reconciliation between applications.

Performance Management Architect has four main components for performing these tasks: a dimension library, dimension mapping, data synchronizer, and the application library. Figure 7-28 shows the interfaces for each of the components.

Architecture of Performance Management Applications

Planning and Profitability and Cost Management are multitiered, web-based applications. Figure 7-29 breaks down the products into their required components.

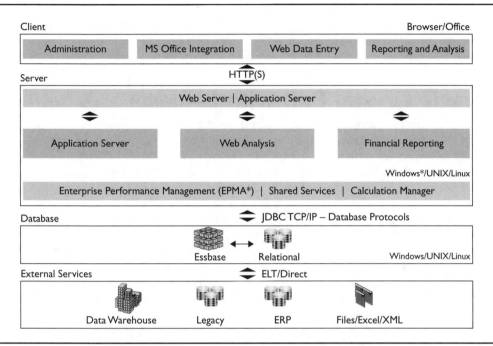

FIGURE 7-29. *Architecture of the performance management applications.*

As shown in Figure 7-29, the architecture has the following tiers:

- **Client tier**   The client tier consists of the Oracle Enterprise Performance Management Workspace (EPM Workspace) web client. The EPM Workspace provides a centralized interface for viewing and interacting with content created using the Oracle Enterprise Performance Management System, including financial applications and reporting content. In addition to viewing and interacting with content, administrators can manage the application through the EPM Workspace.

- **Server tier**   This tier primarily consists of the application server (Planning and Profitability and Cost Management) and the web server. A Hyperion Reporting and Analysis or Hyperion Web Analysis server is optional. The web server, which can be on a separate machine or on the same machine as the application server, lets you access Planning applications from a web client. It uses standard HTTP as the communications protocol and uses Windows security authentication. Client access to the web server is delivered through a standard web browser.

- **Database tier**   This tier consists of a relational database management system (RDBMS) and Essbase.

This concludes our coverage of the packaged performance management applications. With Planning and Profitability and Cost Management, you gain all the advantages of a packaged application, without sacrificing the speed and power of Essbase.

Oracle Crystal Ball with Essbase

Uncertainty makes strategic planning complex. Removing, or even mitigating, uncertainty can create unlimited business value. However, most companies lack the strategic planning infrastructure to rise above the unknown.

Previous sections have illustrated how OLAP tools support management processes and provide key stakeholders with relevant, actionable insight for speed-of-thought analysis. Yet while understanding the past through historic data is necessary for sound decision-making, is it sufficient for forward-looking estimates? Making the right decisions requires you to anticipate and plan for possible changes in the future. A common approach to anticipate these changes is to first assess the company's current position by analyzing historical information to understand the company's past. Occasionally, however, there might be very little or no historical precedent. And even if you do have historical data, it might not extrapolate correctly into the future. For example, let's assume your company wanted to launch a new product or compete in a different market. Your company's past and present state can be a good indicator of future performance, but does not guarantee it. The linkage to making the right actionable decisions still requires additional analysis.

To anticipate possible changes in the future, you must start addressing questions about the future possible outcomes, specifically the following:

- Which outcomes are most likely?

- What are the key risk drivers for those outcomes?

To answer these questions and plan for the right decisions, you must first ascertain the potential range of future results and the probability of different outcomes actually occurring. This type of analysis generally tends to be a limited exercise, concentrating on three common scenarios: best case, worst case, and something in between. Typically worked up in a spreadsheet, these scenarios tend to flex one or two inputs (assumptions) at a time and provide little insight into probable outcomes or drivers, which in the real world; reflect the collective influence of many variables (good and bad) coming together at the same time. Powerful applications such as Planning can use OLAP data to generate and store multiple scenarios, but the process remains slow and manual.

Fortunately, solutions such as Crystal Ball extend traditional OLAP capabilities to help organizations overcome uncertainty and achieve results. Excel-based, Crystal Ball can be used as a stand-alone desktop tool or integrated with Oracle's OLAP technology.

Using the tools of predictive modeling, simulation, and optimization, Crystal Ball gives you insight into the critical factors affecting risk, and calculates the likelihood that you will reach your objectives under even the most uncertain conditions.

Crystal Ball and Monte Carlo Simulation Methods

Monte Carlo simulation, founded upon stochastic analysis, offers the ability to quickly create thousands of what-if scenarios. The ability of Monte Carlo modeling to reflect all outcomes—particularly those dismissed as too unlikely to consider— makes it an objective and vital resource for assessing risk and the effects of uncertainty. These results give the user not only a comprehensive, realistic picture of future possibilities, but also their associated probabilities.

As an example, a company attempting to calculate a certain metric, such as earnings per share for the upcoming quarter, would first input data for various parameters. It would then run an algorithm that uses these inputs to generate outputs of interest, including earnings per share. Monte Carlo simulation is crucial when the exact values for input parameters are unknown or uncertain.

Crystal Ball, using Monte Carlo methods, accommodates uncertainty by allowing the user to define ranges of values (probability distributions) for variable inputs. The program then chooses a value for each assumption according to the given range, and repeats this process as many times as needed—even into the thousands. The result is a rank-ordered list of outcomes from which statistics are calculated. Because values are chosen randomly and the process is repeated many times, the output is statistically significant—a major improvement over a handful of subjective scenarios. Figure 7-30 shows how the output of the simulation would be

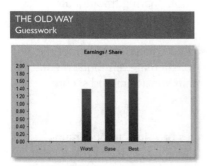

THE OLD WAY
Guesswork

• Limited Scenarios (Worst, Base, Best) = Limited view of risk
• What is the likelihood I'll miss the target?
• What are the most important risk factors?
• What if I want to vary many factors in the forecast at once?

Limited possibilities... No probabilities...

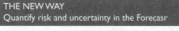

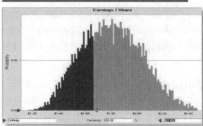

THE NEW WAY
Quantify risk and uncertainty in the Forecasr

• Full range of outcomes-full view of risk
• Understand associated probabilities
• Ranking of key drivers
• Vary as many inputs as needed

Model all possibilities = Forecast with clear probability

FIGURE 7-30. *Crystal Ball generates a full range of outcomes with associated probabilities.*

thousands of values (scenarios) for earnings per share, from which the user could understand the likelihood of, for instance, meeting or exceeding some target value.

Crystal Ball, using Monte Carlo simulation, calculates the probability of achieving any given strategic goal and offers the ability to develop plans that reflect realistic risk and reward. Monte Carlo simulation helps decision makers think about investment and long-term planning, for instance, as a continuum of probabilities rather than a certainty. Therefore, they grow accustomed to responding to change, rather than hoping it will not happen.

Crystal Ball Analysis

Four steps are involved in a Crystal Ball analysis:

- Develop a model of the problem.

- Assign ranges of values to the inputs.

- Calculate the ranges/probabilities of the outputs.

- Analyze and share results.

This section uses the example of a healthcare provider estimating patient revenues to illustrate the workflow of building a Crystal Ball analysis.

Developing a Model of the Problem

Essbase and Excel are both excellent general-purpose, model-building platforms. In the context of integrating Crystal Ball with OLAP technology, we will use an example that takes advantage of the strengths of each tool. Sharing traditional spreadsheet models in an enterprise environment is difficult at best. Broken links, cryptic formulas, and inconsistent application of business rules are just a few of the problems. In Figure 7-31, an Essbase application has been created that defines the relationships (business rules) between inputs in order to calculate reimbursement revenue. Throughout our analysis, our model will remain consistent and secure.

Assigning Ranges of Values to the Inputs

The next step in the modeling process is to assign ranges of values to uncertain inputs. With Smart View, you can access data from a variety of Oracle products for OLAP, such as Essbase and Planning, and bring that data into Excel for further analysis. This OLAP data can be examined either independently using the forecasting tools of Crystal Ball or linked into existing Crystal Ball simulation and optimization models.

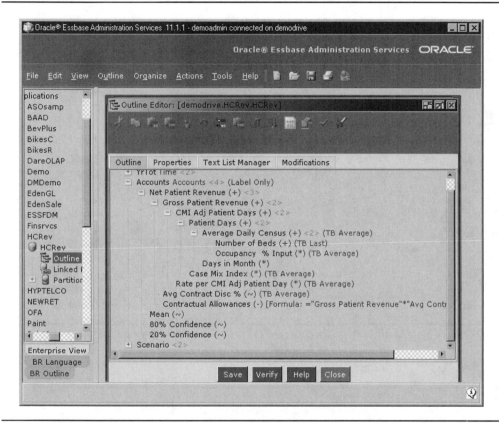

FIGURE 7-31. *Essbase cube calculating net patient revenue based on a variety of inputs*

In Figure 7-32, we have opened an ad hoc query of our Essbase application using Smart View.

We are now ready to apply Crystal Ball. We select a cell containing one of the uncertain inputs (Crystal Ball assumptions). For example, Figure 7-33 shows a selected cell representing the Occupancy % Input for January in the Forecast scenario. Clicking the Define Assumption button on the Crystal Ball ribbon opens a gallery of distributions from which to choose, as shown in Figure 7-34. From the gallery, you can select a distribution type and open a dialog box in which you can specify the parameters, as shown in Figure 7-35.

Crystal Ball offers a great deal of flexibility in assigning distributions, or ranges, to inputs. If there is sufficient historic data, the user can fit a probability distribution

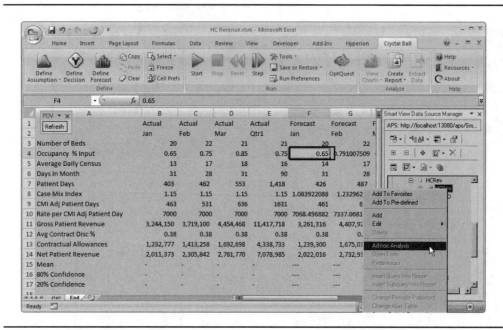

FIGURE 7-32. *Crystal Ball assumption created on top of a Smart View ad hoc query*

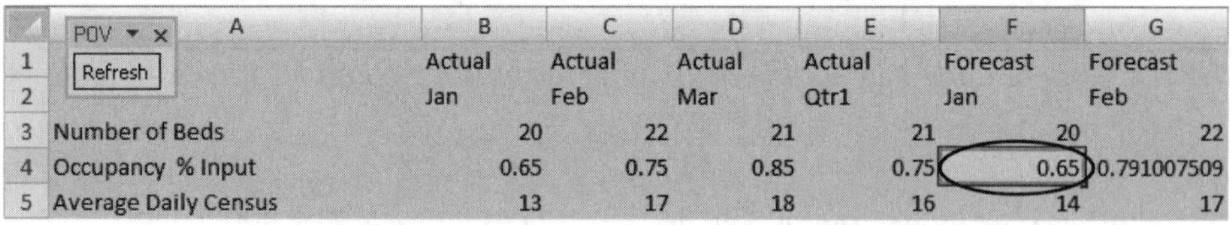

	A	B	C	D	E	F	G
	POV ▾ ×	Actual	Actual	Actual	Actual	Forecast	Forecast
1	Refresh						
2		Jan	Feb	Mar	Qtr1	Jan	Feb
3	Number of Beds	20	22	21	21	20	22
4	Occupancy % Input	0.65	0.75	0.85	0.75	0.65	0.791007509
5	Average Daily Census	13	17	18	16	14	17

FIGURE 7-33. *Select a cell where uncertainty or variability exists.*

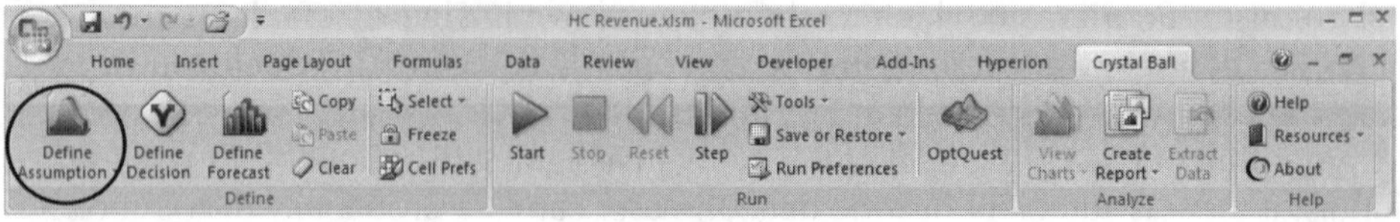

FIGURE 7-34. *Choose Define Assumption from the Crystal Ball ribbon.*

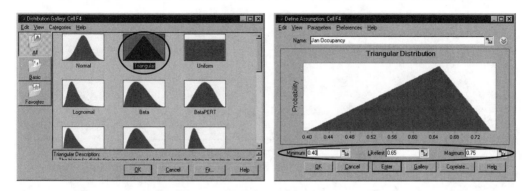

FIGURE 7-35. *Crystal Ball distribution gallery (left) and associated parameters dialog box (right)*

to those values. Range definitions are also available for cases where limited data exist, or where expert opinion might be more appropriate.

In our example, the planner estimates a minimum (0.4), most likely (0.65), and maximum (0.75) value for Occupancy based on expert opinion, and enters these estimates as parameters for the Triangular distribution. Ranges are assigned for the rest of the uncertain inputs in the forecast scenario, and the outputs (Crystal Ball forecasts)—or values targeted for analysis—are identified. By default, assumptions are assigned a green background, and forecasts are assigned a blue background. In this case, we are interested in the Net Patient Revenue for each month as well as Qtr1. The model is now ready to run. Figure 7-36 shows the output.

Calculating the Ranges/Probabilities of the Outputs

Running the model generates 500 what-if scenarios (the number of scenarios can be defined by the user). For each trial, a new value within the defined range is selected for each assumption. These values are submitted back to Essbase, where the Essbase database is recalculated according to the business rules. New results for the outputs are then refreshed in Excel and stored by Crystal Ball for analysis. The histograms in Figures 7-37 and 7-38 represent the range and likelihood of the outcomes for net patient revenue. The higher the bar, the more outcomes were observed in the given range. The boxes at the bottom of the forecast chart can be used to evaluate the certainty of any range of values.

	A	B	C	D	E	F	G	H	I	J
1		Actual	Actual	Actual	Actual	Forecast	Forecast	Forecast	Forecast	
2		Jan	Feb	Mar	Qtr1	Jan	Feb	Mar	Qtr1	
3	Number of Beds	20	22	21	21	20	22	21	21	
4	Occupancy % Input	0.65	0.75	0.85	0.75	0.65	0.76	0.85	0.79302277	
5	Average Daily Census	13	16.5	17.85	15.7833333	13.73112282	17.40216519	18.93159758	16.6882952	
6	Days in Month	31	28	31	90	31	28	31	90	
7	Patient Days	403	462	553.35	1,418	425.6648074	487.2606253	586.8795249	1,500	
8	Case Mix Index	1.15	1.15	1.15	1.15	1.15	1.15	1.15	1.1019211	
9	CMI Adj Patient Days	463.45	531.3	636.3525	1631.1025	461.3874869	600.7740497	580.3527001	1642.51424	
10	Rate per CMI Adj Patient Day	7000	7000	7000	7000	7000	7000	7000	7146.90847	
11	Gross Patient Revenue	3,244,150	3,719,100	4,454,468	11,417,718	3,261,316	4,407,920	4,082,874	11,752,110	
12	Avg Contract Disc %	0.38	0.38	0.38	0.38	0.38	0.38	0.38	0.38	
13	Contractual Allowances	1,232,777	1,413,258	1,692,698	4,338,733	1,239,300	1,675,010	1,551,492	4,465,802	
14	Net Patient Revenue	2,011,373	2,305,842	2,761,770	7,078,985	2,022,016	2,732,911	2,531,382	7,286,308	
15	Mean	-	-	-	-	-	-	-	-	
16	80% Confidence	-	-	-	-	-	-	-	-	
17	20% Confidence	-	-	-	-	-	-	-	-	

FIGURE 7-36. Crystal Ball model with outputs and uncertain variables defined.

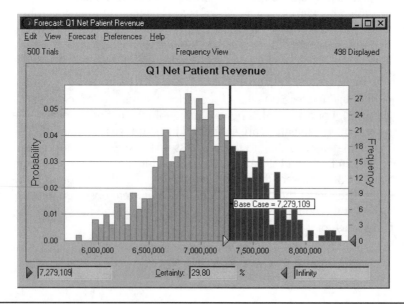

FIGURE 7-37. The likelihood of exceeding the baseline estimate for net revenue is only about 30%.

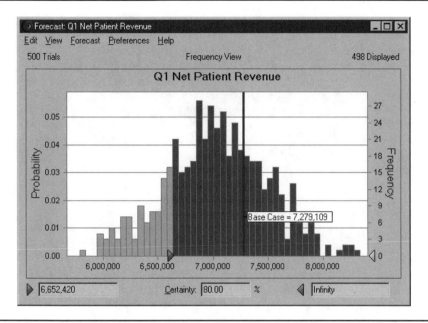

FIGURE 7-38.   *A value of $6.65 M provides 80% certainty—a more confident forecast!*

Analyzing and Sharing Results

The chart in Figure 7-37 shows the likelihood of exceeding the baseline estimate of $7.28 million, which is only about 30 percent. We would like to be more confident in our forecast. The chart in Figure 7-38 shows the same forecast, but now identifies that a value of $6.65 million gives 80 percent certainty, which is a more realistic estimate. Note that key metrics such as mean, 80 percent, and 20 percent confidence levels are members of the Essbase application. Once the simulation is complete, these values are extracted by Crystal Ball and stored in Essbase, giving more meaningful insight to the outcomes used in the Forecast scenario.

The forecast charts answered the question about which outcomes are most likely. A Crystal Ball sensitivity chart identifies which inputs are most significant. It is much more realistic than a tornado chart, because it varies all of the assumptions simultaneously, and each assumption varies according to its own distribution. Figure 7-39 illustrates that the uncertainty around occupancy contributes most to the variability in net revenue. Any "where to focus" discussions for reducing uncertainty and improving forecast accuracy should begin with the sensitivity chart.

In addition to integrating Crystal Ball results directly into OLAP applications, as illustrated in this example, EPM Workspace enables secure sharing of Crystal Ball workbooks and analysis across the enterprise.

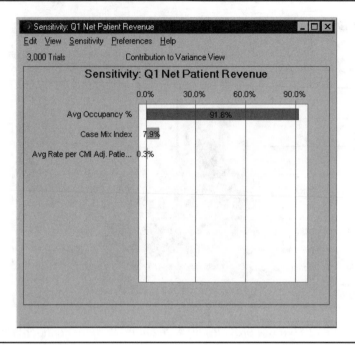

FIGURE 7-39.   *Uncertainty around occupancy has the highest impact on net revenue.*

Crystal Ball with Planning Models

Crystal Ball is also a great extension for Planning models. For example, you can apply Crystal Ball to historic sales data and create future sales predictions by analyzing the levels, trends, and cycles within your data through time-series forecasting and regression methods. These predictions can act as inputs to financial models, which can be simulated and optimized to increase the probability of making your forecasts and reduce the potentials risks in planning assumptions.

Postanalysis of the forecast results can be saved back into your Planning model as scenarios and forecasts. The result is a more accurate forecast with increased confidence.

Crystal Ball Decision Optimizer

Crystal Ball Decision Optimizer adds optimization and substantial processing speed to the power of Monte Carlo simulation. With Decision Optimizer, you can automatically search for your optimal solution to business, finance, and operational spreadsheet models.

Decision Optimizer is easy to use. A wizard guides you through the process of specifying your objectives and defining your constraints and requirements. After you define the optimization parameters, Decision Optimizer quickly pinpoints the set of inputs that best meet your goals, and transfers this to your spreadsheet model. Examples of optimization include finding the asset allocation that maximizes return for a given level of risk, or choosing staffing levels that minimize cost while maintaining required service levels.

This concludes our discussion of Crystal Ball. With this flexible, integrated tool, you can solve problems in which uncertainty and variability have traditionally distorted forecasts and make better decisions to impact the bottom line.

Oracle Smart Space with Essbase

Smart Space, Fusion Edition is a way for people to connect to the whole of the Oracle Business Intelligence Suite Enterprise Edition (OBIEE) stack. It provides direct connectivity to the EPM Workspace (and so to Web Analysis and Financial Reporting documents), OBIEE, and Oracle BI Publisher. Smart Space also provides Essbase developers and administrators easy access to calculations, load rules, and even the status of cubes.

Rather than needing to go to each of the documents of interest, users of Smart Space have the documents come to them! Smart Space uses gadget technology to serve appropriate content directly to the user.

Smart Space is always on, so when you log in to your Windows-based computer, Smart Space automatically connects and shows you what is most interesting to you. Figure 7-40 shows a sample Smart Space desktop.

NOTE
A common misconception is that Smart Space requires Microsoft Windows Vista. This probably came about because Smart Space was used by Microsoft to show off its gadget technology on the original Vista road show in North America. However, Smart Space also works on Windows XP and Windows 2003.

Smart Space Desktops

The core of the user interface is the Smart Space desktop. The desktop allows you to personalize your installation by installing only those gadgets that are relevant to you. In addition, you can have many different desktops, to represent different functions or working practices. For example, the set of gadgets and the list of favorite reports that you use may differ during the month—during the close cycle, you may want access to

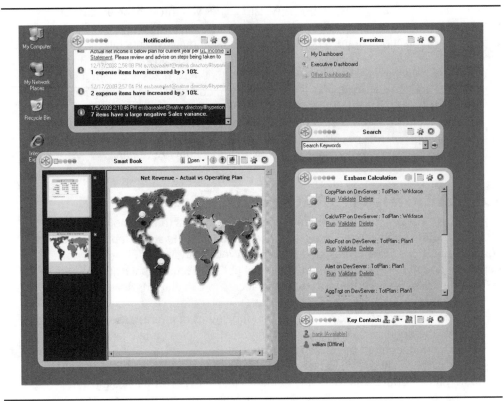

FIGURE 7-40. *Smart Space gadgets on a desktop*

all your statutory reports, but then during a budget reforecast cycle, you may need access to information from your Planning system. By having multiple desktops, you can avoid information overload during key cycles.

You can create, edit, and select desktops using the Smart Space Palette. In Figure 7-41, the current desktop is highlighted, and the default desktop is marked with an asterisk (*). You can add gadgets to the current desktop simply by dragging them from the palette.

Smart Space Gadgets

Oracle supplies a set of standard gadgets with Smart Space. Any number of these gadgets may be flagged as Recommended by the administrator, which means that they will be installed by default. The following are the standard gadgets:

FIGURE 7-41. *Managing desktops with the Smart Space Palette*

■ **Collaboration** The Collaboration gadget allows secure, audited discussions to take place around Oracle Enterprise Performance Management System and OBIEE Plus content using instant messaging technology. Any Smart Space content can be shared within a Collaboration discussion (one to one) or meeting (many users), to ensure that everyone has the same information. For example, let's say that you initiate a conversation with a colleague, Frank, about the Net Revenue Details report. As you can see from Figure 7-42, Frank can open the report directly from the discussion window, ensuring that you are both looking at the same version of the numbers.

■ **Key Contacts** The Key Contacts gadget allows easy communication with your most common contacts. You can see the instant messaging status of your contacts and use the gadget to start a Collaboration discussion or meeting. Figure 7-43 shows how the contacts and their status are displayed.

■ **Notification** The Notification gadget records a history of alerts that have been received. When an alert is triggered, a message is displayed immediately, and the alert is logged in the Notification gadget, as shown in Figure 7-44.

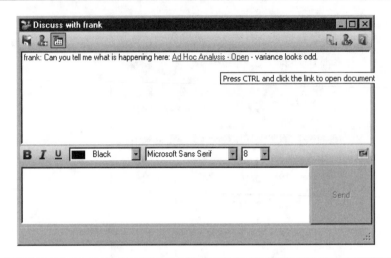

FIGURE 7-42. *Open documents directly from the Collaboration gadget.*

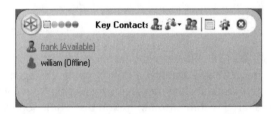

FIGURE 7-43. *Keep your contacts list handy using the Key Contacts gadget.*

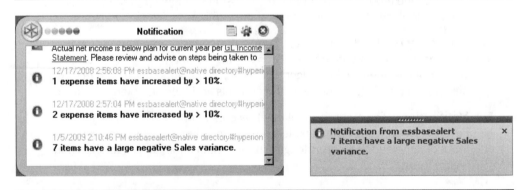

FIGURE 7-44. *An alert message is displayed and logged in the Notification gadget.*

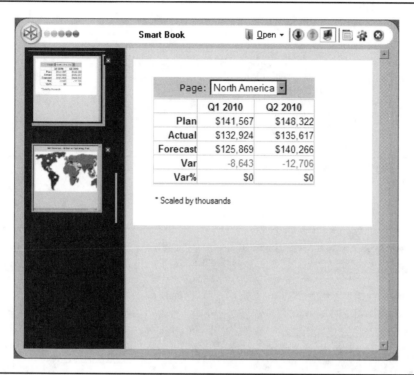

FIGURE 7-45. *A report displayed in the Smart Book gadget*

- **Smart Book**   The Smart Book gadget allows for a selection of Oracle reporting and analysis documents or URLs to be available directly on a user's desktop. Figure 7-45 shows how any reporting documents you add can be (optionally) displayed as a live preview in a preview panel. A selected document can be viewed fully within the Smart Book gadget. Additionally, you can open the item in the EPM Workspace or use it to initiate a discussion through the Collaboration gadget.

- **Favorites**   The Favorites gadget contains a user-defined list of shortcuts to any web-based tool (via a URL) or Smart Space content. Figure 7-46 shows a sample Favorites gadget. The shortcuts can be organized into a folder structure to ease navigation. You can have a different set of favorites within each of your desktops.

- **Search**   The Search gadget allows a quick search of any keywords within the EPM Workspace, without having to open it. Figure 7-47 shows sample search results. You can open any of the resulting items in a viewer or the EPM Workspace, or you can drag an item directly into another gadget, such as a discussion window or Smart Book.

FIGURE 7-46. *The Favorites gadget with some shortcuts*

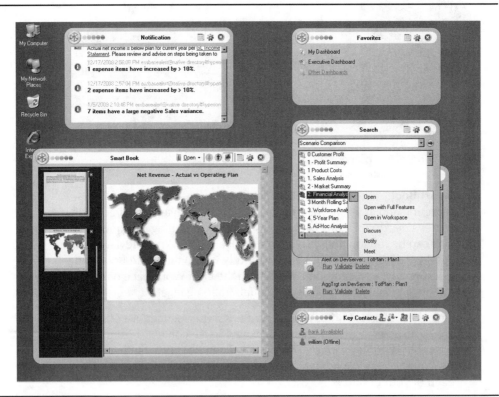

FIGURE 7-47. *Search an EPM Workspace without opening it.*

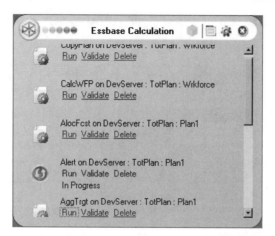

FIGURE 7-48.   *Run Essbase calculations with the Essbase Calculation gadget.*

■ **Essbase Data Load and Essbase Calculation**   These two gadgets enable you
to execute Essbase load rules (to perform both data load and restructures)
and calculation scripts from the desktop with a single click. When initiated,
the icon next to the selected rule/calculation changes to indicate that it is
in progress. Upon completion, the status changes so that you can see the
outcome of the process. For example, Figure 7-48 shows a list of Essbase
calculations, with one calculation underway and others available to be
launched. Any executed calculations would display the appropriate status
(complete, in progress or failed).

In addition to the standard gadgets, Smart Space also makes content available
directly from Windows Explorer. Similar to the Search gadget, you can navigate all of
the EPM Workspace, OBIEE Plus, and BI Interactive Dashboards content, to view
locally, discuss, add to other gadgets, or launch into the EPM Workspace. Figure 7-49
shows how a new folder, called Smart Space Content, is added to Windows Explorer
to allow access to the different sources.

Software Development Kit
Smart Space is designed to be an open, extendable solution to enable partners and
customers to create and publish their own gadgets. The Smart Space Development
Kit provides a software development toolkit (SDK) designed for use with Microsoft
Visual Studio 2005.

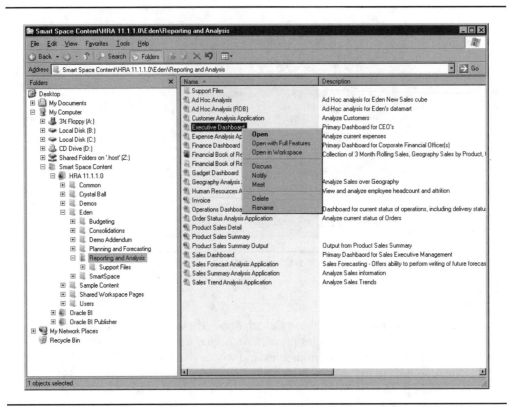

FIGURE 7-49. *Windows Explorer with the Smart Space Content folder displayed*

The SDK offers a full range of functionality, including the following features:

- Gadget user interface for modifying a gadget's user interface

- Security Services for using the user's single sign-on token to launch content

- Catalog and repository access for listing, administering, and launching documents from OBIEE Plus catalogs and repositories

- Collaboration Services for using the Collaboration gadget, including the ability to programmatically send notifications to users from external applications via .NET or Java, and through a web service

The SDK enables you to implement the standard gadgets in ways that suit your business needs. For example, the Notification section in Figure 7-43 (shown earlier) shows an alert message about negative sales variance coming from Essbase. To communicate this information to the appropriate people, a developer created a Java function that calls the SDK's Collaboration Services. The Essbase script that calculates the sales variance was then modified to call the Java function whenever certain conditions were met—in this case, a negative variance.

Developers can also create custom gadgets. The developer of the gadget deploys it using the Smart Space Administration Utility, and your users can then include the custom gadget on their Smart Space desktops. Various Oracle partners have created custom gadgets and deployed them at customer sites. Examples of custom gadgets are the Outline Browser gadget from Applied OLAP and the Cube Freshness gadget from Kerdock.

As you have seen, Smart Space gadgets serve appropriate content directly to the users on their desktop. The Essbase gadgets make it easy to run and monitor calculations scripts and load data, and custom gadgets can be created to manage other Essbase tasks.

Oracle Application Express for Oracle OLAP

Oracle Application Express (APEX) is a web-based application development and deployment tool that comes with the Oracle Database. Developers can use it to create reliable, secure, and easy-to-maintain web applications. The built-in wizards and functionality make it possible to build applications rapidly using relational and Oracle OLAP data. Since the Oracle OLAP data can be represented as SQL views, it is now easier than ever to report on the Oracle OLAP data. By using conditions on the SQL queries, it is possible to return data without the need to use aggregation functions. This greatly increases the performance of querying and retrieving data.

How is this all done? The Oracle OLAP views represent a traditional star schema, where the fact table is represented by the cube view, and the dimension views represent the dimension tables. The data in the cube view represents the data at all levels for all dimensions. So by adding conditions to the WHERE clause to include the level name of the required data, you can retrieve summary data without the time-consuming GROUP BY clause.

APEX allows you to specify these WHERE conditions as drill parameters, so that as you drill down the dimensions, the correct summary data is retrieved from the cube view. This is all done by constructing a parameterized SQL statement. Figure 7-50 shows a query from the Oracle OLAP views that will be used in APEX.

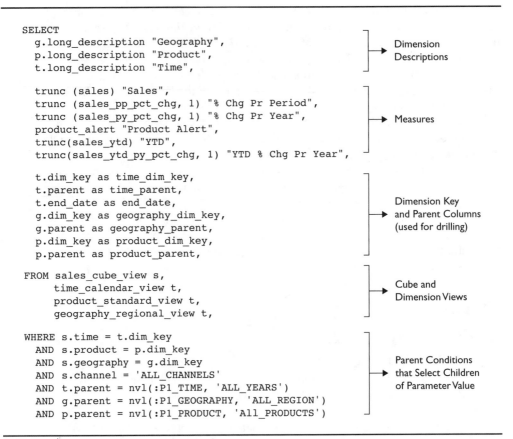

```
SELECT
  g.long_description "Geography",
  p.long_description "Product",
  t.long_description "Time",

  trunc (sales) "Sales",
  trunc (sales_pp_pct_chg, 1) "% Chg Pr Period",
  trunc (sales_py_pct_chg, 1) "% Chg Pr Year",
  product_alert "Product Alert",
  trunc(sales_ytd) "YTD",
  trunc(sales_ytd_py_pct_chg, 1) "YTD % Chg Pr Year",

  t.dim_key as time_dim_key,
  t.parent as time_parent,
  t.end_date as end_date,
  g.dim_key as geography_dim_key,
  g.parent as geography_parent,
  p.dim_key as product_dim_key,
  p.parent as product_parent,

FROM sales_cube_view s,
     time_calendar_view t,
     product_standard_view t,
     geography_regional_view t,

WHERE s.time = t.dim_key
  AND s.product = p.dim_key
  AND s.geography = g.dim_key
  AND s.channel = 'ALL_CHANNELS'
  AND t.parent = nvl(:P1_TIME, 'ALL_YEARS')
  AND g.parent = nvl(:P1_GEOGRAPHY, 'ALL_REGION')
  AND p.parent = nvl(:P1_PRODUCT, 'All_PRODUCTS')
```

Dimension Descriptions

Measures

Dimension Key and Parent Columns (used for drilling)

Cube and Dimension Views

Parent Conditions that Select Children of Parameter Value

FIGURE 7-50. *SQL query to be used in APEX*

This query is pasted into APEX and used as the primary query for a sales report. Figure 7-51 shows the main query entry window in APEX.

Now you can set up the parameters and construct the report based on the query. You can even define stoplight and alert formatting to enhance the report outputs. An example report using this data is shown in Figure 7-52.

Drilling up and down the dimensions is fully supported. APEX also supports graphing of the data. Each task requires little more than creating a simple SQL statement and following an APEX wizard to create a very usable Oracle OLAP-based report.

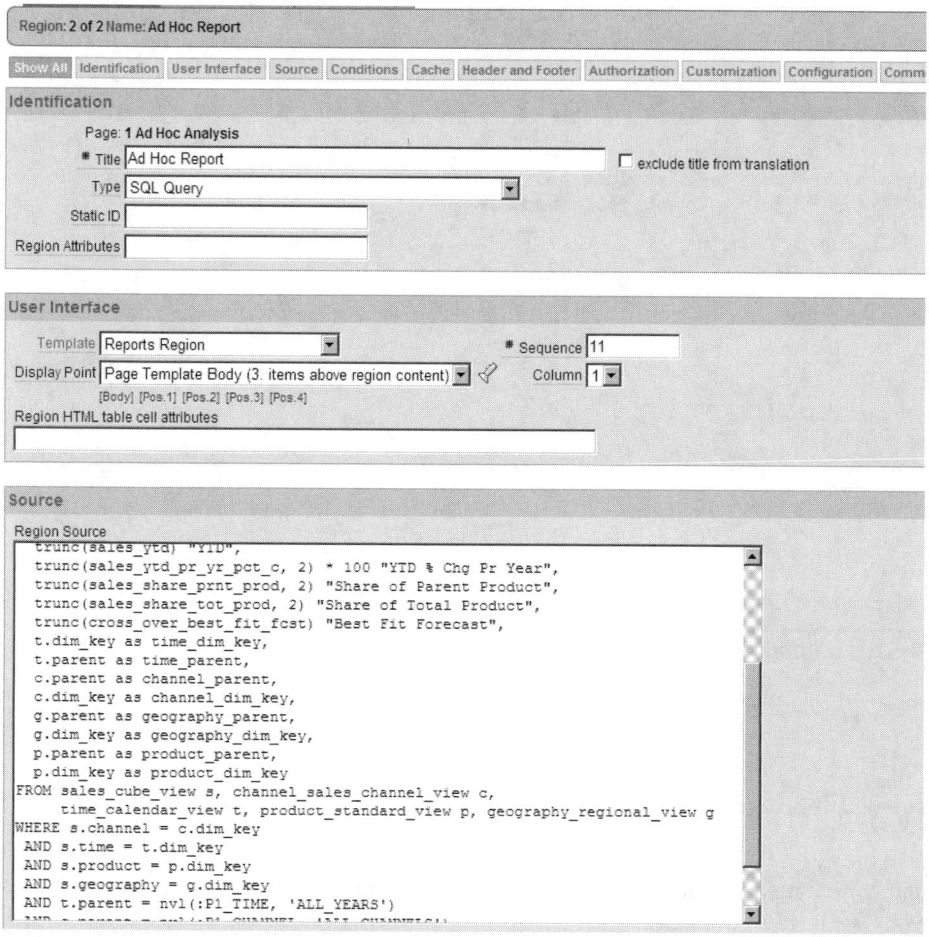

FIGURE 7-51. *APEX report query definition window*

The types of reports and dashboards that can be created from APEX are not as diverse as those produced by OBIEE, but they are still very comprehensive and plentiful. In addition, the skill level requirement is relatively low, and the price is considerably less.

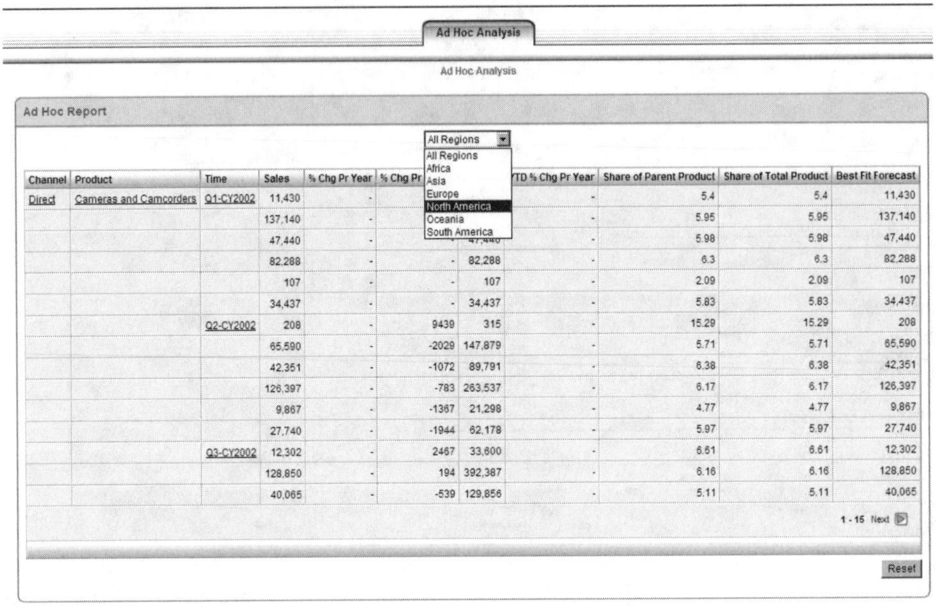

Ad Hoc Analysis

Ad Hoc Analysis

Ad Hoc Report

Regions dropdown: All Regions / Africa / Asia / Europe / North America / Oceania / South America

Channel	Product	Time	Sales	% Chg Pr Year	% Chg Pr	TD % Chg Pr Year	Share of Parent Product	Share of Total Product	Best Fit Forecast
Direct	Cameras and Camcorders	Q1-CY2002	11,430	-		-	5.4	5.4	11,430
			137,140	-		-	5.95	5.95	137,140
			47,440	-	47,440	-	5.98	5.98	47,440
			82,288	-	82,288	-	6.3	6.3	82,288
			107	-	107	-	2.09	2.09	107
			34,437	-	34,437	-	5.83	5.83	34,437
		Q2-CY2002	208	-	9439	315	-	15.29	15.29	208
			65,590	-	-2029	147,879	-	5.71	5.71	65,590
			42,351	-	-1072	89,791	-	6.38	6.38	42,351
			126,397	-	-783	263,537	-	6.17	6.17	126,397
			9,867	-	-1367	21,298	-	4.77	4.77	9,867
			27,740	-	-1944	62,178	-	5.97	5.97	27,740
		Q3-CY2002	12,302	-	2467	33,600	-	6.61	6.61	12,302
			128,850	-	194	392,387	-	6.16	6.16	128,850
			40,065	-	-539	129,856	-	5.11	5.11	40,065

1 - 15 Next ▶

Reset

FIGURE 7-52. *Sample APEX report*

Java Development

Oracle offers Java APIs for both Oracle OLAP and Oracle Essbase. These APIs are public, which means that anyone can develop a custom application to work with one of Oracle's OLAP engines.

Using Oracle BI Beans with Oracle OLAP

Oracle Business Intelligence Beans (BI Beans) is a set of standards-based JavaBeans that provides analysis-aware application building blocks designed for Oracle OLAP. Using Oracle JDeveloper 10*g* and BI Beans, you can build Internet applications quickly and easily. These applications can expose the advanced analytic features of the Oracle Database to both casual information viewers and high-end users who require complete ad hoc query and analysis functionality. The BI Beans components are included in the current 10g version of JDeveloper, but they can also be downloaded separately. BI Beans fall into three categories: presentation, OLAP, and catalog services.

NOTE
Oracle is no longer supporting BI Beans in JDeveloper 11g. While it is possible to use the version 11g OLAP API libraries to access the Oracle OLAP 11g data, the process is not currently certified. This does not prevent the continued use of BI Beans to develop Java applications. In the future, it is anticipated that solutions will be provided to use the JDeveloper ADF components to access Oracle OLAP.

By using BI Beans, application developers can leverage the Oracle technology stack and exploit the advanced analytic features of Oracle OLAP. Using JDeveloper as the integrated development environment (IDE) for BI applications increases application developer productivity.

With Oracle BI Beans, you can do the following:

■ Create boardroom-quality presentations.

■ Leverage advanced analytics of Oracle OLAP.

■ Support collaboration across the enterprise.

■ Rapidly develop BI applications for the Web.

Presentation Beans

When building BI applications, the key piece is the data. The data needs to be presented in such a way that it is easy to identify positive or negative trends. In addition, data presentations are typically created for review by senior management. Presentations need to be easy to build, so any level user within an organization can produce the high-quality reports that senior management expects.

The presentation beans have been through extensive usability testing and are used by other Oracle development groups for products like Oracle Discoverer, Oracle Reports, BI Publisher, and BI Spreadsheet Add-in. For the end user, this provides a consistent look and feel across Oracle products, thus lowering the learning curve as new applications are introduced.

BI Beans provides three flexible data-aware presentation components: graph, crosstab, and table. There is a graph for every occasion, and more than 70 graph types are included with BI Beans. Each graph has hundreds of properties for customizing the graph to give the exact look that you require. User-interface components are provided to make formatting graphs easy. For example, a Graph Type panel, shown in Figure 7-53, is available for end users to change the type of

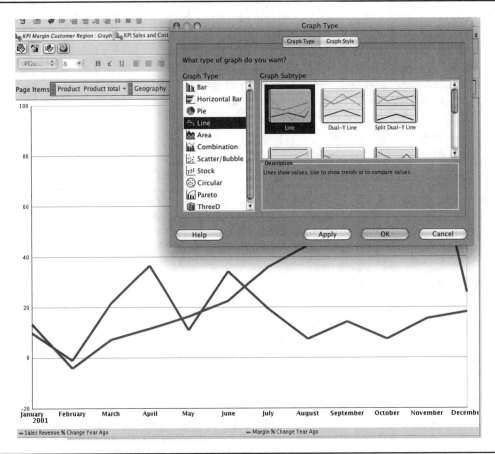

FIGURE 7-53. *The Graph Type panel allows users to change the graph type.*

graph they are currently viewing. The graph has full analytic support as well, which includes drilling, changing the layout, and providing data tips.

The BI Beans table provides a row-oriented view of data, typically used by those who are familiar with relational databases. The crosstab component offers a multidimensional view of data and provides services such as drilling and pivoting. Both table and crosstab components provide page-item-filtering capabilities.

Tables and crosstabs have rich formatting capabilities, down to the cell level. For example, data-driven formatting allows users to highlight data by setting foreground and background colors based on data values within cells. Presentations are completely customizable, down to the details of hiding or showing gridlines, showing titles, and formatting labels.

Not only do application developers have complete control of the look and feel of crosstabs and tables programmatically though the APIs, but BI Beans also present user-interface components for customizing a presentation. Easy-to-use interfaces are available for defining data-driven formatting, and a toolbar gives quick access to commonly used formatting options.

Java and HTML Clients

Depending on the nature and requirements of the application, BI Beans data presentations may be Java-based or HTML-based. This gives developers the option of providing intranet-based users, who have high-bandwidth connections, with full-featured Java applications. If a user population has slower connections, such as a remote sales force using dial-up connections, an HTML application can be deployed for their use.

High-end analytical users who spend a large percentage of their business day analyzing past business performance or developing forecasts of future performance need a highly interactive environment. The Java versions of the presentation beans enable a rich, interactive experience. This includes rotating dimensions in a presentation using drag and drop, formatting through direct manipulation (a formatting toolbar is offered to enhance the interaction), and frozen row and column headers to aid in the navigation of large reports.

The HTML versions of the presentation beans can display custom formats that have been defined and saved using a Java client application, as shown in Figure 7-54. However, they do not require Java to be downloaded to the client. HTML-based tools provide the ability to change among presentation types, change the layout of a presentation, sort the data, and apply queries that have been previously created and saved. The graph bean generates image files on the middle tier, which you can insert into an HTML page just as you would any other image. The thin graph creates image maps that support drilling and tooltips in an HTML application.

BI Beans Catalog

The BI Beans Catalog is used to save, retrieve, and manage all developer-defined and user-defined analytical objects, such as reports, graphs, favorite queries, and custom measures. The BI Beans Catalog is designed to support large, distributed user communities who share analytical objects in collaborative environments. Developers take advantage of the catalog at design time and hook application logic to the catalog, so users can access catalog functionality from the application at run time.

The BI Beans Catalog can be stored in an Oracle Database or in a local file system. From a development standpoint, it may be convenient to store all your objects within your local file system. However, when the time comes to deploy applications, you should export your objects to a database implementation of the catalog. Since the BI Beans Catalog is then in the Oracle Database, it is scalable and secure.

Object definitions are stored in the catalog as XML. This allows developers to store application objects once, and then use the same objects in Java and HTML applications (or, for that matter, in a PDA or WAP application).

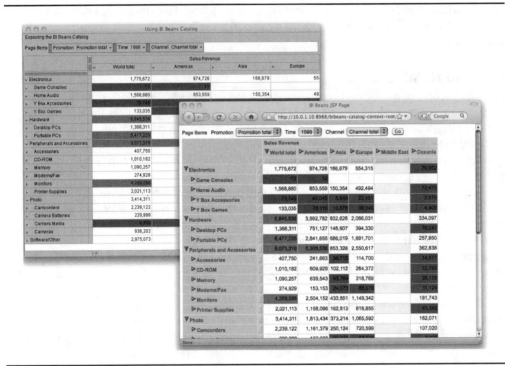

FIGURE 7-54. *Java crosstab with formatting and toolbar (left) and the same crosstab in HTML (right)*

Application Development

Increasing developer productivity is the mission of the BI Beans. This has been accomplished by making JDeveloper the premier environment for developing BI applications. Although BI Beans are standard Java components that can be used with any IDE, using JDeveloper significantly enhances and simplifies the developer experience. Using BI Beans and JDeveloper provides the flexibility to develop applets, applications, servlets, and JSPs.

To speed the process of developing applications and application objects, BI Beans provide a number of wizards in JDeveloper. These wizards allow you quickly to create presentation objects (crosstabs, tables, and graphs), calculations, complete Java applications, and complete HTML applications as servlets. Developers can edit these objects and applications visually in JDeveloper, or they can edit the generated Java code directly.

BI Beans also includes a custom JavaServer Pages (JSP) tag library for embedding BI Beans objects directly into JSPs. For example, a developer could embed a graph in a page by simply inserting a tag referencing a graph that was previously created.

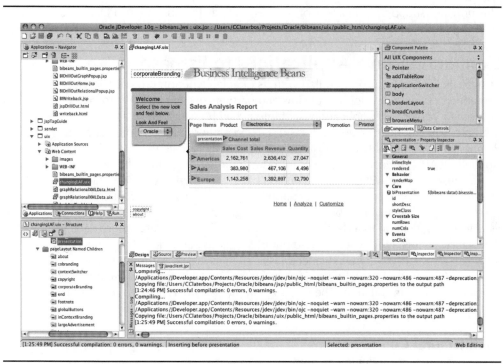

FIGURE 7-55. *Creating a crosstab in JDeveloper with live access to data and formatting*

BI Beans provides a live connection to Oracle OLAP during the JDeveloper application design session, as shown in Figure 7-55. This allows the application developer to see data at design time. This is particularly important with BI applications, because the data content often affects how the analytical objects are designed. For example, being able to see the data at design time allows the developer to make decisions about data selections and formatting in a report.

JDeveloper understands the BI Beans Catalog. This makes it very easy to share analytical objects among many different applications. For example, several different applications could all share the same report. When the report needs to be altered, JDeveloper can be used to make the changes. All the applications that use that report then automatically see the updated report. Other IDEs can be used to do this, but JDeveloper makes the task almost trivial.

In summary, BI Beans provides an application architecture to support any enterprise BI needs. Because BI Bean applications are built using Java, they can be deployed anywhere on the Internet. Java applications can be deployed on any device that can run Java. Servlets can service any device that supports a browser. The application logic is written by the developer on the middle-tier and may be reused by any client application: Java applications, servlets, JSPs, and so on.

This provides support for a variety of devices, such as PCs, browsers, PDAs, and even web-enabled phones like the Apple iPhone and BlackBerry.

Connecting Java Applications to Essbase

Essbase includes a Java API bundled with its Oracle Hyperion Provider Services component. Oracle development teams and partners use the Java API to create distributed, server-side applications that interact with Essbase databases. For example, some of the Oracle products discussed earlier in this chapter, such as Planning and Profitability and Cost Management, incorporate the Java API, as does Applied OLAP's Dodeca, which was introduced in the preceding chapter.

Because the Java API is public, you can have your own development team use the Java API to connect a custom Java application to an instance of an Essbase Server. Programmers can do basic things like sign on to an Essbase Server domain, establish a connection to a database, build dimensions, load data, query data, run calculation scripts, modify a database outline, sign out, and close the connection. They can also perform some advanced tasks, such as create a grid interface.

The API is 100% Java. The ess_japi.jar file is located in the lib directory of your Provider Services installation. The packages in the JAR file reflect the kinds of tasks that you usually do with Essbase.

Architectural Considerations

When designing or modifying an application to work with Essbase, you can follow one of two architectural paths:

- Embed the Java API in your application, as shown in Figure 7-56.

- Implement Provider Services to service calls from the Java API. as shown in Figure 7-57.

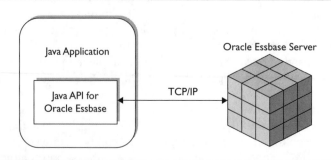

FIGURE 7-56. *Embedded architecture*

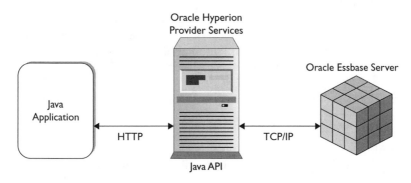

FIGURE 7-57. *Provider Services middle-tier architecture*

As discussed in Chapter 2, Provider Services can also be a data source provider for Smart View, XMLA clients, OBIEE Plus, and Planning (via the Smart View provider). If you are already using one or more of these products, this may be the preferred option for your environment.

Each implementation option offers benefits and drawbacks in terms of supported features. Table 7-1 lists some features and indicates whether they are supported by each option.

You are not bound by your initial architecture decision. Because the reference to the type of implementation is contained within the signOn() method, it is easy to direct your program to use a different architecture should the need arise.

Feature	Supported by Embedded API	Supported by Provider Services
High availability	No	Yes
Clustering	No	Yes
Support Java API client requests from other applications or Oracle Hyperion products	No	Yes
Middle-tier server	No	Yes
Direct TCP/IP connection from application to an Essbase Server	Yes	No
API installed on client machine	Yes	No

TABLE 7-1. *Supported Features by Implementation Method*

Java API Resources

This section provided only a broad overview of the Java API. Essbase ships with a set of sample applications that do a good job of showcasing key methods available to you in the Java API. You can find information about the sample applications, including where to locate them and how to run them, in the *Oracle Hyperion Provider Services Administration Guide.*

You may also find the following resources helpful during your development process:

- **Java API for Oracle Essbase Javadoc** Get details on interfaces, classes, methods, and fields. The Javadoc is installed with Provider Services.

- **Oracle Technology Network: Java Developer Center** Discover Oracle's tools for Java—including JDeveloper and Oracle WebLogic Server—and connect with other Java developers at http://www.oracle.com/technology/tech/java/index.html.

- **Blogs** Benefit from real-world experience as told by industry experts. Find blog postings and presentations on the Internet by using the search term combination "essbase java api."

Conclusion

You may not need to create your own cubes, spreadsheets, and reports to reap the benefits of online analytical processing. In some cases, it may be more appropriate to implement a packaged application to address a particular need, rather than creating your own set of spreadsheets and reports. One or more of the products discussed in this chapter may be exactly what you need to get your OLAP solution up and running quickly. In addition, if a packaged solution does not suit your needs, the public Java APIs for Essbase and Oracle OLAP mean that you can have a custom front-end application built.

In the next chapter, we look at how to make Essbase and Oracle OLAP run more efficiently. As all environments are different, we cannot offer specific solutions. But we can give you some ideas about how to optimize and maintain Oracle OLAP analytic workspaces and Essbase servers and databases.

References

EPM Information Development Team. *Oracle Hyperion Provider Services Administration Guide, Release 11.1.1.* Oracle Corporation, 2008.

Oracle Corporation. Creating Interactive APEX Reports Over OLAP 11g Cubes. Oracle Technology Network (http://www.oracle.com/technology/obe/olap-apex/usingapex4olap.htm).

CHAPTER
8

Keeping It Running

his chapter is intended for database administrators, or anyone implementing or maintaining Oracle OLAP analytic workspaces or Essbase databases. It covers techniques for keeping your OLAP solution running smoothly.

Many factors can affect the performance of your OLAP cubes. By reviewing the advice in this chapter before implementing Oracle OLAP or Essbase, you may be able to design your implementation to minimize performance issues. If you are inheriting an OLAP system that is underperforming, you should find some hints to guide your optimization efforts. However, do note that sometimes performance problems are not related to OLAP, but rather to metadata, source data, or the network. Such problems can result in poor application performance, even when the cubes are performing well.

It is also vital to decide on a backup plan early on in your implementation. You need to ensure that data is never at risk. This chapter describes how to back up Oracle OLAP analytic workspace data, as well as an Essbase database.

Oracle OLAP Care and Maintenance

Because Oracle OLAP runs in the Oracle Database kernel, it inherits all the benefits of the Oracle Database. Many things that are normally done to improve performance or troubleshoot the Oracle Database will affect Oracle OLAP as well. Here, we will focus on how to configure, tune, back up, and troubleshoot Oracle OLAP analytic workspaces.

Configuring and Tuning Oracle OLAP

Oracle OLAP's multidimensional objects use the same database memory, processes, and storage as any other type of object in the database. As a result, Oracle OLAP benefits from the proper tuning and configuration of the Oracle Database itself. For the most part, if the Oracle Database is running efficiently, Oracle OLAP should be functioning efficiently as well. As with an Oracle database, if the Oracle OLAP design is off, the performance is off, so make sure you validate the design. If the design is bad, no amount of tuning can solve the big problem.

In this section, we present recommendations and techniques that we have used over the years to help diagnose problems and optimize the performance of Oracle OLAP analytic workspaces. For general database configuration and tuning recommendations, see the Oracle Database documentation.

Validating the Oracle OLAP Installation

Occasionally, Oracle OLAP is not installed correctly or the installation is invalidated for some reason. For example, installation-related issues can occur if the Oracle database has been migrated from one major release to another, like moving from Oracle Database 10*g* to 11*g*.

To verify that the Oracle OLAP is installed and functioning properly, you should first ensure Oracle OLAP is in the list of installed options, and then run a SELECT statement to ensure that the installation is valid.

Is Oracle OLAP in the List of Installed Options?   When you run SQL*Plus, the header indicates which options are installed on the database. You will see something like the following when you log in:

```
Oracle Database 10g Enterprise Edition Release 11.1.0.7.0 - 64bit
Production With the Partitioning, OLAP and Data Mining options
```

If you do not see OLAP in the list, you need to install Oracle OLAP:

- On Windows-based systems, run the universal installer. Under the custom installation options, select the OLAP option to install Oracle OLAP.

- On UNIX/Linux systems, relink with the OLAP_ON setting using the following commands:

  ```
  cd $ORACLE_HOME/rdbms/lib
  make -f ins_rdbms.mk olap_on
  make -f ins_rdbms.mk ioracle
  ```

Is the Oracle OLAP Installation Valid?   Now you can verify that Oracle OLAP is installed and valid. From SQL*Plus or Oracle SQL Developer, issue the following statement while logged in as as administrator:

```
select comp_id, comp_name, version, status from DBA_REGISTRY where
comp_name like '%OLAP%' or comp_name like '%X%' or comp_name like
'%J%';
```

If Oracle OLAP is installed in the instance, you should see something like the following output:

```
COMP_ID   COMP_NAME                      VERSION      STATUS
--------- ------------------------------ ----------- ---------
JAVAVM    JServer JAVA Virtual Machine   11.1.0.7.0   VALID
CATJAVA   Oracle Database Java Packages  11.1.0.7.0   VALID
XML       Oracle XDK                     11.1.0.7.0   VALID
XDB       Oracle XML Database            11.1.0.7.0   VALID
APS       OLAP Analytic Workspace        11.1.0.7.0   VALID
XOQ       Oracle OLAP API                11.1.0.7.0   VALID
AMD       OLAP Catalog                   11.1.0.7.0   VALID
```

If any of these elements are missing or invalid, you need to reinstall Oracle OLAP. Before reinstalling it, you should ensure that the Java Virtual Machine (JVM), Oracle Database Java packages, Oracle XML Developer Kit (XDK), and Oracle XML DB are installed and valid. Sometimes the installation can be done using the Database Configuration Assistant (DBCA), but this is not usually the case, especially if the database instance is a custom installation. The simplest way to reinstall Oracle OLAP is to run a manual installation.

NOTE
Reinstalling Oracle OLAP does not affect any existing analytic workspaces that are present in an Oracle database.

To reinstall Oracle OLAP manually, follow these steps:

1. Stop the database and restart it in upgrade or restricted mode.

2. Go to command mode and change to the ORACLE_HOME directory.

3. Start SQL*Plus in SYSDBA mode (`sqlplus / as SYSDBA`).

4. Run the following commands.

To install the Java VM, XDK, or XML:

```
conn / as SYSDBA
@?/javavm/install/initjvm.sql;
@?/xdk/admin/initxml.sql;
@?/xdk/admin/xmlja.sql;
@?/rdbms/admin/catjava.sql;
@?/rdbms/admin/catexf.sql;
```

To install Oracle OLAP:

```
@?/olap/admin/olap.sql SYSAUX TEMP;
```

Check the logs to make sure that this procedure properly installed or reinstalled Oracle OLAP. You can verify the installation by rerunning the validation query.

Setting Database Parameters

You can set parameters to improve the performance of Oracle OLAP. Some of these are Oracle Database parameters; others are specific to Oracle OLAP.

Database Parameters That Affect Oracle OLAP Performance   Make sure that the database is set up with the minimum settings to run Oracle OLAP. The parameters that affect the performance of Oracle OLAP are listed in Table 8-1. Adjust the server parameter file or init.ora file to these values, and then restart your database instance.

The recommendations in Table 8-1 assume that the computer is dedicated to Oracle Database and that your database is used predominantly (if not exclusively) for OLAP purposes. If you want to reserve some resources for other applications, first calculate the percentage of resources that are available to Oracle Database. For example, if your computer has 4GB of physical memory and you want to reserve 25 to 30 percent for other applications, you would calculate MEMORY_TARGET (or SGA_TARGET plus PGA_AGGREGATE_TARGET) based on 75 percent of 4GB, which is 3GB.

Parameter	Setting
JOB_QUEUE_PROCESSES	Number of CPUs, plus one additional process for every three CPUs. For example, set JOB_QUEUE_PROCESSES=5 for a four-processor computer.
MEMORY_TARGET	70% of physical memory; also set PGA_AGGREGATE_TARGET=0 and SGA_TARGET=0.
MEMORY_MAX_TARGET	If there is a need in the future to increase MEMORY_TARGET, consider setting this parameter to a maximum value. This allows you to increase the MEMORY_TARGET up to the value you specify for MAX.
PGA_AGGREGATE_TARGET	25% of physical memory (increase up to 50% for builds and major query operations). If using MEMORY_TARGET in Oracle Database 11g, set this value to 0.
SGA_TARGET	50% of physical memory. If using MEMORY_TARGET in Oracle Database 11g, set this value to 0.
SESSIONS	2.5 * maximum number of simultaneous OLAP users.
UTL_FILE_DIR	Directory path where the Oracle Database can write to a file.
UNDO_MANAGEMENT	AUTO

TABLE 8-1.   *Initial Settings for Database Parameter Files*

Oracle OLAP Parameters   Oracle OLAP uses a memory area called the OLAP page pool. The related parameter, called OLAP_PAGE_POOL_SIZE, specifies in bytes (or kilobytes or megabytes) the size of the paging cache to be allocated to an Oracle OLAP session for a user performing any operation against analytic workspaces. This memory is allocated from the User Global Area (UGA).

In Oracle Database 10g and 11g, OLAP_PAGE_POOL_SIZE is set to 0, which means the database dynamically allocates memory to users on an as-needed basis. In some cases, the dynamic allocation can assign too much memory to a single process, leaving little for other users. If this happens, you many need to change the parameter value to reflect the amount of memory required by the users.

If Oracle OLAP is used in a shared server environment, OLAP_PAGE_POOL_SIZE is not dynamic. If the value for OLAP_PAGE_POOL_SIZE is not set, the pool is automatically set to six times the _olap_page_pool_low setting (default of 256KB). In this case, we recommend setting OLAP_PAGE_POOL_SIZE to a fixed value that can accommodate your number of concurrent users, available memory in the System Global Area (SGA), and other resources—between 4MB and 16MB can be a good starting value.

Tuning Oracle OLAP

Before attempting to tune Oracle OLAP, ensure that the server is set up properly and the database is performing well on the relational side. For help completing these tasks, see the *Oracle Database 2-Day + Performance Tuning Guide* available in the DBA Essentials section of the Oracle Database Documentation Library.

Assuming that the server and database have been tuned appropriately, you can focus on Oracle OLAP. Generally, Oracle OLAP performance issues manifest themselves by poor load performance and/or front-end query performance. Load performance can be the most difficult to diagnose, but can also be easiest to fix. This section tells you how to detect poor performance and suggests a few areas where you can improve performance.

Assessing Load Performance   A good place to start your assessment of load performance is the load logs generated by the maintenance process. In Oracle OLAP 10g, the logs are located in the XML_LOAD_LOG table owned by OLAPSYS. In version 11g, each schema has a table called CUBE_BUILD_LOG. These tables have statistics on the loading processes for dimensions and cubes. For either version, look for the rows that specify a LOAD process, and assess the number of rows loaded and the time it took to load the data. As a general rule of thumb, you should expect at least 1 million rows per minute to be loaded by OLAP. Anything less would indicate that you are having an I/O problem or there is some inefficient SQL processing.

If you discover inefficient load processes, you can use DBA tools such as explain plan on the SQL being used to load the data. If the explain plan indicates full table scans and other inefficient behavior, consider fixing these issues. The Automatic Database Diagnostic Monitor (ADDM) can be a big benefit here as well.

The Dimensional Model and Performance   The dimensional model should also be considered as a possible contributor to poor performance. Many implementations create a dimension when it would be more appropriate to define a level, hierarchy, or attribute of an existing dimension. This generally happens when migrating from an existing relational data warehouse or ROLAP tools. We have seen cases where the migrated dimensional model had 50 dimensions. In one particular case, we redesigned a 50-dimension model into a 15-dimension model, and the performance issues were resolved.

Creating surrogate keys in a dimension can also contribute to poor performance. As explained in Chapter 4, Oracle OLAP ensures keys are unique by prefixing the incoming key with the level identifier. Adding a prefix results in larger keys being used in the analytic workspace, which means that it can take longer to store the keys, take up more space, and possibly take more time to retrieve into the front-end tool. If you know that your dimension data contains only unique keys, turn off the surrogate keys option for the dimension. When you do need surrogate keys, use the shortest possible level identifier to minimize the effect of the storage of the data.

Preaggregation: A Balance Between Query Times and Load Performance   While preaggregation of data can improve query performance, it can also increase load times and take additional space. There is a trade-off between space and load time. The best query performance is generally a fully solved cube, but that takes time and space. If load times are too long and space is a concern, further analysis is required. If load times are fast and space is not a concern, then set it to fully solve and check the query performance.

TIP
As mentioned in Chapter 4, with Oracle OLAP 11g, the cost-based aggregation option does not require setting aggregation levels. This is because this version of Oracle OLAP does the analysis for you. Therefore, if you are using version 11g with cost-based aggregation, you might want to let it do the work for you.

You can perform an analysis of how many members are loaded at each level of a hierarchy. This analysis is important in determining which levels of a dimension should be preaggregated and which ones can be aggregated at query time. Let's look at some examples. Table 8-2 shows a simple analysis that should be done on each dimension.

Level	Number of Members	Average # of Children per Member	Preaggregate?
All Products	1	2	Yes
Division	6	3	No
Class	16	4	Yes
Group	55	23	No
SKU	1200	0	Yes

TABLE 8-2. *Product Dimension Example 1*

The number of members and the average number of children per member represent a fairly normal distribution, so standard skip-level aggregation should work well. As we discussed in Chapter 4, in skip-level aggregation, the bottom level is aggregated (in our example, SKU) and every other level above it is aggregated (in this case, Class and All Products). This is the default behavior of the AWM Cube Aggregation wizard.

Table 8-3 shows an example where the bottom two levels have a 1:1 ratio. You do not want to spend the time to aggregate the 400 members of the Group level on the fly, so you should preaggregate this level, along with the SKU level. The compressed composite algorithm will identify the 1:1 ratio automatically and further minimize space by not storing both member keys.

Finally, Table 8-4 shows a much wider distribution. This distribution may take some sample runs to determine the sweet spot with respect to query performance. We recommend starting with the default skip-level aggregation, as shown in Table 8-4.

Level	Number of Members	Average # of Children per Member	Preaggregate?
All Products	1	2	Yes
Division	6	3	No
Class	20	25	Yes
Group	400	1	Yes
SKU	500	0	Yes

TABLE 8-3. *Product Dimension Example 2*

Level	Number of Members	Average # of Children per Member	Preaggregate?
All Products	1	5	No
Division	6	14	Yes
Class	89	4	No
Group	1456	3	Yes
Sub Group	3989	67	No
SKU	120000	0	Yes

TABLE 8-4.   *Product Dimension Example 3*

If this leads to poor performance, then we recommend aggregating the level with the largest number of members, in this case the Sub Group level. If this change still does not improve performance, we would likely use full aggregation instead.

Cube Storage   Cube storage is another important consideration. Using only the amount of storage you need for your data is important for both load and aggregation times. Here are some helpful hints:

■   If your data supports it, use the decimal or integer data type. Even though number is the default, this data type can take up to 3.5 times more space than decimal. Number takes 22 bytes; decimal or integer takes 8 bytes. If your data can be expressed in 8 bytes, you should consider taking advantage of the smaller data storage offered by the other data types.

■   Use compressed composites if possible, because this will always build a smaller more efficient cube. Our experience also indicates that compressed composites load much faster than uncompressed composites. Where possible, consider using compressed composites to improve load performance. Compressed composites are discussed in Chapters 3 and 4.

■   Do not use global composites, which are bigger composites since they are shared across cubes. Note that global composites are unavailable when using compressed composites.

■   Review your sparsity settings. You do not need to have a dense dimension. In fact, extensive testing has shown that defining all dimensions as sparse can result in a dramatic improvement in load and aggregation performance, without a significant degradation of query performance. This is especially true for compressed composites.

Backing Up Oracle OLAP

Because the Oracle OLAP data is contained in the Oracle database, there should already be a backup strategy in place to back up not only the relational data, but also the OLAP data. In addition to the existing Oracle Database backup utilities, Oracle OLAP also contains utilities that can be used to ensure that the data is backed up and secure.

In this section, we touch on the traditional Oracle Database backup processes, and then focus on the Oracle OLAP processes that are available. While manual backups are usually enough for small systems, it is highly recommended that an automatic backup be made on a regular basis.

Full Database Backups

The simplest and most reliable database backup is called a *cold backup*. This consists of shutting down the database instance and copying the directories containing the database files (including Oracle OLAP data) to an archive device, such as tape or other removable media. The challenge is that the database instance must be shut down to perform this type of backup. This is not always possible.

Software products allow for backing up the Oracle database files while they are still open. Recovery Manager (RMAN) is an example of this type of software that is available from Oracle. For more information, see the Oracle Database documentation.

Oracle Database Export Commands

Oracle Data Pump enables fast bulk data and metadata movement between Oracle databases. Data Pump provides parallel export and import utilities (expdp and impdp), as well as a web-based Oracle Enterprise Manager interface. Because the OLAP option is fully integrated into the Oracle Database, it can make use of this facility for backing up and moving data from one machine to another.

RMAN is commonly used to back up, restore, and migrate databases. Again, because Oracle OLAP is fully integrated into the Oracle Database, it can make use of this facility.

A standby database can also be used, provided it is run in Physical mode.

Excluding Analytic Workspace Data for Exports

Analytic workspaces can take up a lot of space and can take time to export. If the analytic workspace can be reconstituted quickly from relational data, or you perform a separate export of the analytic workspace using Data Pump or the OLAP DML export command (discussed in the next section), you may want to exclude the analytic workspace data.

To exclude analytic workspaces from dpexp and exp exports, use this command:

```
select * from sys.exppkgact$ where package IN ('DBMS_AW_EXP',
'DBMS_CUBE_EXP');
delete from sys.exppkgact$ where package IN ('DBMS_AW_EXP',
'DBMS_CUBE_EXP');
```

To restore analytic workspaces exports in dpexp and exp exports, use this command:

```
insert into sys.exppkgact$ values ('DBMS_AW_EXP', 'SYS', 2, 1000);
insert into sys.exppkgact$ values ('DBMS_AW_EXP', 'SYS', 4, 1000);
/* For Oracle Database 11.1, add this syntax: */
insert into sys.exppkgact$ values ('DBMS_CUBE_EXP', 'SYS', 2, 1050);
```

Oracle OLAP Data Export Commands for Analytic Workspaces

The OLAP DML language has a set of utilities that support exporting and importing analytic workspace data to files on the server. These commands copy data and definitions from the analytic workspace to an EIF file contained in the server directory specified by the directory alias. The status of the data's dimensions determines which values are exported from the analytic workspace. These commands are used to copy all or parts of the data contained in the analytic workspace to a file, from which it can be imported into another schema or database instance. These commands perform the same basic functionally as the database export commands, but for analytic workspace objects.

An important feature of the export command is the ability to create subsets of the data, using the LIMIT command, before exporting the data. This can be very important if you want to create a small test set of data. When imported, the analytic workspace will contain all the structures, but only the data needed for the desired functionality. The data can then be imported into a test schema or test server. This is very difficult to do with relational data (although a new feature of Data Pump allows for issuing SELECT statements to do similar limiting of data).

Another handy feature of the Oracle OLAP export command is the ability to exclude aggregated data from the export file. This creates a much smaller export file and still preserves the data. It does require that you aggregate the data once it is loaded again, but this may take less time than the export. To exclude aggregated data, add the noaggr argument to the end of the export command.

The export command has the following syntax:

```
EXPORT export_item TO EIF FILE filename [LIST] [NOPROP] -
[NOREWRITE|REWRITE] [FILESIZE n [K, M, or G]] -
[NOTEMPDATA] [NLS_CHARSET charset-exp] [AGGREGATE | NOAGGR]
```

where `export item` is one of the following:

■ `name [AS newname]`

■ `exp [SCATTER AS scattername [TYPE scattertype]`
  `EXCLUDING (concatbasedim . . .)]`

■ `exp AS name [EXCLUDING (concatbasedim . . .)]`

■ `ALL`

The following example exports the SALESTRACK analytic workspace:

```
CDA olapdir /* change the directory alias to point to olapdir
EXPORT ALL to eif file salestrack.eif
```

If you wanted to do the same thing from a SQL command prompt, you can use the DBMS_AW stored procedure, as follows:

```
exec dbms_aw.execute('cda olapdir;export all to eif file
salestrack.eif');
```

The following is the syntax for the import command:

```
IMPORT import_item FROM EIF FILE filename [INTO workspace] -
    [MATCH [STATUS]|APPEND|REPLACE [DELETE]] [LIST [ONLY]] [DATA] -
    [DFNS] [UPDATE] [NOPROP] [NASKIP] [NLS_CHARSET charset-exp]
```

where `import_item` is one of the following:

■ `name [AS newname]`

■ `ALL`

For example, to import the salestrack.eif file into a new analytic workspace, use this command:

```
CDA olapdir /* change the database alias to point to olapdir
Import ALL from eif file salestrack.eif
```

Troubleshooting Oracle OLAP

A plethora of information pertaining to troubleshooting the Oracle Database is available. Our goal here is to provide some hints on troubleshooting issues related to Oracle OLAP.

Access to the Analytic Workspace

It is not unusual to have users of such tools as OBIEE or Microsoft Excel complain that they are not able to see the Oracle OLAP data. The problem can be traced to user access privileges. As discussed in Chapter 4, the OLAP data stored in an analytic workspace is actually an Oracle table. To allow users access to this table, a simple grant needs to be executed.

For example, consider an analytic workspace table called AW$OLAPTRAIN. To allow Scott to read the OLAP data in SALESTRACK contained in the OLAPTRAIN schema, you issue this command:

```
grant select on AW$SALESTRACK to Scott;
grant OLAP_USER to Scott;
```

The additional grant, OLAP_USER, is used to extend the ability to see OLAP objects. After these grants are made, the user, Scott, can now see the data contained in SALESTRACK AW. See Chapter 4 for additional security settings.

Oracle OLAP Dynamic Performance Tables

The Oracle Database has a series of tables that record the database activity and store information about processes and operations in the database instance. Data in the tables is updated continuously while the instance is running. These tables are called the V$ tables, or the dynamic performance tables, and they are owned by SYS. Any user with the SELECT CATALOG role can access these tables. Additionally, the system creates views from these tables and creates public synonyms for the views. The views are also owned by SYS, but an administrator can grant access to them to any user requiring access.

One set of tables collects data pertaining to the operation of Oracle OLAP. These tables and related views are prefixed with V$AW, as listed in Table 8-5.

View	Description
V$AW_ALLOCATE_OP	Lists the allocation operators available to Oracle OLAP
V$AW_AGGREGATE_OP	Lists the aggregation operators available to Oracle OLAP
V$AW_CALC	Collects information about the cache space usage and the status of dynamic aggregation
V$AW_OLAP	Collects information about the status of active analytic workspaces
V$AW_SESSION_INFO	Contains information about all active sessions that are using Oracle OLAP
V$AW_LONGOPS	Contains information about SQL fetches

TABLE 8-5. *Oracle OLAP Views*

The most important views are V$AW_CALC and V$AW_LONGOPS. The V$AW_CALC view contains data about session usage of caches as well as the status of aggregation processing. You should watch how large the page pool is, as well as cache hits and misses. The more effective the caches are, the better is the response time experienced by users. An ineffective cache (that is, one with few hits and many misses) suggests that the data is not being stored optimally for the way it is being viewed. To improve run-time performance, you may need to reorder the dimensions in the cube to load the larger dimensions sooner than later. The V$AW_CALC view also shows the OLAP DML command that was executed. Knowing which command was executed will help you determine what was being done at the time.

The V$AW_LONGOPS view shows the OLAP DML command being run, such as SQL fetch, import, or execute. The view provides the current state of the operation—whether it is executing, fetching, or finished. It also shows the number of rows that have been acted upon and the time the command started executing.

For additional information about these views and how they can be used, see the *Oracle OLAP User's Guide* under "Administering Oracle OLAP."

Diagnostic Commands

Tables 8-6, 8-7, and 8-8 list of some diagnostic commands that can be used to turn on various features of the database to trace and capture information. These can be used for diagnosing build, query, and program performance problems.

Diagnose	Setting
SQL tracing	`alter session set sql_trace true`
OLAP continuous tracing	`alter session set "_olap_continuous_` `trace_file"=true`
OLAP debug information to trace	`alter session set "_olap_dbgoutfile_` `echo_to_eventlog"=true`
OLAP POutLog (aggregation) to trace	`alter session set "_olap_poutlog_echo_` `to_eventlog"=true`
OLAP SQL import to trace	`alter session set events "37390 trace` `name context forever, level 1"`
OLAP update to trace	`alter session set events "37396 trace` `name context forever, level 1"`

TABLE 8-6. *OLAP Maintain Debugging*

Diagnose	Setting
SQL tracing (binds and waits)	`alter session set events "10046 trace name context forever, level 12"`
CBO decisions	`alter session set events "10053 trace name context forever, level 1"`
OLAP continuous tracing	`alter session set "_olap_continuous_ trace_file"=true`
OLAP table function to trace	`alter session set "_olap_table_ function_statistics"=true`

TABLE 8-7. *Query Debugging*

> **NOTE**
> *In Oracle Database 11g Release 2 (11.2.0), use the DBMS_CUBE_LOG package to manage diagnostic logs.*

These commands should be used with caution. If possible, try them on a nonproduction environment until you are comfortable with their use.

> **NOTE**
> *Regarding the OLAP DML command settings listed in Table 8-8, if you are running OLAP Worksheet, there is no need for the PL/SQL wrapper.*

Diagnose (OLAP DML Commands)	Setting
Details when bad line of code	`exec dbms_aw.execute('BADLINE=yes');`
OLAP program execution	`exec dbms_aw.execute('PRGTRACE=on');`
OLAP model execution	`exec dbms_aw.execute('MODTRACE=on');`
Show error messages	`exec dbms_aw.execute('ECHOPROMPT=yes');`

TABLE 8-8. *Program Debugging*

Helpful DBA Scripts

Analytic workspace access can be summarized as read-many, write-once—only one user at a time can have an analytic workspace open in read-write (RW) mode, but many can have the same analytic workspace open in read-only (RO) mode. You can find out who has RW access by running a SQL `select` statement such as this one:

```
select username,sid,serial#,
owner||'.'||a.aw_name||' ('||decode(attach_mode, 'READ WRITE', 'RW',
'READ ONLY', 'RO','MULTIWRITE', 'MW', 'EXCLUSIVE', 'XW', attach_
mode)||')' aw, generation
from dba_aws a,v$aw_olap b, v$aw_calc c, v$session
where a.aw_number=b.aw_number and sid=b.session_id and c.session_id = sid
order by username, sid, a.aw_name;
```

Notice that this `SELECT` statement makes use of the previously mentioned V$ tables to obtain the session and analytic workspace information. The results of the `SELECT` statement look something like this:

```
USERNAME        SID      SERIAL# AW                                GENERATION
--------------- ---------- ------ ------------------------- ------------
MDT             137      20685   MDT.EMS (RO)                            24
MDT             137      20685   SYS.EXPRESS (RO)                         2
OLAPTRAIN       140      31597   SYS.EXPRESS (RO)                         2
OLAPTRAIN       140      31597   OLAPTRAIN.SALESTRACK (RW)               24
```

These results provide not only a list of all the users that are connected to analytic workspaces, but also their session information. The session is important if you need to kill their session, trace the commands being executed, or just give them a call and ask them to detach from the analytic workspace when they are done.

A more complex query can yield more interesting and useful information. If you want to know about how much of the Program Global Area (PGA) is being used by a session and how well it is using the OLAP page pool, you could use the following script:

```
set lines 110 pages 500
col usn for a23 hea "USER (SID,SERIAL#,SVR)"
col pga_used for 9,990.9 hea "PGA MB|USED"
col pga_max for 9,990.9 hea "PGA MB|MAX"
col olap_pp for 9,990.9 hea "OLAP MB"
col olap_hrate for 99.9 hea "OLAP|Hit %"
bre on REPORT;
comp avg lab Average min lab Minimum max lab Maximum of olap_hrate on
REPORT;
comp avg lab Average sum lab Total min lab Minimum max lab Maximum of
pga_used on REPORT;
comp avg lab Average sum lab Total min lab Minimum max lab Maximum of
pga_max on REPORT;
comp avg lab Average sum lab Total min lab Minimum max lab Maximum of
olap_pp on REPORT;
```

```
select vs.username||' ('||vs.sid||','||vs.serial#||','||
decode(server,'DEDICATED','D','S','SHD','U')||')' usn,
round((pga_used_mem)/1024/1024,1) pga_used, round((pga_max_
mem)/1024/1024,1) pga_max,
round((pool_size)/1024/1024,1) olap_pp,
round(100*((pool_hits)/((pool_hits)+(pool_misses))),1) olap_hrate
from v$process vp, v$session vs, v$aw_calc va
where va.session_id = vs.sid and vp.addr = vs.paddr
order by vs.username, vs.sid, vs.serial#;
```

This script produces output like the following:

USER (SID,SERIAL#,SVR)	PGA MB USED	PGA MB MAX	OLAP MB	OLAP Hit %
MDT (137,20685,D)	6.0	6.5	1.8	98.9
OLAPTRAIN (140,31597,D)	5.9	8.8	1.4	98.8
Average	6.0	7.7	1.6	98.9
Minimum	5.9	6.5	1.4	98.8
Maximum	6.0	8.8	1.8	98.9
Total	11.9	15.3	3.2	

Oracle provides some other handy scripts for the Oracle OLAP administrator on the Oracle wiki site (http://wiki.oracle.com/page/OLAP+option+-+DBA+Sample+Scripts), as shown in Figure 8-1.

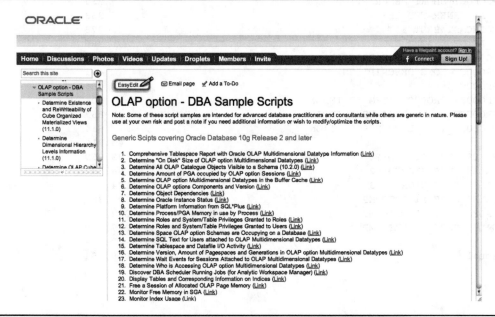

FIGURE 8-1. *Oracle OLAP DBA scripts on the Oracle wiki*

Another interesting site is the Oracle OLAP blog (http://oracleolap.blogspot.com), which includes discussions of basic and advanced OLAP option topics. Another example script demonstrates how to determine the names and size of all the internal AW objects:

```
set lines110 pages 500
col partname for a50 hea AW_OBJECT
col kb for 999,999,990
bre on REPORT;
comp sum lab Total of kb on REPORT;
select partname,

        round(sum(dbms_lob.getlength(awlob))/1024,0) KB
from    olaptrain.aw$salestrack
where   extnum=0
group   by partname
order   by kb;


AW_OBJECT                                                  KB
-------------------------------------------------- ------------
PRODUCT_PRODUCT_TYPE_ID_INDEX                             236
CHANNEL                                                   260
GEOGRAPHY                                                 260
TIME                                                      283
FORECAST_SMSEASONAL                                       291
FORECAST_SEASONAL                                         299
PRODUCT_SHORT_DESCRIPTION                                 338
__AW_GENERATED_153                                        338
FORECAST_BEST_FIT                                         378
__AW_GENERATED_150                                        386
FORECAST_LINEAR_REGRESSION                                386
PRODUCT_LONG_DESCRIPTION                                  401
PRODUCT                                                   496
PRODUCT_PRODUCT_ITEM_ID_INDEX                             504
PRODUCT_ITEM_SHORT_DESCRIPTION                            567
PRODUCT_ITEM_LONG_DESCRIPTION_                            614
                                                       43,716
SALES_CUBE_STORED:P1                                   89,959
SALES_CUBE_STORED:P2                                   96,570
SALES_CUBE_STORED:P3                                  104,174
SALES_CUBE_P1_PRTCOMP                                 197,305
SALES_CUBE_P2_PRTCOMP                                 212,047
SALES_CUBE_P3_PRTCOMP                                 227,569
                                                   ------------
Total                                                1,019,854
```

Flashback with Analytic Workspaces

Oracle OLAP is fully compatible with the Flashback option for the Oracle Database.
Flashback can quickly return a database to the state it was in before the last update
or maintain action. This feature is handy if you are testing designs or debugging
OLAP DML programs. You can use Flashback to help avoid mistakes and save
valuable time.

The following script uses SQL and OLAP DML to demonstrate how to use
Flashback.

```
/* grant flashback to OLAPTRAIN
conn system/manager
grant execute on sys.dbms_flashback to olaptrain;

/* now connect to olaptrain user
conn olaptrain/oracle
set serveroutput on size 9999
begin
dbms_aw.execute('aw attach SALESTRACK rw');
dbms_aw.execute('DEFINE flash_test VARIABLE DECIMAL');
dbms_aw.execute('flash_test = 10');
dbms_aw.execute('update ; commit');
dbms_aw.execute('show flash_test');
dbms_aw.execute('aw detach SALESTRACK');
end;

/* Wait 30 Minutes or so */
begin
dbms_aw.execute('aw attach SALESTRACK rw');
dbms_aw.execute('flash_test = 20');
dbms_aw.execute('update; commit');
dbms_aw.execute('show flash_test');
dbms_aw.execute('aw detach SALESTRACK');
end;

/* Now verify the values */
begin
dbms_flashback.enable_at_time(sysdate - 15/1440); -- go back 15 minutes
dbms_aw.execute('aw attach SALESTRACK ro');
dbms_aw.execute('show flash_test');
dbms_aw.execute('aw detach SALESTRACK');
dbms_flashback.disable;
end;
```

These commands can be run as a script (as shown), run interactively from the SQL prompt, or even run from OLAP Worksheet in SQL or OLAP DML mode.

Essbase Care and Maintenance

In this section, we recommend methods for optimizing an Essbase database and backing up data. The recommendations are general in nature, and some may be inappropriate for your particular situation. You should discuss your specific needs with your consultant before implementing any optimizations.

Optimizing Essbase

It has been said that tuning an Essbase database depends as much on the chef as it does on the recipe. The optimization process requires more than blindly following a specific set of steps. You need an understanding of the data and the users to be able to select the most appropriate optimizations for your system.

There are five key areas for optimization:

- Overall performance (choosing an appropriate data storage model)

- Query performance

- Data load performance

- Calculation performance

- Cache performance

Overall Performance

The most obvious impact on performance can come from the choice of data storage for your Essbase database. As mentioned in Chapter 3, Essbase has two data storage options: aggregate storage option (ASO) and block storage option (BSO). Implementing a storage model that is inappropriate for the data contained in the database can cause performance issues.

When ASO was added to Essbase in 2004, it dramatically changed the performance and scalability landscape. When one beta customer converted an existing BSO application that took more than 3½ hours to aggregate to ASO, the application aggregated in 31 seconds. Early versions of ASO also had a fair number of restrictions. Sadly, myths around these early restrictions remain today, although most of them have been removed, usually many years ago. The result is that many long-time Essbase developers still recommend to new Essbase developers that they start with block storage. We contend that the mindset needs to change from "I will start with BSO, unless it gets too big" to "Is there a reason why I should not use ASO?"

There are still some valid reasons not to choose an ASO solution, such as the need to store/write data to upper levels, or the need to run a procedural calculation script or to call external functions from a script, but this does not preclude a hybrid implementation using the benefits of both storage models. "Should I use ASO or BSO for this model?" is a common question, but the wrong one. "How should I use ASO and BSO together to create my Essbase application?" is a much better starting point. An Essbase application can consist of many databases.

Now that ASO can be the source and target of a partition, creating a composite model that fully satisfies users' requirements is more straightforward, and the resulting solution can leverage the power of both options.

Chapter 3 discussed the advantages of BSO and ASO. We summarize them again here for your review in the context of optimization.

BSO has the following functional advantages:

- You can input data to upper levels. For example, you can input a total charge at the All Markets and All Products levels, and then use an allocation method to push those values down to the individual product SKUs in the individual cities. Upper-level input is particularly useful when you want to do target budgeting or perform allocations (such as a corporate overhead charge).

- You can precalculate every intersection. This means that query times (assuming the data request volume is synonymous) from request to request are consistent. In practice, many intersections of a BSO database are left to calculate dynamically at retrieval time. Total time period values (such as the total at Quarter 1) are often dynamically calculated as an overall efficiency practice.

- Period-to-date reporting capabilities are built into BSO databases.

- You can control calculation behavior down to the cell level. If you need to model a complex calculation process (for example, a goal-seeking calculation), you can control the process in detail with a calculation script.

ASO provides the following advantages:

■ In general, ASO databases are ideal for aggregating large data sets. They can have many millions members, with large dimensionality, and be sourced with hundreds of gigabytes of data.

■ ASO databases are cell-based, and these smaller structures (compared to blocks) tend to load rapidly. Additionally, because you are not aggregating large portions of the database, but rather strategic points, the data is available to your users with less system downtime. Running an aggregation process (while recommended for performance reasons) is optional. Because all upper-level values are dynamic, the values at upper levels calculate on retrieval immediately after loading data.

■ The overall structure of an ASO database is smaller than that of a BSO database. This, coupled with a smaller aggregation footprint, can lead to a disk footprint significantly smaller than with a BSO database.

When designing a database, ensuring proper batch load and calculation times are exceedingly important considerations. If you cannot provide data access to your users in a timely fashion, the deployment is perceived as a failure. Equally important, however, is the concept of query performance, as discussed in the next sections. You need to optimize that database for the types of query executed, the number and frequency of those queries, and the size of the user base. The parameters involved vary from ASO to BSO, and this is where some of the benefits of an ASO database become apparent—the number of things you need to consider is dramatically reduced.

Query Perfomance in Block Storage Databases

Essbase uses a patented storage algorithm for BSO databases that prevents the database explosion that can occur in OLAP databases. Essentially, space is allocated for the members in the dense dimensions whenever data is received against an intersection of sparse members. For example, consider the outline in Figure 8-2. Let's assume that Year, Measures, and Scenario are flagged as dense, while Product and Market are sparse. The others are attribute dimensions and are not flagged.

When a Product is sold in a Market, a data block holding all values for Year, Measures, and Scenario is created. Thus, the dense/sparse setting controls the size of the block of data that is stored, as well as how many blocks are created. If Market was changed to dense, the database would store more information within the block, but there would be fewer blocks: one for each Product, rather than one for each Product/Market combination.

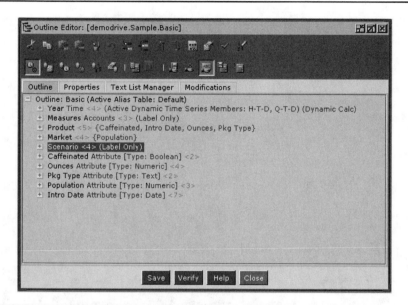

FIGURE 8-2.   *Sample outline for a block storage database*

This is where the tuning of Essbase becomes more of an art. There is no right answer for the block size (although there may be some wrong ones!). The best block size depends on the nature and use of the application, as well as the hardware and operating system being used.

Various statistics are available (as shown in Figure 8-3) to help you understand the application and the data, so you can tune these settings. The volume of data is not necessarily the determining factor, but rather the distribution across the dimensions. The distribution across the sparse dimensions determines how many blocks will be created (before aggregation), while the spread across the dense dimensions will determine the block density (basically, how full the block is).

We mentioned that some of the dimensions in the outline were attribute dimensions. An attribute dimension does not affect storage, as it does not hold any data. It does not exist in its own right, but qualifies another dimension: product A is red; product B is green; the manager for the Eastern region is Jeremy. However, attribute dimensions do allow a greater flexibility of analysis. For example, if you request the total sales of red products, Essbase dynamically calculates the result by retrieving the associated members. Of course, whenever values are calculated at request time, there is a potential impact on retrieval speed.

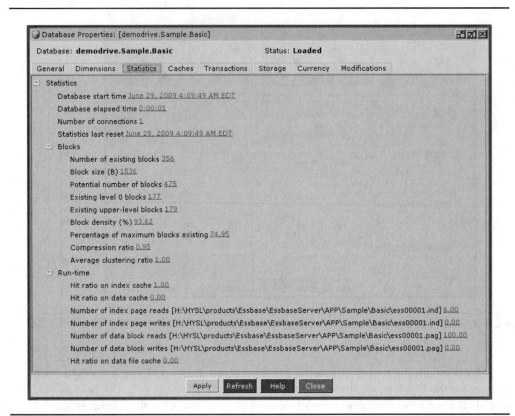

FIGURE 8-3. *BSO statistics in the Administration Services console*

Data Storage Settings Setting dimensions to dense impacts the amount of data stored in each block (that is, the block size). The theoretical block size is calculated by multiplying together the number of members in each dense dimension and then multiplying this by 8 (as each data point requires 8 bytes of storage). Clearly, if you store fewer members, you have a smaller block size, so Essbase allows you to control the storage of individual members. For example, you do not need to store a value for Time, because you can calculate it (and the value of the quarters) from the months. You can flag these members as Dynamic Calc members, so that you are storing 12 members (the months), instead of 17 (the months plus the quarters plus the year). Figure 8-4 shows a sample optimization to reduce the number of stored members.

Based on the dimensional statistics in Figure 8-4, you can calculate the impact of the optimization by comparing the Members in Dimension and Members Stored columns. Using the stored members, you can calculate the block size by multiplying

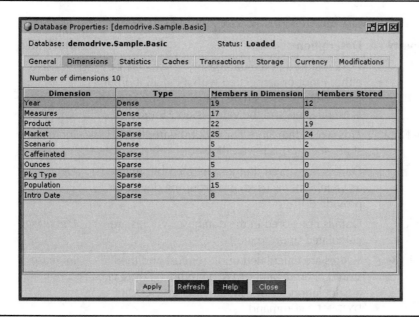

FIGURE 8-4. *Reducing the number of stored members in dense dimensions reduces block size.*

the dense dimensions together (12 * 9 * 2 = 216) and then multiplying by the 8 bytes storage (216 * 8). The result is 1,728 bytes. This compares with the theoretical block size (with no optimizations) of 13,680 bytes (19 * 18 * 5 * 8).

As well as the dynamic calculation setting, there are other options for controlling the size, such as flagging an item as a label. This tells Essbase that it is a placeholder in the outline, but no data will be stored there. Essbase will also automatically try to apply optimizations, so if a member has a single child, it will save space by converting it to an implied share.

Table 8-9 describes the member storage properties that affect block size and states what happens to the block size when each is used on a dense dimension.

For example, consider the following Scenario dimension with five members (recall that Scenario itself counts as a member):

■ Actual

■ Budget

■ Variance, with the formula @VAR(Actual, Budget);

■ Variance %, with the formula @VARPER(Actual, Budget);

Storage Property	Description	Impact on Block Size
Store Data	Data is stored in the database. Values may be either input or associated with a calculation. If the member has a single child, an implicit share is established and the value is not stored.	Increase
Never Share Data	This works like Store Data, but the implicit share scenario is never allowed.	Increase
Label Only	Data is not stored. Rather, the member marked as Label Only is used as a grouping device to provide drill-down.	Decrease
Dynamic Calc	Data is not stored in the database. Values are calculated upon request.	Decrease
Dynamic Calc & Store	Values are calculated upon request and then stored. Stored values may be removed only via a calculation script using the CLEARBLOCK DYNAMIC command.	Increase
Shared Member	Shared members appear to be duplicates. Instead, the duplicate member points to the original member. Thus, the data is "reused." For example, in the Sample Basic database, three diet products occur under their respective product category and a parent called Diet. The Diet member is used for a secondary grouping or rollup.	Decrease

TABLE 8-9. *Properties That Affect Block Size*

If you set Variance and Variance % to Dynamic Calc, the dimension is reduced by two members, which is a reduction of 40 percent. Furthermore, if you set Scenario to Label Only, the dimension is reduced another 20 percent. This reduction has an immediate impact on the size of the block, and in turn, the size of the database, as all blocks are reduced in size.

Choosing Dense or Sparse When determining whether a dimension is dense or sparse, you need to examine the notion of data distribution. Look at each dimension in combination with each of the other dimensions and note where data exists more so than not. As shown in Figure 8-5, when data exists for many combinations, the dimensions are dense. When few combinations contain values, the dimensions are sparse.

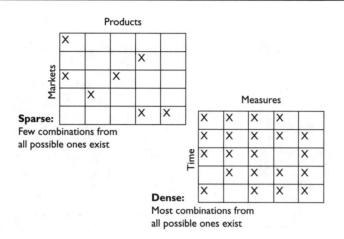

FIGURE 8-5. *Data distribution*

The first distribution diagram in Figure 8-5 reveals that not all products are sold in all markets. For example, a particular drink might sell better in California than in Texas. However, if you have designed your model correctly, you generally have measures across various time periods. The second distribution diagram reflects that while a particular drink may not sell well in Texas as opposed to California, some drinks sell there, and so you have data for sales across time periods.

Block size is the next way to look at dense and sparse. For each application, there should be an optimal size. The *Oracle Essbase Database Administrator's Guide* suggests 8KB to 64KB; however, block sizes larger than 64KB are often better than ones that are less than 8KB. Simply stated, Essbase reads and writes data by block. Therefore, all input, output, and calculation transactions depend on this configuration. As an example, think of a sandy beach and several sizes of shovel. If the task is to move sand from point A to point B, a shovel the size of a teaspoon will be less efficient than one used for gardening by hand. A larger shovel, like one used for snow, can actually work against you, due to the weight of the sand.

As we have said, dimension size has a direct impact on block size. In the preceding examples, you saw that 1,000 accounts by 12 months means 12,000 cells. However, adding another dense dimension, say one with four members, increases the number of cells fourfold. Therefore, adding even a small dense dimension can have a serious impact. Remember that you do not sum the members of a dimension; you multiply them, so the more dimensions you mark as dense, the bigger the block and bigger the impact.

Actual/Budget – Scenario is DENSE   Actual/Budget – Scenario is SPARSE

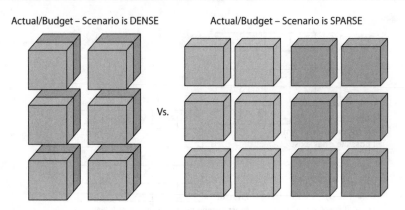

Vs.

FIGURE 8-6. *Scenario tagged as a dense dimension versus as a sparse dimension*

If you can split a block along a smaller dimension, you can quickly reduce the size. For example, you might make Scenario sparse, as shown in Figure 8-6. The reasoning is that frequently you do not need both actual and budget data available at the same time. Assume that you create the budget in the fall, and the actual data does not yet exist. If Scenario were dense, the block would have two times the amount of required data in memory. That means that you need to move more cells into memory than required, which translates to wasted time.

At this point, we will suggest that you review the *Oracle Essbase Database Administrator's Guide* and be prepared to experiment with different dense and sparse scenarios.

Query Performance in Aggregate Storage Databases

ASO databases load data at level 0 and derive all upper-level members and member formulas dynamically. To optimize retrieval performance, you can run an aggregation process on the database to build stored values at some upper-level intersections. After loading data, Essbase analyzes the source data and builds aggregates to optimize those queries that will take the longest to resolve based on the structure of the model. You can also have Essbase monitor query patterns of your user base, and then build aggregations to serve your specific queries more efficiently.

ASO databases have two primary dimension types to consider for optimization: *stored* and *dynamic*. Another dimension type, *multiple hierarchies enabled*, is a hybrid option that allows a portion of one dimension to be stored and other portions to be dynamic. The dimension types come into play when Essbase builds aggregates. Assume you have a database that has the following dimensions and storage properties:

- Time (dynamic)

- Measures (dynamic)

- Markets (stored)

- Customer (stored)

- Products (stored)

- Scenario (stored)

When the ASO engine builds aggregates, it looks at all members (including upper-level members) in stored dimensions to be part of an aggregate view. Suppose you have 4 million customers divided into five geographical regions and then a few hundred subregions. In this dimension, the ASO engine might build a series of aggregate views at the subregion level. In that case, the queries at the five geographical regions would not need to start adding up the entire group of individual customer accounts. Instead, ASO could start the math from the already derived subregions. That aggregation point (based on this example) might be a customer subregion for a given month for a given product line in North America, and be based on the current year scenario.

Because only stored hierarchies are considered for aggregate views, it is much more efficient to have stored dimensions in the outline. With dynamic dimensions, Essbase must derive the entire dimension from the bottom to provide query results (assuming you are querying at upper levels). The multiple hierarchies enabled dimension type would let you have a portion of a dimension be stored and other portions dynamic. You need to use a dynamic hierarchy in the following circumstances:

- To use member formulas in a dimension

- To use consolidation operators other than addition (+)

- To have complex shared member structures (alternate hierarchy dimensions can generally accommodate simple shared hierarchies)

It is best to use dynamic dimension types for smaller dimensions (hundreds or thousands of members), as these can be derived very quickly. From most efficient to least efficient, the dimension types are stored, multiple hierarchies enabled, then dynamic.

Data Load Optimizations

Another important optimization involves streamlining how data is loaded. The first rule of thumb is to try to keep the data manipulation to a minimum. Yes, you can move and split fields in a load rule or replace strings, but this type of manipulation is better suited to a relational database source. When loading data from an SQL source, it is more efficient to present the data fields to Essbase in the correct order, and perform any manipulations and aggregations within the SQL statement.

Sorting for Block Storage Databases   In a BSO application, the most efficient way to load data is to process each block only once. For example, you do not want to write the volume information for each product, and then go back and write the sales value afterwards. Therefore, the optimum sequence for loading data is to sort by the sparse dimensions first, followed by the dense dimensions, so that all the data for a block is processed together, and the block is written only once.

For example, assume that you have a database with Year, Region, Scenario, and Account dimensions. Region and Scenario are flagged as sparse dimensions; Year and Account are dense dimensions. With this configuration, there would be a block of Year by Account data for each combination of Region by Scenario. Figure 8-7 shows two ways to represent the data for load purposes.

In Figure 8-7, the file on the left is much less efficient than the one on the right. The right file is sorted by Region and Scenario, so each group of three records belongs to a particular block. Additionally, the example on the right has more data per record than the one on the left. With more data values in each record, Essbase does not need to process as many records.

Buffers for Aggregate Storage Databases   In an ASO database, the concept of blocks does not exist, and the organization of the data for optimum loading happens automatically in the load buffer. When large volumes of data are being loaded, the size of this buffer can be adjusted to ensure that performance is maintained, setting the Pending cache size limit option, as shown in Figure 8-8. In addition, discrete sets of data can be loaded into individual load buffers, and then the multiple buffers can be committed in a single action.

Calculation Optimizations

As discussed in Chapter 3, one of the principal differences between ASO and BSO is the ability to have procedural calculations. The potential requirement for having a procedural calculation in a deployment is a driving consideration when choosing the data storage model. Of the two models, it is much simpler to optimize ASO aggregations. That is not to say that optimizing calculation scripts is complex, but there is more to consider.

	Year	Region	Scenario	Account	*Data*
1	Jan	East	Actual	Sales	100
2	Jan	West	Budget	Sales	72
3	Jan	East	Budget	Sales	90
4	Jan	West	Actual	Sales	81
5	Jan	East	Actual	Expense	50
6	Jan	East	Budget	Expense	45
7	Jan	West	Actual	Expense	41
8	Jan	West	Budget	Expense	36
9	Jan	West	Budget	Inventory	729
10	Jan	East	Actual	Inventory	1000
11	Jan	East	Budget	Inventory	900
12	Jan	West	Actual	Inventory	810
13	Feb	East	Actual	Sales	125
14	Feb	West	Budget	Sales	91
15	Feb	East	Budget	Sales	113
16	Feb	West	Actual	Sales	101
17	Feb	East	Actual	Expense	60
18	Feb	East	Budget	Expense	54
19	Feb	West	Actual	Expense	49
20	Feb	West	Budget	Expense	44
21	Feb	West	Budget	Inventory	656
22	Feb	East	Actual	Inventory	900
23	Feb	East	Budget	Inventory	810
24	Feb	West	Actual	Inventory	729
25	Mar	East	Actual	Sales	200
26	Mar	West	Budget	Sales	145
27	Mar	East	Budget	Sales	180

	Region	Scenario	Accounts	Jan	Feb	Mar
1	East	Actual	Sales	100	125	200
2	East	Actual	Expense	50	60	90
3	East	Actual	Inventory	1000	900	700
4	East	Budget	Sales	90	113	180
5	East	Budget	Expense	45	54	81
6	East	Budget	Inventory	900	810	630
7	West	Actual	Sales	81	101	162
8	West	Actual	Expense	41	49	73
9	West	Actual	Inventory	810	729	567
10	West	Budget	Sales	72	91	145
11	West	Budget	Expense	36	44	66
12	West	Budget	Inventory	729	656	510
13						

FIGURE 8-7. *Improve data-load efficiency by processing sparse dimensions first.*

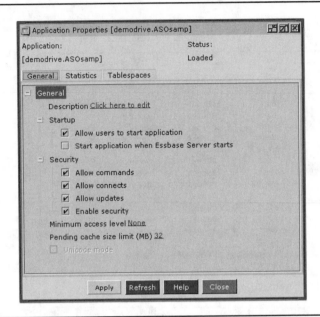

FIGURE 8-8. *Setting the size of the cache*

Aggregations for Aggregate Storage Databases   Within an ASO database, all calculations are dynamic (performed at retrieval time). Performance is maintained by designing aggregations based on the most expensive queries in the database. Based on the data loaded into the database, the ASO engine uses an algorithm to determine those queries that would take the longest. Using our previous example, if we load data for 4 million customers, a query that requests aggregated values across this dimension would require Essbase to add quite a bit of information. The ASO engine would look at the data distribution under this dimension and try to build aggregation points to help query performance across this dimension.

In general, the more aggregations in a database, the faster the performance. Aggregations, however, require disk space. More aggregate values mean more data storage space. As such, there is a point of diminishing returns. It may not benefit you to use an additional 10GB of disk space if the impact on performance might be negligible.

When optimizing the database, you can specify the amount of disk space you want to allow for aggregations. As shown in Figure 8-9, Essbase provides an impact analysis comparing query performance improvement and disk space. This lets you make an educated decision on how much space you use.

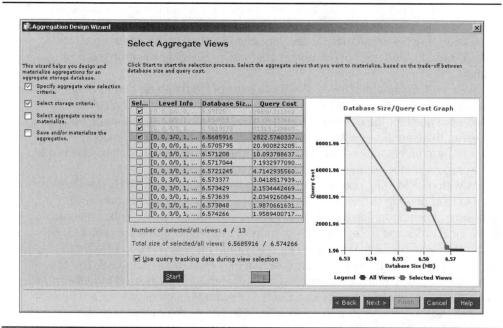

FIGURE 8-9. *Essbase impact analysis*

In Figure 8-9, the horizontal axis on the graph represents the amount of disk space. The vertical axis represents the potential performance gain. In this example, there is a large performance gain over the initial set of aggregations. After that gain, the impact of additional aggregations appears to be somewhat limited.

To quantify the preceding points, a prime way to optimize aggregation behavior in ASO database is to allocate disk space. In addition to leveraging the default aggregation behavior, the administrator can enable query tracking to log which areas of the database are being hit most often, and use this information to overlay or replace the aggregations to fine-tune the performance. In this way, the ASO database becomes self-learning.

Another consideration for ASO aggregation optimization is the amount of time it takes Essbase to build the aggregations. You can optimize this process by allocating RAM to the ASO cache. This cache is used by ASO databases to optimize load and aggregation processes.

Calculation Scripts for Block Storage Databases As we discussed earlier, BSO databases rely on blocks. When running a calculation script on a BSO database, you are creating additional blocks, deriving values for existing blocks, or a combination of both. Remember that even if you are calculating only a single value in a block, the entire block comes into memory. The goal of optimizing a BSO calculation script is to calculate as few blocks and as few cells within those blocks as necessary. In short, do not do more work than is necessary to complete your analysis.

By default, Essbase processes only those parts of the database that have been amended. This behavior is called *intelligent calculation*. Intelligent calculation reduces the need for the developer to think about the process in too much detail. However, there are times when you need to override the default behavior. For example, if a driver value or exchange rate is changed, the whole database needs to be processed, not just those blocks that have been updated.

As with data loading optimization, you want to ensure that Essbase does not need to read or write to any block more than necessary—preferably only once. Therefore, when designing a calculation script, you want to process the database in a logical order and access only those parts of the database that are required. For example, if you load actual numbers for the current month, you do not want to process any of the budget or forecast data that may exist in the database. The IF, FIX, and EXCLUDE commands can be used to control the areas used for either a calculation as a whole or a subsection of it. For example, you could use a statement like FIX(Actual) to ensure that you calculate on only the Actual scenario.

Another key part of calculation performance is ensuring that Essbase has sufficient memory available to the script to be able to perform efficiently. As a starting point, you can design the database outline in what is known as the hourglass shape. An hourglass shape organizes the dense dimensions first, in decreasing order of size, followed by the sparse dimensions, in increasing order of size. Then you ensure that the memory allocated is sufficient to allow Essbase to anchor on the last two sparse dimensions.

You need to consider a series of caches and configuration settings when optimizing calculation processes on BSO database. The best resource for a detailed explanation and instructions of how to calculate these requirements is the *Oracle Essbase Database Administrator's Guide*. That said, the next section provides an overview on the various caches used by Essbase.

One final consideration for calculation script performance is the ability to process calculation tasks in parallel. Essbase can divide a calculation process into multiple tasks, and then run these tasks in parallel. The analysis of whether a script can be run across parallel tasks happens automatically in Essbase; however, you can also set some parameters the Essbase configuration file (essbase.cfg), located in the bin directory of the Essbase installation.

The Essbase configuration file is an optional file that contains a series of commands Essbase reads at startup. Many of these commands apply to the concept of optimization. For example, you can set default parallel calculation settings for all databases. For descriptions of specific settings, see the *Oracle Essbase Technical Reference*.

Optimizing Caches

The caches allow the control of memory allocation to a particular database. Clearly, it is advantageous to allocate as much memory as possible to a database, but this needs to be balanced against the other databases and applications on the server, as well as the total memory available. This is where the 64-bit operating systems provide the greatest performance advantages, with the ability to reference huge quantities of memory. The scope of this memory allows you to lock individual databases completely into memory or to build models that would traditionally be thought too big for an OLAP solution.

BSO databases have separate caches for the index and page file (metadata and data). Figures 8-10 and 8-11 show the related cache settings. To help you judge the settings for both of these caches, statistical information around the effectiveness of the caches is available in Administration Services Console. For more information, see the *Oracle Essbase Database Administrator's Guide*.

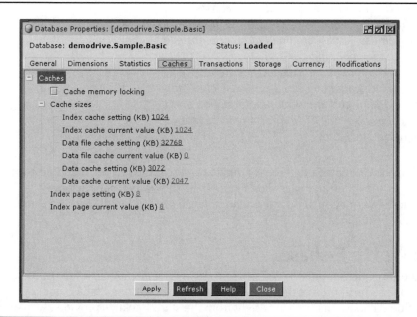

FIGURE 8-10. *Settings for the BSO caches*

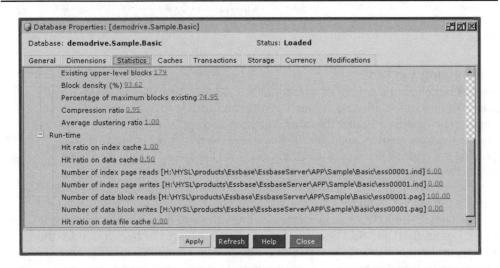

FIGURE 8-11. *Run-time settings for BSO databases*

NOTE
Several other caches exist in BSO databases. The data file cache setting is rarely used, as it relates to when you use Essbase in direct I/O mode, instead of letting the operating system manage the I/O. The calculator and dynamic calc caches are internal behaviors triggered by both the essbase.cfg settings and the outline order. For more information about these caches, see the Oracle Essbase Database Administrator's Guide.

Within an ASO database, there is a single cache, as there is not the same concept of separating the index and page files. Figure 8-12 shows the cache settings.

For more information about the cache settings, see the *Oracle Essbase Database Administrator's Guide.*

Backing Up Essbase

Given the strategic importance of Essbase to many organizations, administrators need to take steps to protect their data. This means integrating Essbase backups into routine database maintenance right from the start. Backups provide a way to restore a specific application or, for that matter, the entire production environment.

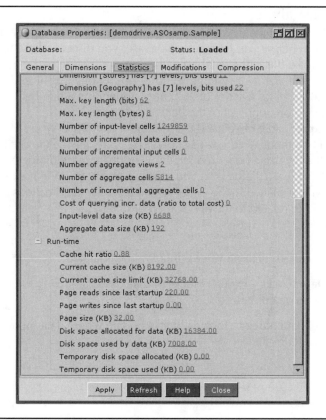

FIGURE 8-12. *Run-time cache settings for ASO databases*

Manual backups are sufficient if created on a regular schedule, but automating your backups offers greater reliability and can provide peace of mind.

In this section, we introduce the various backup strategies that are available for Essbase. We start with the backup strategies that are available for both BSO and ASO databases. Then we examine strategies for BSO databases. We conclude this section with a list of files that need to be backed up in addition to the database.

Creating an Operating System Backup

The traditional approach to backing up servers is an operating system backup. The challenge from an Essbase point of view is that active database files are typically skipped because they are open for read-write access. So, if you can bring your Essbase environment down, this form of backup is fine. Otherwise, you will need to select one of the other backup strategies covered in this section.

Exporting the Database

One of the most common means of backing up BSO or ASO data is a database export. In an export, before you back up a database, you direct Essbase to write the database data to a text file. If the database fails, you can then reload the text file. Because some file management systems do not support large text files, the Essbase server automatically creates a series of 2GB files, appending a number to each file name (01, 02, and so on), until all of the data is exported.

A database export can be executed using Administration Services, MaxL statements, or API methods. Figure 8-13 shows how you can use the context menu associated with the database node to open the Export Database dialog box.

In the Export Database dialog box, you start by specifying a file name. By default, the file will be placed in the folder where all of the applications are stored, rather than in a folder related to the application or database. Next, select one of three export options:

- **All data**   Exports all data values, input and calculated.

- **Level 0 data blocks**   Exports blocks of data associated with the lowest level or leaf nodes of a dimension.

- **Input level data blocks**   Exports blocks of data where data input, manual or mass, has occurred.

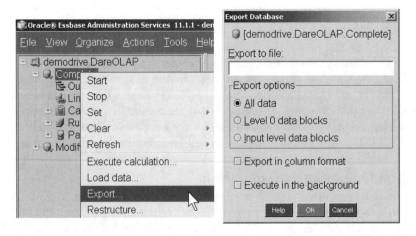

FIGURE 8-13.   *Choosing Database Export in Administration Services*

Finally, you can choose to export data in column format. This creates a tabular output that is particularly useful if the goal is to provide a copy of the data to another application. By default, Essbase exports data in a very compact, quasi-tabular format that can be reloaded very fast. You can also choose to execute the export using a background process, allowing you to continue working in Administration Services.

In the following MaxL example, data is exported to a file called input.txt. By default, only level 0 data is available for export.

```
export database DareOLAP.Complete input data to data_file 'input.txt';
```

To specify a subset of data, you can create and call a report script. The following MaxL example exports a database using the subset described in a report script called input.rep. The output file is input.txt.

```
export database DareOLAP.Complete using report_file 'input.rep' to
    data_file 'input.txt';
```

More modern backup strategies exist for BSO databases. These are discussed in the next section.

Other Backup Strategies for Block Storage Databases

Starting with Essbase release 9.3, new backup methods became available for BSO databases. These include exports through calculation scripts, automated Essbase backup and restore, and transaction replay. All of these methods can be performed manually or automatically.

Creating a Calculation Script   Essbase release 9.3 introduced the ability to export data from BSO databases through calculation scripts. A subset data export enables you to specify with more detail the data you would like to export. You can automate calculation scripts using MaxL.

The following MaxL example executes a calculation script called Export for the database called complete within the application called DareOLAP.

```
execute calculation DareOLAP.Export on database Complete;
```

Three database export targets are available via a calculation script: text, binary, and relational. Here, we will look at examples of how to set data export options for each of the target types using the SET DATAEXPORTOPTIONS command. For more information about this and other commands, see the *Oracle Essbase Technical Reference.*

The following script exports data to a text file. It specifies a data export level of 0 (which means the lowest members in the hierarchy), and then limits output to sales data with values of 1,000 or greater. Next, the script fixes the data slice for the specified dimensions members. Finally, the export target is specified as a text file located at b:\exports\jan.txt. Data will be separated using comma (,) delimiters, and any missing data values are represented by #MI.

```
SET DATAEXPORTOPTIONS
    {
    DataExportLevel "LEVEL0";
    };
DATAEXPORTCOND ("Sales">=1000);
FIX ("100-10","New York","Actual","Sales");
    DATAEXPORT "File" "," "b:\exports\jan.txt" "#MI";
ENDFIX;
```

When you export data using the binary method, Essbase creates the export file using the same bitmap compression technique that is used by the Essbase kernel. This makes for a very fast and efficient export process, using minimal disk storage. Binary exports can be fixed only on sparse dimensions. The following script exports all New York data blocks to a binary file located at b:\backup\newyork.bin.

```
SET DATAEXPORTOPTIONS
    {
    DataExportLevel "ALL";
    };
FIX ("New York");
    DATAEXPORT "BinFile" "b:\backup\newyork.bin";
ENDFIX;
```

In the next example, selected records are inserted directly into the table named NEWYORK in a relational database. All data is exported for the selected dimension members. In the DATAEXPORT statement, a data source name (DSN) is used to establish a connection, commonly via ODBC, to the CUR_SALES relational database. The table name is specified as NEWYORK, followed by the user name and password for the relational database.

```
SET DATAEXPORTOPTIONS
    {
    DataExportLevel "ALL";
    };
FIX("100-10","New York","Actual","Sales");
    DATAEXPORT "DSN" "cur_sale" "newyork" "admin" "password";
ENDFIX;
```

Archiving and Restoring a Database   Beginning with Essbase release 11, administrators can back up and restore BSO databases using the automated Essbase backup and restore capabilities. The automated backup copies the database object and data files to an archive location that you specify, and from which you can quickly restore the database. You must have the Administrator role to use the automated backup feature.

When backing up a database, Essbase performs the following tasks:

- Place the database in read-only mode, protecting the database from updates during the archive process while allowing requests to query the database.

- Write a copy of the database files to an archive file that resides on the computer hosting the Essbase server.

- Return the database to read-write mode.

Figure 8-14 shows how you can use the context menu associated with the database node to open the Archive Database dialog box. In this dialog box, provide the file name. Unless otherwise specified, the file is placed in the ARBORPATH/app folder. Because this process must place the database in read-only mode, the Force archive option may be used to drop users from the database. Users may reconnect to the database, but they will not be allowed read-write access. The Archive in the background option allows you to continue working in Essbase Administration Services while the archive proceeds.

You can use MaxL to automate the archive process. The following example backs up the complete database within the DareOLAP application, overwriting the existing archive file.

```
alter database DareOLAP.Complete force archive to file /Hyperion/
DareOLAP.arc;
```

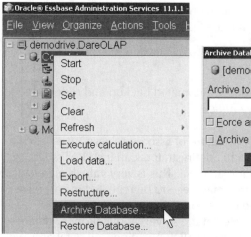
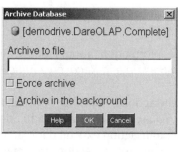

FIGURE 8-14. *Choosing Database Archive in Administration Services*

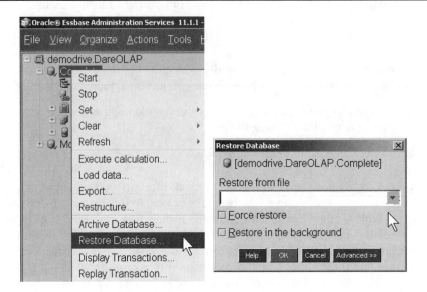

FIGURE 8-15. *Choosing Database Restore in Administration Services*

Restoring a database is the reverse of archiving a database. You must have the Administrator role to terminate active client connections and restore a database. Figure 8-15 shows how to use the context menu associated with the database node to open the Restore Database dialog box. The options in this dialog box work like the corresponding ones in the Archive Database dialog box.

You can also use MaxL to automate the restore process. The following example restores the Complete database within the DareOLAP application.

```
alter database DareOLAP.Complete force restore from file /Hyperion/
DareOLAP.arc;
```

For more information, about Essbase automated backup and restore, see the *EPM System Backup and Recovery Guide*.

Tracking Transactions Another new feature of Essbase release 11 is called *transaction replay*. With this approach, administrators can instruct Essbase to capture each transaction executed for later use. This is very valuable, because you have a single source of all actions that may need to be repeated in case of server or application failure. It eliminates the guesswork.

Transaction capture may be enabled at the server, application, or database level. Essentially, this means that you may specify all applications, all databases within an application, or a specific database. To enable transaction logging, the administrator creates a directory on the Essbase server, and then specifies the directory location via an Essbase configuration setting. The following example shows the essbase.cfg file setting used to enables transaction logging for all databases associated with the DareOLAP application. The log is written to a folder called C:\Hyperion\ trlog.

```
TRANSACTIONLOGLOCATION DareOLAP C:\Hyperion\trlog NATIVE ENABLE
```

To view the transaction history, right-click the database name, choose Display Transactions from the menu, and fill in the Display Transactions dialog box, as shown in Figure 8-16. You can view transactions from the last replay or from a specific date and time. Additionally, you may redirect the output to a file, rather than view it on screen.

To replay transactions, right-click the database name, choose Replay Transactions from the menu, and fill in the Replay Transactions dialog box, as shown in Figure 8-17. You can replay transactions from the last replay or from a specific date and time. Additionally, you may execute the replay in background.

You can use MaxL to automate the replay process. The following example replays the transactions in the DareOLAP. Complete database with sequence IDs 1 through 10 and 20 through 100.

```
alter database DareOLAP.Complete replay transactions using
    sequence_id_range 1 to 10, 20 to 100;
```

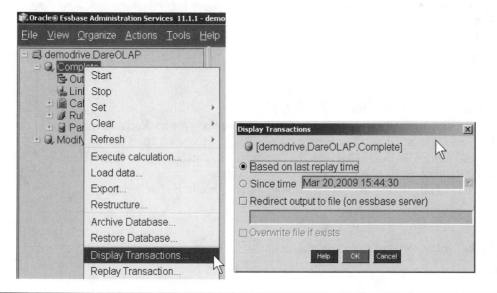

FIGURE 8-16.   *Choosing Display Transactions in Administration Services*

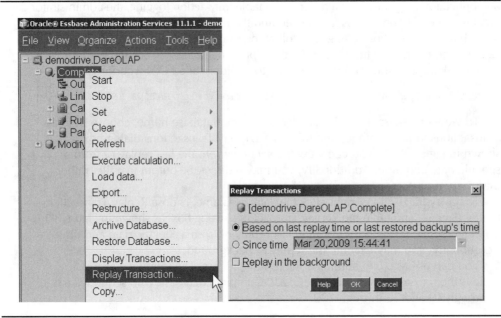

FIGURE 8-17. *Choosing Replay Transaction in Administration Services*

The next example replays all transactions that were logged after a specified date and time.

```
alter database DareOLAP.Complete replay transactions after
    '11_20_2007:12:20:00';
```

Other Important Files to Back Up

The previous sections provided you with many options for backup and restore. However, exporting the data from a database is just part of a good backup strategy. Several other files associated with the applications, databases, and Essbase Server are important for recovery.

In general, all files from the following folders should be backed up:

- ARBORPATH/app/appname

- ARBORPATH/app/appname/dbname

Additionally, the following files should be backed up:

- ESSBASEPATH/bin/essbase.sec (the Essbase security file)

- ESSBASEPATH/bin/essbase.bak (the backup of the Essbase security file)

- ESSBASEPATH/bin/essbase.cfg (Essbase server configuration settings)

You can find the values of ARBORPATH and ESSBASEPATH by examining the environment variables for the server on which Essbase was installed.

Conclusion

Oracle OLAP and Oracle Essbase are significantly different, both in optimization strategies and back up processes. Oracle OLAP, as part of the Oracle database, benefits from the configuration and tuning efforts performed on the database itself. A well-performing database goes a long way to ensuring acceptable load times and query response times for Oracle OLAP data. In addition, when an Oracle database is backed up, so is the Oracle OLAP data. In contrast, Essbase, as a stand-alone multidimensional database, has a variety of optimizations available to tune performance. Many of the optimizations differ based on the data storage model used (ASO or BSO). As with any database, Essbase has its own backup and restore procedures.

In the next and final chapter, we present some real-world examples of how Essbase and Oracle OLAP have been implemented.

References

Oracle Corporation. *Oracle OLAP Developer's Guide 10*g.

Oracle Corporation. *Oracle OLAP Developers Guide 11*g.

Oracle Corporation. "Relevant Diagnostic Parameters for the Oracle OLAP option." Oracle wiki (http://wiki.oracle.com/page/Relevant+Diagnostic+Parameters+for+ the+Oracle+OLAP+option).

EPM Information Development Team. *Oracle Essbase Database Administrator's Guide, Release 11.1.1*. Oracle Corporation, 2008.

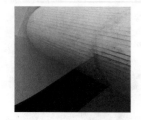

CHAPTER 9

Real-World Examples

n this chapter, we present some real-world examples of how Oracle OLAP and Oracle Essbase have been used to solve analytic challenges. These examples are assembled from a variety of sources, including published stories and our own experiences. In some cases, we exclude the name of the company to protect its privacy; as you might expect, these companies have gained a competitive advantage and want to preserve this advantage.

We start by presenting three Oracle OLAP examples, followed by three Essbase examples. Each example describes a typical challenge that can be addressed using OLAP technology, and then shows how Oracle OLAP or Essbase was used to solve that problem. We do not cover every type of usage, but rather provide a sample of what has been done to give you an idea of the possibilities.

Oracle OLAP Examples

Oracle OLAP is often a part of a larger implementation, but in these examples, we focus on the specific portion involving Oracle OLAP. In this section, we describe how Oracle OLAP has been used for the following purposes:

- Accelerating a data warehouse

- Analyzing projections

- Analyzing financial data

Accelerating a Data Warehouse

As mentioned in Chapter 1, data warehousing with Oracle OLAP can provide the best of both worlds: a single source of analytic data coupled with a multidimensional analysis of the data. The following example comes from a customer story first referenced in an *Oracle Magazine* article titled "Measure. Analyze. Perform." and then published as a follow-up success story in the February 2009 *Oracle OLAP Newsletter*. The company is R.L. Polk & Co. (Polk), and we focus on how adding Oracle OLAP to an existing Oracle Database data warehouse boosted the performance of both the warehouse and the company's BI tools.

Challenge: Improve the Performance of the Data Warehouse for a BI Application

Polk was running an Oracle Database 10*g* data warehouse and using materialized views to create aggregate totals for its BI application. The managers contacted Oracle for assistance in improving data loads, data formatting, and query response times. They were also interested in reducing time spent on maintenance.

Solution: Introduce Oracle OLAP
Cube-Organized Materialized Views

Before making any changes to the data warehouse, Oracle consultants created a baseline by running benchmark tests for user performance and query rewrite using Oracle Real Application Testing and a set of data from the warehouse. Using good experimental design techniques, they ran the same tests with the same data after each major change to the data warehouse, so that they could quantify and isolate any improvements.

In this scenario, the company first upgraded its version of Oracle Database from 10*g* to 11*g*. After the upgrade, they reran the benchmarks. The time to load and aggregate the materialized views decreased from 452 minutes to 385 minutes with version 11*g*.

Then they created an Oracle OLAP cube with four dimensions, based on the design of the original relational materialized views. Unlike the relational materialized views, which were only partially aggregated, the cube-organized materialized views contained fully aggregated data, as well as views for the dimensions themselves. Cube-organized materialized views were also joined to relational tables as necessary at query execution time, which meant that the cube could be integrated into the existing snowflake schema without the need to store all dimension attribute data in the cube itself. When the benchmark tests were rerun using the Oracle OLAP cube-organized materialized views, the results were dramatic. The load and aggregation were computed in just 38 minutes—an improvement of 92 percent over Oracle Database 11*g* alone. Query response times also improved significantly from 552 seconds down to 12 seconds for one sample query.

NOTE
*As discussed in Chapter 4, cube-organized materialized views can dramatically improve performance on normal queries against fact tables. Analytic applications do not need to be modified. The applications simply query the fact tables as usual via SQL, and the Oracle Database 11*g optimizer redirects the queries to the cube-organized materialized views for faster performance and access to data.*

Summary

The benefits of Oracle OLAP as a data warehouse accelerator are clear from this example: improved build times and query times. In addition, as a team member noted, one or a few cube-organized materialized views can replace tens or hundreds of relational materialized views, reducing IT workload and maintenance tasks.

Analyzing Projections

Many of the examples in this book have involved financial data. OLAP technology can be used for other purposes as well. As our next example shows, Oracle Database with Oracle OLAP can be useful for consolidating and analyzing data along multiple dimensions. In this example, the National Petroleum Council (NPC) uses Oracle OLAP to analyze projections for world energy consumption and supply.

Challenge: Analyze Projections for Energy Consumption and Supply

In October 2005, then Energy Secretary of the United States, Samuel W. Bodman, wrote an open letter to Lee Raymond, Chairman of the NPC, an advisory group representing the oil industry. In his letter, Secretary Bodman asked the following questions:

- What does the future hold for global oil and natural gas supply?

- Can incremental oil and natural gas supply be brought online, on time, and at a reasonable price to meet future demand without jeopardizing economic growth?

- What oil and gas supply strategies and/or demand-side strategies does the Council recommend the United States pursue to ensure greater economic stability and prosperity?

His questions precipitated a multiyear study of the problem, pulling information from many experts and organizations, including academic experts, research centers, government agencies, environmental groups, and energy companies. The results were published in 2007 under the title *Facing the Hard Truths about Energy*, available at http://www.npchardtruthsreport.org.

For the study, the organization needed to collect projections from multiple sources and aggregate them in a meaningful way. One of the challenges of the project was privacy. To meet antitrust guidelines set forth by the government, and to ensure no competitive information was exchanged during the study, all information that could identify the source of a projection had to be removed. Indeed, with individual projections being considered very proprietary, technical consultants working on the project were not allowed to access the raw data.

Solution: Implement an Oracle OLAP Analytic Workspace for Survey Data

The Oracle Database data warehouse was designed to be the main analytical tool for the task groups, accepting all data collected from the survey questionnaire and other data sources. To meet privacy concerns, a bonded third party ran Oracle database routines that computed averages, medians, minimums, and maximums, which were used for further analysis.

The multidimensional survey data was then loaded into Oracle OLAP cubes for analysis. The OLAP data was organized into seven dimensions:

- Time (year)

- Geography (country or geographic region)

- Energy type (such as oil, gas, coal, nuclear, or renewable)

- Energy sector (such as commercial or residential)

- Case type (such as business as usual or alternative energy policy)

- Units (applicable unit of measure)

- Source (such as public or proprietary)

The data presented its own issues, such as nonadditive data, skip-level hierarchies, and nonstandard aggregation rules. For example, analyses were conducted at multiple geographic levels. Sometimes the detail data for a given country needed to be obscured because revealing that data would reveal the source of the data. Summary data at a continent level, however, could be revealed, because there were more than three sources for the continent-level data. This led to the need to load data at multiple levels, with special aggregation logic to support higher-level data that was not necessarily the sum of the children.

To analyze the data and draw conclusions, industry experts used Discoverer Plus OLAP. The data was also exported from Oracle BI Discoverer and loaded into Microsoft Excel and PowerPoint for presentations to members of various analysis teams. Study teams were able to investigate relationships in the data during working sessions. The multidimensional nature of the data allowed them to drill down in multiple ways to investigate relationships that otherwise would not have been obvious.

Summary

By storing and analyzing multidimensional survey data using Oracle OLAP, the NPC was able to develop a comprehensive study of the global energy supply and demand through 2030. The privacy of the study contributors was protected because the analysts never had access to the source data, only the aggregated data stored in Oracle OLAP cubes. This project shows that OLAP technology can be used for a wide variety of purposes beyond handling marketing and financial data.

Analyzing Financial Data

Our next Oracle OLAP example is a more typical BI scenario. A company (name withheld for privacy) wanted to help its clients improve their business operations by analyzing their financial data.

Challenge: Provide an Environment for Clients to Analyze Financial Data

In this case, the application was a traditional financial analysis application for reporting financial general ledger data and key business metrics in the healthcare industry. Some of the challenges for this project included the following:

- About 25,000 Account dimension values, with the need to flip the sign of certain accounts for reporting purposes

- Calculated equations for some accounts with interdimension references

- Calculated measures with rules that vary depending on account value

- Need to use Excel in addition to a web-based viewer of reports

Solution: Leverage Oracle OLAP Financial Calculations

While other OLAP products could provide the necessary calculations, this company chose Oracle OLAP specifically so that it could leverage the scalability, reliability, and backup facilities in the Oracle Database that already housed the company's data. The client already had extensive knowledge of the Oracle Database. The reporting requirements would have been difficult to meet using SQL queries to access the relational tables.

By moving the data into a properly designed Oracle OLAP cube, they were able to quickly build reports to include time-series analysis and interdimensional calculations. Because the data is stored at all levels in the cube, the performance of run-time reports improved. By joining the Oracle OLAP data to relational tables, the client was able to easily build reports that drilled to the detail in the relational tables.

The following sections highlight a few of the calculations that were created to meet each challenge and the front-end tools that were used.

Flipping the Sign for Reporting Purposes   Financial reporting has unique requirements. The general ledger stores revenues, liability, and equity accounts as credits, and expenses as debits. The credits are saved as negative numbers, while debits are positive numbers. Using a different sign for credits and debits allows the income statement to be easily derived by aggregating the numbers. For external reporting purposes, however, it is necessary to report all the numbers as positive numbers, changing the sign for credit accounts by multiplying by negative 1 (-1). For example, if a company has a profit of 1 million, this should be reported as +1,000,000 even though it is stored as -1,000,000.

The consultants fulfilled this external reporting need by multiplying all credit accounts and their ancestors by -1 as the data was reported. Moving the responsibility for this data requirement to the Oracle Database ensured that this rule was applied consistently to all reports. For this project, the consultants defined and loaded a one-dimensional measure dimensioned by account called ACCT_REP_SIGN_VAR, which contained a 1 or -1 from a preexisting relational table. The reporting measure ACTUAL was then modified to use the following formula:

```
ACT * ACCT_REP_SIGN_VAR
```

By multiplying the data by a one-dimensional measure that contains a 1 or -1, they were able to "flip the sign" as appropriate for each account.

Calculated Accounts   Simple aggregation handled most of the calculations for the Account dimension, but some accounts needed to be calculated using custom equations. These accounts were calculated using models, as described in Chapter 3.

The business needed to report the cost per day for inpatient hospital care. Oracle OLAP was able to meet this business need by using the following formula, defined in the model:

```
OPEREXP_PER_DAY = OPEREXP / STAY_DAYS
```

This divides the operating expenses by the number of inpatient days to achieve the operating expenses per inpatient day. By defining this key metric in the database, application designers could ensure that this metric was calculated in a consistent way across all reports and analyses.

Calculated Accounts with Interdimensional References   Some more interesting account calculations needed to refer to specific data from two months ago. The business had a cash collection goal for each month. The goal was to collect all net revenue and any bad debt over 60 days. They were able to report the cash collection goal by creating the following model calculation:

```
CASH_COL_GOAL = PATIENT_REV + LAG(BAD_DEBT, 2, PERIOD)
```

Calculated Measures with Rules That Vary   Revenue and expense type accounts can be summed up when calculating a year-to-date measure. Summing balance sheet numbers over periods would grossly overstate the balance sheet. Balance sheet accounts (assets, liability, and equity) are reported as balances as of the end of the period (current month = prior period balance + changes in balance sheet for the current month), requiring no aggregation for year-to-date numbers. In addition, some accounts, like square feet (actual square feet of a building), do not change over time. For both of these examples, a year-to-date measure should report the same as the current month value. The consultants accomplished this requirement by giving these accounts an account type of B and changing the year-to-date formula as follows:

```
EQ if ACCT_TYPE eq 'B' then ACTUAL else {normal YTD formula}
```

End-User Tools   For most of the reporting, Discoverer OLAP was used. BI Discoverer Plus with a Java applet was used to generate reports. BI Discoverer Viewer was used by casual users who wanted to view reports created previously in Discoverer Plus OLAP. Because the cube was built using AWM, the business can take advantage of BI Discoverer, as well as other Oracle reporting tools such as OBIEE and the BI Spreadsheet Add-in to access the same analytic workspace for different customer needs.

Summary

This story highlights how Oracle OLAP can be used for traditional financial analysis applications. Oracle OLAP eases time-series calculations and allows for flexible reporting of the data in a consistent fashion. OLAP models allow for complex models, and insulate the reporting and analysis application from the complexities of data calculations. The business is now able to quickly report on its financials, and easily create formulas and models to meet its needs. The ability to employ models and custom formulas allows Oracle OLAP to be used in a variety of analytical situations.

Essbase Examples

In the preceding section, the Oracle OLAP examples show how a database-centric approach to OLAP effectively solves the challenges faced by these organizations, while at the same time leveraging the features of the Oracle Database. In this section, we present three examples of how Essbase has been used to solve business problems.

You will notice that the Essbase examples take a different approach than the Oracle OLAP examples. An Essbase implementation tends to start with a pilot completed during the discovery process. For a pilot, an Essbase analyst builds an Essbase database using the client's data, and then presents the results to the line-of-business users. The purpose of the pilot is twofold: it shows how Essbase can solve the organization's problem and it demonstrates how quickly Essbase can be implemented.

The examples show Essbase being used for the following purposes:

- Replacing the Excel workbook

- Enhancing an enterprise resource planning (ERP) system

- Replacing custom SQL reports generated by IT

Replacing the Excel Workbook

In Chapter 2, we introduced a phenomenon known as "spreadsheet hell," in which hundreds of manually produced spreadsheets may exist, with no central source for data or calculations. In this scenario, we examine a real-world example of spreadsheet hell and review the Essbase solution.

Challenge: Eliminate Manually Created Spreadsheets

A rental car conglomerate controlled two brand names, operating in several countries. To power business analyses, Excel workbooks were prepared monthly and distributed throughout the organization. The business analysts used spreadsheets for analysis because the software was already available in the organization, they had early success with spreadsheets as analysis tools, and they were already familiar with spreadsheets.

As their use of spreadsheets expanded, the workbooks became more complex and time-consuming to assemble. On a monthly basis, analysts would extract data from disparate sources, including operational systems and the data warehouse, and paste the data into several spreadsheets. These data sheets were then used as the source for report sheets. The report sheets relied on a very complex network of reference-based cell formulas to pull data from the data sheets. All told, it took several business analysts an average of eight business days to perform the data extractions, load the workbooks, and perform some rudimentary tests. This situation caused concern for both the chief operating officer (COO) and chief financial officer (CFO).

The CFO and COO wanted to have access to the data sooner, as well as improve the reliability of the data and calculations. It was also important to them that, whatever solution was implemented, business users would continue to create, maintain, and monitor the application, rather than having IT control administration. The COO and CFO saw IT providing value through data integration and project mentoring.

Solution: Move Data into an Essbase Database

The COO and CFO identified resources from IT and the business community to act as project sponsors. It is a best practice to have representation from both IT and the line of business right from the start. IT has a lot of experience in building systems and managing data, while people from the business side know the business use cases and can identify analytic and reporting requirements. The role of the project sponsors was to assist the Essbase analyst in creating an Essbase database as a pilot project.

The project team created the following plan:

- Schedule a meeting to discuss the business needs and review the existing solution.

- Present a basic technology demonstration to provide a baseline of knowledge for the project sponsors.

- Gather data and reports from which to create the pilot.

- An Essbase analyst from Oracle would create the database and example reports.

- The Essbase analyst would review the pilot with the project sponsors.

- Sponsors would present the final pilot to the COO and CFO for project approval.

The entire pilot process was scheduled over a two-week period. The team selected this time frame to demonstrate that the review process could be completed in less time than was needed to maintain the application monthly.

The first step in proving the proposed solution involved moving the data from the workbooks to an Essbase database. The Essbase analyst built and demonstrated this process. Essbase dimension build rules were used to create the database outline, and data-load rules populated the database with data from the original sources. From there, some ad hoc spreadsheet retrievals validated the dimension structures, calculated values, and demonstrated typical query usage.

After the pilot was complete, the Essbase analyst reviewed the pilot with the project sponsors. The demonstration was executed first with the business cases in mind. Then the methods used to create the database were presented. Most impressive to the sponsors was the speed with which the pilot had been created. From needs analysis to first review took just a few days, while the pilot database itself took the Essbase analyst a mere two hours to build and load with data. And to the amazement of the sponsors, the pilot data matched the production system and the workbooks.

Summary
The COO and CFO wanted reliable data available sooner, but they also wanted a system that could be managed by the business users. On the strength and accuracy

of the pilot, and with the assurance of the sponsors that the system could be managed by the business analysts, the company adopted and implemented the Essbase solution. It took three weeks to complete the production-ready system, including the Essbase database and the end-user reports. Now it takes just one hour a month to load the data from the sources systems and generate end-user reports from the Essbase database.

Enhancing an ERP System

In the next scenario, we look at how Essbase can be used in conjunction with an ERP system. ERP systems use an online transactional processing (OLTP) schema to store data efficiently in a relational database. However, to answer typical analytic questions requires many joins between tables, and the more joins, the slower the query response time. In contrast, OLAP technology stores and aggregates data multidimensionally, which translates into extremely fast query response times and the ability to do ad hoc analyses. Adding Essbase on top of an ERP system enables an organization to take advantage of the strengths of both OLTP and OLAP technologies.

In the following example, the company has a single ERP system. However, because companies often acquire other companies, they can find themselves attempting to manage multiple ERP systems. This is a clear case for a tool like Essbase, which can consolidate data from disparate sources.

Challenge: Create a More Flexible Analytic Environment

One very large consumer packaged goods (CPG) company implemented an ERP system to integrate the data and processes of the organization into a single system. The advantages of an ERP system are many, but for this customer's IT department, the big draw was the ability to provide a single source for all transaction data.

For business analysts, however, an ERP system can present challenges. This particular company's business analysts discovered their limitations very quickly:

- Running analyses was very slow. The ERP application was retrieving detailed data from a relational database management system (traditionally a slow process when done on a production system during business hours) and calculating dynamic values at the time of the query (also time-consuming).

- The analysts could not create custom dimensions. The ERP system came with predefined dimensions and offered little flexibility to modify them to meet analytic needs.

To work around these limitations, the business users needed to analyze the data offline from the ERP, and ended up building very large workbooks using Excel. As in the previous example, updates often took days or weeks, which limited the impact of analyses on the current month and resulted in decisions that were not always based on facts.

Management had been looking for alternatives when a newly hired, senior-level employee mentioned Essbase. He had used Essbase before, and he encouraged management to look at it.

Solution: Add Speed and Flexibility to ERP with an Essbase Database

The pilot process was accomplished very quickly. First, a senior employee was excited about the opportunity to incorporate Essbase into the organization. Second, the Microsoft Office integration available using Oracle Hyperion Smart View for Office was very attractive, as the company's business analysts often used Excel, Word, and PowerPoint to provide information to executives. Once again, a demonstration database was created from an Excel workbook.

In this case, the presentation caused some consternation. When the Essbase analyst presented some reports validating the data, one attendee called into question the revenue for a business unit that had been sold recently. First, the Essbase analyst checked the Essbase outline for accuracy and found that the consolidation used was indeed correct. Then the Essbase analyst checked the formulas in the original Excel workbook for that business unit and discovered the error: Someone had not updated the consolidations from child to parent after the previous quarter's reorganization. The result? The revenues expressed in the workbook were 13 percent understated. Because the workbook had been the only source used to assess the worth of the business unit, the hard truth was that the business unit had been undervalued when it was sold, representing a loss of millions of dollars to the shareholders.

Summary

For the managers, the news of the error was enough to convince them to implement Essbase. For the business analysts, Essbase solved their main challenges with the ERP system. Essbase gave them the flexibility to model dimensions that reflect the way the company is managed, rather than the way the ERP system is configured.

Queries to the Essbase database are now fast—speed-of-thought fast—and the data is reliable. Instead of taking days to weeks before the data is available for reports, it now takes about an hour to load and consolidate the Essbase database.

Replacing Custom SQL Reports

Companies succeed in analytics due, in large part, to a strong working relationship between IT and the rest of the business. A good relationship, however, does not mean that IT should expend valuable resources doing things for business users that, with the right tools, the business users could do for themselves. For example, analysts who understand their business should be able to model the business, build scenarios on the fly, and create their own reports.

The organization in this example is a very large utility conglomerate. As in the previous example, an ERP system was in place, providing a single source of detailed data. Once again, the business users were facing challenges when performing analyses, in this case due to the technical nature of the analytic and reporting tools provided by IT.

Challenge: Empower Business Users to Create Their Own Reports

The IT department members of the utility conglomerate knew business users needed analytics. To meet this need, they had acquired and deployed an add-on analytical application for the ERP system, as well as a SQL-based query and reporting tool. Most of the required content was available through the relational data mart and some 200 standard reports created by IT. However, several ad hoc needs were either ignored or just very difficult to achieve. Because the query and reporting tool required knowledge of SQL, users began to lean on IT resources to create custom reports. This reliance on IT resulted in significant delays in the analysis process, as the analysts were required to wait hours or days for reports to be generated.

Custom reports also contributed to higher workloads for IT personnel. Soon, the IT department was faced with about 3,000 of these custom reports! In many cases, the custom report differed very little from the standard version. However, because the tools provided were technically challenging to the business users, the notion of self-service reporting was merely a dream.

IT management grew concerned about how to handle the thousands of new reports and how to manage the increased demand on their time. A new OLAP reporting solution was required.

Solution: Use Smart View to Create Reports

The Essbase pilot focused on showing how Smart View installed in Excel enabled business users to run their own queries and create their own reports—without using SQL.

Solutions to several previously unidentified reporting issues surfaced during the pilot. For example, simple variance reporting using favorable/unfavorable scenarios meant custom coding in each SQL-based report. The Essbase analyst was able to demonstrate how, with Essbase, the expense reporting property was stored in the database, and so provided this functionality to each report and ad hoc query, eliminating the need for custom coding within the reports themselves. Similarly, balance sheet reporting was modeled in the database, instead of at the report level. Tremendous advantages can be gained when modeling complexities like favorability and balances in the database. Users no longer need to remember to maintain these calculations in every report or query.

Summary

Essbase became part of the solution to the challenges experienced by both the business users and IT. Business users began relying on Smart View for ad hoc reporting, rather than a formal reporting tool. Because ad hoc analysis is driven via business terminology, rather than by SQL, IT was off the hook for supporting all the custom report requests.

Conclusion

The six examples in this chapter were selected to represent typical ways in which Oracle OLAP and Oracle Essbase can solve real-world problems. We demonstrated how Oracle OLAP has been used by organizations to accelerate a data warehouse, analyze projection data from multiple sources, and analyze financial data. The Essbase examples showed how Essbase has been used to replace data stored in Excel workbooks, enhance an ERP system with improved analytics, and replace custom SQL reports generated by IT with self-service reporting. These are just a few of the ways that OLAP systems can be used within an organization. For more examples, see the success stories on the Oracle Technology Network (OTN) web site or contact your Oracle sales consultant.

While the examples in this chapter are specific to each product, it does not mean that Oracle OLAP or Essbase would be unable to meet the *analytic requirements* presented in the other product's examples. That said, it should be clear that each example plays to the strengths of the Oracle product used in the example. If IT wants to speed up response times for analytic SQL-based queries against an Oracle database, Oracle OLAP is the obvious choice, both for its cube-organized materialized views and for its support of SQL. In contrast, when the line of business wants to retain control of the OLAP technology outside the Oracle Database, Essbase is the obvious choice. This is a key point. Both Oracle products are full-featured OLAP offerings; however, each has different strengths that arise from their histories and different development goals. Indeed, the products' differing strengths speak to why Oracle continues to support the development of both products.

Before we conclude this book, let's take a moment to review why OLAP is a cornerstone of BI.

OLAP as a Cornerstone of BI

Chapter 1 stated the five key benefits of an effective OLAP solution: business-focused multidimensional data, business-focused calculations, trustworthy data and calculations, speed-of-thought analysis, and flexible, self-service reporting. Here, we show how Essbase and Oracle OLAP provide these benefits, even though they come at the problem from different points of view.

Recall that Essbase was designed to solve the problems of spreadsheet hell and spread marts faced by people in the line of business. It does so by offering an independent multidimensional database that centralizes data from disparate data sources and arranges that data into dimensions that are intuitive for business users.

Because Essbase offers drill-back to the original data sources, administrators can choose whether to store only summary-level data or detail data as well. Essbase enables administrators to create, store, and run business calculations, ensuring that consistent calculations and results are available across spreadsheets and reports. Essbase includes powerful front-end analysis tools that work within Microsoft Excel, which makes it easy for analysts to query an Essbase database, calculate the database, and create what-if scenarios within the comfort of a familiar user interface. The combination of centralized data, centralized calculations, and front-end tools support speed-of-thought analysis for end users in the line of business. A broad array of user-friendly reporting tools makes flexible, self-service reporting a reality.

Through its ownership by Hyperion, Essbase has evolved into an engine for packaged BI and EPM applications. Essbase supports a variety of packaged reporting tools, BI applications, and EPM applications, such as some of those found in Oracle Enterprise Performance Management System and in OBIEE Plus.

Oracle OLAP is part of the Oracle Database. It resides in the performance layer of the Oracle Database and runs in the Oracle Database kernel. Oracle OLAP benefits from many of the features of the Oracle Database, including data types, SQL support, high availability, scalability, user access management, security, maintenance tasks, and backups.

Oracle OLAP analytic workspaces centralize summary-level data in cubes and present that data in an intuitive star schema, designed for business reporting and analysis. Summary-level OLAP data can be joined to detail-level relational data in the Oracle database with simple table joins. Cubes offer fine control over aggregation to support speed-of-thought analysis for end users. Administrators can maintain business calculations within the analytic workspace, ensuring consistent, trustworthy calculations for an organization. The use of cube-organized materialized views allows for greatly improving the performance of queries and simplification of summary management. End users can continue to use the user-friendly BI applications and reporting tools that they are familiar with, such as those found in OBIEE, Application Express, and third-party SQL-based tools, while enjoying vastly improved performance of end-user analytic queries.

The purpose of any OLAP solution is to solve problems for both business users and IT departments. For business users, it enables fast and intuitive access to centralized data and related calculations for the purposes of analysis and reporting. For IT, an OLAP system enhances a data warehouse or other relational database with aggregate data and business calculations. The needs of both constituencies can be met effectively with either Essbase or Oracle OLAP.

Businesses need BI to compete in today's economy, and OLAP is the cornerstone in an effective BI solution. Oracle offers two market-leading OLAP technologies, each of which provides everything you need to realize the key benefits of OLAP. Whichever technology you choose, our hope is that this book gives you the tools to select, design, construct, and deploy a comprehensive OLAP system—one that empowers the people in your organization to make better, faster decisions for today and more accurate, fact-based predictions for tomorrow.

References

Baum, David. "Measure. Analyze. Perform." *Oracle Magazine*: July/August 2008. Oracle Technology Network (http://www.oracle.com/technology/oramag/oracle/08-jul/o48bi.html).

Oracle Corporation. "Customer Feature." *Oracle OLAP Newsletter*: February 2009. Oracle Technology Network (http://www.oracle.com/technology/products/bi/olap/olapref/newsletter/oracleolapnewsletter_feb09.html).

Committee on Global Oil and Gas, Lee R. Raymond, Chair. *Facing the Hard Truths about Energy*, Appendix A, "Request Letter and Description of the NPC." National Petroleum Council. July 2007.

Glossary

accounts dimension　In Essbase, a dimension type that makes accounting intelligence available. Only one dimension can be defined as the accounts dimension. *See also* dimension.

ad hoc analysis　An online analytical query created on the fly by an end user.

aggregate storage database　In Essbase, the database storage model designed to support large-scale, sparsely distributed data that is categorized into many, potentially large dimensions. Upper-level members and formulas are calculated dynamically, and selected data values are aggregated and stored, typically with improvements in overall aggregation time. Contrast with block storage database.

aggregation　The process of aggregating data from dependent members to parent member. For example, Total US might be an aggregated dimension value aggregated from Western US and Eastern US in the Geography dimension. Also called *rollup* or *consolidation*.

aggregation operator　An operator that defines how values in a hierarchy are aggregated. The default is addition. Oracle OLAP offers a large set of aggregation operators, which are broken down into basic operators (such as sum and average), scaled and weighted operators (such as scaled sum and weighted average), and hierarchical operators (similar to the previous operations, but all children are taken into consideration, even if they do not contain data). In Essbase, aggregation operators are called *consolidation operators*.

alias　An alternative name. For example, for a more easily identifiable column descriptor, you can display the alias instead of the member name.

alternate hierarchy　A way to analyze the same data in a different way. A dimension can have one or more hierarchies that organize and aggregate dimension members in different logical structures. *See also* hierarchy.

analytic workspace　In Oracle OLAP, a container for storing related dimensional objects, such as dimensions and cubes. An analytic workspace is stored in a relational table.

application programming interface (API)　A set of routines, data structures, object classes, and/or protocols that are provided in order to support the building of applications.

attribute　A characteristic that describes a group of dimension members. Users can use attributes to return lists of members that have the specified attribute associated with them. *See also* user-defined attribute and system-defined attribute.

attribute dimension   In Essbase, a special dimension that further defines another (base) dimension. No data is stored against an attribute dimension. *See also* dimension.

block storage database   In Essbase, a way of storing data to optimize data storage. Data is stored in a series of blocks. Each block is an array with storage for every dense dimension member. A block is created for every combination of sparse dimension members for which data exists. Contrast with aggregate storage database.

business intelligence (BI)   A set of concepts and methodologies to improve decision making in business with the use of facts and fact-based systems.

cache   A short-term storage of data to improve speed.

calculated measure   In Oracle OLAP, a measure derived from stored measures and/or other calculated measures. *See also* measure.

calculated value   In Essbase, a value derived from stored values and/or other calculated values. *See also* cell.

calculation   The process of aggregating data or running business calculations.

calculation script   In Essbase, a set of commands that define how a database is consolidated or aggregated. A calculation script may also contain commands that specify allocation and other calculation rules separate from the consolidation process. Compare with dynamic calculation and member formula.

cell   In Essbase or Oracle OLAP, the data value at the intersection of dimension members in a cube. In a spreadsheet, a cell is the intersection of a row and a column.

composite   In Oracle OLAP, a compact format for storing sparse multidimensional data. A composite value exists for each combination of sparse dimensions for which data exists. Oracle OLAP provides two types of composites: a compressed composite for extremely sparse data and a regular composite for moderately sparse data.

compressed cube   In Oracle OLAP, a cube with very sparse data that is stored using a compressed composite.

consolidation   *See* aggregation.

consolidation operator   An operator that defines how values in a hierarchy are aggregated. The default is addition. In Essbase, consolidation operators include the arithmetic operations of addition, subtraction, multiplication, and division, as well as operators for percentage, do not consolidate, and never consolidate. In Oracle OLAP, consolidation operators are called *aggregation operators*.

consolidation order   In Essbase, refers to the default sequence in which dimensions are aggregated, as well as how members are aggregated. *See also* solve order.

cube   A construct used to visualize how OLAP data is stored. Dimensions form the edges of the cube. The intersection of a member from each edge creates a cell that can potentially hold a data value. In Oracle OLAP, an analytic workspace contains multiple cubes with different dimensions. In Essbase, an Essbase multidimensional database is referred to as a cube.

cube schema   In Essbase Studio, the metadata elements, such as measures and hierarchies, representing the logical model of a cube.

cube script   In Oracle OLAP, a sequence of steps that prepare the data for querying, such as loading and aggregating new data.

cube view   In Oracle OLAP, a relational view of the data stored in a cube, which can be queried by SQL. It contains columns for the dimensions, measures, and calculated measures of the cube.

cube-organized materialized view   In Oracle OLAP, a type of materialized view that is organized as a cube. A cube-organized materialized view can be incrementally refreshed through the Oracle Database materialized view subsystem, and it can serve as a target for transparent rewrite of queries against the source tables. A cube-organized materialized view can be used to replace many relational materialized views.

dashboard   A collection of metrics and indicators that provide an interactive summary of your business. Dashboards enable you to build and deploy analytic applications.

data cell   *See* cell.

data cube   *See* cube.

data-load rules   In Essbase, a set of criteria that determines how to load data into a multidimensional database from a text-based file, a spreadsheet, or a relational data set.

data source   In the context of Oracle OLAP and Oracle Essbase, a source of data for OLAP cubes. Source data can be located in relational sources, flat files, or other formats.

data value *See* cell.

data warehouse A central data repository that provides a single source of data for an organization.

dense dimension A dimension that contains data for all (or most) combinations of dimension members. For example, time dimensions with months and years are often dense because they can contain values for all, or many, of the defined periods. *See also* dimension. Contrast with sparse dimension.

dimension A data category used to organize business data for retrieval and preservation of values. Cubes are accessed via their dimensions. *See also* dense dimension, sparse dimension, attribute dimension, accounts dimension, user dimension, and time dimension.

dimension build rules In Essbase, specifications, similar to data-load rules that Essbase uses to modify an outline. The modification is based on data in an external data source.

drill path Navigation through the query result set using a dimensional hierarchy. Drilling down moves the user perspective from aggregated data to detail data. Drilling up navigates from detail to aggregate data. Drill paths can also be used to define links between reports, such as drilling from one dashboard to another.

duplicate member The multiple occurrence of a member name, with each occurrence representing a different member. For example, you could have two members named New York; one member represents New York State, and the other member represents New York City. *See also* member. Contrast with shared member.

extended OLAP (XOLAP) In Essbase, a multidimensional database that stores only the outline metadata and retrieves all data from a relational database at query time.

extract, transform, and load (ETL) Data source-specific rules for extracting data from one database, transforming it, and loading it into another database.

fact table The central table in a star schema. This table typically contains dimension keys that can be joined to dimension tables and numeric data that comprise the facts.

field In the context of a relational database, an area that holds a value, such as a text string, a date, a number, and so on. Records contain fields. *See also* record.

gadget In Oracle Smart Space, a simple, specialized, lightweight application that provides easy viewing of business intelligence and enterprise performance management content and functionality.

genealogy Used to express relationships among members in a hierarchy. Genealogical terms include parent, child, sibling, ancestor, and descendant.

generation In Essbase, a layer in a hierarchical tree structure that defines member relationships in a database. Generations are ordered incrementally from the top member of the dimension (generation 1) down to the leaf members.

hierarchy An arrangement of dimension members into a genealogical structure. Data values are often aggregated up a hierarchy. Users often drill down on a hierarchy. In Essbase and Oracle OLAP, hierarchical relationships are expressed genealogically.

hybrid OLAP (HOLAP) A method of storing data that is a hybrid of multidimensional OLAP (MOLAP) and relational OLAP (ROLAP). Some data is stored multidimensionally (MOLAP), and some data is stored relationally (ROLAP).

IT Information technology department of an organization.

label-only member In Essbase, a member with no data. A label-only member can be used to group other members, in which case it points to the data associated with its first child member. Contrast with member and shared member.

leaf member A member with no children. A leaf member is the lowest point in a hierarchy. In Essbase, a leaf member is also called level 0.

legacy system An old computer system or application program that continues to be used because the user (typically an organization) does not want to replace or redesign it.

level-based hierarchy In Oracle OLAP, a hierarchy with defined levels. For example, Time is usually level-based with levels such as Month, Quarter, and Year. Most hierarchies are level-based. *See also* hierarchy. Contrast with value-based hierarchy.

levels Categorize the members of a level-based hierarchy. In Oracle OLAP, levels in level-based hierarchies define the genealogical structure for dimension members, such as Year, Quarter, and Month. In Essbase, levels are numbered from the bottom of the outline to the top: level 0, level 1, level 2, and so on.

load rule　In Essbase, a rule that can execute as a data-load rule and/or a dimension build rule. *See* data load rule and dimension build rule.

mapping　In Oracle OLAP, a series of specifications that define how Oracle OLAP objects are loaded from relational tables or views.

materialized view　In the Oracle Database, a view often used in data warehousing to provide quick access to summary data by precomputing the rows. Materialized views are refreshed periodically. The Oracle Database can redirect queries to materialized views to improve query performance.

MaxL　In Essbase, the multidimensional database access language consisting of a data definition language (MaxL DDL) and a data manipulation language (MaxL DML). MaxL is used to automated repeated functions or batch together multiple consecutive operations.

MDX (Multidimensional Expression)　A language used to query OLAP data, similar to the use of SQL for relational databases.

measure　In Oracle OLAP, a logical object that contains data.

member　A discrete component within a dimension. A member identifies and differentiates the organization of similar units. For example, a Geography dimension might include the members New York, Dallas, and United States.

member formula　In Essbase, a formula attached to a member.

metadata　Data about the data. A set of data that defines and describes the properties and attributes of the data stored in a database or used by an application. Examples of metadata are dimension names, member names, properties, time periods, and security. Metadata encompasses business and system/technical data.

metadata management　The process of tracking an organization's data and the usage of that data. Metadata management tracks data lineage, data definitions, usage patterns, business rules, and so on.

minischema　A subset of a dimensional schema used for a business purpose to simplify a dimensional schema for a particular audience.

multidimensional　A method of organizing, storing, and referencing data using dimensions. An individual value is the intersection point for a set of dimensions. *See also* dimension.

multidimensional OLAP (MOLAP) MOLAP is the "classic" form of OLAP and is sometimes referred to as just OLAP. *See also* multidimensional.

OLAP DML In Oracle OLAP, the data definition and manipulation language for analytic workspaces.

on the fly Calculated at run time in response to a specific query. Also called *dynamic calculation.*

online analytical processing (OLAP) A multidimensional, computing environment for users who analyze data in real time. OLAP systems feature drill-down, data pivoting, complex calculations, trend analysis, and modeling.

outline The database structure of an Essbase database, including all dimensions, members, tags, types, consolidations, and mathematical relationships. Data is stored in the database according to the structure defined in the outline.

partition In Essbase, an area of data that is replicated, shared, or linked between databases. In Oracle OLAP, you partition along a dimension, usually at a selected level. Partitions enable you to break up and manage data, while at the same time hiding this complexity from applications and end users.

pivot The act of changing your view of the data, such as swapping a dimension from rows to columns.

query A request for data.

ragged hierarchy A hierarchy that contains at least one member with a different base level, creating a "ragged" base level for the hierarchy. Organization dimensions are frequently ragged. Compare with skip-level hierarchy.

record In a database, a group of fields making up one complete entry. For example, a customer record may contain fields for name, address, and telephone number.

relational OLAP (ROLAP) An OLAP system that stores data in a relational database. The base data and the dimension tables are stored as relational tables, and new tables are created to hold the aggregated information.

rollup *See* aggregation.

schema In the Oracle Database, a collection of objects (including analytic workspaces) that belong to a database user.

shared member   In Essbase, a member that shares storage space with another member of the same name, preventing duplicate calculation of members that occur multiple times in an Essbase outline. Contrast with stored member.

skip-level hierarchy   In Oracle OLAP, a hierarchy that contains at least one member whose parent is more than one level above it, skipping a level in the hierarchy. For example, in a Geography dimension with levels for City, State, and Country, Washington D.C. is a city that does not have a State value; its parent is United States at the Country level. Compare with ragged hierarchy.

slowly changing dimension (SCD)   A dimension with values that change slowly over time. For example, an organization's structure changes over time when employees change departments. *See also* dimension.

snowflake dimensional model   A schema design in which a centralized fact table is related to a series of dimension tables that in turn relate to other supporting tables.

software development kit (SDK)   A set of development tools that enables a software developer to create applications for a software package, framework, operating system, and so on. It may contain an application programming interface (API).

solve order   In Essbase, a value against a member in an aggregate storage database used to ensure that formulas are resolved in the correct sequence. *See also* consolidation order.

sparse dimension   A dimension that is unlikely to contain data for all member combinations when compared with other dimensions. For example, not all customers have data for all products. *See also* dimension. Contrast with dense dimension.

spreadsheet application   An application, such as Microsoft Excel, where data is represented in rows and columns.

SQL (Structured Query Language)   A language used to communicate instructions to relational databases, often to request data.

star schema   The simplest data warehouse schema type. The star schema consists of a few fact tables (possibly only one, justifying the name) referencing any number of dimension tables. The star schema is considered an important special case of the snowflake schema.

stored measure In Oracle OLAP, a measure that is stored in the cube. *See also* measure.

stored member In Essbase, another term for member, used to distinguish it from a shared member. Contrast with shared member.

stored value In Essbase, a value that is stored in the cube. *See also* cell.

surrogate key In Oracle OLAP, a way of resolving duplicate members by adding the level name to the member name. *See also* duplicate member.

system-defined attribute In Oracle OLAP, an attribute that is automatically generated for a dimension. *See also* attribute.

TCP/IP (Transmission Control Protocol/Internet Protocol) A standard set of communication protocols linking computers with different operating systems and internal architectures. TCP/IP is used to exchange files, send mail, and communicate in various OLAP products.

time dimension A dimension type that signifies that the dimension contains time-based members, such as fiscal or calendar years and periods. The time dimension can then be used to enable specific time-based calculations and features, such as year-to-date values, time balance averages, change from year ago, and so forth. *See also* dimension.

user dimension In Oracle OLAP, a dimension type other than a time dimension. *See also* dimension.

user-defined attribute (UDA) In Essbase, an attribute attached to a member defined by the administrator. UDAs can be used for selection and in calculations. *See also* attribute.

value-based hierarchy In Oracle OLAP, a hierarchy defined only by the parent-child relationships among dimension members. For example, an employee dimension might have a parent-child relation that identifies each employee's supervisor. *See also* hierarchy. Contrast with level-based hierarchy.

visualization A method for displaying data in meaningful ways using grids, charts, graphs, and other visual techniques.

XML for Analysis (XMLA) A standard that allows client applications to talk to multidimensional or OLAP data sources. The query language used is MDX.

Index

S